ESSENTIALS

A Systematic Approach to Reading, Spelling, and Writing

The LOGIC of ENGLISH

TEACHER'S MANUAL

DENISE EIDE

The Logic of English Essentials Teacher's Manual:
A Systematic Approach to Reading, Spelling, and Writing

Copyright © 2012 Pedia Learning Inc. All rights reserved.
"The Logic of English" is a Registered Trademark of Pedia Learning Inc.
Printed in the United States of America.

Pedia Learning Inc.
10800 Lyndale Ave S. Suite 181
Minneapolis, MN 55420

Cover design: Dugan Design Group
Interior design and typesetting: Katherine Lloyd, The Desk
School Font: David Occhino Design

ISBN 978-1-936706-09-9

First Edition

10 9 8 7 6 5 4 3

www.LogicOfEnglish.com

INTRODUCTION CONTENTS

BEGINNERS TO ADULTS — SAMPLE SCHEDULES

BEFORE YOU BEGIN

TEACHING THE LESSONS

TEACHER RESOURCES

LESSON CONTENTS

SCOPE AND SEQUENCE

Lesson	Phonograms	Exploring Sounds	Spelling Rules	Grammar
Lesson 1	a-z	Consonants and Vowels	11, 21	Nouns, Plurals
Lesson 2	ck, ee, ng, th	Short and Long Vowels	26	Adjectives
Lesson 3	er, or, ea, sh	Syllables	4	Irregular Plurals Non-Count Nouns
Lesson 4	ai, ay, oi, oy	Multi-Letter Consonants and Vowels	3, 9, 10	Article Adjectives
Lesson 5		*Assessment & Review*		
Lesson 6	ar, ch, oo	Broad Vowel Sounds	30, 21	Commas in a Series
Lesson 7	oa, oe	Spellings of Long /ō/		Article Usage
Lesson 8	igh, wh	W and WH	28	Comparative and Superlative
Lesson 9	au, aw, augh	Spellings of /ä/		Possessives
Lesson 10		*Assessment & Review*		
Lesson 11	ou, ow, ough	Spellings of /ow/	22, 24	Verbs, Sentences Subject-Verb Agreement
Lesson 12	tch	Words Ending in -alk	27	Transitive Verbs Direct Objects
Lesson 13	kn, gn	KN and GN	8	Direct Objects Continued
Lesson 14	ir, ur, ear	Spellings of /er/		Common and Proper Nouns
Lesson 15		*Assessment & Review*		
Lesson 16	ed, ew	Hard and Soft C and G	1, 2, 19, 20	Past Tense Verbs
Lesson 17	ui	Long /ū/	12.1, 13	Quotations
Lesson 18	wor, wr	WOR and WR	12.2, 12.3	Indirect Objects
Lesson 19	ph	The /l/ Sound	12.4, 12.5	Subject and Predicate
Lesson 20		*Assessment & Review*		

Lesson	Phonograms	Exploring Sounds	Spelling Rules	Grammar
Lesson 21	ei, ey, eigh	Usage of EI, EY, and EIGH		Subject Pronouns
Lesson 22		Voiced and Unvoiced Pairs	12.6, 12.7, 12.8, 12.9	
Lesson 23	bu, gu	Consonant and Vowel Sounds of Y	6, 7, 15, 16	Possessive Pronoun Adjectives
Lesson 24		Relationship of I and Y	5	Adverbs
Lesson 25	*Assessment & Review*			
Lesson 26	dge	DGE snd GE	25	Commands, Nouns of Direct Address
Lesson 27	ie	The Long /ē/ Sound	23	Linking Verbs, Predicate Nouns, Predicate Adjectives
Lesson 28		Spellings of /ow/		Numbers, Hyphenating Numbers, Ordinal Numbers
Lesson 29	ti, ci, si	Spellings of /sh/	17, 18	Exclamations, Interjections
Lesson 30	*Assessment & Review*			
Lesson 31	cei	Accented Syllables	29	Prepositions
Lesson 32		Single and Double Consonants	14	Prepositions, Paragraphs
Lesson 33		Accented Syllables	14	Helping Verbs, Present Continuous Tense
Lesson 34		Silent L		Helping Verbs, Irregular Present Tense Verbs, Future Tense
Lesson 35	*Assessment & Review*			
Lesson 36		I Says /ē/, Syllable Types	7	Questions
Lesson 37	our	Distorted U Sounds		Coordinating Conjunctions Compound Sentences
Lesson 38	aigh	I Says /y/		Subordinating Conjunctions and Dependent Clauses
Lesson 39	sc	Multi-Syllable Words	Review	Subordinating Conjunctions
Lesson 40	*Assessment & Review*			

INTRODUCTION TO
THE LOGIC OF ENGLISH ESSENTIALS

The Logic of English® Essentials program is designed for students ages eight through adult who want to improve their reading, spelling, and/or sentence level writing abilities. The program systematically teaches how and why English words are spelled in a particular manner and how to build words into phrases and sentences, thereby providing students with the tools needed to decode, spell, and write.

The Logic of English Essentials program may be used to remediate students who are behind in reading, spelling, or sentence level composition or to provide any student with the 104 tools which explain 98% of English words.

Sample lessons are provided for varying ages of readers in the "Beginners to Adults - Sample Schedules" on pages Intro 13 - Intro 22.

Before beginning Lesson 1, students need to have: 1) developed phonemic awareness, 2) learned all the sounds for the A-Z phonograms, and 3) learned how to write the A-Z phonograms. A chapter is devoted to each of these skills in the "Before You Begin" section. For some struggling students, it is best to spend up to one week working on these preliminary skills. For other students, it is possible to review the concepts quickly, in thirty minutes or less, and then proceed to Lesson 1.

KEY TO SYMBOLS

| a | Letters written in a box represent phonogram flashcards. |

A, IGH   Letters written in capital letters represent phonograms. They may be read using the letter names.

/s-ĭ-t/   Letters or words enclosed in slashes represent the sounds. Each sound is separated by a dash.

✎   Activities with a corresponding page in the student workbook.

Ⓚ   Practice activities that have a kinesthetic component.

Ⓥ   Practice activities that have a visual component.

Ⓐ   Practice activities that have an auditory component.

Ⓒ   Practice activities that have a creative component.

MATERIALS NEEDED

- Teacher's Manual
- Student Workbook – 1 per student
- Basic Phonogram Flash Cards
- Red, yellow, green, pink, black, dark blue, and light blue colored pencils.
- Extra paper

OPTIONAL SUPPLEMENTS

- *The Logic of English® Spelling Journal* – 1 per student
- *The Phonogram and Spelling Game Book*
- Phonogram Game Cards - 2 sets
- Timer, for games
- Spelling Rule, Grammar, and Advanced Phonogram Flash Cards
- Phonogram and Spelling Rule Quick Reference
- Index Cards to create Spelling Cards
- Whiteboard, markers, eraser
- Magnetic Letters

BEGINNERS TO ADULTS
SAMPLE SCHEDULES

STRUGGLING READERS AND SPELLERS

8-YEAR-OLD TO ADULT STUDENTS
NOT READING AT GRADE LEVEL

Total Time: 75–130 minutes per day

Schedule: Teach one lesson every one to two days.

Time Frame: Complete *The Logic of English Essentials* in 8-16 weeks.

Before Beginning Lesson 1: Use the first one to five days to develop Phonemic Awareness (see Intro 25 - Intro 32), learn the sounds for A-Z (see Intro 33 - Intro 36), and learn how to write the lowercase letters.

Struggling Readers and Spellers: Older students needing remediation in basic reading and spelling skills should spend a minimum of one and a half to two hours per day, five to six days a week on the material. Splitting the lesson into two 60 minutes sessions per day is ideal.

It is important for parents and educators to understand that every hour invested in reading instruction at this point will save thousands of wasted hours in the future. Investing now in teaching your student to read will also help reverse discouragement.

Tips: Spend up to one week working through the phonemic awareness activities and learning A-Z. However, do not delay longer before beginning Lesson 1. Older students need to see the phonograms at work within words. It is only when the phonogram-to-sound correlation begins to unlock words that students will begin to understand the power of the content taught in The Logic of English Lessons. Students do not need to have mastered all the sounds of A-Z before beginning Lesson 1. Every lesson incorporates phonogram review. Students will be more motivated when they begin to see the phonograms unlocking print.

The biggest hurdles for working with older struggling readers are shame and discouragement. It is often helpful to explain to them that it is not their fault that they have struggled. Rather, it is because they have not been taught in a way that has made sense to them. Many students will need to hear this message reaffirmed many times as they encounter concepts that "click." Gently remind them that their struggles were not their fault. Affirm the legitimacy of their confusion, and point to a new and hopeful way to learn.

Many struggling readers and spellers need additional practice. Utilize the Optional Activities to provide the students with sufficient practice to master the phonograms, spelling rules, and words taught. In addition, many struggling readers and spellers are not natural visual learners. Be sure to incorporate auditory, kinesthetic, and creative learning activities. For mastering spelling, many of these students will find the tips in "Say to Spell" helpful for creating a clear auditory picture of the word.

Once the student can read the sounds of most of the A-Z phonograms, proceed to Lesson 1. A sample schedule for how to utilize each lesson is included below.

Day 1

1. Introduce and practice phonograms. (15 minutes. When the student knows the 74 basic phonograms well, this may be reduced to 2-5 minutes of quick review.)

2. Present Exploring Sounds. (5-15 minutes depending upon the lesson)

3. Teach the new spelling rule. (5-15 minutes depending upon the lesson)

4. 1 Optional Spelling Rule Activity. (5 minutes)

5. Dictate 15 spelling words and analyze the words. (15-25 minutes)

6. Grammar Activity. (10-15 minutes)

7. Dictation. (10 minutes)

8. Composition. (10 minutes)

9. 1-2 Optional Activities. (5-15 minutes)

10. Vocabulary Development. (10-15 minutes)

Optional Day 2

1. Practice phonograms. (15 minutes)

2. Review the spelling rules. (5 minutes)

3. Dictate the Spelling List onto index cards to make Spelling Word Cards. (20 minutes)

4. Choose 2-5 Optional Activities. (30-60 minutes)

STRUGGLING SPELLERS

NINE-YEAR-OLD TO ADULT STUDENTS
READING AT GRADE LEVEL, NEEDING SPELLING REMEDIATION

Total Time: 35–65 minutes per day

Schedule: Teach one lesson every one to two days.

Time Frame: Complete *The Logic of English Essentials* in 8-16 weeks.

Before Beginning Lesson 1: Use the first hour to review Phonemic Awareness (see Intro 25 - Intro 32), learn the sounds for A-Z (see Intro 33 - Intro 36), and review how to write the lowercase letters.

Struggling Spellers: If a student older than eight years old reads at or above grade level but struggles with spelling, a less rigorous approach may be used. In this situation a student should spend 35-65 minutes per day practicing these lessons. Since the inability to spell hinders fluent writing, every minute spent learning how to spell will save countless hours of frustration. It will also provide one of the necessary tools to becoming a fluent writer. Most students using the program for spelling remediation will also experience a significant increase in their reading level as a side benefit.

Tips: Remember that spelling is a deeper level of knowing than reading. Students who can spell a word absolutely know how to read it. However, students who know how to read a word do not necessarily know how to spell it.

Many struggling spellers are not natural visual learners. Be sure to incorporate auditory, kinesthetic, and creative learning activities. For mastering spelling, many of these students will find the tips in "Say to Spell" helpful for creating a clear auditory picture of the word.

Many struggling spellers need additional practice to master the words for spelling. They also often struggle with memorizing the parts of words that have more than one option for spelling. Utilize the Optional Activities to provide the student with sufficient practice to master the phonograms, spelling rules, and words taught. These students will also benefit from creating a *Logic of English Spelling Journal.*

Many struggling spellers also struggle with punctuating sentences. These students will benefit greatly from the grammar lessons incorporated in each lesson. Learning grammar is essential to learning the logic of commas, periods, and capitals. Without grammar, students must rely on intuition or visual memory. If a student is strong in grammar, usage, and punctuation, the Grammar Section may be skipped.

A sample schedule for using the lessons is included below.

Day 1

1. Introduce and practice phonograms. (15 minutes. When the student knows the 74 basic phonograms well, this may be reduced to 2-5 minutes of quick review.)

2. Present Exploring Sounds. (5-10 minutes depending upon the lesson.)

3. Teach the new spelling rule. (5-10 minutes depending upon the lesson.)

4. Dictate 15 spelling words and analyze the words. (15-25 minutes)

5. Teach the Grammar Rules (Optional based upon the needs of the students).

6. Teach the Vocabulary Development Activity. (5-10 minutes).

7. Choose 1-3 Optional Activities from the lesson, as needed by the student.

Optional Day 2

1. Choose 20-45 minutes of Optional Activities and Composition Activities to practice the words learned in the previous lesson.

EMERGING READERS AND SPELLERS

SIX- TO SEVEN-YEAR-OLD STUDENTS

Total Time: 30-60 minutes per day

Schedule: Teach one lesson per week.

Time Frame: Complete *The Logic of English Essentials* in 40 weeks.

Before Beginning Lesson 1: The needs and abilities of students at this age can vary widely. Before beginning Lesson 1 ensure that all students have developed Phonemic Awareness (see Intro 25 - Intro 32), learned the sounds for A-Z (see Intro 33 - Intro 36), and learned how to write the lowercase letters. Depending upon prior experience, plan to dedicate between one and thirty hours to working on this material. For students who have not learned the sounds of A-Z and how to write them, begin by teaching a minimum of one letter per day. Each day play games such as are found in *The Phonogram and Spelling Game Book.*

Emerging Readers and Spellers: Remember that students at this age vary widely in ability and language experiences. Teaching students one-on-one or in a small group will offer the advantage of being able to follow the lead of the students.

Classroom teachers, though, should not short-change the process of developing phonemic awareness and learning the sound and symbol correlations for the A-Z phonograms. This knowledge alone will boost natural readers' abilities.

Tips: Young students also benefit greatly from learning through play and movement. Be sure to incorporate plenty of games in your lessons. Ideas are included in each lesson in the Optional Activities boxes. Additional ideas for practicing phonograms and spelling words designed for young children can be found in *The Phonogram and Spelling Game Book.*

A sample schedule for using the lessons is included below.

Day 1

1. Introduce and practice phonograms. (15 minutes)

2. Present Exploring Sounds. (10 minutes)

3. Teach the new spelling rule. (15 minutes)

4. Independent Work: Practice writing the phonograms five times each, and illustrate the spelling rule.

Day 2

1. Practice phonograms with a game. (15 minutes)

2. Review the spelling rule. (5 minutes)

3. Dictate the spelling list. (15 minutes)

4. Independent Work: Write the plural form or the past tense of each word.

Day 3

1. Practice phonograms with a game. (15 minutes)

2. Grammar lesson. (25 minutes)

3. Phrase/Sentence Dictation. (10 minutes)

4. Independent Work: Choose a grammar worksheet to practice alone.

Day 4

1. Practice phonograms with a game. (15 minutes)

2. Play a spelling game using the list and any desired review words.

3. Vocabulary lesson.

4. Independent Work: Vocabulary practice worksheet.

Day 5

1. Phonogram quiz.

2. Spelling quiz.

3. Composition Activity.

YOUNG EMERGING READERS

FIVE- TO SIX-YEAR-OLD STUDENTS

Total Time: 5-60 minutes per day

Schedule: Teach one lesson every two weeks.

Time Frame: Complete *The Logic of English Essentials* in 80 weeks.

Before Beginning Lesson 1: Plan on dedicating thirty lessons to developing Phonemic Awareness (see Intro 25 - Intro 32), learning the sounds for A-Z (see Intro 33 - Intro 36), and learning how to write the lowercase letters.

Preliminary lessons should consist of: 1) a phonemic awareness activity such as the ones found on Intro 25 - Intro 32; 2) learning how to read and write (large motor skill) one phonogram each day; 3) playing phonogram games such as the ones found in *The Phonogram and Spelling Game Book.*

The first lesson will be very short, five to ten minutes. Teach the first phonogram, its sounds, and how to write it using large motor skills. As phonograms are added, the lessons will grow in length providing students an opportunity to grow in attention span.

Young Emerging Readers and Spellers: During the lessons respect young students' need to learn through play and activity. Also be sure to teach the phonograms using large motor skills by practicing writing with sandpaper letters, salt boxes, whiteboards, and chalkboards. Do not expect them to write on paper.

Once the students have learned the A-Z phonograms and demonstrated basic phonemic awareness, you may begin Lesson 1.

Tips: If the students are ready for writing on paper, you may use the student workbook. If the students' fine motor skills are not well developed, have them write the words with large motor motions on a whiteboard, chalkboard, or in a salt box. Answers for the workbook activities may also be written on whiteboards.

If desired, younger students may skip the grammar lessons, though they will benefit from the Vocabulary Development Activities, Dictation, and Composition.

Students at this age benefit from a lot of direct instruction and teacher participation. Do not expect them to complete activities alone.

Be sure to provide plenty of review through games. Keep it fun.

The following is a suggested schedule to modify the curriculum for young emerging readers and spellers.

Day 1

1. Introduce and practice phonograms. (15 minutes)

2. Present Exploring Sounds. (10 minutes)

3. Teach the new spelling rule. (15 minutes)

Day 2

1. Practice phonograms with a game. (15 minutes)

2. Review the spelling rule and have students illustrate it. (5 minutes)

3. Dictate 5 spelling words and analyze the words. (15 minutes)

4. Optional Activity of choice. (10 minutes)

Day 3

1. Practice phonograms with a game. (15 minutes)

2. Review the spelling rule. (5 minutes)

3. Review words from the previous lesson by writing on vocabulary cards. (5 minutes)

4. Optional Activity of choice. (10 minutes)

Day 4

1. Practice phonograms with a game. (15 minutes)

2. Dictate 5 spelling words and analyze the words. (15 minutes)

3. Grammar lesson. (10 minutes)

4. Read the vocabulary cards. (5 minutes)

Day 5

1. Practice phonograms with a game. (15 minutes)

2. Review the spelling rule. (5 minutes)

3. Review words from the previous lesson by writing on vocabulary cards. (5 minutes)

4. Optional Activity of choice. (10 minutes)

5. Read the vocabulary cards and arrange them into phrases or sentences. (10 minutes)

Day 6

1. Practice phonograms with a game. (15 minutes)

2. Dictate 5 spelling words and analyze the words. (15 minutes)

3. Grammar lesson. (10 minutes)

4. Optional Activity of choice. (5 minutes)

Day 7

1. Practice phonograms with a game. (15 minutes)

2. Review the spelling rule. (5 minutes)

3. Review words from the previous lesson by writing on vocabulary cards. (5 minutes)

4. Optional Activity of choice. (5 minutes)

5. Read the vocabulary cards and arrange them into phrases or sentences. (10 minutes)

Day 8

1. Practice phonograms with a game. (15 minutes)

2. Dictate 2 phrases or sentences from the Dictation Activity. (5 minutes)

3. Composition Activity using the vocabulary cards. (10 minutes)

4. Optional Activity of choice. (5 minutes)

5. Play a spelling game from the *Phonogram and Spelling Game Book.* (10 minutes)

Day 9

1. Practice phonograms with a game. (15 minutes)

2. Dictate 2 phrases or sentences from the Dictation Activity. (5 minutes)

3. Composition Activity in the Workbook. (10 minutes)

4. Teach the Vocabulary Development Activity. (10 minutes)

5. Optional Activity of choice. (5 minutes)

Day 10

1. Practice phonograms with a game. (15 minutes)

2. Dictate 2 phrases or sentences from the Dictation Activity. (5 minutes)

3. Vocabulary Development Activity in the workbook. (5 minutes)

4. Optional Activity of choice. (5 minutes)

5. Read the vocabulary cards. (5 minutes)

6. Play a spelling game from the *Phonogram and Spelling Game Book.* (10 minutes)

ESL STUDENTS

ALL AGES
LEARNING TO READ AND WRITE IN ENGLISH

Total Time: 30-120 minutes per day

Schedule: Varies from one lesson per day to one lesson every ten days, depending upon the ages and needs of students.

Time Frame: Complete *The Logic of English Essentials* in 8-80 weeks

Before Beginning Lesson 1: ESL students benefit greatly from learning the sounds of A-Z in isolation and how to pronounce them. Spend focused time learning how to pronounce the sounds for A-Z, incorporating kinesthetic awareness of how the sounds are produced. Teach students how to write the lowercase letters as they learn to pronounce them. Each day play games such as those found in *The Phonogram and Spelling Game Book*. These lessons may be combined with vocabulary development from another program.

Once students know the sounds of A-Z and how to write them, you may begin teaching Lesson 1.

ESL Students: ESL students benefit greatly from this holistic and systematic approach to learning to read, spell, and write. *The Logic of English Essentials* program is an ideal reading, writing, and grammar course for ESL students. Students will systematically learn the 45 English speech sounds and how they are written, how to build phonograms into words, how words are arranged to construct sentences, and grammar. This program will prepare students to read in English, which is a highly efficient way to further develop vocabulary.

Tips: In addition to gaining English literacy skills, students will become more attuned to the speech patterns of English. When teaching words with unaccented vowels, be certain to explain accented syllables and the schwa sound. This will aid students in developing more natural speech patterns.

Utilize the spelling word lists to develop vocabulary, and rapidly expand students' vocabularies by teaching them how to form derivatives.

ESL students benefit greatly from creating Spelling Cards and using these to form phrases and sentences in English. In addition, the definition of the word may be written on the back of the card, and the cards may then be used for vocabulary drills as well.

ESL students may use any of the sample schedules included above, depending upon the ages and abilities of the students.

BEFORE YOU BEGIN

PHONEMIC AWARENESS

Before you begin to teach the phonograms and their sounds, it is best if students have developed a basic level of phonemic awareness. Phonemes are the individual speech sounds which combine together to form words. The English language has forty-five phonemes.

Phonemic awareness is a clear understanding that words are comprised of individual sounds "glued" together. Though it may seem obvious to a strong reader, this is not a natural concept, and many struggling readers and spellers lack this foundational understanding. Students lacking phonemic awareness often appear to be guessing wildly when "reading." They may even guess a word that does not resemble the targeted word in any way.

Students guess because many programs teach reading using sight words. In this school of thought, students are taught that "the whole word" is a visual representation of a word without understanding that the letters represent a code of sounds. These students are then taught to guess unknown words from context. This sort of teaching produces students who are unaware that the letters in the words represent sounds. Many have never even considered that words are made up of sounds. Their minds have been trained to focus on the word level.

The problem of random guessing is compounded by the students' stage of language development. Babies are natural speech learners. They listen intently to the phonemes in the mother-tongue spoken around them. First, they babble the individual sounds. Then they combine these into short one-syllable words, followed by two-syllable words, and then short sentences. By the time a child is ready to learn to read, he has mastered most if not all of the forty-five phonemes of English, and is now focused on learning new words. In addition, words in the flow of speech are a blend of sounds with variations in color. We do not speak using pure, individual phonemes. It is no wonder many students have never discovered that words are comprised of a sequential blend of individual sounds.

The following activities will heighten awareness of the sounds and teach students to break words into their individual phonemes. As a teacher, your goal is to determine if the student is aware of the phonemes and able to separate words into their individual sounds. If students needs more practice, dwell on the activity until it is easy. For older students who demonstrate a grasp of phonemic awareness, these activities may be used as a quick assessment to demonstrate proficiency.

STEP 1—DEVELOPING A KINESTHETIC AWARENESS OF SOUNDS

A majority of people have not made a strong connection between the auditory and kinesthetic components of speech. This series of questions is designed to heighten students' awareness of the differences in the shape of their mouth as they produce a variety of sounds. This is particularly helpful for students who struggle with auditory processing and/or are kinesthetic learners.

If possible, provide students with a small mirror so they can observe their mouths as they explore the following sounds.

SEE AND FEEL THE SOUNDS

p	*What part of the mouth is used to say /p/?* lips *Put your hand in front of your mouth as you say /p/. What do you feel as you say /p/?* air exploding, or popping out *Can you make /p/ louder and softer?* no Make sure students are not saying /p-ŭ/. Rather, isolate the sound /p/. If they continue to say /ŭ/, isolate the /ŭ/ sound and then ask them to try to remove it from the /p/.
b	*What part of the mouth is used to say /b/?* lips *Put your hand on your throat as you say /p/ and then /b/. What changes when you say /b/?* My throat vibrates. *This is your voice box. You turn your voice box on when you say /b/. /b/ is a voiced sound.* *Can you make /b/ louder and softer?* no Make sure students are not saying /b-ŭ/. Rather isolate the sound /b/.
f	*What part of the mouth is used to say /f/?* teeth and lips *Put your hand in front of your mouth as you say /f/. What do you feel?* air *Keep your hand in front of your mouth. Say /f/ and /p/. How does the air feel different?* With /p/ it explodes. It is fast and then stops. With /f/ it is softer and keeps blowing. *Can you make /f/ louder and softer?* no
v	*Say /v/. What part of the mouth is used to say /v/?* teeth and lips *Compare /f/ and /v/. Put your hand in front of your mouth as you say them, and put your hand on your throat. What is the same and what is different between /f/ and /v/?* The air is soft and blowing with both. /v/ is voiced and /f/ is unvoiced. *Can you make /v/ louder and softer?* no
ŏ	*Say /ŏ/. How is your mouth shaped as you say /ŏ/?* round and open *Can you make /ŏ/ louder and softer?* yes
ō	*Say /ō/. How is your mouth shaped as you say /ō/?* round and open *Compare /ŏ/ and /ō/.* The mouth becomes rounder with /ō/. *Can you make /ō/ louder and softer?* yes

s	*Say /s/. How is your mouth shaped as you say /s/?* slightly open, teeth close together *Where is your tongue and how is it shaped?* The tongue is curved on the sides near the front teeth. *Do you feel the air blowing over your tongue? Feel it with your hand. Compare the air as you say /s/, /f/, /p/.* /s/ and /f/ are steady streams. /p/ is short and popping. *Can you make /s/ louder and softer?* no
z	*Say /z/. Compare the shape of your mouth and tongue to /s/.* They are the same. *What is different?* /z/ is voiced and /s/ is unvoiced. *Can you make /z/ louder and softer?* no
th	*Say /th/ as in "thin." Where is your tongue?* Sticking out slightly between the teeth. *Feel the air.* *Can you make /th/ louder and softer?* no
TH	*Say /TH/ as in "this." What is different from /th/?* /TH/ is voiced, /th/ is unvoiced. *Can you make /TH/ louder and softer?* no
m	*Say /m/. How is your mouth formed?* It is closed, and the lips are pressed together. *Is air coming out of your mouth?* no *What happens if you plug your nose?* I can't say /m/. *Where is the air coming out?* my nose *Can you say /th/, /s/ and /b/ if you plug your nose?* yes
n	*Say /n/. How is your mouth formed?* The tongue is pressing against the roof of the mouth. *Where is the air coming out?* the nose *What happens if you plug your nose?* I can't say /n/.
ē	*Say /ē/. How is your mouth shaped as you say /ē/?* It is open and pulled back in a tense position, or like a smile. My tongue is curled against my teeth in the back.
ĭ	*Say /ĭ/. How is your mouth shaped as you say /ĭ/?* It is open, my lips are forward and relaxed. My tongue is curled against my teeth in the back. *Compare /ē/ and /ĭ/. Is your tongue in the same place?* yes *What changes?* The lips are pulled back further with /ē/, and they relax to say /ĭ/.

STEP 2—GLUING WORDS TOGETHER

The second step to developing phonemic awareness is learning how to hear the individual speech sounds which make up words and "glue" them back together into words. Begin this activity with compound words, proceed to short, one-syllable words, and increase the difficulty until students are gluing together three- and four- syllable words.

Level 1: Compound Words

I am thinking of a word made of two words that are stuck together. I will tell you the two words. You need to glue them together to make the new word.

rain	bow	*rainbow*	water	fall	*waterfall*
foot	ball	*football*	head	ache	*headache*
after	noon	*afternoon*	sail	boat	*sailboat*
back	bone	*backbone*	horse	back	*horseback*
sun	shine	*sunshine*	back	yard	*backyard*
sand	box	*sandbox*	bean	bag	*beanbag*
bed	side	*bedside*	birth	day	*birthday*
blue	bell	*bluebell*	row	boat	*rowboat*
key	board	*keyboard*	fire	fly	*firefly*
red	head	*redhead*	note	book	*notebook*

Level 2: One Syllable Words

I am thinking of a word. I am going to say the word with the sounds un-glued. I want you to glue the sounds back together and tell me the word.

Hint: say the word as the individual sounds, like I said it. Then say it faster and faster, until you blend it together.

The teacher should pronounce each sound with a clear break in between. The objective is to pronounce each sound, not each letter.

/d-ŏ-g/	*dog*	/ĕ-g/	*egg*
/b-oi/	*boy*	/m-ŏ-m/	*mom*
/t-ī-m/	*time*	/h-ō-m/	*home*
/k-ŭ-p/	*cup*	/k-ar/	*car*

/f-ō-n/	phone		/m-ă-n/	man
/p-l-ā-t/	plate		/d-ă-d/	dad
/p-r-ī-z/	prize		/t-ŏ-p/	top
/l-ŭ-n-ch/	lunch		/l-ī-t/	light
/p-l-ā-s/	place		/g-r-ā-t/	great
/s-k-r-ă-p/	scrap		/t-ě-n-t/	tent

Level 3: Two Syllable Words

/ă-p-l/	apple		/t-ā-b-l/	table
/w-ĭ-n-er/	winner		/w-ĭ-n-d-ō/	window
/l-ā-d-ē/	lady		/m-ŏ-TH-er/	mother
/k-ŭ-z-ĭ-n/	cousin		/k-ĭ-t-ě-n/	kitten
/p-ŏ-p-k-or-n/	popcorn		/t-r-ĭ-k-l/	trickle
/t-ĭ-k-l/	tickle		/p-l-ā-er/	player
/d-ŏ-k-t-or/	doctor		/b-ă-s-k-ě-t/	basket
/p-l-ā-g-r-ou-n-d/	playground		/k-ar-t-oo-n/	cartoon

Level 4: Three and Four Syllable Words

/b-ī-s-ĭ-k-l/	bicycle		/c-ŏ-m-p-ū-t-er/	computer
/ě-l-ě-f-ă-n-t/	elephant		/m-ō-t-or-s-ī-k-l/	motorcycle
/r-ě-s-t-ä-r-ä-n-t/	restaurant		/p-ī-n-ă-p-l/	pineapple
/f-or-g-ě-t-f-ŭ-l/	forgetful		/k-ă-m-er-ä/	camera
/k-ar-p-ě-n-t-er/	carpenter		/h-ar-m-ŏ-n-ĭ-c-ä/	harmonica
/h-ŏ-l-ĭ-d-ā/	holiday		/l-ě-m-ŏ-n-ā-d/	lemonade

Games for Additional Practice

Charades

Play Charades. Break action words into their individual sounds. Ask students to blend them back together and then act out the word.

1. /s-ĭ-t/   *sit*
2. /s-t-ă-n-d/   *stand*
3. /j-ŭ-m-p/   *jump*
4. /r-ŭ-n/   *run*
5. /n-ē-l/   *kneel*
6. /k-ĭ-k/   *kick*
7. /s-ĭ-ng/ *sing*
8. /d-ă-n-s/   *dance*

Pick the Object/Picture

Choose a group of objects or pictures and place them on the table. Explain to students that you will say the words with the sounds un-glued. They need to glue the sounds back together and choose the correct object or picture.

/p-ĕ-n/   *pen*
/h-ă-t/   *hat*
/p-ā-p-er/   *paper*
/p-ĕ-n-s-ĭ-l/   *pencil*
/s-p-oo-n/   *spoon*
/b-ŏ-x/   *box*
/k-ō-t/   *coat*
/ē-r-ā-s-er/   *eraser*

Scavenger Hunt

Identify objects in the room. Explain to students that you will say the sounds of a word un-glued. They are to find the object someplace in the room and bring it to you.

STEP 3—UN-GLUING WORDS

When students are able to "glue" together sounds into words, reverse the process by asking students to "un-glue" the words. Choose categories of words such as animals, objects in the room, students' names, or have a set of pictures and ask students to choose a word to "un-glue." This activity may be done with the whole class, with pairs of students, or one-on-one with the teacher.

STEP 4—MANIPULATING WORDS

Level 1: Words that Begin with the Same Sound

To heighten awareness of sounds within words ask students to think of a word that begins with the same sound.

table	cards
ship	queen
lock	money

Level 2: Words that End with the Same Sound

To heighten awareness of sounds within words ask students to think of a word that ends with the same sound.

lock	dad
lip	live
school	true
honey	baby
mom	pass

Level 3: Rhyming

Rhyming demonstrates a more sophisticated level of phonemic awareness. When students rhyme words, they need to recognize that the first sounds of the word can be chopped off and swapped out for another sound. Read the words to the students and ask them to provide a word which rhymes.

cat	tool
dog	all
tap	head
night	sound
cry	nose
fish	ring
snake	hive
floor	true

STEP 5—SYLLABLES

Students need to be able to identify syllable breaks to decode and spell efficiently. Syllable breaks are key to determining the pronunciation of vowels. The following activities will aid students in becoming more proficient at counting the number of syllables in words.

Feel the Chin Movement

Place your hand under your chin. Say a word. Count the syllables by counting the number of times the mouth opens. For more information see Chapter 4 in *Uncovering the Logic of English®* by Denise Eide.

1. ba by
2. pants
3. cop y
4. ti tle
5. ro ses

6. mu sic
7. grand pa
8. tel e phone
9. tooth brush
10. fath er

Hum the Word

Firmly close the mouth, hum each word, and count the number of syllables.

ap ple	hm-hm	two syllables
friend ship	hm-hm	two syllables
pro fes sor	hm-hm-hm	three syllables
hip po pot a mus	hm-hm-hm-hm-hm	five syllables

Move to the Rhythm

Clap, march, stomp, jump to the beat of words.

TEACHING A-Z

Once students have developed phonemic awareness, the ability to segment words into their individual phonemes (sounds) and glue them back together, they are ready to learn the visual representations of the sounds. Each phoneme (sound) is represented by a phonogram, a sound picture. A phonogram may consist of one, two, three, or four letters.

Students should begin learning the single-letter phonograms A-Z. When a phonogram is introduced, students should be taught three things:

1. all the sounds of that phonogram in the order of frequency,

2. the appearance of the lowercase phonogram in book face, (the type of print represented in books), and

3. how to write the lowercase phonogram, preferably in cursive. (See Intro 37 - Intro 38 to learn more about cursive.)

This process uses all four learning modalities, hearing, seeing, doing, and saying, while naturally linking them to reading. Reading is a visual activity in that students must recognize the shapes of the letters. Its auditory component is listening to the sounds. Reading also has a natural kinesthetic component, writing, and is closely linked to the fourth learning modality, speaking. When students use these four modalities simultaneously to learn the phonograms, their learning is faster and deeper. They are able to learn using their strongest modality, while strengthening areas of weakness. In addition, each modality utilizes a separate region of the brain. When all four are activated, synapses are built across the regions and the learning is more effective.

ALL THE SOUNDS OF THE PHONOGRAM
IN ORDER OF FREQUENCY

When a phonogram is introduced, the teacher should tell the student all of its sounds in order of frequency. Too often phonics programs introduce one sound at a time, often over a period of years. These programs rarely draw a connection between the multiple sounds and the phonogram. This generates unnecessary confusion. In addition, when students learn only one sound of a phonogram at a time, they must limit their reading to controlled readers. This "simplified" information creates distress when students try to sound out words from other sources.

Many parents and educators worry that learning more than one sound at a time will overwhelm students. This is simply not the case. The fact that phonograms represent more than one sound is part of the reality of English. It is best for students to learn this from the beginning. It is far more overwhelming to students to discover they have more to learn after the fact, or to learn countless exceptions or sight words to accommodate the simplified sounds.

I often explain the situation to young students by asking, "How many sounds does a dog make?" After the child responds, "barking, whining, growling, etc.," I state, "In the same way, some of our phonograms make more than one sound."

Students who are taught this way from the beginning accept this reality more readily than those of us who need to unlearn misconceptions about English. Struggling students are often relieved when someone is finally honest about the multiple sounds and introduces them in an organized fashion where they can be remembered as a unit.

Students should first be taught the sounds, not the names of the letters. Learning the letter names DEE-OH-GEE does not help a child read the word *dog*. Learning the sounds /d-ŏ-g/ provides the necessary information to decode and spell the word. Students should learn the names of the letters only after the sounds have been mastered. Letter names are important for reading initials, communicating spellings, reading eye charts… however, they are not foundational to reading words.

TEACH LOWERCASE BOOK-FACE LETTERS

Each phonogram should be introduced by showing the students the lowercase phonograms in a book-face style font. This is the style of printing commonly used in books and found on the Basic and Advanced Phonogram Flash Cards. Teaching lowercase letters first provides students with the most vital information they need to be successful in learning to read. Too often we begin by teaching the capital letters. This ignores the fact that a vast majority of the letters we read and write are lowercase; capitals are only found at the beginning of sentences and proper nouns.

Once students have mastered the lowercase letters, they should be taught how to write the capital letters as well as their proper usage. This will help to prevent students from misusing capitals within sentences.

Students should learn the phonograms without additional pictures. The phonograms themselves are pictures of sounds. Adding a picture, for example, of an apple for the phonogram a hinders students in two ways. First, many phonograms, like a , say more than one sound. The picture, though, only represents one of the sounds. Second, students need to create a fast and direct memory link between the phonogram and its sound(s). When a picture is added, students often rely on the process of thinking a stands for apple. Apple begins with /ă/, which is written a . This is far less efficient than learning that the three sounds for a are /ă-ā-ä/.

TEACH HOW TO WRITE THE LOWERCASE LETTERS

As soon as students are shown the phonogram in book face, they should be taught how to write the phonogram, preferably in cursive. (For more information on cursive, see Intro 37 - Intro 38.)

One of the greatest misconceptions about teaching reading is that students should not be taught to write until they have learned to read. This argument is based upon two misunderstandings about writing. First, educators who do not introduce writing at the same time as the sounds fail to recognize that writing is the natural kinesthetic experience of the phonogram. Feeling how the letter is shaped is a necessary component to mastering the shape. This is especially true for kinesthetic learners who learn by touch and doing.

Second, many educators argue that it is best to separate the teaching of writing from reading because many young children do not have well developed fine motor skills. Writing, though, is best taught to **all** students beginning with **large motor** movements. Students should be taught how to form the letters using movements that originate from the elbow, not the fingers. Movements from the elbow are simpler to control. When the large motor patterns are mastered, the transition to fine motor skill will be much easier. Many students who struggle with handwriting also struggle with reading because they do not understand how the letters are shaped; this is partly due to the fact they have not developed the muscle memory for the sequence of strokes necessary for writing.

When teaching a student how to write, always use all four learning modalities: seeing, hearing, doing, and speaking. Show the student how to form the letter (seeing), while providing explicit directions orally (hearing). Then ask the students to repeat the action (doing) while repeating the directions aloud (speaking).

Teach letter formation using large muscle movements originating from the elbow. The motions may be demonstrated on a chart with the index finger. Students may then practice the sequence of movements in salt boxes, on the whiteboard, with chalk, or in the air. Textured letters such as sandpaper letters are also useful as they engage the student's large motor memory with a high sensory experience.

Fluent handwriting is rhythmic with pauses only at the natural stopping or reversal points in the letters. Otherwise, the pencil should continue in a steady motion. When teaching handwriting, it is important to provide students with rhythmic directions that emphasize the natural rhythm of writing. The full, explicit directions in the *Logic of English® Handwriting Series* provide students with clear and explicit directions on how to form each letter. The steps may then be shortened to rhythmic cues which emphasize the natural rhythm of writing.

Students should not be taught how to write through tracing, as tracing hinders the development of a rhythmic, fluid stroke. When writing a lowercase "u" in cursive, the pencil begins on the baseline, moves quickly up to midline, **stops**, drops down to the baseline and curves back up to the midline, **stops**, drops down to the baseline and either **stops** at the end of the word or continues fluidly into the next letter. There are only two or three stopping points. When a student traces, they treat the activity like a connect-the-dot puzzle. The pencil moves in jerky stops to each of the dashes, stopping and starting many times. In this manner, tracing does not aid in developing the fluid muscle memory necessary for writing.

Until students have mastered letter formation, they should not be left alone to practice. Careful teaching and guidance from the beginning will prevent bad habits from forming. If teachers invest time in the beginning to ensure that each student has a clear understanding of how to form each letter and develops the correct muscle memory for each letter, huge amounts of wasted time and pain will be avoided in the future, not only in writing but reading as well. This is because handwriting instruction is formative to not only writing and spelling, but also reading.

Students should not be asked to copy phonograms alone until they have mastered how to form them and are able to write them quickly and with ease. Many students who struggle with visual confusion will begin to write letters backwards when left alone too soon. This results not only in confused handwriting, but also increases confusion in reading.

Students should not be asked to copy words, sentences, or paragraphs until they are reading at a second grade level. When asked to do so sooner, the task is akin to art and void of the valuable language learning that true copy work provides.

BEGIN WITH CURSIVE

At Pedia Learning Inc., we strongly recommend beginning with cursive. Cursive has six primary advantages over print: 1) It is less fine motor skill intensive. 2) All the lowercase letters begin in one place, on the baseline. 3) Spacing within and between words is controlled. 4) By lifting the pencil between words, the beginning and ending of words is emphasized. 5) It is difficult to reverse letters such as b's and d's. 6) The muscle memory that is mastered first will last a lifetime.

As a culture we have been mistakenly led to believe that printing is easier for students than cursive. However, this is simply not the case. Cursive requires far less fine motor skill than printing. Take a moment to write the word *teacher* in both print and cursive. Observe the motions of your fingers and the lifting of the pencil. With cursive the pencil is lifted only between words. With print the up and down motion of lifting the pencil between letters is far more fine motor skill intensive. Cursive was designed for the human hand; printing was designed for the printing press.

One of the most confusing aspects of learning to print is learning where to place the pencil to form each letter. This is because the lowercase print letters begin in seven different places. In contrast, this issue is solved with cursive; all the lowercase letters begin on the baseline. (Uppercase letters in both print and cursive are more difficult to write as they have more starting places.)

In addition, the spacing of letters within words and between words is natural in cursive due to the connections. This is in direct contrast to the difficulty that young students experience with printing. Many students put too little space between words and too much within words.

The connectedness of letters within words also helps to reinforce where words begin and end. Many students struggle to understand this concept when reading and will blend the final sounds of one word with the initial sounds of the next word. These same students frequently make the most errors in spacing their writing as well. By teaching cursive, these problems resolve easily.

Cursive handwriting also emphasizes the direction of reading and writing and makes letter reversals more difficult. Students who first learn to print frequently reverse b's and d's and p's and q's in both reading and writing. Cursive helps to minimize this type of confusion.

The generational problems of our handwriting practices are apparent. Most people in the United States mix print and cursive. This is because writing requires highly developed muscle memory. When students are asked to switch from printing to cursive in second or third grade, they are unable to overcome the prior years of practice. Most people recognize that cursive is faster and therefore end up blending cursive and print. Another significant percentage of students revert back to printing as soon as they are allowed. These students typically found developing the fine muscle memory of printing to be very difficult. They dreaded the demands placed upon them to switch to cursive when they have barely mastered printing. As soon as they are no longer required, they will revert back to printing. Since cursive is faster, it would be far better to develop the life long muscle memory for cursive and later learn to print for specialized uses such as filling out applications.

Although most schools in English speaking countries begin by teaching printing, most other cultures begin with the cursive form. In many non-English speaking countries, children's books are even printed in both print and cursive.

Teaching printing before cursive is one of the reasons for widespread underachievement in handwriting, spelling, and reading. For the reasons stated above, dyslexia and remedial reading centers around the United States recommend teaching cursive handwriting.

Although at Pedia Learning Inc. we believe it is important to begin by teaching students cursive, we understand that not all educators are ready to make the change. Therefore, all of our workbooks will be available in both a cursive and manuscript version.

Cursive Compared to Manuscript

All lowercase cursive letters begin on the baseline.	Lowercase manuscript letters begin in 7 places.
Pick up pencil only between words.	Pick up pencil between each letter.
Cannot put too much space between letters within a word and too little space between words.	Too much space is commonly placed between letters within a word and too little space between words.
Emphasizes where each word begins and ends.	Commonly creates confusion about beginnings and endings of words.
Cannot reverse b's and d's.	Reversals are common.
Historically taught first.	Taught first only for the last 80 years.
Taught first in Europe and Eastern Europe.	Taught only for drafting or not at all in most non-English speaking countries.
Designed for the human hand.	Designed for the printing press.

TEACHING THE LESSONS

Each lesson is divided into three parts. *Part One* includes: Phonograms, Exploring Sounds, and Spelling Rules. In *Part Two* students learn fifteen spelling words and how to analyze their spellings. *Part Three* integrates the spelling words into a Grammar Lesson, Dictation, Composition, and Vocabulary Development Activities. Lessons are designed to provide adequate time to practice new material.

The average student needs to encounter a new concept or word up to thirty times before it is internalized. Therefore, each lesson includes multiple encounters with the words in a variety of contexts. Though there is a consistent structure for the content, each lesson includes a wide variety of unique activities to aid teachers in tailoring the material to their own teaching style and their students' needs. Each lesson includes suggestions for games, directions for which can be found in *The Phonogram and Spelling Game Book*. Activities which include a corresponding page in the student workbook are marked with a ✎. Optional and Challenge activities are also included for students who need further practice or challenge. Many of the optional activities are meant to be assigned as independent or take-home work.

PART ONE OF THE LESSONS

Part One of each lesson consists of three components: Phonograms, Exploring Sounds, and Spelling Rules. Each component is necessary for all students. However, as the students progress in internalizing the phonogram sounds and spellings, phonogram practice time may be reduced to as little as two minutes of review per day.

PHONOGRAMS

The phonogram section of each lesson consists of two parts: introduction and review. Twenty-two lessons include a new phonogram or phonograms to be introduced to the students. In order to create stronger memory hooks, phonograms are often introduced in related groups. Sample teacher and student dialog is included to aid students in comparing and contrasting phonograms and relating new phonograms to previously learned ones.

Each lesson also includes a minimum of twenty previously taught phonograms for students to practice from dictation. The teacher should read the phonogram sounds and any associated spelling aids to clue the students as to which phonogram to write.

Finally, each phonogram section concludes with ideas for phonogram practice using games. Detailed directions may be found in *The Phonogram and Spelling Game Book*.

When students are new to the program, it is recommended that teachers schedule ample time each day for phonogram review and practice. When students have mastered the seventy-four phonograms, teachers may consider the games optional and review the phonograms quickly by reading the phonogram flash cards or writing the phonograms from dictation.

EXPLORING SOUNDS

The Exploring Sounds section includes phonemic awareness activities, lessons on more advanced concepts such as finding the accent, and activities which help students to analyze the options for spelling of sounds that are represented by more than one phonogram. Sample teacher and student dialog is included.

SPELLING RULES

Twenty-three lessons include the teaching of a new spelling rule. The spelling rule lessons are organized so that rules which correspond to a phonogram are taught with the phonogram, and rules which are related are grouped together. Sample teacher and student dialog is included. This section often includes additional workbook activities and optional activities to facilitate student practice.

PART TWO OF THE LESSONS

The second part of every lesson is the introduction of words through spelling dictation and analysis. Students who are not reading will spell their way into reading. Spelling dictation in its most basic form begins with the students hearing the word, then sounding it out, writing it, and finally analyzing why it is spelled in a particular way.

Logic of English® curriculum is laid out to help teachers engage students in learning new words. Each word list is formatted across two pages to facilitate teaching the following steps.

SPELLING DICTATION AND ANALYSIS

The following sample dialog will aid you in understanding the steps to teaching a spelling word. Remember, students hear the word, break it into its individual sounds, write it, and **then** see it for the first time in their own handwriting.

Sample One

Word	Practice Sentence	Say to Spell	# of Syllables	Markings
1. **duck**	*A boy is feeding the duck.*	dŭk	1	du<u>ck</u>

1. The teacher reads the word and uses it in a sentence.

   duck   A boy is feeding the duck.

2. The students repeat the word and say aloud the number of syllables.

   duck 1 syllable

3. The students then sound the word out aloud.

   /d ŭ k/

Option 1: Students may tap their fingers together as they say each sound.

Option 2: The teacher may hold up a finger(s) as the student pronounces each sound. When a sound is spelled with two letters the teacher may clue the student by holding up two fingers. When a sound is spelled with three letters the teacher would hold up three fingers, etc.

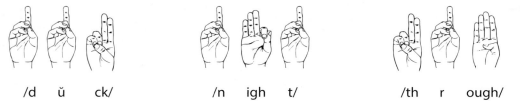

/d   ŭ   ck/   /n   igh   t/   /th   r   ough/

   If there is a sound that needs clarification, the teacher indicates which spelling is used. Students may also ask for clarification.

   Use two letter /k/.

4. The students write the word in their workbook. (If the word has more than one syllable, students should leave a small space between each of the syllables.)

Spelling Hints	Part of Speech	Vocabulary Development
Underline /k/. **26** CK is used only after a single vowel which says its short sound.	N, V	ducks, ducking, ducked, duckling, duckweed

5. Using the Spelling Hints column, teachers guide the students in analyzing the word. (Do **not** require students to learn the numbers for each rule! Rules are numbered only for ease in reference for the teacher.)

How do we mark duck? Underline /k/.

Why? It is a multi-letter phonogram.

Why did we use CK? /ŭ/ is a single short vowel and the rule says, "CK is used only after a single vowel which says its short sound."

6. Do **not** require students to write the part of speech at this time. This will be used in Part Three. The part of speech is included for the teacher's reference on this page.

7. The final column lists common derivatives which utilize the base word. These are not used in Part Two. Derivatives may be assigned to advanced students or used for later review. They also demonstrate to the teacher how learning the one word contributes to overall vocabulary and spelling development.

Sample Two

Many two-syllable words present an additional challenge for spelling. Vowels in unaccented syllables often say the schwa sound, /ə/. In other words, the schwa sound /ə/ can be spelled with any vowel. In traditional spelling programs students must memorize these words visually. The methods used in The Logic of English® provide students the opportunity to form an auditory picture and/or memorize the word kinesthetically by writing the word.

Students will need additional cues from the teacher in order to spell these words correctly from dictation.

Word	Practice Sentence	Say to Spell	# of Syllables	Markings
1. **mother**	*My mother is kind.*	mŏTH er	2	mo<u>th</u> er

1. The teacher reads the word and uses it in a sentence.

   mother My mother is kind.

2. The teacher repeats the word, exaggerating the pronunciation for spelling. (Sounds that commonly need exaggeration are highlighted. An additional tip is also provided under Spelling Hints.)

   /mŏTH er/

3. The students repeat the word with the exaggerated sound and say aloud the number of syllables.

   /mŏTH e r/ 2 syllables

4. The students then sound out the word aloud.

   /m ŏ TH e r/

Option 1: Students may tap their fingers together as they say each sound.

Option 2: The teacher may hold up a finger(s) as the student pronounces each sound. When a sound is spelled with two letters the teacher may clue the student by holding up two fingers. When a sound is spelled with three letters the teacher would hold up three fingers, etc.

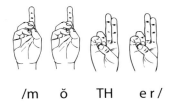

/m   ŏ   TH   e r /

5. If there is a sound that needs clarification, the teacher indicates which spelling is used.

   Use the /er/ of her.

6. The students write the word in their workbooks. (If the word has more than one syllable, students should leave a small space between each of the syllables.)

Spelling Hints	Part of Speech	Vocabulary Development
Say to spell: mŏther. Underline /TH/ and put a 2 over it. /th-TH/ said its second sound. Underline /er/.	N, V	mothers, motherly, mothering, mothered, grandmother

7. Using the Markings and Spelling Hints, teachers guide the students in analyzing the word.

   How do we mark the first syllable /mŏTH/? Underline /TH/.
   What sound of /th-TH/ is it? Second, so I will write a 2 over it.
   How do we mark the second syllable /er/? Underline the /er/.

8. Do **not** require students to write the part of speech at this time. This will be used in Part Three. The part of speech is included for the teacher's reference on this page.

9. The final column lists common derivatives which utilize the base word. These are not used in Part Two. Derivatives may be assigned to advanced students or used for later review. They also demonstrate to the teacher how learning the one word contributes to overall vocabulary and spelling development.

SPELLING MARKINGS

English is a complex code. In the Logic of English® Curriculum students are asked to mark the spelling words as a way to analyze the logic behind the spelling of the word.

1. **Underline multi-letter phonograms** – Forty-eight of the seventy-four phonograms are written with more than one letter. To train student's eyes to see the multi-letter phonograms as a whole, students should be directed to underline multi-letter phonograms in their spelling list.

   eight   *black*   *sharp*   *paint*

2. **Mark the vowel sound** - The single-letter vowels in English each say two or three sounds. Because English has so many vowel sounds, vowels are one of the most difficult aspects of learning to read and spell in English. In *The Logic of English®* materials the phonogram sounds are written in order of frequency. Notice with each of the single-letter vowels that the first sound is the short sound. This is because the short sound is the most common. The short sound will not be marked within words.

The long sound is the second most common sound. Mark long vowel sounds with a line over them. This is the common dictionary marking. In addition to aiding students in analyzing the spelling of a particular word, marking the vowels will teach them how to read the pronunciation key for vowels in a dictionary. When marking the long sound, be sure to have students tell you why the vowel is saying its long sound. This information can be found in the Spelling Hints column of the Teacher's Manual.

sāme   rōpe   tī tle   prō gram

The third vowel sound is called the broad sound. This sound is often written in dictionaries by writing two dots over the vowel.

mä   fäther   dö   püt

3. **Number the sound** - In addition to the single-letter vowels, eighteen additional phonograms make more than one sound. In *The Logic of English®* materials the phonogram sounds are written in order of frequency. Therefore, the first sound is the most common sound heard within words. When the second, third, or fourth sound of a phonogram is heard, the students should write a small number over the phonogram to remind them the phonogram is saying one of its less commonly heard sounds.

is²   sch̲ ool̲ ²   boo̲k²   grou̲p³

Reading Tip: One way to help emerging readers sound out an unknown word is to lightly underline the multi-letter phonograms in pencil and write the number of the sound that is heard above it.

4. **Double underline silent letters** - English words commonly end in a silent final E. In addition, the L and occasionally other letters are silent within the word. A double underline means they are silent.

cave̲̲   live̲̲   ta l̲k   an swer̲̲

5. **Mark the reason for the silent final E** - There are nine reasons to add a silent final E to English words. When a silent E is present, it is important that students understand why it is needed.

When the vowel says its name because of the E, write a line over the vowel to show it is long and double underline the E because it is silent.

cāve̲̲   mīne̲̲   cūte̲̲   tōne̲̲

When the vowel is present for another reason, underline the phonogram that necessitates the E once and double underline the silent E. The reason for the silent E can be found in the Spelling Hints column of the Teacher's Guide.

give̲̲   large̲̲   voice̲̲   table̲̲

PART THREE OF THE LESSONS

Part Three of each lesson consists of four components: Grammar, Dictation, Composition, and Vocabulary Development. These activities are designed to integrate the development of word and sentence level grammar skills into the practice of spelling and reading.

GRAMMAR

Understanding basic grammar is essential to learning how to add suffixes to words and to forming and punctuating sentences. Systematic, explicit teaching ensures that each student has the tools needed to read and write.

While phonograms and spelling rules describe how the letters are organized into words, grammar describes how words are organized into sentences. Once students have learned to read words, they are ready to begin putting these words together into phrases and then into sentences.

The Logic of English® series teaches all levels of language explicitly and systematically. Students are not left to guess or rely on intuition. There are logical reasons and answers given for each step of developing written language, and students are provided with explicit tools which aid them in comprehending while reading and expressing their thoughts in writing.

Many students struggle to express their ideas clearly in writing though they are articulate when speaking. This is because written language is more formal than spoken language. In addition, grammar rules must be learned in order to provide clarity where pauses, tone, facial expression, hand motions, context, and other social cues provide clarity in spoken communication. Although some students seem to naturally absorb many of the rules of written language, all students benefit when the grammar rules which govern written language are taught systematically and explicitly.

In *The Logic of English Essentials*, grammar is taught both as a science and as a tool. Students learn the parts of speech by asking and answering questions. This process of questioning demonstrates to students the relationship between words. This process also provides students the tools to become better writers.

Good writing provides the reader with answers. Fiction writers must provide the reader with the setting (where), plot (what), characters (who), and character development (what are they like?). The author crafts answers in a manner that invites the reader into the fictional world of the story. Excellent expository writers are able to weave in details that make the subject matter come alive.

Too often grammar is taught as an esoteric subject that does not connect to a student's daily life. Grammar, usage, and mechanics are all tools to help us communicate. When we explicitly teach the job of an adjective and the questions it answers, we provide students with the adjective as a tool to improve their writing. Students who know that a subordinating conjunction is a way to connect two related sentences will be able to pull the subordinating conjunctions out of their tool box to improve overly simplistic writing. Students who have learned that a dependent clause is followed by a comma at the beginning of a sentence and is not marked with a comma at the end of the sentence will avoid one of the most common punctuation errors.

Unfortunately many students who attempt to write "naturally" become discouraged as the pieces do not seem to fit together as easily on paper as in their heads. In the Logic of English,® students are systematically taught how to write sentences, punctuate them, and make them more interesting. These foundational skills will aid them in putting their own ideas on paper and provide them with essential information for becoming better writers.

An optional activity of creating Vocabulary Cards is provided in the Grammar Section. This is an excellent activity for kinesthetic students, as the cards are later used to create sentences, organize parts of speech, and play games.

DICTATION

Dictation of phrases and sentences provides students an opportunity to practice spelling and punctuation. Dictation closely mirrors writing, in that it requires students to hold an idea in their minds and translate that thought to paper. The benefit with dictation is that it removes the pressure of the student needing to generate a unique thought and allows for highly controlled practice.

When dictating a sentence, read it two times to the students. Direct students to repeat it back to you and then begin to write.

Students new to dictation will often need to hear the phrase or sentence more than two times. As their skills develop, try to wean them to hearing the sentence only one or two times before writing it.

COMPOSITION

Composition activities are provided to encourage students to use the words they are learning to build sentences. These activities often utilize both the newly learned spelling and the grammar concepts. Initial activities are tightly controlled, allowing students to focus on the process of writing a sentence. Students are provided more creative license as their skills develop. Later activities are also focused on helping students write more complex and interesting sentences.

Teachers should correct the students' spelling, punctuation, and grammar in these activities.

VOCABULARY

The Vocabulary section teaches students how to combine words into compound words, add prefixes and suffixes, and form contractions. Students are taught the meanings of common affixes and roots. They also are taught how to analyze and comprehend the meaning of new words, thereby expanding their vocabulary.

OPTIONAL ACTIVITIES

Each lesson includes numerous optional activities. The Optional Activities are formatted in a blue box so that teachers can easily see that these are non-essential. These activities are designed to provide the teacher with plenty of options to individualize teaching. Most teachers will not use every activity. Each activity is marked with the following symbols to denote the learning styles that are targeted through the activity:

Ⓚ   Kinesthetic - students who learn through movement

Ⓥ   Visual - students who learn through seeing

Ⓐ   Auditory - students who learn through hearing

Ⓒ   Creative - students who learn through creative expression of the material

Some Optional Activities use printed pages in the student workbook.

SPELLING CARDS

An Optional Spelling Cards activity is included in Lessons 1-40. Following the Grammar Section of each Lesson, students write their spelling words onto index cards to create Spelling Cards. The cards can then be rearranged to compose phrases or sentences, or illustrate grammar points such as prepositional phrases, etc. This activity is particularly helpful for students with weak auditory processing skills and those who enjoy kinesthetic activities.

THE LOGIC OF ENGLISH® SPELLING JOURNAL

The Spelling Journal is a highly beneficial activity to aid students in memorizing the sounds which have various options for spelling. *Logic of English® Spelling Journals* may be purchased at www.LogicOfEnglish.com.

ASSESSMENT & REVIEW LESSONS

Every fifth lesson provides assessment and review activities.

Logic of English® assessments are designed to help the students assess their own strengths and weaknesses. The assessments are given via dictation, because dictation better simulates the writing process than spelling individual words or multiple choice questions. Following each assessment, questions are provided to isolate areas that need further practice.

Teachers and students then work together to choose activities that would be most beneficial in clarifying areas of confusion. Ample ideas are also provided for additional practice of words and phonograms.

Assessments should not be used to grade or judge the student. Reading and spelling are subjects that should be taught to the point of mastery for all students. Assessments provide the teacher and students an opportunity to gain insight into what needs more work. The optional activities are ideal for tutors, parents, and other support staff to provide additional practice and instruction that reinforces classroom learning.

Teachers must be aware that some of the concepts have only been introduced in the previous lesson. Since long term retention takes repetition over time, many students will need further review of these concepts. The purpose of a review lesson is to assess what each student has retained and to discover what needs further practice.

If students make fewer than two mistakes, you may skip the review lesson and continue with the next lesson.

If students make more than two mistakes, review activities are provided. Use these activities for one lesson as further practice. DO NOT stop here and wait until all these words are mastered. The concepts will continue to appear and some students, especially older students, need exposure to more words in order to gain mastery.

IMPORTANT TIPS

MANAGING FLASH CARDS

Keep flash cards organized in three stacks, each secured with a rubber band: 1) cards which have not been introduced, 2) cards which students are learning, 3) cards which students have mastered. As phonograms are introduced, move them into the stack of cards students are learning. When students demonstrate consistent mastery of a phonogram, move it into the stack of phonograms which have been mastered. Review this third stack a minimum of once per week.

Review 2x / week

MANAGING PHONOGRAM GAME CARDS

Some of the optional games in *The Phonogram and Spelling Game Book* require more than one stack of Phonogram Game Cards. This can be overwhelming if the cards are not managed well. Nevertheless, the games can be highly motivating to students, and in most situations using these games is highly beneficial and worth the extra effort. Manage the phonogram cards in the same manner as suggested above. Before each lesson make sure that each stack of Phonogram Game Cards has been updated.

OLDER CYNICAL STUDENT

Many older students will be cynical about a new program. This is a healthy response. Do not argue with the student. Simply assure him/her that this program will offer a logical explanation for English reading and spelling. Then move on to teaching the lessons. Some struggling students benefit by seeing the patterns and phonograms in hundreds of words over the course of several weeks. With these students it is very important to keep moving and not get hung up on mastering phonograms. Provide them help by writing a forgotten phonogram on the board and gently reminding them about forgotten rules. Your first goal is to inspire your student that there is a new, logical way to understand words.

STUDENT MISSING TOO MANY WORDS ON THE ASSESSMENT

Many teachers worry when students miss more than two or three words on the end of the week assessment. Use the review lesson to practice the words. Then, especially if the student is cynical, move on. Do not get stuck early in the program. Rules and phonograms will continually reappear for practice. Many students need to see them used in hundreds of words before they begin to "click." Remember, The Logic of English® is not about mastering individual sight words. Students learn to think about the language differently.

Many students will need additional practice on words that have sounds with several options for spelling. *The Logic of English Spelling Journal* is an excellent option for students to create a personal reference.

Some teachers also like to create a review box of spelling words. The spelling box should have two sections, words that are being practiced and words which have been mastered. Write words that are missed on index cards. Direct the students to highlight the troublesome part of the word. Then put the word in a spelling box. Each day review the practice words. When the students have spelled it correctly at least three days in a row, put it in the back of the box. Once every week or two, review the words in the mastered section.

TEACHER RESOURCES

SPELLING LISTS

List 1

1. hat
2. map
3. bag
4. bat
5. bed
6. hand
7. cat
8. leg
9. dog
10. quilt
11. soft
12. fast
13. last
14. pink
15. bad

List 2

1. street
2. sun
3. pond
4. black
5. strong
6. string
7. green
8. truck
9. sick
10. three
11. ten
12. long
13. path
14. tree
15. rock

List 3

1. quick
2. man
3. human
4. clean
5. seven
6. duck
7. clock
8. frozen
9. paper
10. six
11. milk
12. ship
13. forest
14. hero
15. bread

List 4

1. gray
2. oil
3. boy
4. rain
5. favor
6. plain
7. train
8. list
9. paint
10. day
11. toy
12. mail
13. the
14. a
15. an

List 6

1. glass
2. cliff
3. brush
4. all
5. ball
6. school
7. poor
8. car
9. secret
10. moon
11. card
12. book
13. class
14. full
15. sharp

List 7

1. hill
2. rich
3. boat
4. toe
5. tall
6. road
7. room
8. river
9. cheap
10. coat
11. egg
12. soap
13. inch
14. door
15. floor

List 8

1. program
2. tooth
3. night
4. music
5. wheat
6. block
7. bright
8. warm
9. wheel
10. light
11. yard
12. good
13. better
14. best
15. perfect

List 9

1. mother
2. brother
3. son
4. father
5. sister
6. daughter
7. aunt
8. great
9. corner
10. raw
11. year
12. right
13. laughter
14. law
15. author

List 11

1. play
2. pound
3. shout
4. whisper
5. sing
6. agree
7. cough
8. help
9. wait
10. touch
11. sleep
12. fight
13. think
14. destroy
15. open

List 12

1. follow
2. watch
3. enjoy
4. push
5. eat
6. throw
7. match
8. teach
9. want
10. read
11. catch
12. reach
13. call
14. walk
15. talk

List 13

1. sign
2. design
3. know
4. drink
5. meet
6. find
7. pick
8. start
9. pass
10. pull
11. hold
12. sell
13. draw
14. remember
15. need

List 14

1. child
2. woman
3. girl
4. turn
5. old
6. cold
7. flower
8. jump
9. bird
10. hurt
11. ear
12. hear
13. thirteen
14. sail
15. search

List 16

1. cents
2. attend
3. grow
4. get
5. own
6. see
7. pour
8. water
9. lesson
10. wonderful
11. new
12. germs
13. excellent
14. gift
15. shoe

List 17

1. share
2. shine
3. learn
4. state
5. use
6. name
7. suit
8. ride
9. celebrate
10. hide
11. say
12. says
13. said
14. birthday
15. rule

List 18

1. tell
2. write
3. give
4. bring
5. make
6. take
7. save
8. show
9. answer
10. work
11. trace
12. love
13. change
14. blue
15. letter

List 19

1. juice
2. photograph
3. table
4. apple
5. little
6. house
7. large
8. word
9. spell
10. fruit
11. move
12. horse
13. phone
14. like
15. offer

List 21

1. I
2. you
3. they
4. eight
5. wild
6. weigh
7. height
8. type
9. ask
10. breakfast
11. lunch
12. dinner
13. practice
14. add
15. number

List 22

1. her
2. us
3. them
4. simple
5. key
6. price
7. some
8. whole
9. home
10. clothes
11. white
12. knife
13. rescue
14. come
15. yellow

List 23

1. my
2. your
3. its
4. our
5. their
6. happy
7. baby
8. guess
9. study
10. student
11. build
12. cry
13. hungry
14. buy
15. visit

List 24

1. often
2. never
3. slowly
4. yesterday
5. today
6. sometimes
7. accident
8. family
9. careful
10. listen
11. copy
12. beautiful
13. animal
14. story
15. heavy

List 26

1. here
2. there
3. judge
4. person
5. people
6. fly
7. important
8. each
9. circle
10. solve
11. carry
12. example
13. please
14. airplane
15. center

List 27

1. be
2. is
3. are
4. was
5. were
6. always
7. field
8. almost
9. niece
10. cousin
11. husband
12. wife
13. uncle
14. nephew
15. ready

List 28

1. lone
2. alone
3. only
4. one
5. twin
6. twelve
7. twice
8. twenty
9. two
10. four
11. forty
12. five
13. fifty
14. hundred
15. thousand

List 29

1. actions
2. office
3. official
4. invention
5. high
6. expression
7. strange
8. rise
9. directions
10. bridge
11. party
12. this
13. that
14. these
15. those

List 31

1. by
2. over
3. under
4. between
5. above
6. below
7. near
8. ceiling
9. sea
10. window
11. store
12. medicine
13. look
14. hospital
15. mountain

List 32

1. to
2. around
3. beside
4. toward
5. off
6. out
7. through
8. of
9. down
10. across
11. race
12. winner
13. stopped
14. surprise
15. suddenly

List 33

1. beginner
2. prefer
3. receive
4. fix
5. team
6. noise
7. vacation
8. took
9. any
10. many
11. forgetful
12. several
13. present
14. for
15. from

List 34

1. been
2. could
3. would
4. should
5. have
6. do
7. done
8. does
9. may
10. might
11. will
12. decide
13. decision
14. controlling
15. tomorrow

List 36

1. why
2. when
3. where
4. what
5. who
6. how
7. which
8. whose
9. medium
10. believe
11. impossible
12. radio
13. about
14. before
15. after

List 37

1. also
2. too
3. memorize
4. memorization
5. equipment
6. encouraging
7. easy
8. sugar
9. sure
10. unusual
11. measure
12. picture
13. again
14. happen
15. sweet

List 38

1. because
2. although
3. since
4. while
5. whenever
6. until
7. unless
8. eye
9. combination
10. question
11. against
12. straight
13. immediately
14. million
15. country

List 39

1. earth
2. stadium
3. construction
4. science
5. motor
6. motion
7. motive
8. problem
9. enough
10. cent
11. century
12. dollar
13. difference
14. together
15. another

BASIC PHONOGRAMS

The sounds for each phonogram are listed in order of frequency.

Phonogram	Sound		Sample Words		
a	/ă-ā-ä/		mat	table	father
ai	/ā/	Two letter /ā/ that **may not** be used at the end of English words.	laid		
ar	/är/		car		
au	/ä/	Two letter /ä/ that **may not** be used at the end of English words.	author		
augh	/ä-ăf/	Used only at the end of a base word or before a T.	taught	laugh	
aw	/ä/	Two letter /ä/ that **may** be used at the end of English words.	saw		
ay	/ā/	Two letter /ā/ that **may** be used at the end of English words.	play		
b	/b/		bat		
bu	/b/	Two letter /b/.	buy		
c	/k-s/		cat	cent	
ch	/ch-k-sh/		child	school	chef
cei	/sē/		receive		
ci	/sh/	Short /sh/ used only at the beginning of any syllable after the first one.	spacious		
ck	/k/	Two letter /k/ used only after a single, short vowel.	back		
d	/d/		dad		
dge	/j/	Hard /J/ used only after a single, short vowel.	edge		
e	/ĕ-ē/		tent	be	
ea	/ē-ĕ-ā/		eat	bread	steak
ear	/er/	The /er/ of search.	search		
ed	/ed-d-t/	Past tense ending.	traded	pulled	picked
ee	/ē/	Double /ē/.	tree		
ei	/ā-ē-ī/	**May not** be used at the end of English words.	their	protein	feisty
eigh	/ā-ī/	Used only at the end of a base word or before a T.	eight	height	
er	/er/	The /er/ of her.	her		
ew	/oo-ū/	**May** be used at the end of English words.	flew	few	
ey	/ā-ē/	**May** be used at the end of English words.	they	key	
f	/f/		foot		

Phonogram	Sound		Sample Words			
g	/g-j/		bi**g**	**g**ym		
gn	/n/	Two letter /n/ used at the beginning or the end of a base word.	si**gn**			
gu	/g-gw/		**gu**ide	lan**gu**age		
h	/h/		**h**at			
i	/ĭ-ī-ē-y/		**i**t	**i**vy	stad**i**um	on**i**on
ie	/ē/	The /ē/ of field.	fi**e**ld			
igh	/ī/	Three letter /ī/ used only at the end of a base word or before a T.	n**igh**t			
ir	/er/	The /er/ of bird.	b**ir**d			
j	/j/		**j**ob			
k	/k/		**k**it			
kn	/n/	Two letter /n/ used only at the beginning of a base word.	**kn**ow			
l	/l/		**l**ap			
m	/m/		**m**e			
n	/n/		**n**ut			
ng	/ng/		si**ng**			
o	/ŏ-ō-ö/		**o**n	g**o**	d**o**	
oa	/ō/	Two letter /ō/ that **may not** be used at the end of English words.	c**oa**t			
oe	/ō-oo/	**May** be used at the end of English words.	t**oe**	sh**oe**		
oi	/oi/	**May not** be used at the end of English words.	b**oi**l			
oo	/oo-ü-ō/		f**oo**d	t**oo**k	fl**oo**r	
or	/or/		l**or**d			
ou	/ow-ō-oo-ŭ/	**May not** be used at the end of English words.	h**ou**se	s**ou**l	gr**ou**p	c**ou**ntry
ough	/ŏ-ō-oo-ow-ŭff-ŏff/	Used only at the end of a base word or before a T.	th**ough**t b**ough**	th**ough** r**ough**	thr**ough** tr**ough**	
ow	/ow-ō/	**May** be used at the end of English words.	pl**ow**	sn**ow**		
oy	/oi/	**May** be used at the end of English words.	b**oy**			
p	/p/		**p**an			
ph	/f/	Two letter /f/.	**ph**one			
qu	/qu/		**qu**een			
r	/r/		**r**an			
s	/s-z/		**s**ent	a**s**		

Phonogram	Sound		Sample Words			
sh	/sh/	Used only at the beginning of a word and at the end of the syllable. Never used at the beginning of any syllable after the first one, except for the ending -ship.	*sh*e			
si	/sh-zh/	Used only at the beginning of any syllable after the first one.	ses*si*on	divi*si*on		
t	/t/		*t*ip			
tch	/ch/	Three letter /ch/ used only after a single vowel that is not long.	bu*tch*er			
th	/th-TH/		*th*in	*th*is		
ti	/sh/	Tall /sh/ used only at the beginning of any syllable after the first one.	par*ti*al			
u	/ŭ-ū-oo-ü/		*u*p	p*u*pil	fl*u*te	p*u*t
ui	/oo/	Two letter /oo/ that **may not** be used at the end of English words.	fr*ui*t			
ur	/er/	The /er/ of hurt.	h*ur*ts			
v	/v/		*v*an			
w	/w/		*w*all			
wh	/wh/	Used only at the beginning of a base word.	*wh*isper			
wor	/wer/		*wor*m			
wr	/r/	Two letter /r/ used only at the beginning of a base word.	*wr*ite			
x	/ks/		fo*x*			
y	/y-ĭ-ī-ē/		*y*ard	g*y*m	b*y*	bab*y*
z	/z/		*z*ip			

SPELLING RULES

Rule 1 C always softens to /s/ when followed by E, I, or Y.
Otherwise, C says /k/.

Rule 2 G may soften to /j/ only when followed by E, I, or Y.
Otherwise, G says /g/.

Rule 3 English words do not end in I, U, V, or J.

Rule 4 A E O U usually say their names at the end of a syllable.

Rule 5 I and Y may say /ĭ/ or /ī/ at the end of a syllable.

Rule 6 When a one-syllable word ends in a single vowel Y, it says /ī/.

Rule 7 Y says long /ē/ only at the end of a multi-syllable word. I says long /ē/ only at
the end of a syllable that is followed by a vowel.

Rule 8 I and O may say /ī/ and /ō/ when followed by two consonants.

Rule 9 AY usually spells the sound /ā/ at the end of a base word.

Rule 10 When a word ends with the phonogram A, it says /ä/. A may also say /ä/ after a W
or before an L.

Rule 11 Q always needs a U; therefore, U is not a vowel here.

Rule 12 Silent Final E Rules

   12.1 The vowel says its name because of the E.

   12.2 English words do not end in V or U.

   12.3 The C says /s/ and the G says /j/ because of the E.

   12.4 Every syllable must have a written vowel.

   12.5 Add an E to keep singular words that end in the letter S from looking plural.

   12.6 Add an E to make the word look bigger.

   12.7 TH says its voiced sound /TH/ because of the E.

   12.8 Add an E to clarify meaning.

   12.9 Unseen reason.

Rule 13 Drop the silent final E when adding a vowel suffix only if it is allowed by other
spelling rules.

Rule 14   Double the last consonant when adding a vowel suffix to words ending in **one** vowel followed by **one** consonant, only if the syllable before the suffix is accented.*

*This is always true for one-syllable words.

Rule 15   Single vowel Y changes to I when adding any ending, unless the ending begins with I.

Rule 16   Two I's cannot be next to one another in English words.

Rule 17   TI, CI, and SI are used only at the beginning of any syllable after the first one.

Rule 18   SH spells /sh/ at the beginning of a base word and at the end of the syllable. SH never spells /sh/ at the beginning of any syllable after the first one, except for the ending -ship.

Rule 19   To make a verb past tense, add the ending ED unless it is an irregular verb.

Rule 20   ED, past tense ending, forms another syllable when the base word ends in /d/ or /t/. Otherwise, ED says /d/ or /t/.

Rule 21   To make a noun plural, add the ending -S unless the word hisses or changes, then add -ES. Occasional nouns have no change or an irregular spelling.

Rule 22   To make a verb 3rd person singular, add the ending -S, unless the word hisses or changes, then add -ES. Only four verbs are irregular.

Rule 23   Al- is a prefix written with one L when preceding another syllable.

Rule 24   -Ful is a suffix written with one L when added to another syllable.

Rule 25   DGE is used only after a single vowel which says its short (first) sound.

Rule 26   CK is used only after a single vowel which says its short (first) sound.

Rule 27   TCH is used only after a single vowel which does **not** say its name.

Rule 28   AUGH, EIGH, IGH, OUGH. Phonograms ending in GH are used only at the end of a base word or before the letter T. The GH is either silent or pronounced /f/.

Rule 29   Z, never S, spells /z/ at the beginning of a base word.

Rule 30   We often double F, L, and S after a single vowel at the end of a base word. Occasionally other letters also are doubled.

GRAMMAR

NOUNS

N A noun is the name of a person, place, thing, or idea. (1)

A **singular noun** refers to only one person, place, thing, or idea. (1.1)

A **plural noun** refers to more than one person, place, thing, or idea. (1.2)

A **non-count noun** cannot be made plural. (1.3)

Common nouns name general people, places, things, and ideas. (1.4)

Proper nouns name specific people, places, things, and ideas. Capitalize proper nouns.(1.5)

A noun has six jobs: *subject noun, direct object, indirect object, object of the preposition, predicate noun, and noun of direct address. (1.6)*

SN The **subject noun** is who or what the sentence is about.
To find the subject, go to the verb and ask: Who or what _____? (1.7)

DO The **direct object** receives the action of the verb and completes the meaning of the sentence.
To find the direct object, go to the verb and ask: _____ what? _____ whom? (1.8)

IO The **indirect objects** tells to whom or for whom the action is done. The indirect object receives the direct object.
To find the indirect object, go to the verb and ask: To whom did (the subject) _____?
To what did (the subject) _____? (1.9)

OP The **object of the preposition** is the noun or pronoun which follows the preposition.
To find the object of the preposition, go to the preposition and ask: _____ what?
_____ whom? (1.10)

| PN | **Predicate nouns** rename the subject and are linked to the subject with a linking verb. (1.11) |
| NDA | A **noun of direct address** identifies to whom a sentence is directed. Separate a noun of direct address from the rest of the sentence with a comma. (1.12) |

ADJECTIVES

Adj Adjectives modify nouns and pronouns.
Adjectives answer: What kind? How many? Which one? Whose? (2)

| A | A, an, the - tiny **article adjectives** that mark nouns and answer the question: Which? (2.1) |

The article "a" is used only before a consonant. (2.2)

The article "an" is used only before a vowel. (2.3)

| PNA | A **possessive noun adjective** shows ownership and answers the question: Whose? (2.4) |

To turn a noun into a singular possessive noun adjective, add an apostrophe followed by an S. (2.5)

To turn a noun into a plural possessive noun adjective, add an -S to make the noun plural and then add an apostrophe. If the noun has an irregular plural use an apostrophe followed by an S. (2.6)

| PA | **Predicate adjectives** describe the subject and are linked to the subject with a linking verb. (2.7) |

VERBS

V A verb shows action, links a description to the subject, or helps another verb.
To find the verb, go to the subject and ask: What is being said about _____? (3)

| AV | **Action verbs** show actions like run and shout, sit and think. (3.1) |
| TV | A **transitive verb** transfers the action of the verb to the direct object. (3.2) |

| DO | The **direct object** receives the action of the verb and completes the meaning of the sentence. |

To find the direct object, go to the verb and ask: _____ what? _____ whom? (1.8)

IO | The **indirect objects** tells to whom or for whom the action is done. The indirect object receives the direct object.
To find the indirect object, go to the verb and ask: To whom did (the subject) _____? To what did (the subject) _____? (1.9)

LV A **linking verb** connects the subject to additional information about the subject. It may link a noun, pronoun, or an adjective to the subject. (3.3)

PN | Predicate nouns rename the subject and are linked to the subject with a linking verb. (1.11)

PA | Predicate adjectives describe the subject and are linked to the subject with a linking verb. (2.7)

HV | Helping verbs help the main verb by expressing tense, mood, and voice. (3.4)

ADVERBS

Adv An **adverb** modifies a verb, adjective, or another adverb. Adverbs answer: How? When? Where? To what extent? (4)

PREPOSITIONS

P A preposition links a noun or a pronoun to the rest of the sentence. (5)

OP | The **object of the preposition** is the noun or pronoun which follows the preposition. To find the object of the preposition, go to the preposition and ask: _____ what? _____ whom? (1.10)

PRONOUNS

Pro A pronoun takes the place of a noun. (6)

SP | A **subject pronoun** takes the place of a subject noun: I, you, he, she, it, we, they. (6.1)

An **object pronoun** takes the place of an object noun: me, you, him, her, it, us, them. (6.2)

PPA   **Possessive pronoun adjectives** take the place of possessive noun adjectives: my, mine, your, yours, his, her, hers, its, our, ours, their, theirs. (6.3)

Demonstrative pronouns represent a noun. There are four demonstrative pronouns: this, that, these, those. (6.4)

CONJUNCTIONS

C   **Conjunctions connect words, phrases, or sentences together. There are two types of conjunctions: coordinating and subordinating. (7)**

C   **Coordinating conjunctions** connect related words, phrases, or sentences together. Use a comma before a coordinating conjunction: *and, but, or, for, nor, yet, so.* (7.1)

SC   **Subordinating conjunctions** join two sentences together by turning one sentence into a dependent clause (or sentence fragment). (7.2)

When a sentence begins with a dependent clause, separate it from the rest of the sentence with a comma. (7.3)

When a sentence ends with a dependent clause, no comma is needed. (7.4)

INTERJECTIONS

I   **Interjections show strong emotion. They can stand alone. (8)**

I   Separate an interjection from the rest of the sentence with a comma or an exclamation point. If using an exclamation point, capitalize the next word in the sentence. (8.1)

SENTENCES AND CLAUSES

SENTENCE

Sent A sentence must have a capital letter, a subject, a verb, a complete thought, and an end mark. (9)

A sentence has two parts: *the subject and the predicate. (9.1)*

The **simple subject** tells what the sentence is about.
> To find the simple subject, go to the verb and ask: Who or what _____? (9.2)

The **complete subject** includes all the words that modify the simple subject. (9.3)

The **simple predicate** is the verb. The predicate tells what is being said about the subject. (9.4)

The **complete predicate** includes all the words that modify the simple predicate. (9.5)

There are four types of sentences: *statements, command, exclamation, questions (9.6)*

A **statement** ends with a period. (9.7)

A **command** ends with a period or an exclamation point. (9.8)

A **question** ends with a question mark. (9.9)

An **exclamation** shows strong emotion and ends with an exclamation point. (9.10)

There are three sentence styles: *simple, compound, complex. (9.11)*

A **simple sentence** contains a subject(s) and verb(s) and expresses a complete thought. It is also called an independent clause. (9.12)

A **compound sentence** contains two complete sentences (independent clauses) joined together with a comma followed by a coordinating conjunction. (9.13)

A **complex sentence** contains an independent clause joined with one or more dependent clauses. (9.14)

Clause A clause includes a subject and a verb. (10)

An **independent clause** contains a subject(s) and verb(s) and expresses a complete thought. Also called a simple sentence. (10.1)

A **dependent clause** includes a subordinating conjunction, subject, and verb. A dependent clause does not express a complete thought. (10.2)

PUNCTUATION

COMMA RULES 11

1. Use commas to separate the words in a series of three or more. (11.1)

2. Use a comma to separate a direct quote from the rest of the sentence. (11.2)

3. Use a comma to separate a Noun of Direct Address from the rest of the sentence. (11.3)

4. Use commas to separate a parenthetical thought from the rest of the sentence. (11.4)

5. Never use only one comma between the subject and the verb. Two commas may be used between the subject and the verb. (11.5)

6. Use commas in a list of adjectives only if the word "and" makes sense. Otherwise omit the comma. (11.6)

7. Use a comma to separate: city, state; date, year; name, title. (11.7)

CAPITALIZATION RULES 12

1. Capitalize the first word in the sentence. (12.1)

2. Capitalize proper nouns. (12.2)

    These include: days of the week, months of the year, and holidays.

3. Capitalize the first word of a direct quotation. (12.3)

QUOTATION MARKS 13

1. Use quotation marks around direct quotations. (13.1)

    Place commas and periods inside the quotation marks. (13.2)

    Do not use quotation marks if the person is not actually speaking. (13.3)

APOSTROPHES 14

1. Use an apostrophe to denote the sound(s) omitted from a contraction. (14.1)

2. Use an apostrophe to form a possessive noun adjective. (14.2)

NUMBERS 15

1. Hyphenate numbers twenty-one through ninety-nine. (15.1)

2. Hyphenate fractions. (15.2)

3. Spell out numbers zero through one hundred. Use numerals for numbers greater than 100. (15.3)

4. Spell out rounded hundreds and thousands. (15.4)

5. Spell out fractions. (15.5)

6. Spell out years and percentages at the beginning of the sentence; use numerals in the middle of the sentence. (15.6)

7. Write decimals with numerals. (15.7)

8. Spell out times on the hour. Use numerals for exact times that include minutes. Use the lowercase for a.m. and p.m. (15.8)

PARAGRAPH

PARAGRAPH

A paragraph is a closely related group of sentences about a unified topic. (16)

1. Paragraphs begin with an indent. (16.1)

2. Begin a new paragraph when: you start a new topic, you skip to a new time, you skip to a new place, a new person begins to speak, or you want to create a dramatic effect. (16.2)

3. Paragraphs often include three types of sentences: introductory, body, and concluding. (16.3)

THE LESSONS

Lesson 1

1

Phonograms:	A-Z
Exploring Sounds:	Consonants and Vowels
Spelling Rules:	11, 21
Grammar:	Nouns, Plurals

PART ONE

Materials Needed: Phonogram Flash Cards A-Z, 1 deck of Phonogram Game Cards A-Z per student, Spelling Rule Card 11.

Phonograms

New Phonograms — *Review or learn all the sounds for A-Z.*

1. Drill A-Z with flash cards.

2. Show ⬚ qu ⬚. /qu/

   What do you notice about this phonogram? It has two letters.
   Twenty-five of the phonograms have only one letter. There are forty-nine phonograms which have two or more letters. We will learn more about this phonogram later in the lesson.

3. Play Dragon using Phonogram Game Cards A-Z. (*The Phonogram and Spelling Game Book,* p. 10)

4. ✏ *1.1 Phonogram Practice* – Dictate the phonograms to the students. The teacher should say the sound(s) while the students write the correct phonogram. For extra practice, have the students read back the sounds, while you write the correct answers on the board.

1. y	/y-ĭ-ī-ē/	6. c	/k-s/	11. w	/w/
2. a	/ă-ā-ä/	7. m	/m/	12. x	/x/
3. h	/h/	8. o	/ŏ-ō-ö/	13. r	/r/
4. t	/t/	9. u	/ŭ-ū-oo-ü/	14. f	/f/
5. z	/z/	10. i	/ĭ-ī-ē-y/	15. v	/v/

16. p	/p/	20. n	/n/	24. k	/k/
17. g	/g-j/	21. b	/b/	25. l	/l/
18. e	/ĕ-ē/	22. j	/j/	26. qu	/qu/
19. s	/s-z/	23. d	/d/		

The Phonogram QU

Which consonant always has two letters?   qu
This brings us to our first spelling rule. Let's say it together three times.

Spelling Rule	11
Q always needs a U; therefore, U is not a vowel here.	

Read each of the words as I write it on the board.

quit   quest   quilt

From now on, when we find two letters that work together as one phonogram we will underline them. This is to help us remember the letters are working together to make one sound.

qu̲it   qu̲est   qu̲ilt

✎   *1.2 Words Spelled with QU –* **Write three words that use the /qu/ phonogram in your workbook.**

Optional: Spelling Rule Practice

1. Create a reference page to remember this rule. Include sample words.   ©Ⓥ

2. Ask the students to teach this to another student or to a parent.   ©ⓋⓀⒶ

Exploring Sounds

Introducing Consonants and Vowels

Vowels are sounds that are made when our mouths are open. Vowels can be sustained, such as in singing.
What is a vowel? A sound where your mouth is open and that can be sustained such as in singing.

Consonants are sounds that are blocked by the lips, teeth, or tongue. Most consonants cannot be sung.
What is a consonant? Sounds that are blocked and cannot be sung.

(For more information, see *Uncovering the Logic of English,* Chapter 4: Consonants, Vowels, and Syllables.)

Discovering the Consonants and Vowels

Show the students the A-Z Phonogram Flash Cards one by one. Direct the students to say the sound(s). Ask:

> *Can you sing it?*
> *Is your mouth open?*
> *Are your lips, tongue, or teeth blocking the sound? If so, how is it blocked?*

For example:

a	/ă-ā-ä/

> *Can you sing the first sound /ă/?*   yes
> *Is your mouth open?*   yes
> *Then /ă/ is a vowel sound because you can sing it and your mouth is open.*

> *Can you sing the second sound /ā/?*   yes
> *Is your mouth open?*   yes
> *Is it a vowel or a consonant sound?*   vowel

> *Can you sing the third sound /ä/?*   yes
> *Is your mouth open?*   yes
> *Is it a vowel or a consonant sound?*   vowel

b	/b/

> *Can you sing /b/?*   no
> *What is blocking the sound?*   the lips
> *Is it a consonant or a vowel?*   consonant

y	/y-ĭ-ī-ē/

> *Can you sing the first sound /y/?*   no
> *What is blocking the sound?*   the tongue
> *Is it a vowel or a consonant sound?*   consonant

> *Can you sing the second sound /ĭ/?*   yes
> *Is your mouth open?*   yes
> *Is it a vowel or a consonant sound?*   vowel

> *Can you sing the third sound /ī/?*   yes
> *Is your mouth open?*   yes
> *Is it a vowel or a consonant sound?*   vowel

> *Can you sing the fourth sound /ē/?*   yes
> *Is your mouth open?*   yes

Is it a vowel or a consonant sound?   vowel
Y has one consonant sound and three vowel sounds.

Continue in this manner exploring all the A-Z phonograms.

< **Teacher Tip:** *I has three vowel sounds /ĭ-ī-ē/ and one consonant sound /y/.*

Practicing the Consonants and Vowels

1. Provide the students with Phonogram Cards A-Z. Ask them to sort the cards into two stacks: consonants and vowels. Discuss how Y and I have both a consonant and a vowel sound.

2. Identify the vowels as A, E, I, O, U and Y. Practice saying the vowels three times.

3. ✎ *1.3 Single-Letter Vowels* – Direct the students to write the single-letter vowels in their workbooks.

PART TWO

Spelling Dictation

Using Spelling List 1 on pages 6-7, dictate each word following the steps included on pages Intro 42 - Intro 46.

1. Read the word and use it in a sentence.

2. The teacher repeats the word, exaggerating the pronunciation for spelling.

3. The students repeat the word and count the number of syllables.

4. The students then sound out the word aloud, syllable by syllable.

5. If there is a sound that needs clarification, the teacher indicates which spelling is used.

6. ✎ *Spelling List 1* – The students write the word in their workbooks while sounding it out. (The students should leave a space between each syllable.)

7. Guide the students in analyzing each word and marking them as shown under the column Markings. While marking the words, discuss the phonograms and rules used in each word. For more information see the column Spelling Hints.

The final two columns, Part of Speech and Vocabulary Development, are for use in Part 3 and for the teacher's own reference. Do **NOT** have students label the parts of speech or write derivatives at this time.

Tips for Spelling List 1

Words Ending in NK

Some students misspell words ending in the sound /nk/ such as *pink*. Rather than writing an NK these students will often use the phonogram ng (pingk).

If you say the words aloud, it is easy to understand their confusion. To aid students with these words:

1. Affirm their thinking and that it makes sense to you.

2. Explain that when the /n/ and /k/ sounds blend together they make a bit of the nasal sound like the phonogram /ng/. Then explain there are not any words in English spelled NGK or NGC, or NGCK. These combinations of phonograms are not allowed in English. Rather, whenever they hear /n/ or /ng/ followed by the sound /k/ it will be spelled with an N.

3. Model sounding out the word, pronouncing each sound carefully. /th-ĭ-n-k/

4. Practice spelling other words that end in the sound /nk/. *ink, blink, think, stink, rink, chink, sink, link, honk, bonk, bank, skunk, drank, chunk, plunk, hunk, sank, spunk, thank, trunk, shrunk.*

Word	Practice Sentence	Say to Spell	# of Syllables	Markings
1. **hat**	*The hat is on his head.*	hăt	1	hat
2. **map**	*This is a map of our city.*	măp	1	map
3. **bag**	*The bag is full.*	băg	1	bag
4. **bat**	*He hit the ball with the bat.*	băt	1	bat
5. **bed**	*Her bed is soft.*	běd	1	bed
6. **hand**	*His hand is large.*	hănd	1	hand
7. **cat**	*The cat is sleeping.*	căt	1	cat
8. **leg**	*My leg is itchy.*	lěg	1	leg
9. **dog**	*The dog is barking.*	dŏg	1	dog
10. **quilt**	*The warm quilt is on the bed.*	kwĭlt	1	q̲uilt
11. **soft**	*Give the baby the soft blanket.*	sŏft	1	soft
12. **fast**	*The fast dog ran across the street.*	făst	1	fast
13. **last**	*The last piece of candy is in the jar.*	lăst	1	last
14. **pink**	*The girl is wearing a pink dress.*	pĭnk	1	pink
15. **bad**	*The bad sounds hurt my ears.*	băd	1	bad

Spelling Hints	Part of Speech	Vocabulary Development
All first sounds.	N	hats
All first sounds.	N	maps, mapped, mapping, mappable
All first sounds.	N	bags, handbag, bagful, bagpipe, mailbag, schoolbag, windbag, workbag
All first sounds.	N	bats, batting, batted, batter
All first sounds.	N	beds, bedding, daybed, flatbed, hotbed, featherbed, riverbed, roadbed, sickbed, bedsheets, bedside
All first sounds.	N	hands, handed, handing, handful, handy, firsthand, backhand, forehand, handball, handle, handcart, handshake, handspring
All first sounds. **1** C softens to /s/ when followed by an E, I, or Y. Otherwise, C says /k/.	N	cats, bobcat, cattail, catfish, catnap
All first sounds.	N	legs, leggings, bootleg, leggy, legless, legroom, legwork
All first sounds.	N	dogs, dogcatcher, dogleg, doggy, doghouse, dogfish, dogsled, hotdog, dogwood, firedog, watchdog
Underline the /kw/. **11** Q always needs a U; therefore U is not a vowel here.	N	quilts, quilting, quilted
All first sounds.	Adj	softer, softest, softly, softball, soften, softener, softness, softy, softhearted
All first sounds.	Adj	faster, fastest, breakfast, colorfast, fastball, fasting, fasted, steadfast, ultrafast
All first sounds.	Adj	lastly, lasting, lasted, outlast
All first sounds.	Adj	pinker, pinkest, pinkness, pinkish
All first sounds.	Adj	badly

PART THREE

Materials Needed: Grammar Card 1-1.2; Spelling Rule Card 21; red colored pencil.

Grammar

Nouns

1. Recite the rule three times:

Grammar Card 1	N
A noun is the name of a person, place, thing, or idea.	

2. Learn about nouns.

   Most nouns are objects we can see and touch, people, or places.
   What are some words for people? teacher, student, mother, father, sister, firefighter…
   What are some words for places? park, store, school, museum, New York, kitchen…
   What are some words for things? desk, chair, paper, books, dog…
   What are some words for ideas? love, peace, fear, months…

   ✎ *Spelling List 1 – **Let's read our spelling words from today. On your spelling list write a red N***
   next to each word that is a noun.
   hat, map, bag, bat, bed, hand, cat, leg, dog, and quilt.
   Are these nouns people, places, or things? things

Optional: Grammar and Spelling Practice

1. Ask the students to read their spelling list. When they find a word that is a noun, draw a picture of it. ⓒⓥ

2. Show the students a picture dictionary. Ask the students to create a scene using all the words in the list. When the drawing is complete, direct them to label each of the words. ⓒⓥ

Optional: Spelling Cards

1. Dictate the words in Lesson 1 for the students to write on Spelling Cards. Ⓚⓥ

2. Ask the students to identify which words are nouns and draw a red border around them. Ⓚⓥ

Plurals

1. Introduce plurals.

    One way to identify if a word is a noun is to ask: "Can I count it?"
    For example, one hat, two hats, three hats; one map, two maps, three maps.

    Listen carefully. How does the noun change when we have more than one? We add a /s/ sound.

    hat   hats   map   maps

    Yes, we add /s/ to the end of nouns to make them plural.

Read the definitions to the students.

Grammar Card 1.1	N
A singular noun refers to only one person, place, thing, or idea.	

Grammar Card 1.2	N
A plural noun refers to more than one person, place, thing or idea.	

2. Read Spelling Rule Card 21 to the students.

Ask the students to recite it three times together. Say it with a silly voice, say it softly, say it loudly.

Spelling Rule	21
To make a noun plural, add the ending -S unless the word hisses or changes, then add -ES. Occasional nouns have no change or an irregular spelling.	

3. Making words plural by adding -S.

    Read your spelling words and then repeat each word as a plural.

As the students say the words, write the plurals on the board with the S in a different color.

    hat   hats   map   maps

4. ✎ *Spelling List 1* – Write the plural form of each noun next to the spelling words in List 1.

Optional: Plurals Practice

1. Complete *1.4 Extra Practice: Plurals Practice* in the workbook. Answers for first column: *hat, map, cats, dogs, bed, bat, bag, beds, hand.* Second column: *cat, hats, legs, bat, dog, hands, bats.* Ⓥ Ⓐ

2. Practice writing the words in their plural form using oral dictation. Ⓐ Ⓥ

Dictation

✎ *1.5 Dictation* – Read the phrase. Ask the students to repeat it aloud, then write it in their workbooks.

1. bad leg	3. fast cat	5. soft bed
2. last map	4. pink bag	6. last hat

Optional: Dictation

1. Ask the students to use the phrases to create an oral story. Ⓒ Ⓐ

2. Dictate the phrases while the students write them on blank paper. The students may then illustrate each phrase. Ⓒ Ⓥ

Composition

Read the phrases from your dictation aloud.

Notice how the two words worked together. Now make up your own phrases aloud by combining the last five words in the list with the nouns.

✎ *1.6 Composition* – **Write six phrases in your workbook.**

Lesson 2

2

Phonograms:	ck, ee, ng, th
Exploring Sounds:	Short and Long Vowels
Spelling Rules:	26
Grammar:	Adjectives

PART ONE

Materials Needed: Phonogram Flash Cards A-Z, ck , ee , ng , th ; Spelling Rule Cards 26, 11, and 21; pennies to cover the Bingo Chart; 1 set of Phonogram Game Cards per student.

Phonograms

New Phonograms — *ck, ee, ng, th*

Using the Phonogram Flash Cards, introduce the new phonograms and their sounds.

Show ck . /k/ two-letter /k/

> ***What do you notice about this phonogram?*** C and K both say /k/, and they also work together to say /k/.

Show ee . /ē/ double /ē/ always says /ē/

Show ng . /ng/

Show th . /th-TH/

> ***Say /th/ and /TH/. How are they the same?*** My mouth is in the same position.
> ***How are they different?*** /th/ is unvoiced and /TH/ is voiced.
> ***This is a voiced and unvoiced pair.***

Review

1. ✎ *2.1 Writing the Phonograms* – Ask the students to write each phonogram five times while saying the sounds aloud.

2. Drill the phonograms with flash cards.

3. ✎ Play *2.2 Phonogram Bingo* using A-Z and the new phonograms.

4. ✎ *2.3 Phonogram Practice* – Dictate the phonograms to the students. The teacher should say the sound(s) while the students write the correct phonogram. For extra practice, have the students read back the sounds while you write the correct answers on the board.

1. y	/y-ĭ-ī-ē/	10. i	/ĭ-ī-ē-y/	19. ng	/ng/
2. ck	/k/ two-letter /k/	11. w	/w/	20. n	/n/
3. h	/h/	12. x	/ks/	21. a	/ă-ā-ä/
4. t	/t/	13. r	/r/	22. c	/k-s/
5. v	/v/	14. f	/f/	23. z	/z/
6. th	/th-TH/	15. g	/g-j/	24. b	/b/
7. m	/m/	16. j	/j/	25. qu	/qu/
8. o	/ŏ-ō-ö/	17. ee	/ē/ double /ē/		
9. u	/ŭ-ū-oo-ü/	18. e	/ĕ-ē/		

Exploring Sounds

Short and Long Vowel Sounds

What is a vowel? A vowel is a sound that can be sustained, and the mouth is open.
What are the names of the single letter vowels? A, E, I, O, U, Y.

Write them on the board.

a e i o u y

Ask the students to read all of the vowel sounds. /ă-ā-ä/, /ĕ-ē/, /ĭ-ī-ē/, /ŏ-ō-ö/, /ŭ-ū-oo-ü/, /ĭ-ī-ē/

✎ *2.4 Vowels* – **Write the single-letter vowels in your workbook.**

Notice that all of the vowels make more than one sound.
The first sound is called the short sound.
Read only the first sounds of each of the vowels. ă ĕ ĭ ŏ ŭ
In the dictionary this sound is marked with a breve to show that the vowel is saying its short sound.

ă ĕ ĭ ŏ ŭ

Read the short vowels. ă ĕ ĭ ŏ ŭ

✎ *2.5 Short Vowels* – **Write the short vowels including the breve in your workbook. As you write them say their sounds.**

Read the vowels again, but this time read only their second sounds. ā ē ī ō ū
Do you notice anything about the second sound said by each vowel? They say their names.
When a vowel says its name, it is also called the long sound. In the dictionary, the long sound is marked by drawing a line over the vowel.

ā ē ī ō ū

Read the long vowels. ā ē ī ō ū

✎ *2.6 Long Vowels –* **Write the long vowels with the dictionary marking in your workbook. As you write them say their sounds.**

Spelling Rules

Rule 26: When to Use CK

✎ *2.7 Words That Use CK –* **Read the words in your workbook aloud. The words will follow a pattern. Raise your hand when you know the pattern.**

deck	rock	tack
neck	sock	rack
lick	truck	
tick	luck	

What do these words have in common? They all end in two-letter /k/.

Underline the two-letter /k/.

de<u>ck</u>	ro<u>ck</u>	ta<u>ck</u>
ne<u>ck</u>	so<u>ck</u>	ra<u>ck</u>
li<u>ck</u>	tru<u>ck</u>	
ti<u>ck</u>	lu<u>ck</u>	

Do you notice anything about the vowels? They are all short vowel sounds.

Draw a breve over each vowel.

dĕ<u>ck</u>	rŏ<u>ck</u>	tă<u>ck</u>
nĕ<u>ck</u>	sŏ<u>ck</u>	ră<u>ck</u>
lĭ<u>ck</u>	trŭ<u>ck</u>	
tĭ<u>ck</u>	lŭ<u>ck</u>	

This leads to the new spelling rule:

Show the students the spelling rule card. Recite the rule three times.

Spelling Rule	26
CK is used only after a single vowel which says its short (first) sound.	

✎ *2.8 Words That Do Not Use CK –* **Read aloud the second group of words in your workbook.**

cheek	Greek	seek
creek	week	sleek

Why can we not use two-letter /k/ to spell these words? The vowels all say their long sound. (Also these words are not spelled with single vowels. Each of the vowel sounds is spelled with more than one letter.)

Some of our words today will use two letter /k/.
When is it used? only after a single, short vowel
Is it ever used at the beginning of the word? no
Is it ever used after a long vowel? no

Some of the words in our spelling list today will use "two letter /k/." Listen for a short vowel followed by the sound /k/. This is the most common spelling of /k/ after a short vowel at the end of a base word.

Optional: Spelling Journal   Ⓐ Ⓚ Ⓥ

Enter words which use the phonogram CK to spell /k/.

Optional: Spelling Rule Practice

1. Quickly review spelling rules 11, 21, and 26 with the Spelling Rule Cards. Ⓐⓥ

2. Create a reference page to remember this rule. Include sample words. Ⓒⓥ

3. Ask the students to teach this to another student or to a parent. ⒸⓥⒶⓀ

4. **The CK Game** ⓥⒶⓀ

   - Provide each student with a set of Phonogram Game Cards including: A-Z, ck, ee, ng, and th.

   - Ask the students to sort the cards into: vowels, consonants, and multi-letter phonograms.

   - Direct the students to lay out their cards with a ___ | a | ck .

   - Ask the students to find consonant cards which complete the word.

   - Switch the vowel to | e |, | i |, | o |, then | u |.

   - Challenge the students to see how many words they can find that follow the pattern.

   - Optional: Give them one point per word.

   back, black, block, brick, buck, deck, duck, flick, flock, jack, kick, lack, lick, lock, luck, muck, neck, nick, pack, pick, quack, quick, rack, rock, sack, shock, shuck, sick, slack, slick, smack, smock, snack, sock, speck, stick, stock, struck, suck, tack, track, truck, tuck, wick, yuck

PART TWO

Using Spelling List 2 on pages 16-17, dictate each word following the steps included on pages Intro 42 - Intro 46.

	Word	Practice Sentence	Say to Spell	# of Syllables	Markings
1.	**street**	*The store is on Main Street.*	strēt	1	str<u>ee</u>t
2.	**sun**	*The sun is setting.*	sŭn	1	sun
3.	**pond**	*The frog swam in the pond.*	pŏnd	1	pond
4.	**black**	*Wear black pants for the play.*	blăk	1	bla<u>ck</u>
5.	**strong**	*The strong man lifted the heavy weight.*	strŏng	1	stro<u>ng</u>
6.	**string**	*Tie the string on your finger.*	strĭng	1	stri<u>ng</u>
7.	**green**	*My green jacket ripped.*	grēn	1	gr<u>ee</u>n
8.	**truck**	*The truck is driving on the road.*	trŭk	1	tru<u>ck</u>
9.	**sick**	*I feel sick.*	sĭk	1	si<u>ck</u>
10.	**three**	*Three dogs slept.*	thrē	1	<u>th</u>ree
11.	**ten**	*Ten children played.*	tĕn	1	ten
12.	**long**	*The long string is for the tent.*	lŏng	1	lo<u>ng</u>
13.	**path**	*Stay on the path.*	păth	1	pa<u>th</u>
14.	**tree**	*The big tree is bending in the wind.*	trē	1	tr<u>ee</u>
15.	**rock**	*I like to sit on the big rock.*	rŏk	1	ro<u>ck</u>

Spelling Hints	Part of Speech	Vocabulary Development
Underline /ē/. All first sounds.	N	streets, backstreet, streetcar, streetlight, streetwise
All first sounds.	N	suns, sunshine, sunny, sundown, sunrise, sunset, sunburn, sundial, sunscreen, sunroof, suntan, sunup
All first sounds.	N	ponds
Underline /k/. **26** CK is used only after a single vowel which says its short sound.	Adj	blacker, blackest, blacklist, blackjack, blackout, blacktop
Underline /ng/.	Adj	stronger, strongest, strongly, strongbox, stronghold, headstrong
Underline /ng/.	N	strings, stringy, restring, stringless, unstring
Underline /ē/. All first sounds.	Adj	greener, greenest, greenback, greenhorn, greenish, wintergreen
Underline /k/. **26** CK is used only after a single vowel which says its short sound.	N	trucks, trucker, trucking, trucked
Underline /k/. **26** CK is used only after a single vowel which says its short sound.	Adj	sicker, sickest, sickly, airsick, carsick, sickness, homesick, seasick, lovesick, sicken, sickened, sickliest, sicklier, sickroom
Underline /th/. Underline /ē/. All first sounds.	Adj, (N)	threefold, threepence, threescore
All first sounds.	Adj, (N)	tens
Underline /ng/. All first sounds.	Adj	longer, longest, longing, longhorn, longhouse, longitude, prolong, oblong, yearlong, sidelong, longhand
Underline /th/.	N	paths
Underline /ē/. All first sounds.	N	trees, treed, treeless, treetop
Underline /k/. **26** CK is used only after a single vowel which says its short sound.	N, (V)	rocks, rocked, rocking, rocker, bedrock, rockier, rockiest, rocky

PART THREE

Materials Needed: Grammar Card 2; red and blue colored pencils; stuffed animal.

Grammar

Review

> **What is a noun?** A noun is the name of a person, place, thing, or idea.

1. Review nouns by quickly asking the students to name persons, places, and things.

2. ✎ *Spelling List 2* – Read today's spelling list and identify the nouns. Write a red N by each word that is a noun.

Important Teacher Information: Do **not** require the students to identify every possible part of speech. Many words can be used in multiple ways in a sentence. All the options are included for the teacher's reference. The less common grammatical form is included in parenthesis. For example, in List 2, *three* is most commonly used as an adjective, but it may also be used as a noun, as in "The three written on the board is too large." Parts of speech that have not yet been introduced will also be written in parenthesis. For example, *rock* may be used as both a noun and a verb. Since verbs have not been introduced, V is written in parenthesis. The goal of these exercises is for the students to gain an understanding that words have jobs in sentences. It is not to identify every possible job of every word. However, if the students notice other ways a word can be used, affirm their observation.

3. Review how to form plurals.

> street

> **How do I make street plural?** Add -s.

> street — streets

> **What is the rule we learned?** To make a noun plural, add the ending -S unless the word hisses or changes, then add -ES. Occasional nouns have no change or an irregular spelling.

4. ✎ *Spelling List 2* – Direct the students to write the plural form of each noun on their spelling list.

Optional: Plurals Practice

✎ *2.9 Extra Practice: Plurals Practice* – Write the plural for each picture in the workbook. Ⓥ Ⓐ Answers: *suns, trees, trucks, ponds, strings, rocks.*

Adjectives

1. Introduce adjectives.

> *Today we will learn a second part of speech.*
> *An adjective is a word that modifies or describes a noun.*
> *Close your eyes. Picture an apple. Now, picture a green apple. Green is describing the word apple.*
> *Green is an adjective. Now, picture a tiny apple. Tiny is an adjective describing apple. Imagine a*
> *cat. Now, imagine a fat cat. Fat is an adjective modifying cat.*
>
> *Green, tiny, and fat are all adjectives.*

Hold up a stuffed animal.

> *What words would you use to describe this stuffed animal?* Answers will vary.

2. Show Grammar Card 2. Recite the definition of an adjective together three times.

Grammar Card 2	Adj
Adjectives modify nouns and pronouns. **Adjectives** answer: *What kind? How many? Which one? Whose?*	

They

> *I will read a phrase to you. I want you to ask, "What kind," to find the adjective.*

black cat	What kind of cat? Black. Black is an adjective modifying cat.
fast runner	What kind of runner? Fast. Fast is an adjective modifying runner.
beautiful girl	What kind of girl? Beautiful. Beautiful is an adjective modifying girl.

> *Now I want you to ask, "How many?"*

five dolls	How many dolls? Five. Five is an adjective modifying dolls.
six cats	How many cats? Six. Six is an adjective modifying cats.
sixty bugs	How many bugs? Sixty. Sixty is an adjective modifying bugs.

> *Next I will read a phrase, and I want you to ask a question to find the adjective.*

good food	What kind of food? Good. Good is an adjective modifying food.
broken table	What kind of table? Broken. Broken is an adjective modifying table.
cold weather	What kind of weather? Cold. Cold is an adjective modifying weather.

3. Remind the students to use the plural form.

> *I will write two phrases on the board with a mistake. When you find the mistake raise your hand.*

> *ten string*   *three truck*

String and truck should be plural. You need to add an -S.

> *ten strings*   *three trucks*

> **Be careful when using an adjective that tells how many. You will usually need to use the plural form of the noun.**

4. Direct the students to read Spelling Lists 1 and 2 and find the adjectives.

> ✎ *Spelling Lists 1 & 2 – **Identify the adjectives in Spelling Lists 1 and 2. Remember, adjectives are words which answer: What kind? Which one? How many? Whose? Write a blue "Adj." next to words that are adjectives.***

As each adjective is identified, ask the students to use it in a sentence.

Identifying Nouns and Adjectives

> *big tree*   *three rocks*   *long path*

> ✎ *2.10 Identifying Nouns and Adjectives – **I have written the phrases from your workbook on the board. Read the phrases in your workbook. Label each of the nouns and adjectives in your workbook while I label them on the board.***

> *big tree*

> **What is the noun in this phrase?** tree
> **Label tree with an N for noun.**

> N
> *big tree*

> **What kind of tree?** big, adjective
> **Label big with Adj.**

> Adj N
> *big tree*

---

three rocks

What is the noun in this phrase? rocks

N
three rocks

How many rocks? three, adjective

Adj   N
three rocks

---

long path

What is the noun in this phrase? path

N
long path

What kind of path? long, adjective

Adj   N
long path

Optional: Spelling Cards

1. Dictate the words in Lesson 2 for the students to write on Spelling Word Cards.   Ⓥ Ⓚ Ⓐ

2. Sort the cards from Lessons 1 and 2 to find the nouns.   Ⓥ Ⓚ

3. Color a red border around the nouns.   Ⓥ Ⓚ

4. Explain that the rest of the words are adjectives, words that describe nouns. Color a blue border around the adjectives.   Ⓥ Ⓚ

5. Arrange the cards into short adjective-noun phrases.   Ⓥ Ⓚ

Dictation

✎ *2.11 Dictation* – Read the phrase. Tell the students to repeat it aloud, then write it in their workbooks.

1. three trees

2. last street

3. black truck

4. sick dog

5. ten rocks

6. strong string

Optional: Dictation

1. Use the phrases to create an oral story. ©Ⓐ

2. Dictate the phrases onto blank paper. Illustrate each phrase. ⒶⓋ©

Composition

1. Direct the students to find adjectives and nouns from the spelling lists that work together. Compose phrases orally.

2. ✎ *2.12 Composition* – Direct the students to write six two-word phrases in their workbook using words from Lists 1 and 2.

Vocabulary Development

Sometimes two words can be combined together to form a compound word. I will write two words on the board. Read each one, and then combine them to form a compound word. I will then write the new word that is formed.

sun + tan = suntan

long + hand = longhand

hand + spring = handspring

sick + bed = sickbed

bed + sheet = bedsheet

sand + box = sandbox

✎ *2.13 Compound Words* – **Complete the activity in your workbook.**

Lesson 3

Phonograms:	er, or, ea, sh
Exploring Sounds:	Syllables
Spelling Rule:	4
Grammar:	Irregular Plurals Non-Count Nouns

PART ONE

Materials Needed: Phonogram Flash Cards from previous lessons plus er , or , ea , sh ; Spelling Rule Card 4; Phonogram Game Cards.

Phonograms

New Phonograms — *er, or, ea, sh,*

Using the Phonogram Flash Cards, introduce the new phonograms and their sounds.

Show er . /er/, the /er/ of her

Show or . /or/

> **How are these two phonograms alike?** They both have a vowel followed by an R. The /r/ sound is heard in both of them.

Show ea . /ē-ĕ-ā/

Show sh . /sh/

Review

1. ✎ *3.1 Writing the Phonograms* – Ask the students to write each new phonogram five times while saying the sounds aloud.

2. Drill the phonograms with flash cards.

3. Play Phonogram Snatch using the phonograms taught thus far. *(The Phonogram and Spelling Game Book,* 8)

4. ✎ *3.2 Phonogram Practice* – Dictate the phonograms to the students. The teacher should say the sound(s) while the students write the correct phonogram. For extra practice, have the students read back the sounds, while you write the correct answers on the board.

1. a	*/ă-ā-ä/*		8. sh	*/sh/*		15. ng	*/ng/*		
2. ea	*/ē-ĕ-ā/*		9. g	*/g-j/*		16. ee	*/ē/*		
3. u	*/ŭ-ū-oo-ü/*		10. or	*/or/*		17. c	*/k-s/*		
4. s	*/s-z/*		11. ck	*/k/ two-letter /k/*		18. qu	*/qu/*		
5. b	*/b/*		12. th	*/th-TH/*		19. o	*/ŏ-ō-ö/*		
6. er	*/er/, the /er/ of her*		13. y	*/y-ĭ-ī-ē/*		20. f	*/f/*		
7. i	*/ĭ-ī-ē-y/*		14. h	*/h/*					

Exploring Sounds

Syllables

Say the vowel sounds. As you say the vowels, is your mouth open or closed? /ă-ā-ä/, /ĕ-ē/, /ĭ-ī-ē/, /ŏ-ō-ö/, /ŭ-ū-oo-ü/ My mouth is open when I say the vowel sounds.

We open our mouths to say vowel sounds.
Now, repeat these consonant sounds after me. Notice if your mouth is open or closed.

/m/ /m/ closed
/p/ /p/ closed then open
/b/ /b/ closed then open

Repeat these sounds. Tell me what is blocking the sound.
/s/ /s/ tongue
/t/ /t/ tongue
/g/ /g/ tongue
/k/ /k/ tongue

As we speak, our mouths open to say vowels and close in some way to say the consonants. This opening and closing gives the words a rhythm or a beat.

The beats are called syllables.
What are the beats called? syllables
Different words have different numbers of syllables depending upon how many vowel sounds are in the word.

Place your hand under your chin. Repeat the words after me. As you say the words, count how many times your mouth opens. This will tell you both how many syllables are in the word and how many vowel sounds are in the word:

la dy	2	top	1	lem on ade	3
book	1	ta ble	2	win dow	2
light bulb	2	pop corn	2	com pu ter	3
pen cil	2	pine ap ple	3	har mon i ca	4

For more information see *Uncovering the Logic of English,* Chapter 4: Consonants, Vowels, and Syllables.

Optional Practice

1. Clap the syllables.   Ⓐ Ⓚ

2. March to the syllables.   Ⓐ Ⓚ

3. ✏ *3.3 Extra Practice: Long Vowel Sounds* – Dictate the long vowel sounds. Ask the students to write them in their workbook and mark them as long vowels by drawing a line over the top.   Ⓐ Ⓚ Ⓥ

4. ✏ *3.4 Extra Practice: Short Vowel Sounds* – Dictate the short vowel sounds. Ask the students to write them in their workbook and mark them as short vowels by drawing a breve over the top.   Ⓐ Ⓚ Ⓥ

Spelling Rules

Spelling Rule 4: Long Vowel Sounds at the End of Syllables

I will say a word. Count the syllables, then tell me how many syllables are in the word.

After the students identify the number of syllables, sound out the word aloud while you write it on the board. Leave a break between the syllables.

pa per	be tween	ro bot
me ter	o pen	u nit

Read the words to me.
What does the vowel say at the end of the syllable? It says its long sound.
How do we mark a long vowel sound? Put a line over it.

pā per	bē tween	rō bot
mē ter	ō pen	ū nit

Show the students the spelling rule card. Recite the rule three times.

Spelling Rule	4
A E O U usually say their names at the end of the syllable.	

> **Teacher Tip:** *Notice that this rule does not cover the single vowels* `i` *and* `y`. *These will be covered in Rule 5 taught in Lesson 24 and in Rule 7 taught in Lessons 23 and 38.*

Optional: Spelling Rule Practice

1. Quickly review spelling rules 4, 11, 21, and 26 with the Spelling Rule Cards. Ⓐ Ⓥ

2. Create a reference page to remember this rule. Include sample words. Ⓒ Ⓥ

3. Ask the students to teach this to another student or to a parent. Ⓒ Ⓥ Ⓐ Ⓚ

4. **CK Review** Ⓥ Ⓐ Ⓚ

   - Say a word ending in /k/. Ask the students: Does it end in K or CK? Why?

   - **CK is used after a single, short vowel** – *back, black, block, brick, buck, deck, duck, flick, flock, jack, kick, lack, lick, lock, luck, muck, neck, nick, pack, pick, quack, quick, rack, rock, sack, shock, shuck, sick, slack, slick, smack, smock, snack, sock, speck, stick, stock, struck, suck, tack, track, truck, tuck, wick, yuck*

   - **K is used because it is after a long vowel sound** – *beak, leak, peak, speak, sneak, squeak, weak, steak, break, creek, Greek, week, seek, sleek*

   - **K is used after a consonant** – *ink, blink, think, stink, rink, chink, sink, link, honk, bonk, bank, skunk, drank, chunk, plunk, hunk, sank, spunk, thank, trunk, shrunk*

5. Practice dictating some of the words above for students to write on a whiteboard, chalkboard, or in a saltbox. Ask students which form of the sound /k/ they will use. (Provide students with help if needed for using the correct phonogram to spell the long sounds.) Ⓐ Ⓚ Ⓥ

Optional: Spelling Journal　　　　Ⓐ Ⓚ Ⓥ

Enter words where single vowels A, E, O, U say their names at the end of the syllable.

PART TWO

Using Spelling List 3 on pages 28-29, dictate each word following the steps included on pages Intro 42 - Intro 46.

Syllables

Many students struggle to identify the exact location of the syllable break. If needed, provide students with clues for the syllable breaks by pronouncing each syllable with a short pause between them.

Tips for Spelling List 3

Human

One of the difficulties with English spelling is that vowels in unaccented syllables often are pronounced as the schwa sound /ə/. In order to help students create an auditory picture of the word, it is helpful to exaggerate the unaccented vowel. Exaggerate the A in /hū mən/ to /hū măn/. When possible, it is also beneficial to link words to their roots. Point out to students that the words *man* and *human* are related.

Frozen

Say to spell /frō zĕn/ rather than /frō zən/.

To learn more about vowels in unaccented syllables and aiding students in creating an auditory picture of words, see *Uncovering the Logic of English,* 121-128.

	Word	Practice Sentence	Say to Spell	# of Syllables	Markings
1.	**quick**	*The quick dog ran away.*	quĭk	1	q<u>ui</u>ck
2.	**man**	*The man is working hard.*	măn	1	man
3.	**human**	*To err is human.*	hū măn	2	hū man
4.	**clean**	*The clean shirt is on the hook.*	clēn	1	cl<u>ea</u>n
5.	**seven**	*She has seven fish.*	sĕv ĕn	2	sev en
6.	**duck**	*A boy is feeding the duck.*	dŭk	1	du<u>ck</u>
7.	**clock**	*The clock is on the mantel.*	clŏk	1	clo<u>ck</u>
8.	**frozen**	*Ice is frozen water.*	frō zĕn	2	frō zen
9.	**paper**	*Write your name on the paper.*	pā per	2	pā p<u>er</u>
10.	**six**	*Six cats ran.*	sĭx	1	six
11.	**milk**	*The baby wants a bottle of milk.*	mĭlk	1	milk
12.	**ship**	*The ship is in the harbor.*	shĭp	1	<u>sh</u>ip
13.	**forest**	*They walked through the forest.*	for ĕst	2	f<u>or</u> est
14.	**hero**	*The fireman who rescued her is a hero.*	hē rō	2	hē rō
15.	**bread**	*We will have bread for lunch.*	brĕd	1	br<u>ea</u>d²

Spelling Hints	Part of Speech	Vocabulary Development
Underline /qu/. Underline /k/. **26** CK is used only after a single vowel which says its short sound. **11** Q always needs a U; therefore, U is not a vowel here.	Adj	quicker, quickest, quickly, quicken, quickening, quickness, quicksand
All first sounds.	N	manly, men, doorman, mailman, postman, human, woman
Say to spell /hū mǎn/. Put a line above the U. **4** A E O U usually say their names at the end of the syllable.	N	humans, humanly, humanize, dehumanize, inhumane, subhuman, superhuman
Underline /ē/. All first sounds.	Adj	cleaner, cleanest, cleaning, cleaned, cleanable, cleanliest, cleanliness, cleanup, cleanness, housecleaning, preclean, unclean
All first sounds.	Adj (N)	sevens, seventeen, seventy, sevenfold, seventh, seventieth
Underline /k/. **26** CK is used only after a single vowel which says its short sound.	N, (V)	ducks, ducking, ducked, duckling, duckweed
Underline /k/. **26** CK is used only after a single vowel which says its short sound.	N, (V)	clocks, o'clock, clocked, clocking, clocker, clockwise, counterclockwise, clockworks
Say to spell /frō zěn/. Put a line above the O. **4** A E O U usually say their names at the end of the syllable.	Adj	frozenness, prefrozen, refrozen, unfrozen
Put a line above the A. **4** A E O U usually say their names at the end of the syllable. Underline /er/.	N, (V)	papers, newspaper, flypaper, notepaper, paperback, paperboy, paperless, sandpaper, wallpaper, wastepaper
All first sounds.	Adj, (N)	sixes, sixteen, sixty, sixth, sixteenth, sixtieth, sixpence
Milk cannot be spelled with CK. **26** CK is used only after a single vowel which says its short sound.	N, (V)	buttermilk, milked, milker, milky, milkier, milkiness, milkiest, milkmaid, milkman, milkshake, milkweed
Underline /sh/.	N, (V)	ships, shipping, shipped, shipment, shipper, gunship, warship, midshipman, shipyard
Underline /or/.	N	forests, forested, deforest, deforestation, forestry, forester, rainforest, reforestation, reforest
Put a line over /ē/. Put a line over /ō/. **4** A E O U usually say their names at the end of the syllable.	N	heros, (heroes), heroism, heroic, unheroic *The most common spelling is heroes, though heros is now an accepted form in many dictionaries.*
Underline /ĕ/. Put a two over it. /ē-ĕ-ā/ said its second sound.	N	breading, breadbasket, breadboard, gingerbread, sweetbread

PART THREE

Materials Needed: Red and blue colored pencils. Grammar Card 1.3.

Grammar

Review

> **What is a noun?** A noun is the name of a person, place, thing, or idea.

1. Review nouns by quickly asking the students to name persons, places, and things.

2. ✎ *Spelling List 3* – Direct the students to read today's spelling list and identify the nouns. Have them write a red N by each word that is a noun.

    > **Find the nouns that are persons in Lesson 3.** man, human, hero

3. Review adjectives.

    > **What is an adjective?** Adjectives modify nouns and pronouns. Adjectives answer: What kind? How many? Which one? Whose?

    > ✎ *Spelling List 3* – **Find the adjectives in the spelling list and write a blue Adj. next to them.**

4. Review plurals.

    > **What is the rule to make a noun plural?** To make a noun plural, add the ending -S unless the word hisses or changes, then add -ES. Occasional nouns have no change or an irregular spelling.

    paper

    > How do we make this word plural? add -S.

    paper — papers

Irregular Plurals

man

> **How do we make man plural?** men
> **When we do not add -S but the plural changes in some other way, this is called an irregular plural.**

> **What is the rule for making a noun plural?** To make a noun plural, add the ending -S unless the word hisses or changes, then add -ES. Occasional nouns have no change or an irregular spelling.

Non-Count Nouns

Write the following words on the board. Direct the students to read the list. (Help emerging readers sound out the words.)

sand	*water*	*meat*
salt	*dust*	

Does it make sense to say one sand, two sands, three sands? no
Can you count sand? no
Why? There is too much of it. It is too tiny.
Sand is a non-count noun. We cannot count it but we can measure it. How could we measure sand? inches, buckets, tons, bags…

Non-count nouns are often measured rather than counted.
Since these nouns cannot be counted, they cannot be made plural.

Re-read the words in this list. After you read each word answer the question: Can you count it?
Circle the two non-count nouns in today's spelling list.
Hint: try counting each noun one ___, two ___ . milk, bread

Grammar Card 1.3

A non-count noun cannot be made plural.

✎ *Spelling List 3 – Write the plural form of each noun on Spelling List 3. If a noun is a non-count noun and does not have a plural, leave it blank.*

Optional: Spelling Cards

1. Dictate the words in Lesson 3 for the students to write on Spelling Word Cards.   ⒶⓋⓀ

2. Color a red border around the nouns and a blue border around the adjectives.   ⓋⓀ

3. Arrange the cards into short adjective noun phrases.   ⓋⓀ

Dictation

✎ *3.5 Dictation* – Read the following phrases one time. Ask the students to repeat it aloud, then write it in their workbooks.

1. quick humans	3. last forest	5. six clean papers
2. seven pink ducks	4. frozen bread	6. three clocks

Composition

1. Find adjectives and nouns from previous spelling lists that work together. Compose phrases orally.

2. Write all the adjectives in Lists 1, 2, and 3 which answer, "How many?" on the board.

ten   *six*   *seven*   *three*

3. Compose phrases orally that include a number, adjective, and noun, for example, *three black cats*.

4. ✎ *3.6 Composition* – Direct the students to compose six adjective noun phrases in their workbook. Encourage the students to write three phrases which include a number, adjective, and noun.

Vocabulary Development

Writing O'Clock Times in Words

Write *o'clock* on the board.

Why does the O say /ō/? Because it is at the end of the syllable.

The O stands for "of the" clock.

Point to the apostrophe.

This mark is called an apostrophe. It takes the place of the words "of the." Notice that the apostrophe is written like a small hook. It begins at the top line.
Look at Lessons 1-3. What numbers have we learned to spell so far? ten, six, seven, three
These can be combined with o'clock to write the time.

ten o'clock   *six o'clock*   *seven o'clock*

✎ *3.7 O'clock Times* – **Write the times shown in your workbook.**

Review Compound Words

Words in English can combine to form new words called compound words.
Learning one word in English can often provide us with clues to the meanings and spellings of many different words.
For example, what do we get if we combine sand and paper? sandpaper

sandpaper

✎ *3.8 Compound Words* – **Combine the words in your workbook to form new words.**

Optional: Vocabulary Development

1. Direct the students to read the words in their spelling lists. After reading each word ask, "Can you think of a compound word which uses this word?" Ⓐ

2. Draw pictures of the compound words. Label each picture. ⒸⓋ

Lesson 4

Phonograms:	ai, ay, oi, oy
Exploring Sounds:	Multi-Letter Consonants and Vowels
Spelling Rules:	3, 9, 10 Spellings of Long /ā/
Grammar:	Article Adjectives

PART ONE

Materials Needed: Phonogram Flash Cards from previous lessons plus ai , ay , oi , oy ; Spelling Rule Cards 3, 9, 10; 1 game piece per student; 1 die per student; 1 set of Phonogram Game Cards per student.

Phonograms

Today we will learn a new spelling rule that will help us understand today's phonograms.

Recite it together three times.

Spelling Rule	3
English words do not end in I, U, V, or J.	

New Phonograms — *ai, ay, oi, oy*

Using the Phonogram Flash Cards, introduce the new phonograms and their sounds.

Show ai . /ā/

Two letter A that may not be used at the end of English words.
Why can't we use it at the end? English words do not end in I, U, V, or J.

Show ay . /ā/

> **Two letter A that may be used at the end of English words.**

Show ay and ai .

> **What is the same between these two phonograms?** They both say /ā/. They both begin with the letter A.
> **What is different?** One ends in I, the other in Y.
> **Which one may be used at the end?** ay
> **Which one may not?** ai
> **Why?** English words do not end in I, U, V, or J.
> **I and Y are related in English. Y often stands in for I at the end of English words.**

Repeat with oy and oi . /oi/

Review

1. Drill the phonograms with flash cards.

2. ✎ *4.1 Writing the Phonograms* – Ask the students to write each new phonogram five times while saying the sounds aloud.

3. ✎ *4.2 Phonogram Practice* – Dictate the phonograms to the students. The teacher should say the sound(s) while the students write the correct phonogram. For extra practice, have the students read back the sounds, while you write the correct answers on the board.

1. oy */oi/ that you may use at the end of English words.*	7. a */ă-ā-ä/*	14. ng */ng/*
	8. ay */ā/ Two-letter ā that may be used at the end of English words.*	15. c */k-s/*
2. h */h/*		16. th */th-TH/*
3. ea */ē-ĕ-ā/*	9. i */ĭ-ī-ē-y/*	17. ai */ā/ Two-letter ā that may not be used at the end of English words.*
4. n */n/*	10. o */ŏ-ō-ö/*	
5. sh */sh/*	11. or */or/*	18. k */k/*
6. oi */oi/ that you may not use at the end of English words.*	12. e */ĕ-ē/*	19. er */er/ the /er/ of her*
	13. ck */k/ two-letter /k/*	20. ee */ē/ double /ē/*

4. ✎ *4.3 Phonogram Board Game* – Roll the die. Advance the number of spaces forward as shown on the die. While passing each space, read the phonogram. If a phonogram sound is missed, the player must go back to the space where he began. If the player reads all the sounds correctly, he may stay on that space and play advances to the next player.

Exploring Sounds

Multi-Letter Consonants and Vowels

You will need all the multi-letter phonogram flash cards learned so far, excluding | er | and | or |.<

> **Teacher Tip:** *The R controlled phonograms represent both a consonant and a vowel sound. (For more information see* Uncovering the Logic of English *page 82.)*

What is a vowel? A sound where your mouth is open and you can sustain or sing the sound.
What is a consonant? A sound that is blocked by the tongue, teeth, or lips.

As I show you the cards, read the sounds. Decide if the phonogram is a multi-letter vowel or a multi-letter consonant?

Show | th |.

    /th-TH/ It is a consonant. My teeth are blocking the sound.

Show | ee |.

    /ē/ It is a vowel sound. My mouth is open and I can sing it.

Show | ng |.

    /ng/ It is a consonant. The tongue is at the top of the mouth. I can say it with my mouth closed.

Show | ck |.

    /k/ It is a consonant. My tongue is blocking the sound.

Show | oi |.<

    /oi/ It is a vowel. Nothing is blocking the sound. It can be sustained.

> **Teacher Tip:** *We often do not think of /oi/ as a vowel sound. This is because most of us have been taught that the only vowels are: A, E, I, O, U and sometimes Y. Words such as* boil *and* boy, *however, clearly show that /oi/ is a vowel sound.*

Optional: Sounds Practice

1. ✎ *4.4 Extra Practice: Consonants and Vowels* – Complete the activity in the work-book. Ⓥ Ⓐ Ⓚ

2. Using the Phonogram Game Cards, ask the students to sort all the phonograms learned so far into vowels or consonants. (Exclude OR and ER for now.) Ⓚ Ⓥ Ⓐ

3. Ask the students to create a vowel collage and a consonant collage using all the phonograms learned so far. The collage may be done with markers, colored pencils, or by cutting phonograms out of old magazines. © Ⓥ

Spelling Rules

Spellings of the sounds /ā/ and /ä/

1. Spellings of the long /ā/ sound

    Which phonograms spell the long /ā/ sound? /ă-ā-ä/, two letter /ā/ that we may use at the end of English words, two letter /ā/ that we may not use at the end of English words, and /ē-ĕ-ā/.

    As your students list them, write them across the top of the board.

a	ay	ai	ea

    Which of these phonograms cannot be used at the end of a word? Two letter /ā/ that may not be used at the end of English words.

    Why can't we use AI at the end of the word? English words do not end in I, U, V or J.

2. Words that use the phonogram EA to spell the long /ā/ sound

    Only nine words use the phonogram EA to say the long /ā/ sound. Read them as I write them on the board. I will write them in blue to help us remember EA is not a common spelling of the long /ā/ sound.

a	ay	ai	ea	
			steak	wear
			great	tear
			bear	pear
			break	swear
			yeah	

    Where is /ē-ĕ-ā/ used to say the long /ā/ sound? In the middle of the word.
    /ē-ĕ-ā/ is not used for the long /ā/ sound at the end of the word.

    > **Teacher Tip:** *"Yeah" may also be spelled "yea." If you choose to introduce this spelling, simply state it is the only word where EA appears at the end of the word.*

3. Single-vowel A at the end of the word

    I will read a rule which will eliminate another phonogram from spelling the long /ā/ sound at the end of the word.

Spelling Rule	10
When a word ends with the phonogram A, it says /ä/. A may also say /ä/ after a W or before an L.	

✏️ *4.5 A Says /ä/ – **Read the words in your workbook.***

mä	pä	sofä	spä
orcä	datä	lavä	togä

What sound does single-letter A make at the end of the word? /ä/
We will mark the third sound of A, /ä/, by putting two dots over it.
Mark each of the words in your workbook.

4. AY spells long /ā/ at the end of the word.

   What is the only spelling of long /ā/ that may be used at the end of English words? /ā/ two-letter
   A that may be used at the end of English words.

Show Spelling Rule Card 9 and recite.

Spelling Rule	9

AY usually spells the sound /ā/ at the end of a base word.

How do we spell long /ā/ at the end of a word? ay

Read the words as I write them on the board.

a	ay	ai	ea	
	day		steak	wear
	clay		great	tear
	play		bear	pear
	tray		break	swear
			yeah	

5. Single vowel A is the most common spelling of long /ā/ at the end of a syllable.

   What rule have we learned that helps us spell the long /ā/ sound at the end of a syllable?
   A E O U usually say their long sounds at the end of a syllable.
   How do we spell long /ā/ at the end of a syllable? single vowel A
   This is the most common spelling of long /ā/ in the middle of the word at the end of a syllable.

   Read the words as I write them on the board.

a	ay	ai	ea	
bā ker	day		steak	wear
pā per	clay		great	tear
flā vor	play		bear	pear
mā jor	tray		break	swear
			yeah	

When spelling a word with the long /ā/ sound it is important to think about where the sound is located in the word.

6.   AI is the most common spelling of long /ā/ in the middle of the syllable.

What do you think is the most common spelling of the long /ā/ sound in the middle of the syllable? ai
Notice I said "most common." What other spelling of long /ā/ is sometimes used in the middle of the syllable? ea

Read the words as I write them on the board.

a	ay	ai	ea	
bā ker	d<u>ay</u>	j<u>ai</u>l	steak	wear
pā per	cl<u>ay</u>	n<u>ai</u>l	great	tear
flā vor	pl<u>ay</u>	p<u>ai</u>n	bear	pear
mā jor	tr<u>ay</u>	st<u>ai</u>rs	break	swear
			yeah	

Practice reading each of the lists of words with the long /ā/ sound.

✎   *4.6 Spellings of the Long /ā/ Sound* – As students answer the questions, direct them to write the answers in their workbook. This page is a useful reference tool for spelling the long /ā/ sound.

Write the spellings of the long /ā/ sound in your workbook.

Which spelling of /ā/ is most common at the end of a syllable?   A
Write it in your workbook.

Which spelling of /ā/ is most common in the middle of the syllable?   AI
Write it in your workbook.

Which spelling of /a/ is occasionally used in the middle of the syllable?   EA

Which spelling of /ā/ is most common at the end of the word?   AY
Write it in your workbook.

End of Syllable	Middle of the Syllable	End of the Word
a	ai (ea)	ay

There are only nine words which use EA to spell /ā/. Write them in your workbook.
Highlight the EA with color to help you remember how these are spelled.

Optional: Spelling Journal   Ⓐ Ⓚ Ⓥ

Enter sample words using A, AI, AY, and EA to spell the long /ā/ sound.

Optional: Spelling Rule Practice

1. Quickly review Spelling Rules 3, 4, 9-11, 21, and 26 using the flash cards.   Ⓐ Ⓥ

2. Create a reference page to remember these rules. Include sample words.   Ⓒ Ⓥ

3. Ask the students to teach this to another student or to a parent.   Ⓒ Ⓥ Ⓐ Ⓚ

4. Ask students to form words ending in A and AY with the Phonogram Game Cards.   Ⓚ Ⓐ Ⓥ

5. Create a sentence using the EA words as a memory device. For example: Yeah, the great breaking bears wearing pants with tears swear to eat only steaks and pears. Ⓒ Ⓐ

6. **The Long /ā/ Game** Ⓥ Ⓐ Ⓚ

   • Provide each student with a whiteboard and marker.

   • Explain that you will say a word. Students need to decide which spelling of long /ā/ is used within the word, write the word on the whiteboard, and then explain why they chose that spelling.

   • They get one point for writing the correct spelling of /ā/, one point for spelling the rest of the word correctly, and one point for correctly explaining why /ā/ was spelled that way.

   • **A spells /ā/ at the end of the syllable** – *paper, baker, flavor, major, razor, bacon, basin, laser*

   • **AI spells /ā/ in the middle of the syllable** – *bait, mail, bail, gait, hair, jail, maid, pain, pair, rail, rain, sail, tail, wail, wait*

   • **AY spells /ā/ at the end of the word** – *play, day, way, lay, say, ray, sway, stay, jay, way*

   • **EA** – *steak, great, bear, break, wear, tear, pear, swear, yeah*

PART TWO

Using Spelling List 4 on pages 42-43, dictate each word following the steps included on pages Intro 42 - Intro 46.

Tips for Spelling List 4

Gray

One of the differences between American and British spellings is the word *gray/grey*. If you are teaching British spelling, teach the spelling of the color *grey* after Lesson 21. Substitute instead the word *clay*.

Favor

In order to help students create an auditory picture of the word, it is helpful to exaggerate the unaccented vowel. Therefore exaggerate the ⟨or⟩ so that / fā **ver**/ sounds like / fā **vor**/.

To learn more about vowels in unaccented syllables and aiding students in creating an auditory picture of words, see *Uncovering the Logic of English*, 121-128.

The

The rhythmic nature of English also applies to words within sentences. Important words such as nouns, verbs, adjectives, and adverbs are stressed, whereas common grammatical terms such as articles, prepositions, and helping verbs are not. Therefore, many of the vowels in common grammatical terms are pronounced as the schwa sound /ə/.

To aid students in spelling these words, it is helpful to exaggerate the vowel for spelling purposes, in this case "the" becomes /THē/.

Though it is no longer as common in American speech, it was once considered proper English to pronounce *the* as /THē/ before a vowel as in /THē/ inspector or /THē/ apple, and /THə/ before a consonant as in /THə/ grapes or /THə/ hat.

A

For the same reasons as explained above, teach *a* as /ā/.

PART THREE

Materials Needed: Grammar Card 2.1; red, blue, and light blue colored pencils.

Grammar

Review

What is a noun? A noun is the name of a person, place, thing, or idea.

1. Review nouns by quickly asking the students to name persons, places, and things.

2. ✎ *Spelling List 4* – Direct the students to read today's spelling list and identify the nouns. Write a red N by each word that is a noun. Some students will be unsure if *favor* and *day* are nouns. Ask them: Can you count favors? One favor, two favors? Can you count days? One day, two days? Then they are nouns because they have a plural and you can count them.

3. Review adjectives.

    What is an adjective? Adjectives modify nouns and pronouns. Adjectives answer: What kind? How many? Which one? Whose?

    ✎ *Spelling List 4* – **Find the adjectives in the spelling list and write a blue Adj. next to them.**

4. Review non-count nouns.

    What is a non-count noun? A non-count noun is a noun that cannot be counted.
    Can you make a non-count noun plural? no

    ✎ *Spelling List 4* – **There are four non-count nouns in today's spelling list. Find the non-count nouns in Spelling List 4 and circle them.** oil< , rain, paint< , mail.

    < Teacher Tip: *Oil and paint may both be used as a count or a non-count noun. Consider the difference between: Is that the olive oil? The oils I most commonly use are olive oil and canola oil. The paint is dry. The paints are in the cupboard.*

5. Review plurals.

    How do we make a noun plural? To make a noun plural, add the ending -S unless the word hisses or changes, then add -ES. Occasional nouns have no change or an irregular spelling.

    ✎ *Spelling List 4* – **Write the plural form of each noun in Spelling List 4. If a noun is a non-count noun and does not have a plural, leave it blank.**

Article Adjectives

Write the following phrases on the board.

the desk	*a cat*	*an ant*
the pen	*a dog*	*an egg*

Word	Practice Sentence	Say to Spell	# of Syllables	Markings
1. **gray**	*The sky is gray today.*	grā	1	gr<u>ay</u>
2. **oil**	*The olive oil is in the cupboard.*	oil	1	<u>oi</u>l
3. **boy**	*The boy ran fast.*	boy	1	b<u>oy</u>
4. **rain**	*The rain is falling from the sky.*	rān	1	r<u>ai</u>n
5. **favor**	*He did me a favor.*	fā **vor**	2	fā v<u>or</u>
6. **plain**	*Her plain sweater is her favorite one.*	plān	1	pl<u>ai</u>n
7. **train**	*The train sped down the track.*	trān	1	tr<u>ai</u>n
8. **list**	*Write a list of the supplies you need.*	lĭst	1	list
9. **paint**	*They paint beautifully.*	pānt	1	p<u>ai</u>nt
10. **day**	*What a day it has been!*	dā	1	d<u>ay</u>
11. **toy**	*The baby is playing with a soft toy.*	toy	1	t<u>oy</u>
12. **mail**	*She will mail the letter today.*	māl	1	m<u>ai</u>l
13. **the**	*The boys are noisy.*	THē	1	th<u>e</u>²
14. **a**	*A girl is playing.*	ā	1	a
15. **an**	*An apple a day keeps the doctor away.*	ăn	1	an

Spelling Hints	Part of Speech	Vocabulary Development
Underline /ā/. **3** English words do not end in I, U, V, or J.	Adj	grayish, grayed, graying, grayer, grayest
Underline /oi/. Do not double the L because OI is a two letter vowel. **30** We often double F, L, and S after a single vowel at the end of a base word. Occasionally other letters also are doubled.	N, (V)	oils, oily, oiliest, oilier, oilcloth
Underline /oy/. **3** English words do not end in I, U, V, or J.	N	boys, boyish, boyhood, boyishness, busboy, choirboy, cowboy, schoolboy, tomboy, tomboyish
Underline /ā/.	N, (V), (Adj)	rain, rained, raining, rainy, rainiest, rainier, rainbow, raincoat, raindrop, rainfall, rainstorm, rainforest, rainmaker, rainwater
Say to spell /fā vor/. Put a line above the A. **4** A E O U usually say their names at the end of the syllable. Underline /or/.	N	favors, favorite, favorites, disfavor, favorable, favorably, favoritism, unfavorable, unfavorably
Underline /ā/.	Adj, N	plainer, plainest, plainness, plainly, plains, plainspoken
Underline /ā/.	N, (V)	trains, detrain, overtrain, retrain, trainable, trainee, trainer
All first sounds.	N, (V)	lists, listing, listed, enlist, enlisted, enlistment
Underline /ā/.	N, (V)	painter, painted, painting, paintbrush, repaint, unpainted
Underline /ā/. **3** English words do not end in I, U, V, or J.	N, (Adj)	days, today, daybed, daybreak, daydream, daydreamer, everyday, daytime, doomsday, holiday, payday, someday, today, weekday
Underline /oi/. **3** English words do not end in I, U, V, or J.	N, (V)	toys, toying, toyed
Underline /ā/. Do not double the L because AI is a two letter vowel. **30** We often double F, L, and S after a single vowel at the end of a base word. Occasionally other letters also are doubled.	N, (V)	mailman, mailer, mailing, mailed, airmail, blackmail, email, mailbag, mailbox
Say to spell /THē/. Underline /TH/. Put a 2 over it. /th-TH/ said its second sound. Draw a line above /ē/. **4** A E O U usually say their names at the end of the syllable.	A	
Say to spell /ā/. **4** A E O U usually say their names at the end of the syllable.	A	
All first sounds.	A	

Ask the students:

Which desk? the desk
Which pen? the pen
Which cat? a cat
Which dog? a dog
Which ant? an ant
Which egg? an egg

A, an, *and* the *are called article adjectives. They answer the question, "Which"; therefore they are tiny adjectives describing the noun.*

Show Grammar Card 2.1 and recite the definition three times.

Grammar Card 2.1	A
A, An, The — Tiny article adjectives that mark nouns and answer the question: Which?	

✎   *Spelling List 4 – **Write a light blue A next to the article adjectives in your spelling list. We will make them blue because they are adjectives. We will make them light blue because they are a special kind of adjective.***

the desk   the pen   a cat

Look at the phrases on the board. What comes after "A" and "the?" a noun

"A, an, the" are also called noun markers. This is because whenever you hear one of these tiny words, a noun will follow close by.

Find all the words in List 4 that make sense with "the." the oil, the boy, the rain, the train, the list, the paint, the day, the toy, the mail.
Notice that all the nouns make sense with "the".
This is another way to decide if a word is a noun. Ask yourself, "Does it makes sense with the article "the?"" If the answer is yes, it is a noun.

Read the spelling words in Lesson 4 and locate all the words that make sense with the article "a." a boy, a train, a list, a day, a toy.

Why can't we say a rain? "A" means one; it is like counting. We do not use "a" with a non-count noun.

✎   *4.7 Article Adjectives – **Write the three article adjectives in your workbook.***

Identifying Nouns and Adjectives

✎ *4.8 Identifying Nouns and Adjectives* – **Read the phrase in your workbook. I will write it on the board. Then we will answer questions to label the parts of speech. Label each part of speech in your workbook as I write it on the board.**

the gray paint

> **What is the noun in this phrase?** paint

      N
the gray paint

> **What kind of paint?** gray, adjective

   Adj N
the gray paint

> **Which paint?** the, article adjective

A Adj N
the gray paint

---

a long train

> **What is the noun in this phrase?** train
> **What kind of train?** long, adjective
> **Which train?** a, article adjective

A Adj N
a long train

the plain oil

> **What is the noun in this phrase?** oil
> **What kind of oil?** plain, adjective
> **Which oil?** the, article adjective

A   Adj   N
the plain oil

Challenge

The purpose of this activity is to demonstrate to the students that words can do different jobs in a sentence. Though *toy* and *mail* are often used as nouns, they may also be used as adjectives.

the toy train

> **What is the noun in this phrase?** train
> **What kind of train?** toy, adjective
> **Which train?** the, article adjective

A   Adj   N
the toy train

In this sentence is "toy" acting as a noun or an adjective? adjective
How do you know? It answers the question, "What kind?"

✎ *You may add a blue Adj. for adjective next to toy on your spelling list. Some words may be different parts of speech depending upon how they are used in the sentence.*

a mail truck

> **What is the noun in this phrase?** truck
> **What kind of truck?** mail, adjective
> **Which truck?** a, article adjective

A   Adj   N
a mail truck

In this sentence is mail acting as a noun or an adjective? adjective
How do you know? It answers the question, "What kind?"

✎ *You may add a blue Adj. next to mail on your spelling list.*

Vocabulary Development

A suffix is a group of letters added to the end of a base word to change the meaning.

gray + er

What new word is formed when the suffix -er is added to gray? grayer
Use grayer in a sentence. Answers vary. For example, "That paint is grayer than the other paint."

gray + er = grayer

plain + er

What new word is formed when -er is added to plain? plainer
Use plainer in a sentence. Answers vary. For example, "That sweater is plainer than the other one."

plain + er = plainer

Look back at the words in Spelling List 2. What words can we add the suffix "er" to? blacker, stronger, greener, sicker, longer
Do we add the suffix -er to nouns or to adjectives? Adjectives
What does it mean? -er changes the word so that we can compare.
I will write another suffix on the board. Read it to me.

gray + est =

What new word is formed when -est is added to gray? grayest
Use grayest in a sentence. Answers vary. For example, "That one is the grayest cat."

gray + est = grayest

Are there any words in Spelling Lists 2-4 that make sense when we add the suffix "est?" blackest, strongest, greenest, sickest, longest, plainest, grayest, quickest, cleanest
What is the difference between stronger and strongest? Stronger is used to compare two things. Strongest means that it is the most strong of all.
Use strongest in a sentence.

✎ *4.9 Vocabulary Development –* **Complete the activity in the workbook.**

Dictation

✎ *4.10 Dictation –* Read the following phrases one time. Ask the students to repeat each phrase aloud, then write it in their workbooks.

1. a gray day	4. the plainest toy
2. the strongest hero	5. oil paints
3. a bad rain	6. the long list

Composition

✎ *4.11 Composition* – Direct the students to use the words in lessons 1-4 to write six phrases following the pattern: article, adjective, noun.

Lesson 5 – Assessment & Review

5

Create an atmosphere where it is acceptable to make errors.
Model the attitude and strategies to move forward in practice.

PREPARATION

Many students, especially those who have struggled with reading, become discouraged when they are assessed. These students see assessments as a judgement upon themselves. When they do poorly, these students often believe they are stupid and incapable, and then struggle emotionally to remain engaged with the lessons. For these reasons, it is vital that teachers help students develop a new perspective towards learning to read and towards assessments.

These assessments are meant to help the teacher and the student know what needs more practice. There is no shame in needing to practice material again. Learning is a process of remembering and forgetting. In order to master material for lifelong retention, it must be practiced daily over a long period of time — years. As the teacher, consider subjects you studied in school but have not used for years. You will not know this material as well as you did when you were taking the course.

These lessons are designed to provide flexibility so that teachers and students can work together to practice the words and concepts that have not been mastered.

Before giving the assessment, ask students the following questions:

- *When will you use reading in your life?*

- *When will you use spelling?*

- *How do you feel when you misspell or misread a word? Why?*

Then discuss the following points:

- *Reading and spelling are an important part of everyday life. Without knowing how to read and spell, you will waste a lot of time and become frustrated.*

- *People need to practice a new word an average of forty times before it is mastered.*

- *Every fifth lesson we will review and practice the words and rules we have learned so far.*

- *Needing to practice the words more is expected. You do not need to feel badly about it.*

- *Some of the words on the assessment were words taught in the previous lesson. You may not have mastered them yet.*

- *To begin you will take an assessment. This helps us know which words and rules you need to practice. This is not to judge you. Based upon your mistakes, we will play games and do fun activities to practice the words.*

- *Tell me if there are words, phonograms, or spelling rules you want to review or practice.*

SPELLING ASSESSMENT

Materials Needed: Red colored pencil.

1. ✎ *5.1 Assessment* – Dictate the phrases to the students while they write them in their workbook.

1. the quickest cat	6. three green trees	11. a toy train
2. stronger legs	7. the gray ships	12. the last days
3. bad paints	8. six paper maps	13. seven ducks
4. black rocks	9. the sickest boy	14. rain
5. the longest path	10. a clean bag	15. faster trucks

2. Direct the students to read the phrases aloud while you write them on the board. Sound out each word and model the thought process. The students should mark corrections in red. Encourage the students to discuss what they missed. Create an atmosphere where it is acceptable to make errors. Model the attitude and strategies to move forward in practice. For example:

    the quickest cat

    > */THē/ /quĭck/ Use two letter CK because it is after a single short vowel /ĕst/ /căt/.*
    > **Which spelling of /k/ did I use?** Two letter ck.
    > **Why?** Because it is after a single short vowel.
    > **Did you spell the suffix /ĕst/ correctly?**

    stronger legs

    > */strŏnger lĕgs/ Did you use ER to spell /er/?...*

3. Recheck the students' work. Note the words and concepts which need further practice.

4. Did the students:

    > _____ *use CK after a single short vowel?*
    > _____ *use the phonogram ER to spell the /er/ sound?*
    > _____ *use AY to spell the long /ā/ sound at the end of the word?*
    > _____ *use AI to spell the long /ā/ sound in the middle of the syllable?*
    > _____ *use a single-vowel A to spell the long /ā/ sound at the end of the syllable?*
    > _____ *add an -S to make words plural?*

5. ✎ *5.2 Reading* – Ask the students to read the following words and phrases. Note the words they did not read fluently.

1. bat	6. a pink quilt	11. dog
2. hat	7. a hero	12. forest
3. list	8. ten strings	13. plain oil
4. frozen milk	9. mailman	14. clock
5. soft bed	10. street	15. favor

16. human hands   18. ponds   20. the hot sun

17. bread   19. rainforest

6. ✎ *5.3 Words to Practice* – Ask the students to read the words in the list and mark which ones they would like to practice further.

7. Using the assessment and your knowledge as a teacher, identify words to dictate onto index cards.

1. ____ a	21. ____ green	41. ____ quick
2. ____ an	22. ____ hand	42. ____ quilt
3. ____ bad	23. ____ hat	43. ____ rain
4. ____ bag	24. ____ hero	44. ____ rock
5. ____ bat	25. ____ human	45. ____ seven
6. ____ bed	26. ____ last	46. ____ ship
7. ____ black	27. ____ leg	47. ____ sick
8. ____ boy	28. ____ list	48. ____ six
9. ____ bread	29. ____ long	49. ____ soft
10. ____ cat	30. ____ mail	50. ____ street
11. ____ clean	31. ____ man	51. ____ string
12. ____ clock	32. ____ map	52. ____ strong
13. ____ day	33. ____ milk	53. ____ sun
14. ____ dog	34. ____ oil	54. ____ ten
15. ____ duck	35. ____ paint	55. ____ the
16. ____ fast	36. ____ paper	56. ____ three
17. ____ favor	37. ____ path	57. ____ toy
18. ____ forest	38. ____ pink	58. ____ train
19. ____ frozen	39. ____ plain	59. ____ tree
20. ____ gray	40. ____ pond	60. ____ truck

SPELLING WORD REVIEW

Materials Needed: Index cards, highlighter, timer, whiteboard, markers, eraser.

1. Dictate the missed words onto index cards. Have the students highlight the part of the word that was difficult.

2. Choose from the review activities below or use an activity found in the *The Phonogram and Spelling Game Book*.

1.   Play Spelling Snap *(The Phonogram and Spelling Game Book, 36)*.

2.   Play Guess My Word *(The Phonogram and Spelling Game Book, 37)*.

3.   Practice using Blind Spelling *(The Phonogram and Spelling Game Book, 42)*.

OPTIONAL SPELLING RULE REVIEW

Materials Needed: Spelling Rule Cards 3, 4, 9, 10, 21, 26; whiteboard, marker, eraser; Phonogram Cards AY, AI, OY, and OI.

Use the following mini-lesson to review the concepts as needed.

Spelling Rule 3

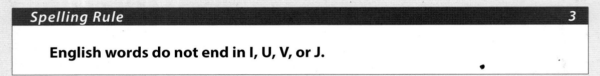

Spelling Rule	3
English words do not end in I, U, V, or J.	

1.   Review the rule by reciting it. Discuss the sample words on the back of the card.

2.   Show | ay | and | ai |.

   How does this rule apply to these phonograms? AY may be used at the end of the word. AI may not be used at the end of the word.

3.   Show | oy | and | oi |.

   How does this rule apply to these phonograms? OY may be used at the end of the word. OI may not be used at the end of the word.

4.   Dictate the following words as the students write them on a whiteboard: *pay, paint, toy, toil, soy, soil, plain, play, tray, train, day, boy, boil, way, wail, may, mail, main.*

Spelling Rule 26

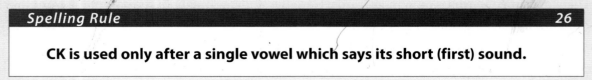

Spelling Rule	26
CK is used only after a single vowel which says its short (first) sound.	

1.   Review the rule by reciting it. Discuss the sample words on the back of the card.

2.   Write the following words on the board:

quick, tack, rock, sock, lick, trick, lock, luck, truck, deck

Read each word. What is the same between each of these words? They all end in CK. They all have a single vowel. The single vowels all say their short sound.

3. Write the following words on the board:

    plank, stink, leak, peak, milk, cheek, shrink

    Read each word. What is the same between each of these words? They all end in K.
    Do any of them have a single short vowel before the K? No

4. Direct students to write the words in activities 2 and 3 on index cards. When finished, have the students draw a card, read the word, state what form of /k/ was used and why. To turn it into a game, give one point for correct reading, one point for identifying the type of /k/, and one point for identifying why that form of /k/ was used.

Spelling Rule 4

Spelling Rule	4
A E O U usually say their names at the end of a syllable.	

1. Review the rule by reciting it. Discuss the sample words on the back of the card.

2. Write the following words on the board: *major, favor, meter, open, robot, unit.* Discuss where the syllable breaks and why each word is read with a long vowel.

3. ✎ *5.4 Extra Practice: Vowels at the End of Syllables* – Have the students practice reading the words in their workbook. Direct them to draw a line between the syllables and mark the long and short vowel sounds. *pep/per, pa/per, af/ter, fa/vor, of/fer, o/pen, hap/pen, pop/per, sup/per, cof/fin, ca/per, to/paz, fro/zen, hu/man*

4. Dictate the following words as students write them on a whiteboard: *frozen, human, favor, supper, cupid, pepper, happen, topaz, sofa, defog, solo, coffin, paper, zebra.* As they write each word, ask them to explain why the vowel says its long or short sound.

Spelling Rule 21

Spelling Rule	21
To make a noun plural, add the ending -S unless the word hisses or changes, then add -ES. Occasional nouns have no change or an irregular spelling.	

1. Review the rules by reciting them. Discuss the sample words on the back of the card.

2.   Write the following words on the board: *quilt, cat, tree, train, forest, paint.*

> ***Read each word.***
> ***How do you make them plural?*** add -S
> ***Read the plural form:*** quilts, cats, trees, trains, forests, paints

man

> ***What is the plural of man?*** men
> ***This is called an irregular plural. Why?*** Because we did not add -s. The word changed.

3.   Orally practice making words plural using nouns from Spelling Lists 1-4.

4.   ✎ *5.5 Extra Practice: Plurals* – Dictate the following words: *boys, trains, lists, toys, men, humans, papers, forests, strings, streets, paths, rocks, quilts, ponds, trees.* Direct students to write the singular word in the first column and the plural form in the second column.

Spelling Rules 9 and 10

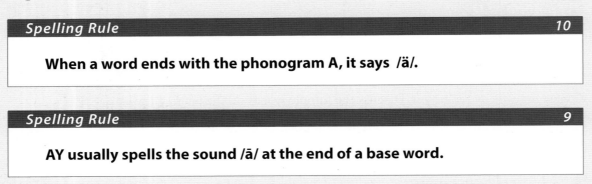

Spelling Rule	10
When a word ends with the phonogram A, it says /ä/.	

Spelling Rule	9
AY usually spells the sound /ā/ at the end of a base word.	

1.   Review the rules by reciting them. Discuss the sample words on the back of the card.

2.   Write the following words on the board: *pay, stay, day, ray, may, okay, jay, play.*

> ***Read each word. How are these words alike?*** They all end in AY.

Write the following words on the board: *ma, pa, zebra, cola.*

> ***Read each word. How are these words alike?*** They all end in A.
> The A says /ä/.

3.   Give each student an AY and an A phonogram card. Tell them you will say a word, and they need to hold up the phonogram which spells the last sound in the word. *lava, ray, tuna, tray, way, tuba, play, say, workday, ultra, ma, pa, stay, zebra*

OPTIONAL PHONOGRAM ASSESSMENT & REVIEW

Materials Needed: Whiteboard, marker, and eraser; Phonogram Game Cards.

Phonograms

✎ *5.6 Extra Practice: Phonogram Quiz* – Dictate the phonograms to the students.

1. l	/l/		14. or	/or/		27. i	/ĭ-ī-ē-y/
2. th	/th-TH/		15. d	/d/		28. t	/t/
3. a	/ă-ā-ä/		16. oi	/oi/		29. j	/j/
4. m	/m/		17. p	/p/		30. u	/ŭ-ū-oo-ü/
5. ea	/ē-ĕ-ā/		18. e	/ĕ-ē/		31. k	/k/
6. b	/b/		19. qu	/qu/		32. v	/v/
7. sh	/sh/		20. f	/f/		33. ee	/ē/
8. y	/y-ĭ-ī-ē/		21. g	/g-j/		34. w	/w/
9. n	/n/		22. ng	/ng/		35. er	/er/
10. c	/k-s/		23. r	/r/		36. ai	/ā/
11. ck	/k/		24. h	/h/		37. oy	/oi/
12. o	/ŏ-ō-ö/		25. ay	/ā/		38. x	/ks/
13. z	/z/		26. s	/s-z/			

Optional Phonogram Practice

Practice the phonograms as needed using the following game suggestions, or choose other games from *The Phonogram and Spelling Game Book*.

1. ✎ *5.7 Extra Practice: Phonogram Blitz* – *(The Phonogram and Spelling Game Book*, 29)

2. Practice the phonograms with Phonogram Sky Writing (*The Phonogram and Spelling Game Book*, 23).

3. Play Eraser Race (*The Phonogram and Spelling Game Book*, 28).

Lesson 6

6

Phonograms:	ar, ch, oo
Exploring Sounds:	Broad Vowel Sounds
Spelling Rules:	30, 21
Grammar:	Commas in a Series

PART ONE

Materials Needed: Phonogram Flash Cards from previous lessons and ar , ch , oo ; Phonogram Game Cards and cloth bag; Spelling Rule Card 30.

Phonograms

New Phonograms — *ar, ch, oo*

Show ar . /är/

> **What sound does /ă-ā-ä/ say in this phonogram?** /ä/ is the third sound of A.

Show ch . /ch-k-sh/

Show oo . /oo-ü-ō/

Review

1. Drill the phonograms with flash cards.

2. ✎ *6.1 Writing the Phonograms* – Direct the students to write each new phonogram five times while saying the sounds aloud.

3. ✎ *6.2 Phonogram Practice* – Dictate the phonograms to the students. The teacher should say the sound(s) while the students write the correct phonogram. For extra practice, have the students read back the sounds, while you write the correct answers on the board.

1. or   /or/
2. u   /ŭ-ū-oo-ü/
3. th   /th-TH/
4. ai   /ā/ that you may not use at the end of English words.
5. ch   /ch-k-sh/
6. ck   /k/ two-letter /k/
7. ea   /ē-ĕ-ā/

8. g   /g-j/
9. ay   /ā/ that you may use at the end of English words.
10. sh   /sh/
11. oo   /oo-ü-ō/
12. c   /k-s/
13. oi   /oi/ that you may not use at the end of English words.

14. ar   /är/
15. oy   /oi/ that you may use at the end of English words.
16. d   /d/
17. ng   /ng/
18. er   /er/ the /er/ of her
19. ee   /ē/ double /ē/
20. y   /y-ĭ-ī-ē/

4. Play Rotten Egg (*The Phonogram and Spelling Game Book,* 13).

Exploring Sounds

Broad Vowel Sounds

1. Write *a* on the board.

> *How many sounds does this phonogram make?* three
> *What are they?* /ă-ā-ä/
> *How do we mark the short sound /ă/?* Draw a breve or a curved line over it.

ă

> *How do we mark the long sound /ā/?* Draw a line over it.

ā

> *What is the third sound?* /ä/
> */ä/ is called the broad sound. It is marked with two dots.*

ä

> *The broad sound for the letter A is /ä/. What other single vowel says the same sound?* O
> *O is the most common spelling of the /ŏ/ sound.*

Write *o* on the board.

> *How many sounds does this phonogram make?* three
> *What are they?* /ŏ-ō-ö/
> *How do we mark the short sound /ŏ/?* Draw a breve or a curved line over it.
> *How do we mark the long sound /ō/?* Draw a line over it.
> *What is the third sound /ö/ called?* The broad sound.
> *How is it marked?* With two dots.

ŏ ō ö

Write *u* on the board.

> *How many sounds does this phonogram make?* four
> *What are they?* /ŭ-ū-oo-ü//
> *How do we mark the short sound /ŭ/?* Draw a breve or a curved line over it.
> *How do we mark the long sound /ū/?* Draw a line over it.
> *What is the same and what is different between the sounds /ū-oo/?* /ū/ starts with a /y/ sound.
> /oo/ does not start with /y/. They both say /oo/.
> *These are both variations on the long sound. Sometimes the /y/ sound is dropped. We will mark*
> *them both by drawing a line over the top to show it is a long sound.*
> *The fourth sound /ü/ is the broad sound.*
> *How is it marked?* With two dots.

ŭ ū ū ü

2. ✎ *6.3 Reading the Vowel Sounds* – Read the vowel sounds found in your workbook.

1. ŭ	4. ü	7. ă	10. ā
2. ŏ	5. ä	8. ē	
3. ě	6. ö	9. ū	

3. ✎ *6.4 Writing the Vowel Sounds* – Dictate the following vowel sounds. Direct the students to write them with the markings in their workbook.

1. ä-ŏ (two spellings)	3. ō	6. ă	9. ā
2. ě	4. ū	7. ē	10. ö
	5. ŭ	8. ü	

Spelling Rules

Doubling Letters at the End of Words

staff	tall	class
sniff	call	mess
scoff	pill	miss
off	ball	moss
huff	fall	glass
puff	pull	pass
scruff	hill	bass

✎ *6.5 Discover the Rule* – **Read each of the words in your workbook.**
What do you notice about each of these words? The last letters are doubled.
Which letters are doubled? F, L, S
What do you notice about the vowels? They are all single vowels.

Do most of the vowels make their long, short, or broad sound? short
Find four words where the vowel does not make its short sound and circle them. tall, call, ball, fall
What is the same about all these words? They all are spelled *all* and the A is saying /ä/.
One of the places A often says its third sound /ä/ is before an L.

This leads us to the rule:

Spelling Rule	30
We often double F, L, and S after a single vowel at the end of a base word. Occasionally other letters also are doubled.	

Do we always double F, L, and S? no
What vowel sound is F, L and S most often doubled after? a short vowel sound
What does A usually say before an L? / ä/

Optional: Spelling Rule Practice

1. Review spelling rules 3-4, 9-11, 21, 26, and 30 with the Spelling Rule Cards.   Ⓐ Ⓚ Ⓥ

2. Provide students with a set of phonogram game cards which includes all the phonograms learned so far. Direct students to sort the phonograms into consonants and vowels.   Ⓐ Ⓚ Ⓥ

3. ✎ *6.6 Extra Practice: Consonants and Vowels* – Direct students to write the consonants and vowels in the correct columns in the workbook.   Ⓐ Ⓚ Ⓥ

4. Create a reference page to remember this rule. Include sample words.   Ⓒ Ⓥ

5. Ask the students to teach this rule to another student or to a parent.   Ⓐ Ⓚ Ⓥ Ⓒ

6. Say a word. Ask the students to name words that rhyme: *ball, class, hill, ruff, pull, toss*…   Ⓐ

Optional: Spelling Rule Practice Continued

7. Write _ill on the board. Ask students to name as many words as possible that end in _ill – *hill, mill, pill, fill, kill, trill, chill, bill, dill, drill, frill, gill, shrill, thrill, still, will.* Write them on the board as the students list them. Ⓐ Ⓚ Ⓥ

    *   **_all** – *ball, fall, call, hall, wall, mall, stall, tall, thrall*

    *   **_ell** – *bell, dell, dwell, fell, sell, spell, shell, smell, well, yell*

    *   **_ull** – *hull, dull, bull, cull, full, pull, scull, skull*

    *   **_ass** – *bass, brass, class, grass, glass, sass, pass*

    *   **-ess** – *less, mess, dress, chess, bless, press, stress, unless*

    *   **-iss** – *miss, bliss, hiss, kiss, Swiss*

PART TWO

Using Spelling List 6 on pages 62-63, dictate each word following the steps included on pages Intro 42 - Intro 46.

Tips for Spelling List 6

Secret

One of the difficulties with English spelling is that vowels in unaccented syllables often are pronounced as the schwa sound /ə/. In order to help students create an auditory picture of the word, it is helpful to exaggerate the unaccented vowel. Therefore exaggerate the vowel so that /sē krə t/ sounds like /sē krĕt/.

To learn more about vowels in unaccented syllables and aiding students in creating an auditory picture of words, see *Uncovering the Logic of English,* 121-128.

Word	Practice Sentence	Say to Spell	# of Syllables	Markings
1. **glass**	*The glass is full of water.*	glăs	1	glass
2. **cliff**	*Look at the big cliff.*	clĭf	1	cliff
3. **brush**	*Put my brush on the table.*	brŭsh	1	<u>brush</u>
4. **all**	*All the dogs are barking.*	äl	1	äll
5. **ball**	*The ball rolled down the hill.*	bäl	1	bäll
6. **school**	*The school is just down the street.*	skool	1	sch<u>oo</u>l²
7. **poor**	*They are very poor.*	poor	1	p<u>oo</u>r
8. **car**	*He drove the red car.*	cär	1	c<u>ar</u>
9. **secret**	*I have a secret to tell you.*	sē krĕt	2	sē cret
10. **moon**	*There is a full moon tonight.*	moon	1	m<u>oo</u>n
11. **card**	*Let's buy mom a birthday card.*	card	1	c<u>ar</u>d
12. **book**	*I read a good book.*	bük	1	b<u>oo</u>k²
13. **class**	*Our class has ten students.*	clăs	1	class
14. **full**	*The bucket is full.*	fŭl	1	full
15. **sharp**	*Be careful with the sharp knife.*	sharp	1	sh<u>ar</u>p

Spelling Hints	Part of Speech	Vocabulary Development
30 We often double F, L, and S after a single vowel at the end of a base word. Occasionally other letters also are doubled.	N, Adj	glasses, eyeglasses, fiberglass, glassful, glassy, sunglasses, wineglass, hourglass
30 We often double F, L, and S after a single vowel at the end of a base word. Occasionally other letters also are doubled.	N	cliffs, cliffhanger
Underline /sh/.	N, (V)	brushes, airbrush, paintbrush, brushed, brusher, brushing, hairbrush, sagebrush, toothbrush, underbrush
Put two dots over the /ä/. /ă-ā-ä/ said its third sound /ä/. Hint: The letter A often says /ä/ before an L. **30** We often double F, L, and S after a single vowel at the end of a base word.	Adj	
Put two dots over the /ä/. /ă-ā-ä/ said its third sound /ä/. Hint: The letter A often says /ä/ before an L. **30** We often double F, L, and S after a single vowel at the end of a base word.	N	balls, basketball, balloon, cannonball, baseball, butterball, handball, meatball, pinball, racquetball, volleyball
Underline /k/ and put a 2 over it. It is the second sound of /ch-k-sh/. Underline /oo/. We cannot use CK because the /k/ sound is not after a single, short vowel at the end of the base word.	N, Adj	schools, schooling, schoolbook, preschool, schoolboy, schoolgirl, schoolhouse, schoolmate, schoolroom
Underline /oo/.	Adj	poorly, poorer, poorest, poorhouse
Underline /är/.	N	cars, carpool, caravan
Say to spell: / sē krĕt/. Put a line over /ē/. **4** A E O U usually say their names at the end of the syllable.	N, Adj	secrets, secretary
Underline /oo/.	N	moons, moonlight, honeymoon, moonbeam, moonlighting, moonstruck
Underline /är/.	N, (V)	cards, bankcard, carded, discard, flashcard, postcard, timecard, placard
Underline /ü/. Put a 2 over it. /oo-ü-ō/ said its second sound. We cannot use CK because it is a multi-letter vowel. **26** CK is used only after a single vowel which says its short sound.	N, (V)	books, booked, bookish, bookends, bookkeeping, booklet, bookmark, bookmobile, bookstore, bookshelf, textbook
30 We often double F, L, and S after a single vowel at the end of a base word. Occasionally other letters also are doubled.	N	classes, classy, classic, classical, classify, classification, classroom, classless, outclass, classmate, underclassman
30 We often double F, L, and S after a single vowel at the end of a base word. Occasionally other letters also are doubled.	Adj	fuller, fullest, fully
Underline /sh/. Underline /är/.	Adj	sharper, sharpest, sharpen, sharpening, sharpener, sharpness, sharpshooter, sharpy

PART THREE

Materials Needed: Grammar Cards 7, 11.1; red, blue colored pencils; Spelling Rule Card 21.

Grammar

Review

What is a noun? A noun is the name of a person, place, thing, or idea.

1. Review nouns by quickly asking the students to name persons, places, and things.

2. ✎ *Spelling List 6* – Direct the students to read today's spelling list and identify the nouns. **Write a red N by each word that is a noun. Test words by deciding if you can make them plural and if it makes sense with the article "the."**

3. Review adjectives.

   What is an adjective? Adjectives modify nouns and pronouns. Adjectives answer: What kind? How many? Which one? Whose?

   ✎ *Spelling List 6* – **Find the adjectives in the spelling list and write a blue Adj next to them.**

Challenge

There are two words in our list that can be both a noun and an adjective. Can you find them? glass, secret
Use glass in a sentence where it is a noun. The glass is sitting on the table.
Use glass in a sentence where it is an adjective. The glass bowl broke.
Use secret in a sentence where it is a noun. I know five secrets.
Use secret in a sentence where it is an adjective. The secret door is over there.

Optional: Spelling Cards

1. Dictate the words in Lesson 6 for the students to write on index cards. Ⓐ Ⓚ Ⓥ

2. Ask the students to color a red border around the nouns. Ⓚ Ⓥ

3. Direct them to put a blue border around the adjectives. Ⓚ Ⓥ

Plurals

1. Write the following words on the board.

   boy   *camp*   *coin*   *day*

Read each word and then say the plural form.   boy, boys; camp, camps; coin, coins; day, days.
What did you do to form the plural? add S

Write the following words on the board.

| class | brush | bench | box |

Read the first word and then say the plural form. class, classes
Did you just add the sound /s/? no
What did you do to form the plural? add /ĕs/
Why do we need to add /ĕ/ before the /s/? Could we say class-s and be able to hear the extra /s/ without putting /ĕ/ before it? No

Write *-es* after *class* in another color to form *classes.*

Read the next word and say the plural. brush, brushes
What did you do to form the plural? add /ĕs/
Why do we need to add /ĕ/ before the /s/? We cannot say brush-s. The /ĕ/ is added so that we can hear the plural /s/ sound.
Continue in the same manner with the remaining words.

| classes | brushes | benches | boxes |

Spelling Rule   21

To make a noun plural, add the ending -S unless the word hisses or changes, then add -ES. Occasional nouns have no change or an irregular spelling.

---

2. *Spelling List 6* – Direct the students to write the plural form of each of the nouns on their spelling list.

Optional – Plurals Practice

1. *6.7 Extra Practice: Plurals* – Complete the plurals exercise in the workbook. Ⓐ Ⓚ Ⓥ
Answers: *books, glasses, cards, cars, balls, brushes.*

2. Review the definitions of singular and plural with Grammar Cards 1.1-1.2. Ⓐ Ⓥ

Identifying Parts of Speech

6.8 Identifying Parts of Speech – Read the phrase in your workbook. I will write it on the board. Then we will answer questions to label the parts of speech. Label each part of speech in your workbook as I write it on the board.

a full moon

What is the noun in this phrase? moon

N
a full moon

What kind of moon? full, adjective

Adj   N
a full moon

Which moon? a, article adjective

A Adj   N
a full moon

---

the secret classroom

What is the noun in this phrase? classroom

What kind of classroom? secret, adjective

Which classroom? the, article adjective

A   Adj   N
the secret classroom

---

a glass ball

What is the noun in this phrase? ball

What kind of ball? glass, adjective

Which ball? a, article adjective

A Adj   N
a glass ball

Commas in a Series

✎ *6.9 Commas in a Series* – Direct the students to read the lists in their workbook aloud.

sun and moon

cars and trucks

balls, cards, toys, and books

paper, paint, and paintbrushes

seven men, three boys, and ten kids

black trucks, red cars, and gray trains

What do you notice about each list? When there are only two words in the list, there are no commas. When there are three or more words in the list, each word in the list is separated by a comma. The word "and" is used before the last item in the list.

Circle each of the commas in your workbook.

This leads to our first comma rule:

Grammar Card 11.1	Comma Rule 1
Use commas to separate the words in a series of three or more.	

The word "and" is a conjunction.

Grammar Card 7	C
Conjunctions connect words, phrases, or sentences together.	

Notice how the word "and" is joining the words in the list together.

Optional: Comma Practice

1. ✎ *6.10 Extra Practice: Commas in a Series* – Direct students to add commas where needed to the lists in their workbooks. Ⓚⓥ

2. Write four commas on small sticky notes. Write "and" on another sticky note. Direct students to arrange the spelling cards into lists placing commas between each item. Ⓚⓥ

Dictation

✎ *6.11 Commas in a Series* – Read the phrase one time. Ask the students to repeat it aloud, then write it in their workbooks.

1. the hot sun and the full moon
2. all the secret books
3. the poorest school
4. cliffs, ponds, and paths
5. toy cars, toy trains, and balls
6. the paintbrushes

Vocabulary Development

Balloon – a common word in children's books

Write the words *ball* and *balloon* on the board. Ask the students to read them. Provide help as needed.

> ***How are these words related?*** They both have the word ball. A balloon is shaped like a ball.
> ***What was added to the end of ball to form balloon?*** oon

> ✎ *6.12 Vocabulary Development –* **Write balloon in your workbook.**

Compound Words

> ***What is a compound word?*** Two words joined together to form a new word.

1. Direct the students to orally form compound words with the words in List 6.

2. ✎ *6.13 Compound Words* – Direct students to write new compound words using the words in their workbooks.

Answer Key: *sunglasses, basketball, cannonball, meatball, schoolbook, schoolboy, schoolroom, classroom, flashcard, bookend, bookmark, bookshelf, textbook, paintbrush, toothbrush, hairbrush*

Challenge

Write the suffix *-let* on the board. Write the words: *booklet, piglet, droplet*.

> ***What does -let mean?*** something small

Composition

1. Using the words in the workbook, ask the students to orally compose lists. Look at the sample together. Remind the students that each word in a list is separated by a comma.

2. ✎ *6.14 Composition* – Direct the students to write six lists in their student workbook.

Lesson 7

Phonograms:	oa, oe
Exploring Sounds:	Spellings of the Long /ō/ Sound
Spelling Rules:	
Grammar:	Article Usage

PART ONE

Materials Needed: Phonogram Flash Cards from previous lessons and oa , oe ; 1 Set of Phonogram Game Cards per student, bell or buzzer.

Phonograms

New Phonograms — *oa, oe*

Show oa . */ō/*

Show oe . */ō-oo/*

> ***What do you notice about these phonograms?*** They both begin with an O. They both say /ō/. One ends in an A, and one ends in E.

I will write words using these phonograms on the board. Raise your hand when you see a pattern.

toe	*board*
doe	*coach*
hoe	*foam*
oboe	*oak*

OE is used at the end of the word, OA is used in the middle of the word.

Review

1. Drill the phonograms with flash cards.

2. ✎ *7.1 Writing the Phonograms* – Ask the students to write each new phonogram five times while saying the sounds aloud.

3. Direct the students to arrange all the phonograms learned so far in ABC order. This may be done with the flash cards, game cards, or on paper.

4. ✎ *7.2 Phonogram Practice* – Dictate the phonograms to the students. The teacher should say the sound(s) while the students write the correct phonogram. For extra practice, have the students read back the sounds, while you write the correct answers on the board.

1.	g	/g-j/	9.	ea	/ē-ĕ-ā/	15.	oa	/ō/ two-letter /ō/	
2.	oe	/ō-oo/	10.	or	/or/	16.	oi	/oi/ that you may not use at the end of English words.	
3.	th	/th-TH/	11.	ay	/ā/ that you may use at the end of English words.				
4.	er	/er/ the / er/ of her				17.	oy	/oi/ that you may use at the end of English words.	
5.	ch	/ch-k-sh/	12.	sh	/sh/				
6.	ng	/ng/	13.	ai	/ā/ that you may not use at the end of English words.	18.	d	/d/	
7.	y	/y-ĭ-ī-ē/				19.	ar	/är/	
8.	ck	/k/ two-letter /k/	14.	oo	/oo-ü-ō/	20.	ee	/ē/ double /ē/	

5. Play Teacher Trouble (*The Phonogram and Spelling Game Book*, 29).

Exploring Sounds

Spellings of the Long /ō/ Sound

List the phonograms that say the long /ō/ sound. o, oa, oe, oo

Write the sounds at the top of the board so they form columns.

o	oa	oe	oo

Vowel sounds are some of the most difficult to spell because there are many choices. When we learn the Logic of English®, there are still some spellings we will need to memorize. Today we will analyze the spellings of /ō/. Though we often need to memorize which spelling is used, we will discover which spellings are the most common.

oo	*is the least common spelling. It is used in only 2 words.*

Write these two words under OO in a different color to highlight that they are the only words which spell the long /ō/ sound, OO.

o	oa	oe	oo
			door
			floor
			(poor)<

> ← Teacher Tip: *In some dialects poor is pronounced with a long /ō/ sound. Include poor if it is helpful to your students.*

That leaves O, OA, and OE.

Which of these three spellings say the long /ō/ sound at the end of the syllable? O
What is the spelling rule? A E O U usually say their names at the end of the syllable.

Under the O, I will write a few examples of how O spells the long /ō/ sound at the end of the syllable. Read each word as I write it.

o	oa	oe	oo
o pen			door
o kay			floor
mo tor			(poor)<
to tal			

Which of the spellings says the long /ō/ sound in the middle of the syllable? OA.

Under OA, in the second column, write the following words.

o	oa	oe	oo
o pen	boat		door
o kay	coat		floor
mo tor	toad		(poor)<
to tal	soap		

Which of these spellings may be used at the end of the word? oe, o
`oe` **is not very common. There are only 7 common words which use** `oe` **.
Read them as I write them.**

Write them under OE and in a different color to highlight that they are the only words which end in OE.

o		oa	oe		oo
o pen		boat	doe	oboe	door
o kay		coat	aloe	foe	floor
mo tor		toad	toe	hoe	(poor)<
to tal		soap	woe		

When you hear /ō/ at the end of the word, it is usually spelled O.

o		oa	oe		oo
o pen	no	boat	doe	oboe	door
o kay	so	coat	aloe	foe	floor
mo tor	tomato	toad	toe	hoe	(poor)<
to tal	bingo	soap	woe		

Practice reading the lists of words with the long /ō/ sound.
Which two spellings of /ō/ are the most common? O and OA

✎ *7.3 Spellings of the Long /ō/ Sound –* **What are the spellings of long /ō/?** o, oa, oe, oo
Write them in your workbook.

Which spelling of O is most common in the middle of the syllable? OA
✎ **Write it in your workbook.**

Which spelling of O is most common at the end of a syllable and at the end of the word? O
✎ **Write it in your workbook.**

Middle of the syllable	End of the syllable
oa	o

Which words do you think are the most important for you to remember that use OE and OO?
Answers will vary.

✎ **Write the words in your workbook that use the OE and OO phonogram that are the most important for you to remember.**
Highlight the OE and the OO with color to help you remember how these are spelled.

Optional: Spelling Journal   Ⓐ Ⓚ Ⓥ

Enter sample words using O, OA, OE, and OO to spell the long /ō/ sound.

Optional: Spelling Rule Practice

1. Review spelling rules 3-4, 9-11, 21, 26, and 30 with the Spelling Rule Cards.   Ⓐ Ⓚ Ⓥ

2. ✎ *7.4 Extra Practice: Plurals Practice* – Read the word. Write the plural form. Ⓐ Ⓚ Ⓥ

3. ✎ *7.5 Optional: Double F, L, and S* – Set the timer for 2-4 minutes. Tell students they are to think of as many words as possible to complete the patterns, and write them in their notebooks. Ⓐ Ⓚ Ⓥ

   - **_ill** – *hill, mill, pill, fill, kill, trill, chill, bill, dill, drill, frill, gill, shrill, thrill, still, will*
   - **_all** – *ball, fall, call, hall, wall, mall, stall, tall, thrall*
   - **_ull** – *hull, dull, bull, cull, full, pull, scull, skull*

PART TWO

Using Spelling List 7 on pages 74-75, dictate each word following the steps included on pages Intro 42 - Intro 46.

Tips for Spelling List 7

Floor and Door

These are the only two words which use the phonogram OO to spell the long /ō/ sound. After teaching these two words, draw attention to the spelling. Ask students how the meaning of *floor* and *door* are related and how they could use that to help remember how to spell them.

Word	Practice Sentence	Say to Spell	# of Syllables	Markings
1. **hill**	The cat ran up the hill.	hĭl	1	hill
2. **rich**	The man is very rich.	rĭch	1	ri<u>ch</u>
3. **boat**	We will go on a boat ride tonight.	bōt	1	b<u>oa</u>t
4. **toe**	He stubbed his toe.	tō	1	t<u>oe</u>
5. **tall**	The tall man walked under the tree.	täl	1	täll
6. **road**	The road is blocked.	rōd	1	r<u>oa</u>d
7. **room**	You may sleep in this room.	room	1	r<u>oo</u>m
8. **river**	The river is at flood stage.	rĭv <u>er</u>	2	riv <u>er</u>
9. **cheap**	This store sells cheap coffee.	chēp	1	<u>cheap</u>
10. **coat**	Bring your coat.	cōt	1	c<u>oa</u>t
11. **egg**	The recipe calls for one egg.	ĕg	1	egg
12. **soap**	Wash your hands with soap.	sōp	1	s<u>oa</u>p
13. **inch**	Sal grew one inch last year.	ĭnch	1	in<u>ch</u>
14. **door**	Open the door carefully.	dōr	1	d<u>oo</u>r³
15. **floor**	Set your bag on the floor.	flōr	1	fl<u>oo</u>r³

Spelling Hints	Part of Speech	Vocabulary Development
30 We often double F, L, and S after a single vowel at the end of a base word. Occasionally other letters also are doubled.	N	hills, hilly, anthill, downhill, uphill, foothill, hillside, hilly, hillier, hilliest, hilltop, molehill
Underline /ch/.	Adj	riches, enrich, enrichment, richer, richest, richly, richness, superrich
Underline /ō/.	N	boats, boater, boating, boated, boathouse, boatman, boatswain, iceboat, rowboat, motorboat, riverboat, sailboat, tugboat
Underline /ō/.	N	toes, tiptoe, toed, toeing
Put two dots over the /ä/. /ă-ā-ä/ said its third sound /ä/. Hint: The letter A often says /ä/ before an L. **30** We often double F, L, and S after a single vowel at the end of a base word.	Adj	taller, tallest, tallness
Underline /ō/.	N	roads, railroad, roadbed, roadblock, roadrunner, roadside, roadwork, byroad, crossroad, highroad, inroad
Underline /oo/.	N	rooms, bedroom, bathroom, roomy, ballroom, classroom, courtroom, darkroom, homeroom, lunchroom, playroom
Underline /er/.	N	rivers, riverbank, riverbed, riverfront, riverside, riverboat, upriver
Underline /ch/. Underline /ē/.	Adj	cheaper, cheapest, cheaply, cheapness, cheapen, cheapskate
Underline /ō/.	N	coats, coating, coated, raincoat, turncoat, undercoat, overcoat, waistcoat, greatcoat, housecoat
30 We often double F, L, and S after a single vowel at the end of a base word. Occasionally other letters also are doubled.	N	eggs, eggshell, eggplant, eggnog, eggy
Underline /ō/.	N	soaps, soapy, soapbox, soaped, soaping, soapier, soapiest, soapiness, soapstone, soapsuds
Underline /ch/. All first sounds.	N	inches, inching, inched, inchworm
Underline /ō/. Put a 3 over it. /oo-ŭ-ō/ said its third sound. /oo/ is the most common sound. /ō/ is used in only two words. Since it is not common, it is listed last.	N	doors, doorbell, doorknob, doorjamb, doorkeeper, doorman, doormat, doorstep, doorway, indoor, outdoor, outdoorsman
Underline /ō/. Put a 3 over it. /oo-ŭ-ō/ said its third sound. /oo/ is the most common sound. /ō/ is used in only two words. Since it is not common, it is listed last.	N	floors, floored, flooring

PART THREE

Materials Needed: Grammar Cards 2.2 and 2.3; red and blue colored pencils.

Grammar

Review

> *What is a noun?*   A noun is the name of a person, place, thing, or idea.

1. Review nouns by quickly asking the students to name persons, places, and things.

   ✎ *Spelling List 7 –* **Read today's spelling list. Identify the nouns. Write a red N by each word that is a noun.**
   Test words by deciding if you can make them plural and if it makes sense with the article "the." Inch is a noun. It is an idea. "The inch" makes sense and you can count inches.

2. Review adjectives.

   > *What is an adjective?* Adjectives modify nouns and pronouns. Adjectives answer: What kind? How many? Which one? Whose?

   ✎ *Spelling List 7 –* **Find the adjectives in the spelling list and write a blue Adj next to them.**

   Review the definitions of a noun, adjective, and article adjective using the Grammar Flash Cards.

3. ✎ *Spelling List 7 –* Review the plurals rule, Spelling Rule 21. Direct the students to write the plural form of each of the nouns on their spelling list. Notice that the word *inch* hisses and needs an -ES.

Optional: Spelling Cards

1. Dictate the words in Lesson 7 for the students to write on index cards.   Ⓐ Ⓚ Ⓥ

2. Ask the students to color a red border around the nouns.   Ⓚ Ⓥ

3. Direct them to put a blue border around the adjectives.   Ⓚ Ⓥ

Definite and Indefinite Articles

> *I will read two sentences. I will change only one word. Tell me how the meaning changes.*

> *I want a black dog.*
> *I want the black dog.*   "A dog" means any dog. "The dog" means a particular dog.

I would like a cup of tea.
I would like the cup of tea.   "A cup of tea" means any cup of tea. "The cup of tea" means a particular cup.

She went to a party.
She went to the party.   "A party" means any party. "The party" means a particular party.

Using A and An

✎   *7.6 Articles – Read the phrases in your workbook.*

a river	an ant
a hill	an egg
a road	an inch
a cheap coat	an open door
a clean room	an oil lamp

When do we use "a"? before a consonant
Hint: look at the first letter of each word.
When do we use "an"? before a vowel
Circle the consonant that follows "a" red and circle the vowel that follows "an" blue in each of the phrases in your workbook.

Recite the rule:

Grammar Card 2.2	A
The article a is used only before a consonant.	

Grammar Card 2.3	A
The article an is used only before a vowel.	

✎   *7.7 A and An – Complete the phrases in your workbook using "a" or "an."*

Identifying Parts of Speech

✎   *7.8 Identifying Parts of Speech – Read the phrase in your workbook. I will write it on the board. Then we will answer questions to label the parts of speech. Label each part of speech in your workbook as I write it on the board.*

a boat, a car, and a truck

What are the nouns in this phrase? boat, car, truck

Which boat? a, article adjective
Which car? a, article adjective
Which truck? a, article adjective

What is the word "and" called? conjunction
What does a conjunction do? It connects words, phrases, or sentences together.

A N   A N C A N
a boat, a car, and a truck

---

a long road and a short hill

What are the nouns in this phrase? road, hill

What kind of road? long, adjective
Which road? a, article adjective

What kind of hill? short, adjective
Which hill? a, article adjective

What is the word "and" called? conjunction
What does a conjunction do? It connects words, phrases, or sentences together.

A Adj N   C A Adj N
a long road and a short hill

---

a red, black, and green coat

What is the noun in this phrase? coat

What kind of coat? red, adjective
What kind of coat? black, adjective
What kind of coat? green, adjective
Which coat? a, article adjective

What is the word "and" called? conjunction
What does a conjunction do? It connects words, phrases, or sentences together.

A Adj Adj   C Adj N
a red, black, and green coat

Dictation

✎ *7.9 Dictation* – Read the phrase one time. Ask the students to repeat it aloud, then write it in their workbooks.

1. an inch long boat
2. hills, rivers, and roads
3. oil, milk, and soap
4. an egg
5. the secret room
6. doors and floors

Vocabulary Development

Compound Words

What is a compound word? Two words joined together to form a new word.

1. Direct the students to orally form compound words with the words from Lessons 6 and 7.

2. ✎ *7.10 Compound Words* – Write new compound words using the words in the workbook.

door	bell mat step way

sail tug motor river	boat

bed class bath play	room

Optional: Vocabulary Practice

1. Illustrate each compound word. Ⓚ Ⓥ Ⓒ

2. ✎ *7.11 Extra Practice: The Suffixes -er and -est* – Write the new words formed by adding the suffixes -er and -est. Ⓚ Ⓥ Ⓐ

Composition

✎ *7.12 Composition* – Direct the students to write short phrases using *a* and *an* + adjective + noun using the sample words provided in the workbook.

Lesson 8

Phonograms:	igh, wh
Exploring Sounds:	W and WH
Spelling Rules:	28
Grammar:	Comparative and Superlative

PART ONE

Materials Needed: Phonogram Flash Cards from previous lessons and igh , wh , w ; pennies to cover the Bingo Chart; Spelling Rule Card 28.

Phonograms

New Phonograms — *igh, wh*

Introduce igh . /ī/

> **What do you notice about** igh **?** It has three letters. The first letter is I and it says /ī/. The GH is silent.

Introduce wh . /wh/

Exploring Sounds

W and WH

Depending upon your dialect, some students may pronounce /w/ and /wh/ differently. The /wh/ has a more airy sound. Other English speakers pronounce them exactly the same. The goal of this activity is to attune students to the fact that some people distinguish these sounds in their speech. Students do not need to change how they pronounce the words, but it helps them to understand the logic of the spellings when they realize that some people distinguish these sounds. Also if they do pronounce W and WH differently, they will know which spelling is used.

✎ *8.1 The Phonogram WH* – **This phonogram is limited in where it is used in the word. Read the words in your workbook. Underline the WH. Where is it used in the word?** WH is used only at the beginning of a base word.

when	*whip*	*wheel*	*whisk*
wheat	*whiff*	*which*	*whimper*

Show the students ⬚ w ⬚ and ⬚ wh ⬚ .

> **Do you pronounce these phonograms differently?**
> **Some people do.**

✎ *8.2 The Phonogram W* – **Compare how you say the words which start with the phonogram W to the words which start with the phonogram WH.**

water	*week*	*wool*	*wall*
warm	*wing*	*wind*	*wax*

Optional: Listen to this recording of the two pronunciations. http://www.macmillandictionary.com/dictionary/american/when.

> **Some dialects pronounce these two phonograms differently. The difference is subtle, so do not be concerned if you cannot hear it. What is most important is that you understand there is a reason for the two distinct spellings. If you do not pronounce them differently, you will need to memorize which words use the phonogram WH at the beginning.**

Phonograms

Review

1. Drill the phonograms with flash cards.

2. ✎ *8.3 Writing the Phonograms* – Ask the students to write each new phonogram five times while saying the sounds aloud.

3. ✎ *8.4 Phonogram Practice* – Dictate the following phonograms while the students write them onto the Bingo Chart.

1. igh	/ī/	10. i	/ĭ-ī-ē-y/	19. sh	/sh/		
2. ee	/ē/	11. wh	/wh/	20. u	/ŭ-ū-oo-ü/		
3. t	/t/	12. ng	/ng/	21. oo	/oo-ü-ō/		
4. oe	/ō-oo/	13. oi	/oi/	22. z	/z/		
5. or	/or/	14. ai	/ā/	23. th	/th-TH/		
6. er	/er/	15. o	/ŏ-ō-ö/	24. ck	/k/		
7. l	/l/	16. ea	/ē-ĕ-ā/	25. a	/ă-ā-ä/		
8. ch	/ch-k-sh/	17. oa	/ō/				
9. oy	/oi/	18. ay	/ā/				

4.   ✎   *8.4 Phonogram Practice* – Using the Bingo Chart created by each student, direct the students to take turns calling out a phonogram to cover. When someone has five-in-a-row, they may call Bingo. For greater challenge, the students must have two Bingos or cover the whole board.

Spelling Rules

Phonograms Ending in GH

✎   *8.5 Phonograms Ending in GH –* **Read the words in your workbook. What is the same in each word?** They all include the phonogram IGH.
Read them again to yourself and underline the three letter / ī/.
Three letter /ī/ is only used in two places in a word.
Where is three letter /ī/ used? Three letter /ī/ is used only at the end of a base word or before a T.

bight	fright	nigh	sight
blight	high	night	slight
bright	knight	plight	tight
fight	light	right	thigh
flight	might	sigh	

This leads to a new rule.

Spelling Rule	28
Phonograms ending in GH are used only at the end of a base word, or before the letter T. The GH is either silent or pronounced /f/.	

What sound do sigh, thigh, high, and nigh end in? /ī/.
Do English words end in I? No
Why not? English words do not end in I, U, V, or J.
This is one spelling for /ī/ at the end of a word. These are the only four words that use IGH to spell /ī/ at the end. The most common way to spell /ī/ at the end of the word is with a Y. We will learn more about this in a later lesson.
IGH is not a common spelling of the long /ī/ sound. There are over two million words in English.
Guess how many base words use the phonogram IGH?
It is found in only nineteen common base words.
It is important to learn IGH because it is found in some very common words.

Read the list again. Put an X next to the ones which are the most important to remember.

Optional: Spelling Journal Ⓐ Ⓚ Ⓥ

Add words spelled with IGH.

Optional: Spelling Rule Practice

1. Review rules 3-4, 9-11, 21, 26, 28, and 30. Ⓐ Ⓥ

2. Create a reference page to remember this rule. Include sample words.   Ⓒ Ⓥ

3. Ask the students to teach this to another student or to a parent.   Ⓒ Ⓐ Ⓚ Ⓥ

4. Think of a silly sentence or story to help remember the words which use IGH.   Ⓒ Ⓐ

5. Provide students with the igh, th, b, f, h, l, m, n, p, r, s, and t Phonogram Game Cards. Ask them to arrange the cards into the words spelled with IGH.   Ⓐ Ⓚ Ⓥ

6. Write the IGH words on the board. Ask students to read them. Then erase one, see if they can recite the list. Keep erasing one word seeing if students can remember the whole list.   Ⓐ Ⓥ

7. After playing games with the IGH words, ask students to see how many they can write from memory on a blank piece of paper.   Ⓐ Ⓥ Ⓚ

8. ✎ *8.6 Extra Practice: Write the IGH Words* – Write the eighteen words that use the phonogram IGH. Cross out the phonograms as you write the words.   Ⓐ Ⓥ Ⓚ

PART TWO

Using Spelling List 8 on pages 86-87, dictate each word following the steps included on pages Intro 42 - Intro 46.

PART THREE

Materials Needed: Red and blue colored pencils.

Grammar

Review

> **What is a noun?**   A noun is the name of a person, place, thing, or idea.

1. Identify the nouns.

    ✎ *Spelling List 8 – **Read today's spelling list. Write a red N by each word that is a noun. Test words by deciding if you can make them plural and if they make sense with the article "the."***

2. Review adjectives.

    What is an adjective? Adjectives modify nouns and pronouns. Adjectives answer: What kind? How many? Which one? Whose?

    ✎ *Spelling List 8 – **Find the adjectives in the spelling list and write a blue Adj next to them. Review the definitions of a noun, adjective, and article using the Grammar Flash Cards.***

3. ✎ *Spelling List 8* – Review the plurals rule, Spelling Rule 21. Direct the students to write the plural form of each of the nouns on their spelling list. Notice that *music* and *wheat* are non-count nouns, and *tooth* has an irregular plural: *teeth*.

    What is the plural of tooth? teeth
    Can you count music? No, it is a non-count noun. It does not have a plural.
    Can you count wheat? No, there is too much of it. We measure it.

Optional: Spelling Cards

1. Dictate the words in Lesson 8 for the students to write on index cards.   Ⓐ Ⓚ Ⓥ

2. Ask the students to color a red border around the nouns.   Ⓚ Ⓥ

3. Direct them to put a blue border around the adjectives.   Ⓚ Ⓥ

	Word	Practice Sentence	Say to Spell	# of Syllables	Markings
1.	**program**	*We will watch the program at 2 o'clock.*	prō grăm	2	prō gram
2.	**tooth**	*The girl's tooth fell out last night.*	tooth	1	tooth
3.	**night**	*The moon and stars come out at night.*	nīt	1	night
4.	**music**	*The violinist played beautiful music.*	mū zic	2	mū sic²
5.	**wheat**	*This bread is made out of wheat flour.*	whēt	1	wheat
6.	**block**	*We live on the first block.*	blŏk	1	block
7.	**bright**	*The light is bright.*	brīt	1	bright
8.	**warm**	*The soup is warm.*	warm	1	warm
9.	**wheel**	*Roll the wheel to me.*	whēl	1	wheel
10.	**light**	*Please turn off the light.*	līt	1	light
11.	**yard**	*The swing is in the yard.*	yard	1	yard
12.	**good**	*That is a good book.*	güd	1	good²
13.	**better**	*This book is better.*	bĕt ter	2	bet ter
14.	**best**	*This is the best book.*	bĕst	1	best
15.	**perfect**	*She got a perfect score on her test.*	per fĕct	2	per fect

Spelling Hints	Part of Speech	Vocabulary Development
Draw a line above /ō/. **4** A E O U usually say their names at the end of the syllable.	N	programs, programmer, programming, programmable
Underline /oo/.	N	toothache, toothbrush, toothpaste, toothless, toothy, toothpick, teeth, teethe, teething
Underline /ī/. **28** Phonograms ending in GH are used only at the end of a base word or before the letter T. The GH is either silent or pronounced /f/.	N	nights, nightly, fortnight, nightcap, nightclothes, nightgown, nightfall, nightie, overnight, tonight, weeknight
Draw a line above /ū/. **4** A E O U usually say their names at the end of the syllable. Put a 2 above /z/. /s-z/ said its second sound.	N	musical, musicality, musically, musician, musicology
Underline /wh/. Underline /ē/.	N	buckwheat
Underline /k/. **26** CK is used only after a single vowel which says its short sound.	N	blocks, blocker, blocked, blocking, blockade, blockage, sunblock, unblock, woodblock
Underline /ī/. **28** Phonograms ending in GH are used only at the end of a base word or before the letter T. The GH is either silent or pronounced /f/.	Adj	brighter, brightest, brighten, brightening, brightly, brightness, overbright
Underline /ar/.	Adj	warmed, warmer, warmest, warming, lukewarm, rewarm, warmblooded, warmly, warmness, warmth
Underline /wh/. Underline /ē/.	N	wheels, wheelie, cartwheel, flywheel, pinwheel, waterwheel, wheelbarrow, wheelchair, wheelwright
Underline /ī/. **28** Phonograms ending in GH are used only at the end of a base word or before the letter T. The GH is either silent or pronounced /f/.	N	lights, lighter, lightest, lighten, lightening, lightened, lighted, lightness, candlelight, sunlight, floodlight, headlight, twilight
Underline /ar/.	N	yards, yardage, backyard, barnyard, courtyard, dockyard, shipyard, vineyard, yardstick
Underline /ü/. Put a 2 above it. /oo-ü-ō/ said its second sound.	Adj	goodbye, goodwill
Underline /er/.	Adj	betterment
All first sounds.	Adj	
Underline /er/.	Adj	perfection, perfectly, imperfect, imperfectly, perfection, perfectionist, perfectionism, perfectness

Identifying Parts of Speech

✎ *8.7 Identifying Parts of Speech – **Read the phrase in your workbook. I will write it on the board. Then we will answer questions to label the parts of speech. Label each part of speech in your workbook.***

---

the best coat

    What is the noun in this phrase? coat
    What kind of coat? best, adjective
    Which coat? the, article adjective

    A   Adj   N
    the best coat

---

good wheels, bright lights, and the best music

    What are the nouns in this phrase? wheels, lights, music
    What kind of wheels? good, adjective
    What kind of lights? bright, adjective
    What kind of music? best, adjective
    Which music? the, article adjective

    What is the word "and" called? conjunction
    What does a conjunction do? It connects a words, phrases, or sentences together.

    Adj   N   Adj   N   C   A Adj N
    good wheels, bright lights, and the best music

---

a perfect day and a perfect night

    What are the nouns in this phrase? day, night

    What kind of day? perfect, adjective
    Which day? a, article adjective
    What kind of night? perfect, adjective
    Which night? a, article adjective

    What is the word "and" called? conjunction
    What does a conjunction do? It connects a words, phrases, or sentences together.

    A   Adj   N C A Adj   N
    a perfect day and a perfect night

Comparative and Superlative

Write the suffixes "-er" and "-est" on the board

✎ *8.8 Comparison – **Many adjectives can be used to compare. Read the phrases in your workbook.***

a warm coat   a warmer coat   the warmest coat

What endings were added to the word warm? the endings -er and -est
Underline the suffixes -er and -est.
Put an A over the article adjectives in each phrase. How did the article change? It changed from "a warmer coat" to "the warmest coat."
Read the next group of phrases.

a clean room   a cleaner room   the cleanest room

Does it makes sense to say "a cleanest room?" no
Why? Because if it is the cleanest room, it is a particular one.
Underline the suffixes -er and -est.
Put an A over the article adjectives in each phrase.

When we add the suffix -er to a word, such as "cleaner," we are making a comparison. This form of an adjective is called the comparative, because it compares.

comparative

Do you see/hear the word compare in comparative?
When we add the suffix -est to a word such as "cleanest," we are saying it is the best. This form is called the superlative.

superlative

We can remember what superlative means when we look at the root. Notice that superlative begins with the same letters as the word "super." What do we mean when we say someone or something is super? that they are the best

How do I change bright to compare? brighter, brightest
How about sharp? sharper, sharpest

How about good? better, best
Notice, we do not say gooder and goodest. Gooder and goodest are not words. Instead what do we say? better and best
Use each of these in a sentence.

How about the word perfect? This is a perfect paper. Can we compare and say perfecter or perfectest? no
Why? It is already perfect. There cannot be anything better than perfect.

Optional: Vocabulary and Usage Practice

1. Use words in Lessons 1-8 and orally practice forming phrases or sentences using the degrees of comparison. ©Ⓐ

2. Write phrases using comparisons. Draw a picture of each phrase. ©ⓀⓋ

3. ✎ *8.9 Extra Practice: Proof Reading* - Complete the activity in the workbook. Find the mistake in each phrase. Rewrite the phrase correctly on the lines below. ⒶⓋⓀ

Dictation

✎ *8.10 Dictation* – Read the following phrase one time. Ask the students to repeat it aloud, then write it in their student workbooks.

1. the cheapest wheat bread
2. legs, hands, and teeth
3. a perfect music program
4. a good day and night
5. the brightest light
6. better truck wheels

Composition

✎ *8.11 Composition* – Direct the students to choose a word from each column in their workbooks and compose six phrases.

Optional: Spelling Cards

Arrange the cards into phrases using degrees of comparison. ⓀⓋ

Vocabulary Development

Adding the Suffixes -ish, -ness

If working with second language learners, bring props to illustrate each word.

Read the words as I write them on the board.

pink   gray   green
boy   sick

Write the suffix "-ish" on the board.

What do these words change to when we add the suffix -ish? pinkish, boyish, grayish, sickish, greenish.

As the students say them, add the ending *-ish* in a different color.

pinkish   *grayish*   *greenish*

boyish   *sickish*

How is the meaning changed? Pinkish is not fully pink, but it has a hint of pink, etc.

Use each of the roots and the derivatives in a sentence. The hat is pink. The pinkish brown hat is sitting on the table.

Read the words as I write them on the board.

sick   *frozen*   *bright*

quick   *sharp*   *light*

clean   *cheap*

What kind of words are each of these, nouns or adjectives? adjectives

How do you know? They answer which one? or what kind?

sick + ness

What new words are formed with the suffix -ness? sickness, quickness, cleanness, frozenness, sharpness, cheapness, brightness, lightness

What does sickness mean? The state of being sick.

Use each of the derivatives in a sentence.

sick + ness = sickness

boy + ish

What word is formed? boyish

What does boyish mean? boy-like.

Use it in a sentence. He gave me a boyish smile.

boy + ish = boyish + ness

What word is formed if we add -ness to boyish? boyishness

boy + ish = boyish + ness = boyishness

How many suffixes are in boyishness? two

Some words have more than one suffix.

What does boyishness mean? The act of being boyish.

Use it in a sentence. His boyishness led him to great adventure.

✎ *8.12 Vocabulary Development* – Direct the students to complete the activity in the workbook.

Challenge

Use sick and sickness in a sentence. Answers will vary. The boy is sick. The sickness came on quickly.

Listen to this phrase: The sick boy

What kind of boy? sick

Sick is an adjective because it answers the question, what kind?

Listen to this sentence. The sickness makes the boy cough.

Does "the sickness" make sense? yes

Since sickness makes sense with the noun marker "the," it is a noun.

Is "sickness" a person, place, thing, or idea? idea

The ending -ness changes an adjective into a noun.

Lesson 9

Phonograms:	au, aw, augh
Exploring Sounds:	Spellings of the Sound /ä/
Spelling Rules:	
Grammar:	Possessives

PART ONE

Materials Needed: Phonogram Flash Cards from previous lessons and `au`, `aw`, `augh`; Slips of paper, basket, and buzzer.

Phonograms

New Phonograms — *au, aw, augh*

Show `au`. /ä/

Show `aw`. /ä/

> *How are these related?* They both begin with the letter A. They both say /ä/.
> *How are they different?* One ends with the letter U and one ends with the letter W.
> *Which one may I use at the end of English words?* AW
> *Which one may I not use at the end of English words?* AU
> *Why?* English words do not end in I, U, V, or J.

Show the phonogram `augh`. /ä-ăf/

> *This says /ä-ăf/.*

Show `augh`, `au`.

> *How are these related?* They both say /ä/. They both have the letters AU.
> *How are they different?* One has a GH and it also says /ăf/.
> *What sound is GH saying in the sound /ăf/?* /f/
> *What other phonogram do we know that ends in GH?* Three letter /ī/.

The GH is either silent or pronounced /f/.
What is the rule that governs phonograms that end in GH? Phonograms ending in GH are used only at the end of a base word, or before the letter T. The GH is either silent or pronounced /f/.

✎ *9.1 AUGH Words – AUGH is not used in very many words. AUGH is found in only ten base words. A few of the words are very common. The most common words which use AUGH are written in your workbook. In the first group of words, AUGH will say /ä/. Read the words and underline the /ä/.*

caught	slaughter	onslaught
daughter	taught	haughty ˂
distraught	fraught	naughty ˂

There is only one commonly used base word that is pronounced /ăf/.

laugh ˂

We can also add the suffix -ter to this word to form:

laughter

Read the words in your workbook and underline the /ăf/.

˂ Teacher Tip: *Since students have not been taught Y at the end of the word you may choose not to include haughty and naughty. Or you may simply tell students, "Y often says its /ē/ sound at the end of a multi-syllable word." Draught also uses AUGH to spell /ăf/.*

Show au .

Can AU be used at the end of the word? no
Why? English words do not end in I, U, V, or J.

✎ *9.2 AU Words – Read the words. Put a line between each syllable and underline the AU.*

au/thor	caulk	haunt
aunt	fault	taunt
au/to	maul	launch
au/to/mat/ic	vault	sum/mer/sault
haul	res/tau/rant	

Where is AU used? AU is used at the end of the syllable or in the middle of a syllable.

Show aw .

Can AW be used at the end of the word? yes

✎ *9.3 AW Words – **Read the words in your workbook. Underline the AW as you read them.***

claw	crawl	dawn	awful
jaw	shawl	fawn	awkward
flaw	awl	drawn	awning
raw	brawl	pawn	hawk
law	drawl	sawn	squawk
saw		yawn	gawk
straw		lawn	
draw			

Where is AW most commonly used? At the end of the base word, before an N and before an L.

Phonogram Review

1. Drill the phonograms with flash cards.

2. ✎ *9.4 Writing the Phonograms* – Direct the students to write each new phonogram five times while saying the sounds aloud.

3. ✎ *9.5 Phonogram Practice* – Dictate the following phonograms. For extra practice, have the students read them back. Write the correct answers on the board as the students check their answers.

1. ai */ā/*	8. ay */ā/*	15. ee */ē/*
2. ng */ng/*	9. er */er/*	16. or */or/*
3. ea */ē-ĕ-ā/*	10. ar */är/*	17. sh */sh/*
4. ch */ch-k-sh/*	11. au */ä/*	18. oi */oi/*
5. oy */oi/*	12. augh */ä-ăf/*	19. u */ŭ-ū-oo-ü/*
6. wh */wh/*	13. aw */ä/*	20. g */g-j/*
7. igh */ī/*	14. oo */oo-ŭ-ō/*	

4. ✎ *9.6 Phonogram Tic-Tac-Toe* – Play Phonogram Tic-Tac-Toe. Each student has six game boards in their workbook. (For directions see *The Phonogram and Spelling Game Book*, 26).

Exploring Sounds

Spellings of the Sound /ä/

What are two ways the /ä/ sound is marked in the dictionary? ä and ŏ. A with two dots over it and O with a curved line or a breve over it.

ä ŏ

List the phonograms that say the broad /ä/ sound. a, o, au, aw, augh

Write the sounds at the top of the board so they form columns.

a	o	au	aw	augh

Vowel sounds are some of the most difficult to spell because there are many choices. The /ä/ sound has a lot of options in English and you will need to memorize the correct spelling for writing. Knowing these sounds will allow you to read any word you encounter with the /ä/ sound. Knowing your options for spelling also will aid you in looking up unknown words in the dictionary and fixing words that you misspell on the computer. Words with the /ä/ sound need to be memorized. Today we will analyze the spellings of /ä/ and discover which spellings are the most common.

Which spelling of /ä/ is not very common? augh

What are the most commonly used words that are spelled with AUGH? caught, slaughter, fraught, daughter, taught, distraught, (haughty, naughty)

a	o	au	aw	augh
				caught
				slaughter
				fraught
				daughter
				taught
				distraught
				onslaught

Which spellings of /ä/ do we know are commonly used at the end of the word? A and AW
Let's write some words that include AW.

a	o	au	aw	augh
			saw	caught
			law	slaughter
			straw	fraught
			raw	daughter
			draw	taught
				distraught
				onslaught

Is AW used in any other part of the word? In the middle of the syllable.
Read the words as I add them to the list.

a	o	au	aw	augh
			saw	caught
			law	slaughter
			straw	fraught
			raw	daughter
			draw	taught
			lawn	distraught
			crawl	onslaught

What does single-letter A say at the end of a baseword? /ä/
Which rule does it follow? When a word ends with the phonogram A, it says /ä/.
Read the words as I write them on the board.

a	o	au	aw	augh
pa			saw	caught
ma			law	slaughter
sofa			straw	fraught
soda			raw	daughter
			draw	taught
			lawn	distraught
			crawl	onslaught

There are two other places where A often says the /ä/ sound. Read the words in your workbook to discover where.

✎ *9.7 A says /ä/ – Read the words in your workbook and put two dots over the /ä/. Tell me when you see where A is saying the sound /ä/.* A says /ä/ after a W and before an L.

water	wash	ball	fall
wasp	walnut	call	wall

Let's add some sample words to our chart. Read them as I write them.

a	o	au	aw	augh
pa			saw	caught
ma			law	slaughter
sofa			straw	fraught
wash			raw	daughter
water			draw	taught
call			lawn	distraught
fall			crawl	onslaught

When does O say /ŏ/? In the middle of the syllable.
Why can't O say /ŏ/ at the end of the syllable? A E O U usually say their names at the end of the syllable. ◄

Let's add some sample words to our chart. Read the words as I write them.

◄ **Teacher Tip:** *Some students will ask, then why can A say /ä/ at the end of the syllable? Explain to them that vowels sometimes say their third or broad sounds at the end of the syllable, but they do not say their short sounds at the end of syllables.*

a	o	au	aw	augh
pa	top		saw	caught
ma	pot		law	slaughter
sofa	lot		straw	fraught
wash	rock		raw	daughter
water	sock		draw	taught
call	popcorn		lawn	distraught
fall	stop		crawl	onslaught

Finally, where is AU used? At the end of the syllable and in the middle of the syllable.

a	o	au	aw	augh
pa	top	au thor	saw	caught
ma	pot	au to	law	slaughter
sofa	lot	aunt	straw	fraught
wash	rock	taunt	raw	daughter
water	sock	haunt	draw	taught
call	popcorn	launch	lawn	distraught
fall	stop	fault	crawl	onslaught

✎ *9.8 Spellings of the /ä/ Sound –* **Write the spellings of /ä/ in your workbook.**

a   o   au   aw   augh

✎ *9.9 Most Common Spellings of /ä/*

Which spelling of /ä/ do you use at the end of the syllable? au
Write it on your chart.

Which spellings of /ä/ are used in the middle of the syllable? o, au, aw
Write them on your chart.

When you hear the sound /ä/ in the middle of the syllable you need to pay careful attention for spelling.

Which spellings of /ä/ are used at the end of the word? a and aw

End of the Syllable	Middle of the syllable	End of the Word
au	*o, au, aw*	*a, aw*

When you hear the sound /ä/ in a word it is important to think carefully about the spelling options. Many of these words will need to be memorized.

Optional: Spelling Journal   Ⓐ Ⓚ Ⓥ

Add words where A, O, AUGH, AU, and AW spell the sound /ä/.

Spelling Rules

Optional: Spelling Rule Practice

1. Review rules 3-4, 9-11, 21, 26, 28, and 30 using the Spelling Rule Cards. Ⓐⓥ

2. Create a sentence to remember the words which use AUGH. ©Ⓐ

3. Write the AUGH words on the board. Ask students to read them. Then erase one, see if they can recite the list. Keep erasing one word seeing if students can remember the whole list. Ⓐⓥ

4. After playing games with the AUGH words, ask students to see how many they can write from memory on a blank piece of paper. ⒶⓀⓥ

5. Draw pictures of words that use the various spellings of /ä/. Label each picture. ©ⓥ

6. Draw a collage of the spellings of the /ä/ sound. Include sample words. ©Ⓐⓥ

7. Play a game such as Spelling Basketball (*The Phonogram and Spelling Game Book,* 43) to practice words with the /ä/ sound. ⓀⒶⓥ

PART TWO

Using Spelling List 9 on pages 102-103, dictate each word following the steps included on pages Intro 42 - Intro 46.

Tips for Spelling List 9

Mother, Brother, Son

Notice that in each of these words the phonogram ⌐o⌐ is pronounced as a schwa sound /ə/. Exaggerate the short /ŏ/ sound in each of the words for spelling purposes. /mŏTH er/, /brŏTH er/, /sŏn/.

Author

In order to help students create an auditory picture of the word, it is helpful to exaggerate the unaccented vowel. Therefore exaggerate the vowel so that /ä thər/ sounds like /ä thor/.

To learn more about vowels in unaccented syllables and aiding students in creating an auditory picture of words, see *Uncovering the Logic of English,* 121-128.

PART THREE

Materials Needed: Grammar Cards 2.4, 2.5, 2.6; red and blue colored pencils.

Grammar

Review

1. Review nouns

    What is a noun? A noun is the name of a person, place, thing, or idea.

    ✎ *Spelling List 9 – **Read today's spelling list. Identify the nouns. Write a red N by each word that is a noun. Test words by deciding if you can make them plural and if it makes sense with the article "the."***

    How many nouns in this list refer to people? eight
    Which nouns in this list refer to ideas? laughter, year, law
    You can test each of these by seeing if they make sense with the noun marker "the." The laughter, the year, the law all make sense. Therefore, they are nouns.

2. Review adjectives.

    What is an adjective? Adjectives modify nouns and pronouns. Adjectives answer: What kind? How many? Which one? Whose?

    ✎ *Spelling List 9 – **Find the adjectives in the spelling list and write a blue Adj next to them. Review the definitions of a noun, adjective, and article using the Grammar Flash Cards.***

3. ✎ *Spelling List 9* – Review the plurals rule, Spelling Rule 21. Direct the students to write the plural form of each of the nouns on their spelling list.

Optional: Spelling Cards

1. Dictate the words in Lesson 9 for the students to write on index cards.   Ⓐ Ⓚ Ⓥ

2. Ask the students to color a red border around the nouns.   Ⓚ Ⓥ

3. Direct them to put a blue border around the adjectives.   Ⓚ Ⓥ

---

4. Write the articles *a* and *an* on the board.

    What are these? article adjectives
    When do we use the article "an"? before a vowel
    When do we use the article "a"? before a consonant

    Read the nouns in the spelling list and combine them with the correct article. a mother, a brother, an aunt...

	Word	Practice Sentence	Say to Spell	# of Syllables	Markings
1.	**mother**	*My mother is kind.*	mŏTH er	2	mot͜h er
2.	**brother**	*Our brother is sick today.*	brŏTH er	2	brot͜h er
3.	**son**	*I saw your son at the park.*	sŏn	1	son
4.	**father**	*Her father is in Europe.*	fä THer	2	fä t͜her
5.	**sister**	*His sister is six years old.*	sĭs ter	2	sis te͟r
6.	**daughter**	*Their daughter plays the violin.*	dä ter	2	dau͟gh ter
7.	**aunt**	*My aunt plays the piano.*	änt	1	au͟nt
8.	**great**	*That is a great story.*	grāt	1	gre͟at
9.	**corner**	*Turn right at the corner.*	cor ner	2	co͟r ne͟r
10.	**raw**	*Raw fruits and vegetables are healthy.*	rä	1	ra͟w
11.	**year**	*Next year we will go to Hawaii.*	yĕr	1	yea͟r
12.	**right**	*My right hand hurts.*	rīt	1	ri͟ght
13.	**laughter**	*Laughter filled the house.*	lăf ter	2	lau͟gh te͟r
14.	**law**	*You must stop at the light. It is the law.*	lä	1	la͟w
15.	**author**	*Who is the author of this book?*	ä thor	2	au͟ thor

Spelling Hints	Part of Speech	Vocabulary Development
Say to spell /mŏther/. Underline /TH/ and put a 2 over it. /th-TH/ said its second sound. Underline /er/.	N	mothers, motherly, mothering, mothered, grandmother, motherhood, motherland, stepmother, motherless
Say to spell /brŏther/. Underline /TH/ and put a 2 over it. /th-TH/ said its second sound. Underline /er/.	N	brothers, brotherly, stepbrother, brotherhood, brotherliness
Say to spell /sŏn/. All first sounds.	N	sons, stepson, grandson, godson, sonny, sonless
Put 2 dots over /ä/. /ă-ā-ä/ said its third sound. Underline /TH/ and put a 2 over it. /th-TH/ said its second sound. Underline /er/. How was /ä/ spelled in father? **a**.	N	fathers, fatherly, fathering, grandfather, fatherless, fatherhood, stepfather, forefather, fatherliness, fatherland
Underline /er/.	N	sisters, sisterly, stepsister, sisterhood
Underline /ä/. Underline /er/.	N	daughters, daughterly, granddaughter, stepdaughter, daughterless
Underline /ä/. Dialects which pronounce /ănt/ will need to say to spell to create a strong auditory picture.	N	aunts, auntie
Underline the /ā/. Put a 3 over it. /ē-ĕ-ā/ said its third sound.	Adj	greater, greatest, greatly, greatness, greathearted, greatcoat
Underline /or/. Underline /er/.	N	corners, cornered, cornering, cornerstone
Why can't we use AU? **3** English words do not end in I, U, V, or J. Underline /ä/.	Adj	rawer, rawest, rawhide
Underline /ē/.	N	years, yearbook, yearling, yearlong, yearly, midyear, semiyearly, biyearly, multiyear
Underline /ī/. **28** Phonograms ending in GH are used only at the end of a base word or before the letter T. The GH is either silent or pronounced /f/.	Adj (N)	rightly, rightful, righteous, righteousness, righted, rightful, rightfully, upright, downright, forthright, copyright
Underline /ăf/ and put a 2 over it. /ŏ-ăf/ said its second sound. Underline /er/.	N	laugh, laughed, laughing, laughable, laughingly, laughingstock, laughableness
Why can't we use AU? **3** English words do not end in I, U, V, or J. Underline /ä/.	N	laws, lawyer, sister-in-law, brother-in-law, bylaw, lawful, lawsuit, lawmaker, lawbreaker, lawgiver, lawless, lawlessness, outlaw
Say to spell /ä thor/. Underline /ä/. Underline /th/. Underline /or/. Notice that author ends in -or. This is someone who does something.	N	authors, authoring, authored, authorized, authoritarian, authority, coauthor, unauthorized

Possessives

Write the following phrases on the board. As you write them explain:

This hook is called an apostrophe. We add an apostrophe to show that something belongs to someone.

mother's hat   *father's coat*

Read each phrase out loud.
What do you notice about each of the phrases? They each include an apostrophe S.
Another way to say "mother's hat" is "a hat belonging to mother."
What is another way to say "father's coat?" a coat belonging to father

How do we write the plural form of brother? Add an S.

brothers

What if two brothers shared a bedroom? To make the word brothers show possession, we would add an apostrophe after the S.

brothers' room

When the apostrophe is placed after the S it shows that the word is plural and that more than one brother owns the room. Notice that though we are talking about more than one brother, we do not say /brother-s-es/. Since we do not say /s/ twice, we do not write it twice.

the sisters' laughter

How many sisters are laughing? more than one

the authors' books

How many authors? more than one

the author's books

Now how many authors? one

the men's room

What happens if it is an irregular plural? Add an apostrophe followed by an S.

Repeat the rules.

Grammar Card 2.4   PNA

A possessive noun adjective shows ownership and answers the question: Whose?

Grammar Card 2.5   PNA

To turn a noun into a singular possessive noun adjective, add an apostrophe followed by an S.

Grammar Card 2.6   PNA

To turn a noun into a plural possessive noun adjective, add an -S to make the noun plural and then add an apostrophe. If the noun has an irregular plural use an apostrophe followed by an S.

Identifying Parts of Speech

✎ *9.10 Identifying Parts of Speech –* **Read the phrase in your workbook. I will write it on the board. Then we will answer questions to label the parts of speech. Label each part of speech in your workbook.**

the author's greatest book

What is the noun in this phrase? book
What kind of book? greatest, adjective
Whose book? the author's
Author's is a possessive noun adjective. It is an adjective that is showing posses-sion. Write a PNA over it.
Which book? the, article adjective

A   PNA   Adj   N
the author's greatest book

the room's darkest corner

What is the noun in this phrase? corner
What kind of corner? darkest, adjective
Whose corner? room, possessive noun adjective
Which corner? the, article adjective

A   PNA   Adj   N
the room's darkest corner

> *mother's laughter*
>
> **What is the noun in this phrase?** laughter
> **Whose laughter?** mother's, possessive noun adjective
>
> PNA   N
> *mother's laughter*

Optional: Grammar Practice

1. Using spelling lists 1-9, direct the students to orally form phrases using the possessive + noun. Write them on the board as the students say the phrases. Emphasize the 's and s' by writing them in a different color. For example, the cat**'s** yard, the authors**'** book.   Ⓐ Ⓚ Ⓥ

2. Using spelling lists 1-9, direct the students to orally form phrases using a possessive noun + adjective + noun. Write them on the board as the students say the phrases. Emphasize the 's and s' by writing them in a different color. For example:

   the man's clean yard

   the sisters' best coats

3. ✎ *9.11 Extra Practice: Possessives Practice* – Complete the activity in the workbook.

4. ✎ *9.12 Extra Practice: Article Review* – Complete the activity in the workbook.   Ⓐ Ⓚ Ⓥ

5. ✎ *9.13 Extra Practice: Editing* – Complete the activity in the workbook. Find the mistake in each phrase. Rewrite the phrase correctly on the lines below.   Ⓐ Ⓚ Ⓥ

6. Review the Grammar concepts taught so far using Grammar Cards 1-1.3; 2-2.6; 7; 11.1.   Ⓐ Ⓥ

Composition

✎ *9.14 Composition* – Direct the students to write eight phrases using the words found in their workbooks.

Optional: Spelling Cards

Write an apostrophe on a sticky note. Direct students to organize the cards into phrases following the pattern: article + possessive noun + adjective + noun. Make sure they add the apostrophe in the correct place.   Ⓐ Ⓚ Ⓥ Ⓒ

Vocabulary Development

Compound Words

Which words in our list refer to family members? mother, brother, son, father, sister, daughter, aunt

What do you call your mother's mother? grandmother
What did we add to mother to form grandmother? grand

grandmother

What do you call your mother's father? grandfather

grandfather

What other two spelling words can you add grand to? granddaughter, grandson

granddaughter, grandson

Notice the two d's in granddaughter. This is because we are joining the two words grand and daughter to form a compound word.

What do you call your father's grandmother? great-grandmother

great-grandmother

Notice the hyphen between great and grandmother. The hyphen shows these words are connected. Some compound words are written together, like grandmother. Others are written with a hyphen like great-grandmother.

What do you call your father's grandfather? great-grandfather
What do we need between great and grandfather? a hyphen

great-grandfather

What do we call your mother's great-grandfather? great-great-grandfather
How many hyphens did we use? two

great-great-grandfather

Which family words can be combined with step? stepmother, stepfather, stepdaughter, stepson

stepmother, stepfather, stepdaughter, stepson

What is a stepmother? When your father remarries, his new wife is your stepmother.

✎ *9.15 Vocabulary Development –* **Complete the activity in your workbook.**

Homophones

Sometimes words sound alike but are spelled differently. These are called homophones.

Write *homophone* on the board.

Homo means same and phone means sound. Homophones are two words that sound the same but are spelled differently. Find a word that is a homophone, or sounds the same, as a word from last week. son – sun

✎ *9.16 Son and Sun – Draw a picture of each in your workbook and label them.*

Challenge

Read the words as I write them on the board. What do you notice about each word? They all have the words in-law. In-law is written with a hyphen.

mother-in-law   father-in-law   sister-in-law   brother-in-law
son-in-law   daughter-in-law

What is an in-law? Someone who is related by marriage.
Notice that a hyphen joins these compound words. These are called hyphenated compounds. Compare these to the following words.

sailboat   grandmother   schoolroom   toothbrush

These are closed compounds. They are written with no space.
In addition some words, though they may seem to go together, are not compound words.

school bus   corner store   full moon

The only way to know for certain if a word is a hyphenated compound, an open compound written without a hyphen, or a closed compound written without a space, is to look it up in the dictionary.

Dictation

✎ *9.17 Dictation* – Read the following phrases one time. Ask the students to repeat it aloud, then write it in their student workbooks.

1. the author's best book
2. a sharp corner
3. grandmother's perfect bread
4. raw eggs
5. the daughter's laugh
6. grandfathers, fathers, and sons

Materials Needed: red pencil, index cards, highlighter.

1. ✎ *10.1 Assessment* – Dictate the phrases to the students while they write them in their workbooks.

   1. cars, trucks, and boats
   2. the author's good books
   3. the school's best classroom
   4. the perfect night
   5. three sisters' secrets
   6. all the fullest glasses

   7. a sharp right corner
   8. the richest laughter
   9. cliffs, rivers, roads, and hills
   10. the mother's son and daughter
   11. a better toothbrush
   12. great-grandfather's yard

2. Direct the students to read the phrases aloud while you write them on the board. Sound out each word and model the thought process. The students should mark corrections in red. Encourage the students to discuss what they missed. Create an atmosphere where it is acceptable to make errors. Model the attitude and strategies to move forward in practice. For example:

   cars, trucks, and boats

   /carz/ /Did you use a /k-s/ at the beginning of cars? /k-s/
   How do we make cars plual? To make a noun plural add the ending -S unless the word hisses or changes, the add -ES. Occasional nouns have no change or an irregular spelling.

   What do we need after cars? comma
   Why? This is a list.

   /trŭks/ What form of /k/ do we need? Two-letter /k/
   Why? Two-letter /k/ is used only after a single vowel which says its short sound.

   What do we need after truck? comma
   Why? This is a list.

   /ănd/

   /bōts/ What form of the long /ō/ sound will I use? OA
   Why? OA is the most common spelling in the middle of the syllable.

3. Recheck the students' work. Note the words and concepts which need further practice.

4. Did the students:

_____ add an -S to make words plural?

_____ add an -ES to make words plural that hiss?

_____ double the FF, LL, and SS after a single, short vowel?

_____ use IGH and AUGH only at the end of a word and before the letter T?

_____ use CK only after a single, short vowel?

_____ add an apostrophe S to show possession?

_____ add an S apostrophe to plural nouns to show possession?

_____ use a comma in a series?

_____ spell the suffixes -est and -er correctly?

5. ✎ *10.2 Reading* – Ask the students to read the following words and phrases aloud. Note the words they did not read fluently.

1. cheaper cards
2. seven warm coats
3. the music program
4. raw eggs
5. clean floors
6. the pink door
7. the black truck's wheels
8. good laws
9. bright moonlight
10. six years, three weeks, and ten days
11. grandmothers, mothers, sisters, and aunts
12. ten toes
13. brother's toy blocks
14. tall men
15. poor
16. wheat, soap, and eggs
17. ball
18. six inches

6. ✎ *10.3 Words to Practice* – Ask the students to read the words in the list and mark which ones they would like to practice further.

7. Using the assessment and your knowledge as a teacher, identify words to dictate onto index cards.

1. _____ all
2. _____ aunt
3. _____ author
4. _____ ball
5. _____ best
6. _____ better
7. _____ block
8. _____ boat
9. _____ book
10. _____ bright
11. _____ brother
12. _____ brush
13. _____ car
14. _____ card
15. _____ cheap
16. _____ class
17. _____ cliff
18. _____ coat
19. _____ corner
20. _____ daughter
21. _____ door
22. _____ egg
23. _____ father
24. _____ floor
25. _____ full
26. _____ glass
27. _____ good
28. _____ great
29. _____ hill
30. _____ inch
31. _____ laughter
32. _____ law
33. _____ light
34. _____ moon
35. _____ mother
36. _____ music
37. _____ night
38. _____ perfect
39. _____ poor

40. _____ program   47. _____ school   54. _____ toe
41. _____ raw   48. _____ secret   55. _____ tooth
42. _____ rich   49. _____ sharp   56. _____ warm
43. _____ right   50. _____ sister   57. _____ wheat
44. _____ river   51. _____ soap   58. _____ wheel
45. _____ road   52. _____ son   59. _____ yard
46. _____ room   53. _____ tall   60. _____ year

SPELLING WORD REVIEW

Materials Needed: Index cards, highlighter, timer, paper, pencil.

1. Dictate the missed words onto index cards. Have the students highlight the part of the word that was difficult.

2. Choose from the review activities below or use an activity found in the *The Phonogram and Spelling Game Book*.

Optional Spelling Word Practice

1. ✎ *10.4 Word Search* – Create a Spelling Word Search. Dictate ten spelling words. The students write them in the grid and then fill in letters to hide the words. When finished, have the students exchange papers to find the words. (*The Phonogram and Spelling Game Book*, 52)

2. Practice using Speed Writing (*The Phonogram and Spelling Game Book*, 37).

3. Direct the students to write the words on index cards. Put the words in a pile in front of each student. They read the word, turn it upside down, then try to write it. Then check if they have written it correctly. If they spelled it incorrectly, they should put the card back into the pile. If they spelled it correctly, they may proceed with the next card.

OPTIONAL SPELLING RULE REVIEW

Materials Needed: Phonogram cards; paper, pencil; whiteboard, marker, eraser; magnetic letters.

Use the following mini-lessons to review the concepts as needed.

Spelling Rule 21

Spelling Rule	21

To make a noun plural, add the ending -S unless the word hisses or changes, then add -ES. Occasional nouns have no change or an irregular spelling.

1. Review the rule by reciting it. Discuss the sample words on the back of the card.

2. Discus the meaning of hissing words. Read the following words to the students. Direct the students to raise their hand if the word hisses at the end: *chair, table, class, match, song, lunch, bush, box, rug, sofa, step, fox, wall, camera, lock, class, desk, lamp, flash, computer, toothbrush, sink, soap, book, mess.*

3. Provide the students with a set of phonogram cards which include all the phonograms that have been learned so far. Separate the phonograms into two piles: ones that hiss and ones that do not. *s, z, ch, sh, (tch)* Ⓥ Ⓐ Ⓚ

4. Ask the students to name words that hiss at the end.

5. Dictate the following words while the students write them on white boards: *maps, inches, classes, cats, dogs, glasses, books, rooms, schools, brushes.*

6. ✎ *10.5 Extra Practice: Plurals Review* – Complete the activity in the workbook.

Spelling Rule 30

Spelling Rule	30

We often double F, L, and S after a single vowel at the end of a base word. Occasionally other letters also are doubled.

1. Review the rule by reciting it. Discuss the sample words on the back of the card.

2. **Double the consonant game:** Say a word aloud. The students should write it on a small white board. Award one point for spelling the word correctly. (Provide spelling hints for the multi-letter vowels if needed.) Award one point for knowing why the last consonant could or could not be doubled.

    -   **Double the last consonant after a single vowel** – *tall, ball, fall, wall, call, staff, bluff, stuff, cliff, off, drill, sill, mill, trill, will, grill, sell, shell, well, tell, class, mass, mess, less, kiss, miss, hiss, toss, loss*

    -   **Do not double the last consonant after a multi-letter vowel** – *feel, steel, wheel, beef, reef, mail, nail, hail, pail, rail, trail, oil, boil, spoil, soil, pool, stool, school, spool, coal, goal, loaf*

3. Form the ending pattern using magnetic letter tiles. Ask the students to form new words by adding the beginning consonants.

- **_all** – ball, fall, call, hall, wall, mall, stall, tall, thrall
- **_ell** – bell, dell, dwell, fell, sell, spell, shell, smell, well, yell
- **_ill** – hill, mill, pill, fill, kill, trill, chill, bill, dill, drill, frill, gill, shrill, thrill, still, will
- **_ull** – hull, dull, bull, cull, full, pull, scull, skull
- **_ass** – bass, brass, class, grass, glass, sass, pass
- **_ess** – less, mess, dress, chess, bless, press, stress, unless
- **_iss** – miss, bliss, hiss, kiss, swiss

4. Direct the students to make a collage of words ending in FF, LL, or SS. They may do so by writing the words in patterns or by cutting words or letters out of newspapers and magazines and arranging them.

Spelling Rule 28

Spelling Rule	28
Phonograms ending in GH are used only at the end of a base word, or before the letter T. The GH is either silent or pronounced /f/.	

1. Review the rule by reciting it. Discuss the sample words on the back of the card.

2. Review the words which use IGH. Write them on the board. Direct the students to read them. Erase a word, challenge them to still recall the list. When all the words have been erased, ask the students to write the words using IGH on a piece of paper.

blight	high	plight	tight
bright	light	right	thigh
fight	might	sigh	
flight	nigh	sight	
fright	night	slight	

3. Review the words which use AUGH. Write them on the board. Direct the students to read them. Erase a word, challenge them to still recall the list. When all the words have been erased, ask the students to write the words using AUGH on a piece of paper.

caught	taught	haughty
daughter	fraught	naughty
slaughter	aught	

Spelling Rule 26

Spelling Rule	26
CK is used only after a single vowel which says its short (first) sound.	

1. Review the rule by reciting it. Discuss the sample words on the back of the card.

2. Write _ack_ on the board. (Or use magnetic tiles.) Ask the students to find letters that complete the word: *back, sack, tack, rack, lack, mack...*

   - Write _ick_ on the board. Ask the students to find letters that complete the word: *tick, quick, sick, lick, rick, nick, hick, kick...*

   - Write _uck_ on the board. Ask the students to find letters that complete the word: *duck, buck, luck...*

3. **CK Review**

   - Say a word ending in /k/. Ask the students: does it end in K or CK? Why? Have them write it on a whiteboard.

   - **CK is used after a single, short vowel** – *back, black, block, brick, buck, deck, duck, flick, flock, jack, kick, lack, lick, lock, luck, muck, neck, nick, pack, pick, quack, quick, rack, rock, sack, shock, shuck, sick, slack, slick, smack, smock, snack, sock, speck, stick, stock, struck, suck, tack, track, truck, tuck, wick, yuck*

   - **K is used after a long vowel sound** – *beak, leak, peak, sneak, speak, squeak, weak, steak, break, creek, Greek, week, seek, sleek*

   - **K is used after a consonant** – *ink, blink, think, stink, rink, chink, sink, link, honk, bonk, bank, skunk, drank, chunk, plunk, hunk, sank, spunk, thank, trunk, shrunk*

OPTIONAL GRAMMAR REVIEW

Re-teach or practice the rules as needed using the activities below.

Possessives

Grammar Card 2.5	PNA
To turn a noun into a singular possessive noun adjective, add an apostrophe followed by an S.	

Grammar Card 2.6	PNA
To turn a noun into a plural possessive noun adjective, add an -S to make the noun plural and then add an apostrophe. If the noun has an irregular plural use an apostrophe followed by an S.	

1. Review the rule by reciting it. Discuss the sample phrases on the back of the card.

2. Discuss the meaning of the following phrases:

the helper's hat   *the teacher's books*

the author's pen   *the boy's trains*

Compare and contrast these to the plural forms.

the helpers' hats   *the teachers' books*
the authors' pens   *the boys' trains*

Notice that the plural form of each word is written before the apostrophe.

helpers   *teachers*   *authors*   *boys*

Since the plural of man is irregular, to form the possessive noun adjective we will add an apostrophe followed by an S.

men's

3. Illustrate each of the eight phrases above and label them with the correct possessive form.

4. ✎ *10.6 Extra Practice: Possessives* – Complete the activity in the workbook.

5. ✎ *10.7 Extra Practice: More Possessives* – Complete the activity in the workbook.

Commas in a Series

Grammar Card 11.1	Comma Rule 1
Use commas to separate the words in a series of three or more.	

1. Review the rule by reciting it. Discuss the sample phrases on the back of the card.

2. Demonstrate where to put a comma with phrases on the board.

a car, a truck, and a train

bread, milk, and eggs

3. Dictate the following lists to the students.

- *mother, father, son, and daughter*

- *cats, dogs, and ducks*

- *ship, train, car, and truck*

- *oil, eggs, bread, and milk*

4. Provide the students with sticky notes that have commas written on them and the word *and*. Ask the students to arrange their spelling cards into lists. Have them place the comma and the word *and* in the correct place.

OPTIONAL PHONOGRAM ASSESSMENT & REVIEW

Phonograms

✎ *10.8 Extra Practice: Phonogram Quiz* – Dictate the following phonograms by reading the sounds and spelling aids.

1.	wh	/wh/	15.	oi	/oi/ *that you may not use at the end of English words.*	31.	e	/ĕ-ē/
2.	th	/th-TH/				32.	j	/j/
3.	a	/ă-ā-ä/	16.	r	/r/	33.	ar	/är/
4.	au	/ä/ *that you may not use at the end of English words.*	17.	er	/er/ *the /er/ of her*	34.	z	/z/
			18.	f	/f/	35.	ee	/ē/
5.	o	/ŏ-ō-ö/	19.	s	/s-z/	36.	l	/l/
6.	igh	/ī/ *three -letter/ī/*	20.	oa	/ō/	37.	w	/w/
7.	b	/b/	21.	g	/g-j/	38.	oo	/oo-ü-ō/
8.	ay	/ā/ *two-letter /ā/ that you may use at the end of English words.*	22.	t	/t/	39.	k	/k/
			23.	h	/h/	40.	augh	/ä-ăf/
			24.	sh	/sh/	41.	x	/ks/
9.	p	/p/	25.	u	/ŭ-ū-oo-ü/	42.	ch	/ch-k-sh/
10.	c	/k-s/	26.	ea	/ē-ĕ-ā/	43.	m	/m/
11.	or	/or/	27.	i	/ĭ-ī-ē-y/	44.	ck	/k/ *two-letter /k/*
12.	qu	/kw/	28.	ng	/ng/	45.	y	/y-ĭ-ī-ē/
13.	d	/d/	29.	v	/v/	46.	oe	/ō-oo/
14.	aw	/ä/ *two letter /ä/ that you may use at the end of English words.*	30.	ai	/ā/ *two-letter /ā/ that you may not use at the end of English words.*	47.	n	/n/
						48.	oy	/oy/

Optional Phonogram Practice

Practice the phonograms as needed using the following game suggestions, or choose other games from the *The Phonogram and Spelling Game Book*.

1. ✎ *10.9 Extra Practice: Speed Bingo* (*The Phonogram and Spelling Game Book*, 26, Variation 2).

2. Practice using Blind Writing (*The Phonogram and Spelling Game Book*, 23).

3. Play Team Up (*The Phonogram and Spelling Game Book*, 14).

Lesson 11

Phonograms:	ou, ow, ough
Exploring Sounds:	Spelling the /ow/ Sound
Spelling Rules:	22, 24
Grammar:	Verbs, Sentences, Subject-Verb Agreement

PART ONE

Materials Needed: Phonogram flash cards from previous lessons and ou , ow , ough ; game pieces, one per student; die, one for every two students.

Phonograms

New Phonograms — *ou, ow, ough*

> *Today we will learn new phonograms which are related. I want you to tell me how they are related.*

Show ou . /ow-ō-oo-ŭ/.

> *Repeat the sounds.* /ow-ō-oo-ŭ/
> *How many sounds does /ow-ō-oo-ŭ/ make?* four

Show ow . /ow-ō/

> *Repeat the sounds.* /ow-ō/
> *How many sounds does /ow-ō/ make?* two

Show ou and ow .

> *How are these related?* They both begin with the letter O. They both say /ou-ō/.
> *How are they different?* One ends with the letter U and one ends with the letter W.
> *Which one may I use at the end of English words?* OW
> *Which one may I not use at the end of English words?* OU
> *Why?* English words do not end in I, U, V, or J.

Show ⬚ough⬚ . /ŏ-ō-oo-ow-ŭff-ŏff/

> ***Repeat the sounds.*** /ŏ-ō-oo-ow-ŭff-ŏff/
> ***How many sounds does /ŏ-ō-oo-ow-ŭff-ŏff/ make?*** six

Show ⬚ou⬚ and ⬚ough⬚ .

> ***How are these phonograms related?*** They both start with the letters OU.
> They share the sounds: /ow-ō-oo/. ŏ

Show ⬚ough⬚ /ŏ-ō-oo-ow-ŭff-ŏff/.

> ***What rule applies to this phonogram?*** Phonograms ending in GH are used only at the end of a base word, or before the letter T. The GH is either silent or pronounced /f/.

Phonogram Review

1. Drill the phonogram sounds with the flashcards.

2. ✎ *11.1 Writing the Phonograms* – Write each new phonogram five times while saying the sounds aloud.

3. ✎ *11.2 Phonogram Practice* – Dictate the following phonograms. For extra practice, have the students read them back. Write the correct answers on the board as the students check their answers.

1. igh	6. ch	11. ow	16. ar
2. ou	7. ck	12. oo	17. oi
3. aw	8. ai	13. er	18. oa
4. wh	9. au	14. ea	19. oe
5. ough	10. ng	15. ay	20. augh

4. ✎ *11.3 Phonogram Board Game* – Play a phonogram board game. Provide the students with die. The students roll the die and advance the correct number of spaces. As they pass each phonogram they must read it. If they misread a sound, the player returns to the spot they began and play passes to the next player. Optional: When the students roll a 3 they must go back three spaces.

Exploring Sounds

Reading Words with OW

Show ⬚ow⬚ .

> ***What does this say?*** /ou-ō/
> ✎ *11.4 Reading Words with OW* – ***Read the words in your workbook aloud. Underline the /ow-ō/.***

ow		ō	
cow	town	throw	window
brown	crown	thrown	show
down	powder	grow	snow
frown	tower	grown	crow

What do you notice about /ow-ō/? It is most often used before an N and at the end of the word. **Notice that /ow/ and /ō/ are both common sounds.**

Reading Words with OU

Show ou .

What does this say? /ow-ō-oo-ŭ/

✎ *11.5 Reading Words with OU –* **Read the words in your workbook aloud. Underline the /ow-ō-oo-ŭ/.**

/ow/	/ō/	/oo/	/ŭ/
out	your	tour	young
count	soul	group	touch
cloud			
shout			
found			
ground			
noun			

Looking at your list of words, which sound is the most common for /ow-ō-oo-ŭ/? /ow/
Which sounds are not very common sounds of /ow-ō-oo-ŭ/? /ō-oo-ŭ/
Can we use ou **to spell /ow/ at the end of the word?** no
Why not? English words do not end in I, U, V, or J.

< *Teacher Tip: OU commonly says the /ŭ/ sound with the suffix -ous. For example: cautious, curious, gracious, frivolous, serious… These words are all derived from Latin roots.*

Reading Words with OUGH

Show ough .

What does this say? /ŏ-ō-oo-ow-ŭff-ŏff/

All the words which use OUGH are listed in your workbook. Are there very many? no
You will need to memorize which words are spelled with OUGH.

✎ *11.6 Reading Words with OUGH* – **Read the words and underline the phonogram OUGH.**

/ŏ/	/ō/	/oo/	/ow/
bought	although	through	bough
brought	dough		drought
thought	borough		plough
fought	furlough<		
ought	thorough	**/ŭf/**	**/ŏf/**
nought	though	enough	cough
sought		rough	trough
wrought<		tough	

< **Teacher Tip:** *"Wrought" and "furlough" also use OUGH. However, the phonograms WR and UR have not been taught yet.*

Spelling Words with the /ow/ Sound

Which three phonograms say /ow/? OU, OW, and OUGH
Which one is not common? OUGH, it is only found in three words:6 bough, drought, and plough.

When we hear the sound /ow/ at the end of the word, how is it spelled? OW
How is /ow/ spelled in the middle of the syllable? OU or OW
When we hear /ow/ in the middle of the word we will need to pay careful attention for spelling purposes.

There are only two known common words that start with the /ow/ sound. Can you think of them? owl and out

owl   out

✎ *11.7 Most Common Spellings of /ow/* – **Add the sounds to the chart in your workbook.**

Middle of the Syllable	End of the Word
ou, ow	ow

Optional Spelling Journal   Ⓐ Ⓚ Ⓥ

Add words with the phonograms OW, OU, and OUGH to the Spelling Journal under the sounds /ow/, /ō/, /oo/, /ŭ/ /ŭff/, /ŏff/.

Optional Sounds Practice

1. Create a silly sentence or saying to memorize which words are spelled with OUGH. ⒶⓀⓋⒸ

2. Write words using the phonograms OU, OW, and OUGH on index cards. Have the students practice reading them. ⒶⓋ

3. Direct the students to create a collage of OU, OW, and OUGH words. The students may either use words only or they may include pictures for each word. ⒸⓋⓀ

4. Direct the students to write a crossword maze with words that are spelled with OU, OW, and OUGH. (*Phonogram and Spelling Game Book*, 53) ⒶⓀⓋ

5. Write the OUGH words on the board. Ask the students to read them. Then erase one, see if they can recite the list. Keep erasing one word seeing if the students can remember the whole list. ⒶⓋ

6. After playing games with the OUGH words, ask the students to see how many they can write from memory on a blank piece of paper. ⒶⓀⓋ

7. Draw pictures of words that use the various spellings of /ow/. Label each picture. ⒸⓋ

Optional Review of Vowel Sounds

What are the single letter vowels? a, e, i, o, u, and y
Today we will focus on a, e, o, u

a, e, o, u

Which of these makes only two vowel sounds? E

What are the sounds of the letter E? /ĕ-ē/
What is the first sound /ĕ/ called? the short sound
How is it marked? with a breve

ĕ

What is the second sound /ē/ called? the long sound
How is it marked? with a line

ē

Which of these vowels make three vowel sounds? A, O
What are the first vowel sounds /ă-ŏ/ called? the short sounds
How are they marked? with a breve

ă ŏ

What are the second sounds /ā-ō/ called? the long sounds
How are they marked? with a line

ā ō

What are the third vowel sounds /ä-ö/ called? broad sounds
How are they marked? with two dots

ä ö

Which of these vowels has four sounds? U
What is the first sound /ŭ/ called? the short sound
How is it marked? with a breve

ŭ

What are the sounds /ū-oo/ called? long sounds
How are they both marked? with a line

ū

What is the fourth sound /ü/ called? the broad sound
How is it marked? with two dots

ü

Optional Review of Vowel Sound   Ⓐ Ⓚ Ⓥ

Dictate the vowel sounds for the students to write on a separate sheet of paper.

Optional Spelling Rule Practice   Ⓐ Ⓚ Ⓥ

Review rules 3-4, 9-11, 21, 26, 28, 30 using the Spelling Rule Cards.

PART TWO

Using Spelling List 11 on pages 124-125, dictate each word following the steps included on pages Intro 42 - Intro 46.

Tips for Spelling List 11

Agree

One of the difficulties with English spelling is that vowels in unaccented syllables often are pronounced as the schwa sound /ə/. In order to help the students create an auditory picture of the word, it is helpful to exaggerate the unaccented vowel. Therefore exaggerate the vowel so that /ə grē/ sounds like /ā grē/.

To learn more about vowels in unaccented syllables and aiding the students in creating an auditory picture of words, see *Uncovering the Logic of English*, 121-128.

Word	Practice Sentence	Say to Spell	# of Syllables	Markings
1. **play**	*The children play outside.*	plā	1	pl<u>ay</u>
2. **pound**	*I pound the nail with a hammer.*	pownd	1	p<u>ou</u>nd
3. **shout**	*Do not shout.*	showt	1	<u>sh</u>out
4. **whisper**	*Try to whisper.*	whĭs per	2	<u>wh</u>is p<u>er</u>
5. **sing**	*They will sing a song.*	sĭng	1	si<u>ng</u>
6. **agree**	*They agree it is a good idea.*	ā grē	2	ā <u>gree</u>
7. **cough**	*She has a bad cough.*	cŏf	1	<u>cough</u>
8. **help**	*The boy cried for help.*	hĕlp	1	help
9. **wait**	*I will wait for you.*	wāt	1	w<u>ai</u>t
10. **touch**	*Do not touch the wet paint.*	tŭch	1	t<u>ou</u>ch⁴
11. **sleep**	*You will sleep in the guest room.*	slēp	1	sl<u>ee</u>p
12. **fight**	*Do not fight.*	fīt	1	fi<u>gh</u>t
13. **think**	*Think carefully before you answer the question.*	thĭnk	1	<u>think</u>
14. **destroy**	*Gophers destroy the grass.*	dē stroy	2	dē str<u>oy</u>
15. **open**	*I will open the door for you.*	ō pĕn	2	ō pen

Spelling Hints	Part of Speech	Vocabulary Development
Underline /ā/. **3** English words do not end in I, U, V, or J. **9** AY usually spells the sound /ā/ at the end of a base word.	V, N	player, played, playing, playful, playmate, downplay, horseplay, outplayed, playable, playability, playwright, replay, playroom
Underline /ow/.	V, N	pounded, pounds, pounding, pounder, impound, compound
Underline /sh/. Underline /ow/.	V, N	shouted, shouting, shouts
Underline /wh/. Underline /er/.	V, N	whispered, whispering, whispers, whispery
Underline /ng/.	V	sang, sung, singing, singer, singsong, singable
Say to spell /ā grē/. Put a line over the /ā/. **4** A E O U usually say their names at the end of the syllable. Underline /ē/.	V	agreed, agreeing, agreement, agreeable
Underline /of/.	V, N	coughed, coughing
All first sounds.	V	helper, helped, helping, helpful, helpfulness, helpless, helplessness, helpmate, unhelpful
Underline the /ā/.	V	waiter, waitress, waited, waiting, awaited
Underline the /ŭ/ and put a 4 over it. /ow-ō-oo-ŭ/ said its fourth sound. Underline /ch/.	V, N	touched, touches, retouch, touchable, touching, touchy, touchstone, untouched, untouchable
Underline /ē/.	V	sleeps, slept, sleeping, sleeper, sleepy, sleepless, asleep, oversleep, overslept, sleepwalk, sleepwalker, sleepwalking
Underline /ī/. **28** Phonograms ending in GH are used only at the end of a base word or before the letter T. The GH is either silent or pronounced /f/.	V, N	fought, fighting, fighter, bullfight, firefighter, gunfight, infighting, prizefight, prizefighters, refight
Underline /th/.	V	thought, thinker, thinking, thinkable, unthinkable, rethink, freethinker, outthink, unthinkably, unthinkingly
Put a line over the /ē/. **4** A E O U usually say their names at the end of the syllable. Underline /oy/. **3** English words do not end in I, U, V, or J.	V	destroyer, destroyed, destroying, destroys
Put a line above the O. **4** A E O U usually say their names at the end of the syllable.	V, Adj	opener, opening, opened

PART THREE

Materials Needed: Grammar Rule Cards 1.7, 3, 3.1, 9; green colored pencil; Spelling Rule Cards 22 and 24.

Grammar

Review

What is a noun? A noun is the name of a person, place, thing, or idea.
What is an adjective? Adjectives modify nouns and pronouns. Adjectives answer: What kind? How many? Which one? Whose?
What is an article? A, An, The. Tiny article adjectives that mark nouns and answer the question: Which?

Verbs

Today we will learn a new part of speech, the verb.

1. Show card and recite the rule:

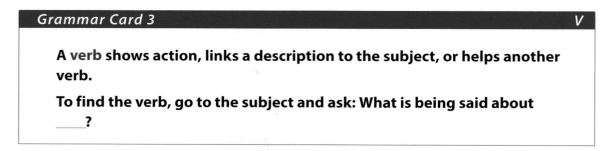

We will begin by focusing on action verbs. Each of the words in today's list shows an action. They are action verbs.

I will call out an action verb and I want you to act it out: jump, spin, crawl, hop, whisper, think... Now it is your turn to name action verbs.

2. ✎ *Spelling List 11* – Read List 11 and discuss the action that is shown by each word or have the students act out each word. Direct the students to write a green V next to each verb on the spelling list to indicate it is a verb.

Optional Spelling Cards

1. Dictate the words in Lesson 11 for the students to write on index cards.   Ⓐ Ⓚ Ⓥ

2. Color a green border around the verbs.   Ⓚ Ⓥ

Optional Grammar Practice

1. Play Charades using the verbs in List 11. The students must write their guess on a small white-board.   Ⓚ Ⓐ

2. Call out a word. Ask the students to decide if it is a noun, verb, article or adjective: *sing, the, blue, car, letter, shout, stand, desk, pencil, green, fifteen, sit, whisper, a, big, small, house, park, walk.* Ⓐ

3. Review the Grammar concepts taught so far using Grammar Cards 1-1.3; 2-2.6; 3-3.1; 7; 11.1. Ⓐ Ⓥ

Sentences

Until now we have been writing only phrases. Today we will learn about sentences.

Show the grammar card and recite the rule:

Grammar Card 9	Sentence
A sentence must have a capital letter, subject, verb, complete thought, and an end mark.	

Let's look at each of the requirements for a sentence.
What is a capital letter? an upper-case letter
What is a subject?   Answers will vary.
I have a grammar card that will help us to define the subject.

Grammar Card 1.7	SN
The subject noun is who or what the sentence is about.	
To find the subject, go to the verb and ask: Who or what _____?	

What is a verb? A verb shows action, links a description to the subject, or helps another verb.
What is a complete thought? It makes complete sense and includes all the information.

I will read some sentences and fragments. A fragment is not a complete thought. Tell me if it is a complete sentence or a fragment.

Father sails. sentence

Grandmothers whisper. sentence

Old fragment

hard kicks fragment

The girl is coughing. sentence

the good man fragment

The men help. sentence

dogs fragment

jump fragment

The children sing. sentence

Five kangaroos jump. sentence

the sleeping man fragment

The author writes books. sentence

an excellent meal fragment

What is an end mark? End marks are periods, questions marks, and exclamation points.

Write the three types of end marks on the board. At this time do not discuss when each one is used.

. ? !

Identifying Parts of Speech

✎ *11.8 Identifying Parts of Speech* – ***Look at the first sentence in your workbook. Read it aloud. We will compare it to the definition of a sentence.***

> *The daughters sing.*
>
> ***The daughters sing. To find the noun we will ask who or what about the verb.***
> ***Who sings?*** the daughters
> ***Daughters is the subject noun.***
> ***The subject is who or what the sentence is about.***
>
> ```
>      SN
> The daughters sing.
> ```
>
> ***Which daughters?*** the, article adjective
>
> ```
>  A    SN
> The daughters sing.
> ```
>
> ***To find the verb we ask:***
> ***What is being said about daughters?*** Daughters sing.
> ***Sing is the verb.***
>
> ```
>  A    SN     V
> The daughters sing.
> ```

Does it begin with a capital letter? yes
Does it have a subject? yes, daughters
Does it have a verb? yes, sing
Is "The daughters sing" a complete thought? yes
Does it end with an end mark? Yes, it ends with a period.
This is a correctly written sentence.

The boys play.

Who plays? boys
Boys is the subject noun.

SN
The boys play.

Which boys? the, article adjective

A   SN
The boys play.

To find the verb ask:
What is being said about boys? Boys play. Play is the verb.

A   SN   V
The boys play.

Is this a sentence? yes
Does it begin with a capital letter? yes
What is the subject? boys
What is the verb? play
Is "The boys play" a complete thought? yes
Then it is a correctly written sentence.

---

a long train

What is the subject? train
What kind of train? long , adjective
Which train? a, article adjective

A Adj   SN
a long train

Is this a sentence? No
Why not? It does not have a verb, and it is not a complete thought.

sing, shout, play

> **What is the subject?** there is none
> **Who sings, shouts, and plays?** no one
> **Is this a sentence?** no
> **Why not?** It does not have a subject, and it is not a complete thought.

Optional Grammar Activity

1. ✎ *11.9 Extra Practice: Sentences and Fragments* – Complete the activity in the workbook. Rewrite the sentences with a capital letter and end mark. Do not write anything if it is a fragment. Ⓥ Ⓐ Ⓚ

2. ✎ *11.10 Extra Practice: Sentences and Fragments* – Write S for sentence and F for fragment next to each line. Ⓐ Ⓚ Ⓥ

3. ✎ *11.11 Extra Practice: Reading Practice* – Practice reading the sentences in the workbook. Ⓥ Ⓐ Ⓚ

Subject Verb Agreement

I will say a noun. Find a verb from List 11 to make it into a sentence. I will write the sentences on the board. (Begin by providing only plural nouns.)

For example:

Mothers agree.

Sisters play.

Brothers wait.

Write the samples on the board, demonstrating how every sentence must begin with a capital letter and end with an end mark.

Begin to provide singular nouns and write the sentences across the board from the ones with plural nouns.

Mothers agree.	*Mother helps.*
Sisters play.	*Sister coughs.*
Brothers wait.	*Brother shouts.*

Once you have gathered a number of examples, ask the students to compare what was written.

Using a colored marker, highlight the S in each column.

Mothers agree.   *Mother sits.*

Sisters play.   *Sister wants.*

Brothers wait.   *Brother plays.*

What do you notice about these words? When the noun is plural, the verb does not have an S. When the noun is singular the verb adds an S.

This is called subject-verb agreement.

A boy march____.

What do we add to march? -es to make marches
Why? It hisses.

The snake hiss____?

What do we add after hiss? -es.
Why? It hisses.

The bee buzz____?

What do we add after buzz? -es.
Why? It hisses.

This leads to our new spelling rule. Before I read it you need to know that 3rd person singular is referring to the type of verbs we are using.

Spelling Rule	22

> **To make a verb 3rd person singular, add the ending -S, unless the word hisses or changes, then add -ES. Only four verbs are irregular.**

What rule does this remind you of? To make a noun plural, add the ending -S unless the word hisses or changes, then add -ES. Occasional nouns have no change or an irregular spelling.

◁ Teacher Tip: *Third person singular refers to verbs which make sense with the singular pronouns: he, she, and it. First person singular refers to I. Second person singular refers to you. We will learn more about the person of verbs in Lesson 21. Irregular: have - has, do - does, go - goes, am - is. Notice that though the formation of these four verbs is irregular, they all end with -S or -ES in the 3rd person singular.*

✎ *11.12 Subject-Verb Agreement* – Complete the activity in the workbook. Add the correct ending, if needed, to each word so that the subject and verb agree.

Dictation

✎ *11.13 Dictation* – Read each sentence twice. Ask the students to repeat it aloud, then write it in their workbooks.

1. The daughters agree.
2. Three sisters play.
3. The sick brother coughs.

4. Strong heroes shout.
5. Grandmother whispers.
6. The boys help.

Composition

1. Ask the students to combine words from List 9 with List 11 to make short, oral sentences. Listen for subject verb agreement. As the students create sentences, write them on the board. For example:

   Sisters play.

   Father pounds.

   The author waits.

   The sons agree.

2. ✎ *11.14 Composition* – Instruct the students to write six sentences in their workbooks using words from Lists 9 and 11. Remind them to capitalize the first letter and add an end mark.

Challenge: Adding Adjectives to Write more Interesting Sentences

Sisters play.

This sentence is very simple. To make the sentence more interesting, we can add an adjective to describe the noun.
What questions do adjectives answer? What kind? How many? Which one? Whose?
What kind of sisters play? Good sisters play.

Good sisters play.

How many sisters play? Six sisters play.

Six sisters play.

Which sisters play? The six sisters play.

The six sisters play.

What kind of sisters play? The six talented sisters play.

The six talented sisters play.

✎ *11.15 Challenge: Writing with Adjectives* – Direct the students to underline the subject noun. Then have them answer: what kind, which one, or how many about the subject. Ask the students to write a new sentence that includes an adjective describing the subject.

Optional Spelling Cards

1. Provide the students with the light blue article cards, the red noun cards, the green verb cards and sticky notes with the letters S and ES written on them. Direct the students to choose an article, noun, and verb to form a sentence. The student should then place the S or ES after either the noun or verb so that the subject and verb agree. Then read the sentence.   Ⓚ Ⓥ

2. Add blue adjective cards to form sentences in the pattern: Article – Adjective – Noun – Verb.   Ⓚ Ⓥ

Vocabulary Development

Adding the Suffixes -ful and -less

> *Read the words as I write them on the board.*

tooth   *daughter*   *sleep*   *help*

Write -*less* on the board.

> *What new words are formed when we add -less to each of these words?* toothless, daughterless, sleepless, helpless

toothless   *daughterless*   *sleepless*   *helpless*

> *What does it mean if someone is toothless?* They have no teeth.
> *What does daughterless mean?* They do not have any daughters.
> *What does it mean if someone is sleepless?* They cannot sleep.
> *How about helpless?* They cannot help themselves.

bagful   *glassful*

> *Read each of these words. What suffix did I add and how does it changes the meaning?* You added the suffix -ful. It means that something is full.

playful   *helpful*

> *What does playful mean?* someone who is full of play
> *What does helpful mean?* someone who helps a lot or is full of help

> *What word does the suffix -ful remind you of?* Full

-ful   *full*

> *How is the word full different from the suffix -ful?* The word has two L's and the suffix has only one L.

There is a spelling rule which helps us to remember that the suffix is written with one L.

Spelling Rule	24
-Ful is a suffix written with one L when added to another syllable.	

✎ *11.16 Vocabulary Development –* **Form new words using the suffixes -less and -ful in your workbook.**

Optional Vocabulary Activity

1. Use each of the new words in a sentence orally. Ⓐ

2. Ask the students to list as many words as they can think of that end in -less and -ful. Write them on the board as they think of them. The lists below are not complete. Each word in the list includes words that use only the phonograms and rules taught so far. If the students list a word not included, write it on the board, sounding it out while you write it. Ⓐ

   - *armful, bagful, barrelful, bowlful, bucketful, cupful, cheerful, colorful, delightful, disrespectful, dreadful, eventful, flavorful, forkful, frightful, glassful, gleeful, helpful, houseful, joyful, lapful, lawful, meaningful, mindful, mournful, needful, playful, powerful, pocketful, prayerful, restful, rightful, roomful, sackful, shovelful, skillful, spoonful, successful, trustful, truthful, watchful, youthful.*

   - *aimless, armless, artless, bottomless, boundless, brainless, breathless, charmless, cheerless, chinless, cloudless, colorless, comfortless, dinnerless, faithless, fearless, fatherless, flavorless, flowerless, groundless, heatless, heedless, jobless, leafless, mindless, motherless, numberless, restless, seamless, snowless, strapless, spotless, thoughtless, windowless.*

3. Write -ful and -less on index cards. Write 15-25 of the base words from the list above on index cards. Ask the students to pick a card, read the word, then choose the suffix -ful or -less to add, and read the new word that is formed. ⒶⓀⓋ

4. Dictate words with the suffix -ful and -less as the students write them on a white board. Provide clues as to which phonograms are used when needed. ⒶⓀⓋ

Lesson 12

Phonograms:	tch
Exploring Sounds:	Words Ending in -alk
Spelling Rules:	27
Grammar:	Transitive Verbs & Direct Objects

PART ONE

Materials Needed: Phonogram flash cards from previous lesson and tch ; Phonogram Game Cards, two sets per group of two-four students.

Phonograms

New Phonograms — *tch*

Show tch . /ch/

> **What do you notice about this phonogram?** The CH says /ch/ and the T is silent.
> **Repeat the sound.** /ch/

Review

1. Drill the phonogram sounds with the flashcards.

2. ✎ *12.1 Writing the Phonograms* – Write the new phonogram five times while saying the sound aloud.

3. ✎ *12.2 Phonogram Practice* – Dictate the following phonograms. For extra practice, have the students read them back. Write the correct answers on the board as the students check their answers.

1. ou	6. aw	11. igh	16. oe
2. au	7. ay	12. oo	17. ch
3. ai	8. oy	13. ar	18. ea
4. oi	9. ough	14. oa	19. or
5. ow	10. augh	15. wh	20. sh

4. Play Phonogram Memory using the Phonogram Game Cards (*The Phonogram and Spelling Game Book*, 8).

Exploring Sounds

Words Ending in -alk

I will write four words on the board. As I write each word, I will read it. When I am finished writing it, read it back to me. Look for a pattern.

talk   chalk   balk
walk   stalk

Read each word again.
What do you notice about these words? They all end in alk. The A says /ä/. The L is silent.
These are all the words that end in alk.
When we see a silent letter in a word, we will underline it twice to show that it is silent.

ta_l_k   cha_l_k   ba_l_k
wa_l_k   sta_l_k

How many sounds does A make? three /ă-ā-ä/
What rule do we know that tells us when A says its third sound /ä/? When a word ends with the phonogram A, it says /ä/. A may also say /ä/ after a W or before an L.
In each of these words the L reminds us to say the third sound.
How do we mark the third sound? Put two dots over it.

tä_l_k   chä_l_k   bä_l_k
wä_l_k   stä_l_k

✎ *12.3 Words Ending in -alk* – Read the words. Underline the L twice to show it is silent. Mark the third vowel sound with two dots.

Optional Spelling Journal   Ⓐ Ⓚ Ⓥ
Add words with ALK to the sound /ä/.

Spelling Rules

When to use the Phonogram TCH

Today we will learn the limits to the phonogram TCH.

✎ *12.4 TCH Words – Read the words in your workbook which use three letter /ch/. Underline three letter /ch/. Mark the sound of the vowel. What do you notice about these words?*

cătch	ĭtch	skĕtch	swĭtch
fĕtch	mătch	scrătch	wätch
hŭtch	pătch	stĭtch	bütcher

Do these words contain single-letter vowels, multi-letter vowels or both? only single-letter vowels

Which vowel sounds are heard in these words? the short sound and the broad sound

What would be a good rule? answers vary

Let's compare your rule to this one:

Spelling Rule	27

TCH is used only after a single vowel which does not say its name.

Optional Spelling Rule Practice ⒸⒶⓀⓋ

1. Quickly review rules 3-4, 9-11, 21-22, 24, 26-28, 30 using the Spelling Rule Cards. ⒶⓋ

2. Create a reference page to remember these rules. Include sample words. ⒸⓋ

3. Ask the students to teach this to another student or to a parent. ⒸⓋⒶⓀ

4. Read the following words aloud while the students write them using magnetic letter tiles: *stitch, hatch, latch, watch, patch, fetch, etch, crutch, twitch, clutch.* ⓀⒶⓋ

5. Write _atch on the board. Direct the students to find how many words complete this pattern. Continue with the other vowels. ⒶⓀⓋ

   - **_atch** - *batch, catch, hatch, latch, scratch, swatch*

   - **_etch** - *etch, stretch, wretch*

   - **_itch** - *itch, ditch, hitch, glitch, pitch, snitch, switch, witch*

   - **_otch** - *botch, scotch, splotch*

   - **_utch** - *clutch, crutch, Dutch, hutch*

6. Dictate words from the list above for the students to write on white boards or to spell using the phonogram game cards. ⒶⓀⓋ

Spelling Journal ⒶⓀⓋ

Add words using TCH to spell /ch/.

PART TWO

Using Spelling List 12 on pages 140-141, dictate each word following the steps included on pages Intro 42 - Intro 46.

Tips for Spelling List 12

Enjoy

Vowels are the most difficult aspect of English spelling. Many people say /ĭn joy/ though the word is spelled /ĕn joy/. For spelling purposes it is helpful to clearly articulate words, however, students do not need to change their pronunciation in daily speech.

PART THREE

Materials Needed: Grammar Rule Cards 1.8 and 3.2; green colored pencil.

Grammar

Review

1. Review:

   What is a noun? A noun is the name of a person, place, thing, or idea.
   What is an adjective? Adjectives modify nouns and pronouns. Adjectives answer: What kind? How many? Which one? Whose?
   What is an article? A, An, The. Tiny article adjectives that mark nouns and answer the question: Which?

2. Review the definition of a sentence:

   Name the parts of a sentence. A sentence must have a capital letter, subject, verb, complete thought, and an end mark.

3. Review the definition of a verb:

   What is a verb? A verb shows action, links a description to the subject, or helps another verb.
   What kind of words are listed in List 12? verbs
   ✎ *Spelling List 12 –* ***Write a green V next to each word in List 12 to show they are verbs.***

Optional Spelling Cards

1. Dictate the words in Lesson 12 for the students to write on index cards. Ⓐ Ⓚ Ⓥ

2. Color a green border around the verbs. Ⓚ Ⓥ

3. Combine the cards from Lists 11 and 12. Put them in a pile face down. Direct the students to draw a word, read it, and act it out. Optional: Ask other students to guess which word they read by writing the word on a small whiteboard. Ⓐ Ⓚ Ⓥ

Transitive Verbs & Direct Objects

This section is about direct objects. Direct objects receive the action of the verb. Act out the sentences so that the students can see the direct object receiving the action of the verb.

The boy throws.

Let's ask a few questions to decide if this is a sentence.

	Word	Practice Sentence	Say to Spell	# of Syllables	Markings
1.	**follow**	*They follow the trail.*	fŏl lō	2	fol l<u>ow</u>²
2.	**watch**	*Will you watch the baby while I go out?*	wäch	1	wät<u>ch</u>
3.	**enjoy**	*The cats enjoy laying in the sun.*	ĕn joy	2	en j<u>oy</u>
4.	**push**	*Push open the door.*	pŭsh	1	pü<u>sh</u>
5.	**eat**	*We will eat lunch at one o'clock.*	ēt	1	<u>ea</u>t
6.	**throw**	*Throw me the ball.*	thrō	1	<u>thr</u>o<u>w</u>²
7.	**match**	*You need to match your socks.*	măch	1	mat<u>ch</u>
8.	**teach**	*I will teach you how to spell it.*	tēch	1	<u>tea</u>ch
9.	**want**	*I want a sandwich for lunch.*	wänt	1	wänt
10.	**read**	*They read good books in that class.*	rēd	1	r<u>ea</u>d
11.	**catch**	*How many fish did you catch?*	căch	1	cat<u>ch</u>
12.	**reach**	*Reach for the rope with one hand.*	rēch	1	r<u>ea</u>ch
13.	**call**	*Grandma and Grandpa call at seven p.m. on Sunday.*	käl	1	cäll
14.	**walk**	*We will walk to the park.*	wäk	1	wäl̲k
15.	**talk**	*We will talk at the park.*	täk	1	täl̲k

Spelling Hints	Part of Speech	Vocabulary Development
Underline /ow/. **3** English words do not end in I, U, V, or J. Put a 2 over the /ō/. /ow-ō/ said its second sound.	V, N	followed, following, follower
Put two dots over /ä/. /ǎ-ā-ä/ said its third sound after a W. Underline /ch/. **27** TCH is used only after a single vowel which does not say its name.	V, N	watched, watching, watchful, watchband, watchcase, watchdog, watchfulness, watchmaker, watchmen
Say to spell / ĕn joy/. Underline /oy/. **3** English words do not end in I, U, V, or J.	V	enjoyed, enjoying, enjoyment, enjoyable
Underline /sh/. Put two dots over the /ü/. /ǔ-ū-oo-ü/ said its broad sound.	V, N	pusher, pushed, pushing, pushy
Underline the /ē/.	V	eating, eaten, ate, eatable, eatery, eateries
Underline /th/. Underline /ō/. Put a 2 over /ow-ō/ because it said its second sound.	V, N	throwing, threw, overthrow, throwaway, throwback, thrower, thrown
Underline /ch/. **27** TCH is used only after a single vowel which does not say its name.	V, N	matched, matches, matching, matchbook, matchbox, matchless, matchlock, matchmaker, mismatch, rematch
Underline the /ē/. Underline the /ch/. **27** TCH is used only after a single vowel which does not say its name. EA is a multi-letter vowel.	V	taught, teaches, teacher, teaching, reteach, schoolteacher, teachable, unteachable, teachableness
Put two dots over the /ä/. Hint: The letter A often says /ä/ after the letter W.	V	wanted, wanting, unwanted
Underline /ē/.	V	reads, reading, readable, proofread, reader, readership, unread, unreadable, copyreader
Underline /ch/. **27** TCH is used only after a single vowel which does not say its name.	V, N	caught, catches, catcher, catchall, catchphrase, catchword, dogcatcher, cowcatcher, flycatcher, catchable
Underline the /ē/. Underline /ch/.	V	reacher, reached, reaching, outreach, overreach, reachable, unreached
Put two dots over the /ä/. Hint: The letter A often says /ä/ before an L. **30** We often double F, L, and S after a single vowel at the end of a base word. Occasionally other letters also are doubled.	V, N	caller, called, calling, birdcall, callback, callable
Put two dots over the /ä/. /ǎ-ā-ä/ said its third sound. Double underline the L. It is silent. A said /ä/ after a W and before an L.	V, N	walked, walker, walking, crosswalk, cakewalk, jaywalk, sidewalk, skywalk, sleepwalk, walkingstick, walkway
Put two dots over the /ä/. /ǎ-ā-ä/ said its third sound. Double underline the L. It is silent. A said /ä/ before an L.	V, N	talked, talking, talker, shoptalk, talkative, talkativeness, talkie

Does it begin with a capital letter? yes
Does it have a subject noun? yes, boy
Does it have a verb? yes, throws
Does it make complete sense or is something missing? Something is missing.
We are left wondering, what does the boy throw?

The boy throws the ball.

Is this a complete thought? yes
Some verbs need a second noun to make the thought complete. These types of verbs are called transitive verbs.

Transitive Verb

Listen to the words "transitive" and "transfer." What do they have in common? They both begin with trans-.

transfer

What do you do when you transfer something? You move it from one place to another.
A transitive verb transfers the action of the verb to the direct object.

Act this out as you say the following:

For example: I move the chair.

I am transferring the action to the chair. Chair is the direct object.

Grammar Card 3.2	TV
A transitive verb transfers the action of the verb to the direct object.	

The noun that receives the action is called the direct object.

Grammar Card 1.8	DO
The direct object receives the action of the verb and completes the meaning of the sentence. **To find the direct object, go to the verb and ask: ____ what? ____ whom?**	

What else could the boy throw? Tell me the answer in a complete sentence. For example: The boy throws the toy.
Toy is the direct object. It is receiving the action of the verb.
What else could the boy throw? Tell me the answer in a complete sentence. For example: The boy

throws the paper.
Paper is the direct object. It is receiving the action of the verb…

What is the direct object? A direct object is a noun that receives the action of the verb.
All of the verbs in List 12 need a direct object. Therefore, they are all transitive verbs.

Read each verb in List 12 aloud. Then use it in a sentence including a subject and a direct object. For example: The woman follows the boy.

> ⟨ Teacher Tip: *Verbs that need a direct object are called transitive verbs. Direct objects are often called complements because they complete or complement the meaning of the verb.*

Identifying the Parts of Speech

✎ *12.5 Identifying Parts of Speech –* ***Label the parts of speech in your workbook as we discuss each sentence and I label it on the board.***

The man pushes the swing.

Who pushes? man, subject noun
Which man? the, article adjective
What is being said about the man ? man pushes, verb
Pushes what? swing, direct object
Which swing? the, article adjective
Is there a direct object receiving the action of the verb? yes
Then it is a transitive verb. Write a T next to the V to show the type of verb.

　A　SN　TV　A　DO
The man pushes the swing.

The sisters enjoy the book.

Who enjoys? sisters, subject noun
Which sisters? the, article adjective
What is being said about sisters? sisters enjoy, verb
What do they enjoy? book, direct object
Which book? the, article adjective
Is there a direct object receiving the action of the verb? yes
Then it is a transitive verb. Write a T next to the V to show the type of verb.

　A　SN　TV　A　DO
The sisters enjoy the book.

Mother opens the green box.

Who opens? mother, subject noun
What is being said about mother? mother opens, verb
What does mother open? box, direct object
Which box? the, article adjective
What kind of box? green, adjective
Is there a direct object receiving the action of the verb? yes
Then it is a transitive verb. Write a T next to the V to show the type of verb.

SN   TV   A   Adj   DO
Mother opens the green box.

The three boys eat bread and jam.

Who eats? boys, subject noun
How many boys? three, adjective
Which boys? the, article adjective
What is being said about the boys? boys eat, verb
What do they eat? bread, direct object
What else do they eat? jam, direct object
What is the word "and"? conjunction
How many direct objects are in this sentence? two
What joins them together? the conjunction "and"
Is there a direct object receiving the action of the verb? yes
Then it is a transitive verb. Write a T next to the V to show the type of verb.

A   Adj   SN   TV   DO   C   DO
The three boys eat bread and jam.

Optional Grammar Activities

1. ✏ *12.6 Extra Practice: Reading Sentences* – Direct the students to read the sentences in the workbook aloud. Ⓐ Ⓥ

2. ✏ *12.7 Extra Practice: Subject-Verb Agreement* – Complete the activity in the workbook. Add the correct ending if needed to each word so that the subject and verb agree. Ⓐ Ⓚ Ⓥ

3. ✏ *12.8 Extra Practice: Sentences and Fragments* – Write an S next to the complete sentences. Write an F next to the fragments. Ⓐ Ⓚ Ⓥ

Vocabulary Development

The Suffix -er

Today we will use the suffix -er to form new words.

work + er

What new word is formed when we add "work" and /er/? worker

work + er = worker

What is a worker? Someone who works.
Use worker in a sentence. For example: The worker ate lunch.

play + er

What word is formed when we add the suffix -er to play? player

play + er = player

What is a player? Someone who plays.
Use player in a sentence. For example: The first player up to bat struck out.

open + er

What word is formed when we add the suffix -er to open? opener

open + er = opener

What is an opener? something used to open
Use opener in a sentence. For example: The can opener is in the kitchen.

How does the suffix -er change the meaning of open, play and work? It changes a verb to a person or thing which does the action. In other words the suffix -er changes a verb into a noun.

Read through the verbs in Lessons 11 and 12. Which ones take the suffix -er?

player	fighter	watcher	catcher
pounder	thinker	destroyer	caller
singer	walker	thrower	
helper	talker	reader	
waiter	follower	opener	

✎ *12.9 Vocabulary Development* – Complete the activity in your workbook.

Optional Vocabulary Activities

1. Write action verbs on index cards. Write the suffix -er on an index card. Direct the students to form new words using the cards.   Ⓐ Ⓚ Ⓥ

2. Dictate verbs with the suffix -er for the students to write on a whiteboard, chalkboard, or with magnetic letters. Emphasize the spelling of the suffix.   Ⓐ Ⓚ Ⓥ

3. Play Charades. Write the verbs + er from Lists 11 and 12 on index cards. One student draws a card, reads it, and acts it out. The other students guess the correct answer by writing it on a whiteboard.   Ⓐ Ⓚ Ⓥ

Dictation

✎ *12.10 Dictation* – Read each sentence twice. Ask the students to repeat it aloud, then write it in their workbooks.

1. The man catches the ball.
2. The boy pushes the toy truck.
3. Mother enjoys the music.
4. A helper opens the black door.
5. The class watches the program.
6. The teacher reads a book.

Composition

Today we will write sentences following the pattern: Subject, Verb, Direct Object.
What is a direct object? a noun that receives the action of the verb

✎ *12.11 Composition* – **Using the words in your workbook, form sentences which include a subject, verb, and direct object.**

Optional Spelling Cards   Ⓐ Ⓚ Ⓥ

Provide the students with the light blue article cards, the red noun cards, and the green verb cards. On a sticky note write the endings -S and -ES. Direct the students to choose a noun, verb and direct object to form a sentence. Add in articles as needed. The students should then place the -S or -ES after either the noun or verb so that the subject and verb agree. Then read the sentence aloud.

Challenge: Adding Adjectives to Write More Interesting Sentences

Both the subject and the direct object are nouns. To make the sentence more interesting, we can choose an adjective to describe the subject. For example:

The man catches the ball.

To add an adjective describing man, we ask what kind of man? the tall man

The tall man catches the ball.

We can also add an adjective describing ball by answering the question, what kind of ball? the green ball

The tall man catches the green ball.

Which sentence provides more information and is more interesting? The man catches the ball; or The tall man catches the green ball.

✎ *12.12 Writing with Adjectives* – Direct the students to underline the subject noun and the direct object. Then have them answer: what kind, which one, or how many about the subject, then repeat and ask: what kind, which one, or how many about the direct object. Ask the students to write a new sentence that includes adjectives describing both the subject and direct object.

Lesson 13

Phonograms:	kn, gn
Exploring Sounds:	KN and GN
Spelling Rules:	8
Grammar:	

PART ONE

Materials Needed: Phonogram flash cards from previous lessons, kn and gn , a colored pencil for each student.

Phonograms

New Phonograms — *kn, gn*

Show kn . /n/

Show gn . /n/

> *Repeat the sound.*
> *How are these phonograms the same?* They both say /n/. They both have an N as the second letter.
> *How are they different?* One begins with a K, the other begins with a G.
>
> *Neither KN nor GN is a very common phonogram. The most common spelling of the sound /n/ is the letter N.*

Exploring Sounds

KN and GN

> *Both KN and GN are limited in how they are used.*
> ✎ *13.1 Words with KN and GN – Read some of the most common words which use KN and GN in your workbook. Underline the KN and the GN.*

Discuss the meaning of unknown words as your students read them aloud.

knead	*gnat*
knack	*gnaw*
knight	*gnarl*
know	*gnash*
knock	*gnome*
knob	*campaign*
knot	*sign*
knit	*design*
knee	

When is KN used? KN is used only at the beginning of the word.
When is GN used? GN is used both at the beginning and the end of the word.

Show kn .

/n/ Two letter /n/ used only at the beginning of a base word.

Show gn .

/n/ Two letter /n/ used both at the beginning and the end of a base word.

Looking at the list would you guess KN or GN is more common? KN
Why? It's used in more common words.
There are only eighteen base words that begin with KN and only seven that begin with GN.

Spelling Journal   Ⓐ Ⓚ Ⓥ

   Enter words spelled with KN and GN.

Phonogram Review

1. Drill the phonogram sounds with flashcards.

2. ✎ *13.2 Writing the Phonograms* – Write each new phonogram five times while saying the sounds aloud.

3. ✎ *13.3 Phonogram Practice* – Dictate the following phonograms. For extra practice, have the students read them back. Write the correct answers on the board as the students check their answers.

1. oi	4. kn	7. aw	10. ay
2. oe	5. tch	8. wh	11. gn
3. igh	6. oa	9. ee	12. ow

13. ai   15. ng   17. ea   19. ar

14. ou   16. oo   18. au   20. ough

4. Play Phonogram Snap using the Phonogram Game Cards (*The Phonogram and Spelling Game Book*, 10).

Spelling Rules

I and O May Say /ī/ and /ō/ When Followed By Two Consonants

What is the long sound of I? /ī/
How is it marked? Draw a line over it.

ī

What is the long sound of O? /ō/
How is it marked? Draw a line over it.

ō

✎ *13.4 I and O – Together we will read the words in your workbook. In each of these words the I and the O will say their long sounds. After you read the word, mark the vowel as long. Look for a pattern that might explain why they say their long sound.*

wild	bold
child	cold
mild	gold
blind	roll
kind	both
sign	bolt

Are the long /ī/ and /ō/ at the end of the syllable? no
How many consonants do you see after the long /ī/ and /ō/? two
This leads to a new rule:

Spelling Rule	8
I and O may say /ī/ and /ō/ when followed by two consonants.	

Does the rule state the I and O **always** *says /ī/ and /ō/ before two consonants?* No, they may say /ī/ and /ō/ before two consonants.

✎ *13.5 I and O Continued* – **Read the words in your workbook. Mark the vowel as short.**

bĭll   lŏck

mĭlk   gŏlf

sĭck   dŏll

drĭnk   sŏck

Optional Spelling Rule Practice

1. Create a reference page to remember this rule. Include sample words. Ⓒ Ⓥ

2. Ask the students to teach this to another student or to a parent. Ⓒ Ⓥ Ⓐ Ⓚ

3. Quickly review rules 3-4, 8-11, 21-22, 24, 26-28, 30 using the Spelling Rule Cards. Ⓐ Ⓥ

4. Write _ind, _ild, _old, _olt _ick, _ock, _ink, _ong, _ing on the board. Ask the students to find letters that complete the words. (Or use the Phonogram Game Cards or magnetic letters.) Ⓐ Ⓚ Ⓥ

   • _ind: *blind, kind, rind, bind, hind, wind, find, behind, mind*

   • _ild: *child, mild, wild*

   • _old: *bold, cold, gold, mold, sold, hold, told, scold, fold*

   • _olt: *bolt, colt, molt*

   • _ick: *tick, trick, brick, sick, stick, lick, rick, nick, thick, click*

   • _ock : *lock, rock, frock, knock, sock, cock, dock, flock*

   • _ink: *clink, sink, rink, brink, link, mink, blink*

   • _ong: *long, along, belong, dong, gong, song, strong*

   • _ing: *king, ping, ring, sing, wing, zing, bring, cling, fling, sting, sling, swing, thing, string*

5. Dictate words in the list above for the students to write on a whiteboard or in a saltbox. Ⓐ Ⓚ Ⓥ

6. Say a word. Ask the students to find the words that rhyme. They may write suggestions on a whiteboard or the teacher may write the list on the board for the class to see. Ⓐ Ⓚ Ⓥ

7. ✎ *13.6 Extra Practice: Rhyming* – Challenge the students to write as many words as they can think of that rhyme with the word at the top of the column. Optional: provide the students a limited amount of time for each column, such as 30 or 60 seconds. Ⓐ Ⓚ Ⓥ

8. Nonsense Words – Discuss the writing of Dr. Suess. Read a sample if appropriate. Ask the students to create nonsense words that rhyme with the words in Activity 4. Ⓐ Ⓚ Ⓥ Ⓒ

PART TWO

Using Spelling List 13 on pages 154-155, dictate each word following the steps included on pages Intro 42 - Intro 46.

PART THREE

Materials Needed: Green colored pencil.

Grammar

Review

1. Verbs

    What is a verb? A verb shows action, links a description to the subject, or helps another verb.
    One way to find an action verb is to ask, "Can I do it?"
    What kind of words are listed in List 13? verbs

    ✎ *Spelling List 13 –* **Write a green V next to each word in List 13 to show they are verbs.**

    ### *Optional Spelling Cards*

    Dictate the words in Lesson 13 for the students to write on index cards. Color a green border around the verbs.   ⒶⓀⓋ

    ---

2. Sentences

    Name the parts of a sentence. capital letter, subject, verb, complete thought, and an end mark.

    ✎ *13.7 Sentences and Fragments –* **In your workbook, write an S next to the complete sentences. Write an F next to the fragments.**

3. Adjectives, Articles, and Nouns

    What does an adjective do? An adjective modifies a noun or a pronoun. An adjective answers: What kind? How many? Which one? Whose?

    What does an article do? It is a tiny adjective that marks nouns and answers the question: Which?
    What are the articles? a, an, the

    What is a noun? A noun is a person, place, thing, or idea.

Word	Practice Sentence	Say to Spell	# of Syllables	Markings
1. **sign**	*Sign your name on the line.*	sīn	1	sī<u>gn</u>
2. **design**	*He will design the card.*	dē zīn	2	dē sī<u>gn</u>²
3. **know**	*I know where to find the book.*	nō	1	<u>kn</u>ow²
4. **drink**	*It is important to drink enough water.*	drĭnk	1	drink
5. **meet**	*Meet me at the store.*	mēt	1	m<u>ee</u>t
6. **find**	*I hope you find your keys.*	fīnd	1	fīnd
7. **pick**	*Did you pick strawberries today?*	pĭk	1	pi<u>ck</u>
8. **start**	*We will start tomorrow.*	stärt	1	st<u>ä</u>rt
9. **pass**	*Pass this to him.*	păs	1	pass
10. **pull**	*We will pull the trailer.*	pŭl	1	pull
11. **hold**	*Hold on to your hat.*	hōld	1	hōld
12. **sell**	*These stores sell good bread.*	sĕl	1	sell
13. **draw**	*The students will draw you a picture.*	drä	1	dr<u>aw</u>
14. **remember**	*Remember to bring your coat.*	rē mĕm ber	3	rē mem b<u>er</u>
15. **need**	*We need to bring a lunch.*	nēd	1	n<u>ee</u>d

Spelling Hints	Part of Speech	Vocabulary Development
Put a line over the I. Underline two letter /n/ used at the end of the word. **8** I and O may say /ī/ and /ō/ before two consonants.	V, N	signed, signing, assign, assignment, design, signal, signify, signature, signpost, significant, insignificant, signet, signer
Put a line over the /ē/. **4** A E O U usually say their names at the end of the syllable. Put a 2 over the /z/. Put a line over the I. **8** I and O may say /ī/ and /ō/ before two consonants. Underline two letter /n/ used at the end of the word.	V, N	designed, designing, designer, designate, designation, codesign, redesign
Underline /n/. Underline /ō/. Put a 2 over it. /ow-ō/ said its second sound.	V	knew, knowledge, acknowledge, acknowledgement, foreknow, knowable, knowingly, known, unknown
All first sounds.	V	drinks, drinking, drinkable, drinker, overdrink
Underline /ē/.	V, N	met, meeting, meets, meetinghouse
Draw a line over the I. **8** I and O may say /ī/ and /ō/ before two consonants.	V, N	found, finder, finding, finds, pathfinder, viewfinder, faultfinder
Underline /k/.	V	picked, picker, picking, handpick, nitpick, picky, pickier, picket, picketing, pickpocket, pickup, toothpick
Underline /ar/.	V, N	started, starting, starter, restart, upstart
30 We often double F, L, and S after a single vowel at the end of a base word. Occasionally other letters also are doubled.	V	passed, passing, passer, bypass, overpass, underpass, passbook, passenger, passage, passerby, passable, passover, passport
30 We often double F, L, and S after a single vowel at the end of a base word. Occasionally other letters also are doubled.	V	pulled, pulling, outpull, pullback, puller, pulley, pullman, pullout, pullover
Put a line over the /ō/. **8** I and O may say /ī/ and /ō/ before two consonants.	V, N	holding, held, behold, beholden, foothold, holdout, holdover, holdup, household, shareholder, withhold, uphold
30 We often double F, L, and S after a single vowel at the end of a base word. Occasionally other letters also are doubled.	V	sold, selling, sells, bookseller, outsell, undersell, resell, sellout, outsold, undersold
Underline /ä/.	V	drew, drawing, drawings, drawable, drawback, drawbridge, drawn, outdraw, redraw, withdraw, overdrawn
Put a line over the /ē/. **4** A E O U usually say their names at the end of the syllable. Underline the /er/.	V	remembered, remembering
Underline the /ē/.	V, N	needed, needing, needful, needy, needfully, needless, needlessly, neediness, unneeded

Nouns can perform six different jobs in a sentence. We have already learned two of those jobs. What are they? A noun can be the subject and the direct object.

This is like people. For example a person may work at a school as a teacher during the school year and have a second job in a store on the weekend.

Identifying Parts of Speech

English grammar is about word order. In some languages words can be arranged in any order because endings on the words show the meaning. In English the word order indicates the meaning.

I will write two sentences on the board. Tell me when you notice what is different between them.

The cat drinks the milk.

The milk drinks the cat.

Discuss with the students how the meaning changes by switching the order of the words.

Let's label the jobs for each word in the sentence.

The cat drinks the milk.

Who drinks? cat, subject noun
Which cat? the, article adjective
What is being said about cat? cat drinks, verb
What does the cat drink? milk, direct object
Which milk? the, article adjective
Is there a direct object receiving the action of the verb? yes
Then what kind of verb is it? a transitive verb
Write a T next to the V to show the type of verb.

  A SN TV A DO
The cat drinks the milk.

The milk drinks the cat.

In this sentence what drinks? milk, subject noun
Does this make sense? no
Which milk? the, article adjective
What is being said about milk? milk drinks, verb
What does the milk drink? cat, direct object
Is there a direct object receiving the action of the verb? yes
Then what kind of verb is it? a transitive verb
Write a T next to the V to show the type of verb.

  A SN TV A DO
The milk drinks the cat.

By changing the position of the words "cat" and "milk" we changed their jobs in the sentence and therefore changed the meaning of the sentence.

✎ *13.8 Identifying Parts of Speech – **Read the first two sentences in your workbook and tell me how they are different.***

The grandmother knows the boy.

The boy knows the grandmother.

In the first sentence, the grandmother knows. In the second sentence, the boy knows.

Write each sentence on the board. Ask the students the questions to aid them in identifying the parts of speech. As the students become more proficient, have them ask the questions. Mark the part of speech on the board. Direct the students to write them in their workbooks.

We will now identify the parts of speech in each sentence. The parts of speech tell us the job of each word in the sentence.

The grandmother knows the boy.

> **In this sentence who knows?** grandmother, subject noun
> **Which grandmother?** the, article adjective
> **What is being said about grandmother?** grandmother knows, verb
> **Who does grandmother know?** boy, direct object
> **Which boy?** the, article adjective
> **Is there a direct object receiving the action of the verb?** yes
> **Then what kind of verb is it?** a transitive verb
> **Write a T next to the V to show the type of verb.**

> A   SN   TV   A   DO
> *The grandmother knows the boy.*

The boy knows the grandmother.

> **In this sentence who knows?** the boy, subject noun
> **Which boy?** the, article adjective
> **What is being said about the boy?** boy knows, verb
> **Who does the boy know?** grandmother, direct object
> **Which grandmother?** the, article adjective
> **Is there a direct object receiving the action of the verb?** yes
> **Then what kind of verb is it?** a transitive verb
> **Write a T next to the V to show the type of verb.**

> A   SN   TV   A   DO
> *The boy knows the grandmother.*

The brothers sell good books.

Who sells? brothers, subject noun
Which brothers? the, article adjective.
What is being said about the brothers? brothers sell, verb
What do the brothers sell? books, direct object
What kind of books? good, adjective
Is there a direct object receiving the action of the verb? yes
Then what kind of verb is it? a transitive verb
Write a T next to the V to show the type of verb.

A   SN   TV   Adj DO
The brothers sell good books.

The six men sell cheap cars and trucks.

Who sells cars? men, subject noun
How many men? six, adjective
Which men? the, article adjective
What is being said about men? men sell, verb
What do they sell? cars, direct object
What else do they sell? trucks, direct object
What kind of cars and trucks? cheap, adjective
What is the word "and?" conjunction
Is there a direct object receiving the action of the verb? yes
Then what kind of verb is it? a transitive verb
Write a T next to the V to show the type of verb.

A   Adj SN TV Adj DO   C   DO
The six men sell cheap cars and trucks.

1. Review commas in a series using Grammar Card 11.1. Discuss the samples on the back of the card. Ⓐ Ⓚ Ⓥ

2. Write the following sentence on the board. Ⓐ Ⓥ

   Grandfather sells boats cars and trucks.

      What is wrong with it? It needs a comma after boats and cars.

   Grandfather sells boats, cars, and trucks.

3. ✎ *13.9 Extra Practice: Subject-Verb Agreement* – Complete the activity in the workbook. Ⓐ Ⓚ Ⓥ

4. ✎ *13.10 Extra Practice: Editing* – Complete the activity in the workbook. Find the mistakes in each sentence. Rewrite the sentence correctly on the lines below. Ⓐ Ⓚ Ⓥ

5. Review Grammar Cards 1-1.3; 1.7-1.8; 2-2.6; 3-3.2; 7, 9, 11.1. Ⓐ Ⓥ

Dictation

✎ *13.11 Dictation* – Read each sentence twice. Ask the students to repeat it aloud, then write it in their workbooks.

1. The author signs the books.
2. The man designs cars.
3. Mother needs milk, bread, and eggs.
4. The class draws the ducks.
5. The player passes the ball.
6. Father remembers the man.

Composition

✎ *13.12 Composition* – Using the words in the workbook, write six sentences that follow the pattern Subject Noun + Verb + Direct Object.

Provide the students with the light blue article cards, the red noun cards, and the green verb cards. On a sticky note write the endings -S and -ES. Direct the students to choose noun, verb and direct object to form a sentence. Add in articles as needed. The students should then place the -S or -ES after either the noun or verb so that the subject and verb agree. Then read the sentence aloud. Ⓚ Ⓥ Ⓐ

Vocabulary

The Prefixes pre- and re-

> **What is suffix?** a letter or letters added to the end of a word
> **Today we will add a prefix. A prefix is a letter or letters added to the beginning of the word.**

prefix

> **What is the root word of prefix?** fix
> **What letters have been added to the beginning?** PRE
> **Read the words as I write them on the board.**

precook	*preheat*	*preteen*
precut	*presoak*	*pretest*

> **What do you think the suffix PRE means?** before

> **Therefore a prefix is letters added before the root word.**

re + sell =

> **What new word is formed when we add "re-" to "sell"?** resell

re + sell = resell

> **What does it mean to resell something?** to sell it again
> **Read the list of words in your workbook. What do you think the prefix re- means?**

replay	*resell*	*recall*	*reopen*

Re- means to do something again.
> **What do we call the letters we add to the beginning of the word?** prefix
> **When we add a prefix to the word, did anything in the base word change?** no
> **Adding prefixes is easy. Just add it to the beginning of the base word.**
> **Use each of these words in a sentence aloud.**

✎ *13.13 Vocabulary – **Practice forming words with the prefix re- in your workbook.***

Lesson 14

Phonograms:	ir, ur, ear
Exploring Sounds:	Spellings of /er/
Spelling Rules:	
Grammar:	Common and Proper Nouns

PART ONE

Materials Needed: Phonogram flash cards from previous lessons and er , ir , ur , and ear ; Pennies or other small objects to cover the Bingo chart.

Phonograms

New Phonograms — *ir, ur, ear*

Show ir . */er/*

Show ur . */er/*

Show ear . */er/ three letter /er/*

What multi-letter vowel do you see in three letter /er/? /ē-ĕ-ā/

Show er , ir , ur , ear .

> *What is the same between each of these phonograms?* They all say /er/. They all have an R in them.
> *Which form of /er/ have we been using until now?* ER
> *This is the most common spelling. It is found in more than 80% of the words.*
> *IR and UR are the next most common and EAR is the least common.*
>
> *When you encounter words with IR, UR, or EAR, they will need to be memorized for spelling. These are good words to add to your Spelling Journal.*

Exploring Sounds

/r/ and /er/

Say the sound /r/ as in read.
Can you sustain or sing it? no
Say the sound /er/ as in her.
Can you sing it? yes
The R colors the vowel that is next to it.
Read the following words out loud as I write them on the board. Listen carefully to the vowels.

turn	girl	early
hurt	swirl	earth

What is the written vowel in each of these words: turn – U; hurt – U; girl – I; swirl – I; early – EA; earth – EA.

t<u>u</u>rn	g<u>i</u>rl	<u>ea</u>rly
h<u>u</u>rt	sw<u>i</u>rl	<u>ea</u>rth

What are the sounds of U? /ŭ-ū-oo-ü/.
Can you hear one of these sounds in turn? no
How about in hurt? no
Which letter drowns out the vowel sound? R
Words with an R are called R-controlled words. The R drowns out the vowel sound.

What is the most common spelling of /er/? ER
Remember, when you see a word that has the sound /er/ spelled with an IR, UR, or EAR, you will need to pay extra attention and memorize which spelling of /er/ is used.

✎ *14.1 Spellings of /er/ – In your workbook you have a list of some of the common words that use IR, UR, and EAR to spell /er/. Read each word and underline the phonogram used to spell the sound /er/.*

first	fur	earth
bird	burn	learn
skirt	hurt	pearl
stir	turn	earn
shirt	church	yearn
squirrel	burst	search
birth	curl	heard

EAR is the least common. There are only 13 common base words which use the phonogram EAR. You have seven of them listed in your workbook.

How are syllables and vowels related? Opening and closing the mouth to say the vowels is what forms the syllables.

How many vowel sounds are in each syllable? one

Many people feel confused about when to use R or a spelling of /er/ within a word.

✎ 14.2 R or a Spelling of /er/? – **Read the pairs of words in your book aloud. As you read them, compare the vowel sounds.**

| print | perch | | train | turn | | drip | dirt |
| track | term | | brow | burn | | brand | bird |

What do you notice about the vowel sound in words that use single-letter R? The vowel is clearly pronounced.

What do you notice about the vowel sound in words that use ER, IR, or UR? The R distorts the vowel sound.

Help me to spell the word drain. How many syllables is drain? one
How many vowels sounds will there be? one
Can I hear the vowel sound clearly? Yes, it is a long /ā/ sound.
Why can I not spell it like this:

derain

Because then it would have two syllables. Each of the vowels forms a new syllable.

Therefore I must use the single-letter R.

drain

Is AI one or two vowel sounds? One. It is a multi-letter vowel.

Help me to sound out the word learn.
How many syllables in learn? one
How many vowel sounds will it have? one
Is the vowel sound clear? no
Will I use the letter R or a spelling of /er/? ER, IR, UR, or EAR
In learn we will use the three-letter /er/.

learn

All of the words I say will either be spelled with R or with /er/. Listen to the word and tell me which spelling is used. *Optional: Direct the students to write the words on a small whiteboard.*

| trim | fern | creep | perch |
| her | cram | herd | brain |

Now let's consider words with more than one syllable.

✎ 14.3 R or a Spelling of /er/? – **Read the pairs in your workbook aloud. Draw a line between the syllables. As you read the words, compare the vowel sounds.**

| per/son | pre/pay | | fur/nish | fright/en |
| tur/bo | trum/pet | | trip/let | tur/nip |

How does the syllable spelled with R differ from the syllable spelled with ER, IR, UR, or EAR? The vowel sound is clearly pronounced in the syllable when it is spelled with a single-vowel R. The vowel sound is distorted with the R when it is spelled with ER, IR, UR, or EAR.

In order to cue the students which spelling of /er/ is heard within a word, the teacher and students need to agree on sample words. You can either use the words *her, bird, hurt,* and *search* as found on the back of the cards, or you can pick four words that you will use as a class.

To help me cue you which sound of /er/ you are to write, we will memorize a word that uses each spelling.

✎ *14.4 Spelling Cues – Write the sample words we will use for the spellings of /er/ in your workbook.*

Spelling Journal   Ⓐ Ⓚ Ⓥ

Enter words spelled with ER, IR, UR, and EAR.

Phonogram Review

1. Drill the phonograms with flashcards.

2. ✎ *14.5 Writing the Phonograms* – Write the new phonogram five times while saying the sound aloud.

3. ✎ *14.6 Phonogram Practice* – Dictate the following phonograms. For extra practice, have the students read them back. Write the correct answers on the board as the students check their answers.

1. kn	6. oe	11. ay	16. ow
2. igh	7. au	12. gn	17. oa
3. sh	8. augh	13. ough	18. aw
4. ar	9. oo	14. wh	19. oi
5. ai	10. ou	15. tch	20. ch

4. ✎ *14.7 Phonogram Bingo* – Play Phonogram Bingo (*The Phonogram and Spelling Game Book*, 26).

Review Spelling Rules

Optional Spelling Rule Practice

Quickly review rules 3-4, 8-11, 21-22, 24, 26-28, 30 using the Spelling Rule Cards.   Ⓐ Ⓥ

PART TWO

Using Spelling List 14 on pages 166-167, dictate each word following the steps included on pages Intro 42 - Intro 46.

Tips for Spelling List 14

Woman

At first glance the common pronunciation of the word "woman," /wə mĭn/, appears to have no relation to the spelling of the word. Nevertheless there is a deeper connection. Notice that the root of woman is "man." In order to draw a stronger connection to the spelling of the word, it is helpful to clearly point out the root.

In order to help the students create an auditory picture of this word, it is beneficial if they exaggerate the sounds for spelling purposes to /wō măn/.

PART THREE

Materials Needed: Grammar Rule Cards 1.4 and 1.5; green, red, and blue colored pencils.

Grammar

Review

✎ *Spelling List 14 – **The words in Spelling List 14 include nouns, adjectives, and verbs. Today we will sort them into their parts of speech.***

1. Find the nouns.

   What is a noun? A noun is a person, place, thing, or idea.

   We will begin by finding the nouns.
   As you look through spelling list 14, how will you identify the nouns? Look for persons, places, things, or ideas. See if the article "the" makes sense with the word. See if I can make the word plural.
   Write a red N next to each noun.
   Use each one in a sentence aloud.

Write the nouns on the board as they are identified. Words in parenthesis can be nouns or verbs. Based upon the ages of the students, decide if you will point that out or allow them to identify them solely as verbs.

child	(turn)	bird	(sail)
woman	flower	(hurt)	(search)
girl	(jump)	ear	

	Word	Practice Sentence	Say to Spell	# of Syllables	Markings
1.	**child**	*This is my child.*	chīld	1	ch<u>ī</u>ld
2.	**woman**	*I know that woman from work.*	wō mǎn	2	wō man
3.	**girl**	*The girl is a fast runner.*	gerl	1	g<u>ir</u>l
4.	**turn**	*Turn to page ten.*	tern	1	t<u>ur</u>n
5.	**old**	*How old are you?*	ōld	1	ōld
6.	**cold**	*It has been a cold winter.*	cōld	1	cōld
7.	**flower**	*The flower is beautiful.*	flow er	2	fl<u>ow</u> <u>er</u>
8.	**jump**	*The dogs jump over the fence.*	jŭmp	1	jump
9.	**bird**	*The birds are singing.*	berd	1	b<u>ir</u>d
10.	**hurt**	*He hurt his leg.*	hert	1	h<u>ur</u>t
11.	**ear**	*My ear hurts.*	ēr	1	<u>ear</u>
12.	**hear**	*I hear a drum pounding.*	hēr	1	h<u>ear</u>
13.	**thirteen**	*She is turning thirteen in June.*	ther tēn	2	th<u>ir</u>t<u>ee</u>n
14.	**sail**	*The boats sail at night.*	sāl	1	s<u>ai</u>l
15.	**search**	*We will search for the answer.*	serch	1	<u>sear</u>ch

Spelling Hints	Part of Speech	Vocabulary Development
Underline /ch/. Put a line over the /ī/. **8** I and O may say /ī/ and /ō/ before two consonants.	N	children, childlike, childlikeness, childbearing, childish, childishness, childless, childlessness, grandchild
Say to spell /wŏ mǎn/. Draw a line over the /ō/. **4** A E O U usually say their names at the end of the syllable.	N	women, womanhood, congresswoman, businesswoman, anchorwoman, womanly, womanliness, womanlike
Underline /er/.	N	girls, girlfriend, girlhood, girlish, girly, girlishness, schoolgirl
Underline /er/.	V, N	turned, turning, downturn, return, returnable, returning, turnoff, turnkey, turnstile, turntable, upturn
Draw a line above the /ō/. **8** I and O may say /ī/ and /ō/ when followed by two consonants.	Adj	older, oldest, oldie, oldish
Draw a line above the /ō/. **8** I and O may say /ī/ and /ō/ when followed by two consonants.	Adj	colder, coldest, colds
Underline /ow/. Underline /er/.	N, V	flowers, flowering, cauliflower, cornflower, flowery, flowerpot, mayflower, sunflower, wallflower
All first sounds. G may soften to /j/ before E, I, and Y. Here the /j/ sound is before a U therefore it must be spelled with a J.	V, N	jumper, jumped, jumping, jumpy, jumpiest
Underline /er/.	N	birds, bluebird, seabird, birdbath, birdhouse, birdseed, blackbird, lovebird, mockingbird, birdie, jaybird, jailbird, songbird
Underline the /er/.	V, N, Adj	hurting, hurtful, hurtfully, hurtfulness, unhurt
Underline the /ē/.	N	ears, earring, earache, eardrum, earful, earlobe, earmuff, earshot, earsplitting
Underline the /ē/. Notice that **hear** uses EA to spell the /ē/ like **ear**. An easy way to remember the correct spelling of hear is to think **"ears hear."**	V	hearing, heard
Underline /th/. Underline /er/. Underline /ē/.	Adj, N	thirteenth
Underline /ā/. Do not double the L. **30** We often double F, L, and S after a single vowel at the end of a base word. Occasionally other letters also are doubled.	V, N	sailor, sailed, sailing, assail, parasailing, sailboat, sailcloth, sailfish, sailplane, topsail
Underline /er/. Underline /ch/.	V, N	searched, searching searchable, researcher, researching, searchingly, searchlight, unsearchable

What is the plural of child? children

children

Why does the I say /ī/ in child? I and O may say /ī/ and /ō/ before two consonants.
Does I always say /ī/ before two consonants? no
What does I say in children? /ĭ/

What is the plural of woman? women
Just as we say to spell /wōmăn/ for spelling purposes, so we will say /wōmĕn/ to help us remember how to spell the plural form.

2. Find the verbs.

What is a verb? A verb shows action, links a description to the subject, or helps another verb.
To find a verb, ask the question: Can I _____?

Can I _____?

When you find a verb, write a green V by it in your workbook.
Can I child? no
Can I turn? yes...

turn	*hurt*	*sail*
jump	*hear*	*search*

3. Find the adjectives.

What is an adjective? An adjective modifies a noun or a pronoun. An adjective answers: What kind? How many? Which one? Whose?

To test if a word is an adjective ask: What kind?
Write a blue Adj. next to each word that is an adjective.

old	*cold*	*hurt*

Are there any adjectives that answer: How many? thirteen
Label thirteen with an Adj.

thirteen

Optional Spelling Cards

1. Dictate the words in Lesson 14 for the students to write on index cards. Ⓚ Ⓥ Ⓐ

2. Ask the students to color a green border around the verbs, a red border around the nouns, and a blue border around the adjectives. If a word can be used as more than one part of speech, color two borders. Ⓚ Ⓥ

Proper Nouns

What is a noun? A noun is the name of a person, place, thing or idea.
Today we will learn about two types of nouns.

Grammar Card 1.4	N
Common nouns name general people, places, things, and ideas.	

Grammar Card 1.5	N
Proper nouns name specific people, places, things, and ideas. Capitalize proper nouns.	

I will write some nouns on the board. Read them as I write them.

woman   park

child   restaurant

girl   book

town   hotel

These are common nouns.
A proper noun names a particular person, place, thing, or idea.
For example, woman can mean any woman, but Jennifer names a particular woman. When we write a proper noun, we capitalize the first letter.

woman   Jennifer

Child is a common noun. Name other children.

Write the names as children say them. Capitalize the first letter of each name.

child   Jacob Brown

Continue directing children to name other proper nouns while you list them on the board.

girl   Jill Baker, Morgan Evans,

town   Denver...

park   Grant Park...

restaurant   China Star...

book   Good Night Moon...

hotel   The March Inn

Notice that when you write a proper name of a person, both words are capitalized. In titles of books, the first word and all the important words are capitalized.

✎ *14.8 Proper Nouns – Write the first and last names for five people in your family (class).*

< Teacher Tip: *Capitalize words such as Mother, Father, Brother, Sister, Grandmother... when they are used in place of a person's name. Do not capitalize them when they follow an article adjective or a possessive pronoun adjective such as my, your, his, her...*

Titles of Respect

Often when we write people's names we will need to use a title of respect such as Mr. Johnson, Ms. Carter, Mrs. Verner, and Dr. Conners.

Rather than writing out the words Mister and Doctor, they are usually abbreviated.

I will write a word on the board. Tell me if you know how to write the abbreviation.

Mister	Mr.		Doctor	Dr.
	Mrs.			Ms.

There are two additional titles of respect that are commonly used. They only have an abbreviated form. Ms. is said "Miss." Ms. is a title of respect of a any woman - married or unmarried. Mrs. is said "Misses." Mrs. is a title of respect for a married woman.

What is the difference between Ms. and Mrs.? Mrs. means the woman is married. Ms. may be used for a married or an unmarried woman.

✎ *14.9 Titles of Respect – Write the abbreviations for the titles of respect in your workbook as I read them aloud: Mrs. Dr. Ms. Mr.*

Optional Grammar Practice

1. ✎ *14.10 Extra Practice: Reading –* Read the sentences in your workbook aloud. Underline the proper nouns. Ⓐ Ⓚ Ⓥ

2. ✎ *14.11 Extra Practice: Editing –* Complete the activity in the workbook. Find the mistakes in each sentence. Rewrite the sentence correctly on the lines below. The number of mistakes is noted beside each sentence. Ⓚ Ⓥ

3. Practice writing the first, middle, and last names of family members. Ⓚ Ⓥ

4. Review Grammar Cards 1-1.5; 1.7-1.8; 2-2.6; 3-3.2; 7, 9, 11.1.

Identifying Parts of Speech

✎ *14.12 Identifying Parts of Speech –* **Read the phrase in your workbook. I will write it on the board. Then you will answer questions to label the parts of speech. Label each part of speech in your workbook as I write it on the board.**

The old woman sells birds.

Who sells? woman, subject noun
What kind of woman? old, adjective
Which woman? the, article adjective
What is being said about the woman? woman sells, verb
Sells what? birds, direct object
Is there a direct object receiving the action of the verb? yes
Then what kind of verb is it? a transitive verb
Write a T next to the V to show the type of verb.

A   Adj   SN   TV   DO
The old woman sells birds.

The children jump.

Who jumps? children, subject noun
Which children? the, article adjective
What is being said about the children? children jump, verb
Is there a direct object receiving the action of the verb? no

A   SN   V
The children jump.

The girl hears birds.

Who hears? girl, subject noun
Which girl? the, article adjective
What is being said about the girl? girl hears, verb
What does the girl hear? birds, direct object
Is there a direct object receiving the action of the verb? yes
Then what kind of verb is it? a transitive verb
Write a T next to the V to show the type of verb.

A   SN   TV   DO
The girl hears birds.

The boy's ear hurts.

> ***What hurts?*** ear, subject noun
> ***What is being said about the ear?*** ear hurts, verb
> ***Whose ear?*** the boy's ear
> ***Boy's is acting as an adjective. However, notice that it is also a possessive noun. We will call this a possessive noun adjective. Write a PNA over it for Possessive Noun Adjective.***
> ***Which ear?*** the, article adjective
> ***Is there a direct object receiving the action of the verb?*** no

>   *A PNA SN   V*
> *The boy's ear hurts.*

Forming Possessive Noun Adjectives with Irregular Plurals

the birds wing　　　　*the sailors ship*　　　　*the childs turn*

What is wrong with these phrases? You need to add an apostrophe before the S to show that it is an adjective showing possession.

the bird's wing　　　　*the sailor's ship*　　　　*the child's turn*

> ***How many birds are we talking about?*** one
> ***How many sailors?*** one
> ***How many children?*** one

What if I wanted to talk about the wings on three birds. How would I need to change it? Move the apostrophe to after the S.

three birds' wings

Why? Because you would first form the plural by adding an -S and then add the apostrophe.
We do not say /bird-s-es/. We do not say the -S sound twice, therefore we do not write another -S.
What if I want to talk about ten sailors? *Move the apostrophe to after the S.*

ten sailors' ships

What about six children? **Change child to children and add an apostrophe followed by an S.**

six children's turns

woman

How do I form the plural possessive noun adjective for "woman?" Write women, apostrophe, S.

women's

✎ *14.13 Possessives –* **Complete the activity in your workbook.**

Answer Key: 1. a boy's ear 2. a girl's flowers 3. thirteen women's designs 4. three children's toys 5. ten teachers' books

Vocabulary Development

Compound Words

What is a compound word? A compound word is two words joined together to form another word.

What new words are formed with:

school + girl =

schoolgirl

school + girl = schoolgirl

book + seller = bookseller

✎ *14.14 Compound Words –* **Complete the activity in your workbook.**

Answer Key: 1. sailboat 2. seabird 3. birdbath 4. songbird 5. blackbird 6. flowerpot 7. sunflower 8. grandchild 9. congresswoman 10. watchdog

Dictation

✎ *14.15 Dictation –* Read each sentence twice. Ask the students to repeat it aloud, then write it in their workbooks.

1. The girls pick flowers.
2. The children jump the river.
3. Ella sails the boat.
4. Thirteen old men talk.
5. The hurt bird jumps.
6. Adam, Ethan, and Gavin search Grant Park.

Composition

We learn grammar to help us write better sentences. Knowing the parts of speech helps us to know if there is something wrong with a sentence and how to fix it. It also helps us to write more interesting sentences.

One way to write a more interesting sentence is to add adjectives that answer: what kind, which one, or how many.

The dogs bark.

To make this sentence more interesting, we could answer: What kind of dogs bark? for example, black

We could also ask: How many dogs bark? six

The six black dogs bark.

Which sentence is more interesting?   the one with adjectives describing dog

✎   *14.16 Composition – Read the sentences in your workbook. Add an adjective to describe the noun in bold.*

Lesson 15 — Assessment & Review

SPELLING ASSESSMENT

Materials Needed: red colored pencil.

1. ✎ *15.1 Assessment* – Dictate the sentences while the students write them in their workbooks.

   1. The thoughtful girls pick flowers.
   2. The child watches the hurt bird.
   3. The woman reads the book, starts the program, and teaches the children.
   4. The playful children shout, jump, and fight.
   5. Thirteen helpers remember the papers.
   6. The old dog follows the cat.
   7. The sisters eat good bread and drink cold milk.
   8. Grandmother opens the door, searches the yard, and finds the cat.
   9. Ears hear.
   10. The girls walk and talk.

2. Direct the students to read the sentences aloud while you write them on the board. Sound out each word and model the thought process. The students should mark corrections in red. Encourage the students to discuss what they missed. Create an atmosphere where it is acceptable to make errors. Model the attitude and strategies to move forward in practice.

3. Recheck the students' work. Note the words and concepts which need further practice.

4. Did the students:

   _____ *add an -S and -ES to make words plural?*
   _____ *add an -S and -ES to form the singular verb?*
   _____ *spell the suffix -ful with one L?*
   _____ *use TCH only after a single vowel which does not say its name?*
   _____ *spell long I and O correctly?*
   _____ *capitalize the first letter of the sentence?*
   _____ *put a period at the end of the sentence?*
   _____ *use a comma in a series?*

5. ✎ *15.2 Reading* – Ask the students to read the following words and phrases. Note the words they did not read fluently.

   1. The men agree.
   2. The child catches the bird and holds it.
   3. The cold sailors reach land.
   4. Grandfather coughs.
   5. The children design and draw toy cars.
   6. Asher pulls, pushes, and turns the knob.
   7. Parker starts and Taylor waits.
   8. Samantha enjoys swim meets.
   9. Hudson knows the signs.
   10. The loud sound destroys the song.
   11. Mother whispers a secret.

12. Father pounds the nail.

13. Touch the ball and pass it on.

14. Quinn wants and needs sleep.

15. The socks match.

16. School starts at three o'clock.

17. The students think.

6.   ✎   *15.3 Words to Practice* – Ask the students to read the words in the list and mark which ones they would like to practice further.

7.   Using the assessment and your knowledge as a teacher, identify words to dictate onto Spelling Word Cards.

1. ____ agree	21. ____ help	41. ____ search
2. ____ bird	22. ____ hold	42. ____ sell
3. ____ call	23. ____ hurt	43. ____ shout
4. ____ catch	24. ____ jump	44. ____ sign
5. ____ child	25. ____ know	45. ____ sing
6. ____ cold	26. ____ match	46. ____ sleep
7. ____ cough	27. ____ meet	47. ____ start
8. ____ design	28. ____ need	48. ____ talk
9. ____ destroy	29. ____ old	49. ____ teach
10. ____ draw	30. ____ open	50. ____ think
11. ____ drink	31. ____ pass	51. ____ thirteen
12. ____ ear	32. ____ pick	52. ____ throw
13. ____ eat	33. ____ play	53. ____ touch
14. ____ enjoy	34. ____ pound	54. ____ turn
15. ____ fight	35. ____ pull	55. ____ wait
16. ____ find	36. ____ push	56. ____ walk
17. ____ flower	37. ____ reach	57. ____ want
18. ____ follow	38. ____ read	58. ____ watch
19. ____ girl	39. ____ remember	59. ____ whisper
20. ____ hear	40. ____ sail	60. ____ woman

SPELLING WORD REVIEW

1. Dictate the words students missed onto Spelling Word Cards or index cards. Have the students highlight the part of the word that was difficult.

2. Choose from the review activities below or use another activity found in the *The Phonogram and Spelling Game Book*.

Optional Spelling Word Practice

1. Play Spelling Snap (*The Phonogram and Spelling Game Book*, 36).

2. Play Spelling Word Memory (*The Phonogram and Spelling Game Book*, 39).

3. Write the words with Sky Writing. Or play a guessing game using Sky Writing. One person "writes" the letter in the air, while another tries to "read" what was written. (*The Phonogram and Spelling Game Book*, 45)

OPTIONAL SPELLING RULE REVIEW

Materials Needed: Spelling Rule Cards 8, 22, 24, and 27; paper, pencil; whiteboard, marker, eraser; magnetic letters; Phonogram Game Cards.

Use the following mini-lessons to review as needed.

Spelling Rule 8

Spelling Rule	8
I and O may say /ī/ and /ō/ when followed by two consonants.	

1. Review the rule by reciting it and discussing the samples on the back of the card.

2. Write the words on the board. Have the students practice reading them.

bold	volt	hind	blink
poll	find	pint	link
bind	child	doll	milk
sign	sold	bonk	rich
cold	stroll	sock	brink
roll	kind	rock	drill
mind	mild	bill	print
wild	gold	dish	sling
told	both	hiss	stick

3. Choose words and direct the students to write them with magnetic letters.

4. Choose a word in the list. Say the word. Ask the students to write a list of the words that rhyme.

    - child, mild, wild

    - cold, bold, fold, hold, gold, old, scold, sold, told

    - bind, blind, find, hind, kind, mind, wind

    - poll, roll, toll

    - rock, cock, flock, lock, sock, stock, shock

    - blink, clink, drink, ink, mink, pink, rink, sink, think, wink

    - bill, chill, dill, fill, frill, gill, grill, hill, ill, kill, mill, pill, quill, shrill, sill, skill, spill, still, thrill, till, trill, twill, will

Spelling Rule 24

Spelling Rule	24
-Ful is a suffix written with one L when added to another syllable.	

1. Review the rule by reciting it and discussing the samples on the back of the card.

2. Write the words on the board. Have the students practice reading them aloud. As they read the words, have them identify the base word.

armful	cupful	painful	potful
bagful	glassful	pailful	pocketful
blissful	forgetful	mouthful	spoonful
basketful	joyful	lapful	teaspoonful
capful	lawful	needful	thoughtful

3. Direct the students to choose a word from the list and use it aloud in a sentence.

4. Direct students to illustrate the rule on a separate page. Students must use at least five sample words.

5. Dictate words from the list above while the students write them on a small white board. Encourage the students to consider the base word before adding the suffix -ful.

6. ✎ *15.4 Extra Practice: Adding the Suffix -Ful* – Complete the activity in the workbook.   Ⓥ Ⓐ Ⓚ

Spelling Rule 27

Spelling Rule	27
TCH is used only after a single vowel which does not say its name.	

1. Review the rule by reciting it and discussing the samples on the back of the card.

2. Read the following words aloud while the students write them on a small white board. The students get one point for spelling it correctly and one point for correctly explaining why to use CH or TCH. Play to 10 or 15 points. If needed, provide the students with clues for spelling the vowel sounds. Ⓚ Ⓐ Ⓥ

   - **TCH after a single vowel that does not say its name** – *stitch, hatch, latch, watch, patch, fetch, etch, crutch, twitch, clutch*

   - **CH after a consonant** – *lunch, hunch, porch, ranch, punch, brunch, French, torch, arch, birch, church, search*

   - **CH after a multi-letter vowel** – *pouch, touch, couch, ouch, beach, bleach, each, teach, reach, peach, leech, speech, poach, coach, roach*

3. Dictate the words below. Students should write them with magnetic letter tiles or the Phonogram Game Cards. Ⓐ Ⓚ Ⓥ

   - **_atch** - *batch, catch, hatch, latch, scratch, swatch*

   - **_etch** - *etch, stretch, wretch*

   - **_itch** - *itch, ditch, hitch, glitch, pitch, snitch, switch, witch*

   - **_otch** - *botch, scotch, splotch*

   - **_utch** - *clutch, crutch, Dutch, hutch*

Spelling Rule 22

Spelling Rule	22
To make a verb 3rd person singular, add the ending -S, unless the word hisses or changes, then add -ES. Only four verbs are irregular.	

1. Review the rule by reciting it and discussing the samples on the back of the card.

2. Practice writing verbs with the correct ending on the board. Write each sentence with a blank. Direct the students to fill in the correct ending if one is needed.

   The woman design____ books.

   The sisters play____ games.

   The boy throw____ the ball.

   The man watch____ the bird.

   The authors laugh____ .

3. ✎ *15.5 Extra Practice: Subject-Verb Agreement* – Complete the activity in the workbook. Ⓥ Ⓐ Ⓚ

OPTIONAL GRAMMAR REVIEW

Materials Needed: Grammar Rule Cards 2.5, 2.6, 9, and 11.1.

Re-teach or practice the rules as needed using the activities below.

Sentences

Grammar Card 9	Sent
A sentence must have a capital letter, subject, verb, complete thought, and an end mark.	

1. Review the rule by reciting it and discussing the samples on the back of the card.

2. Practice writing the capital letters.

3. ✎ *15.6 Extra Practice: Sentences* – Rewrite the sentences in the workbook with a capital letter and end mark.

4. ✎ *15.7 Extra Practice: Sentences and Fragments* – Complete the activity in the workbook.

Possessives

Grammar Card 2.5	PNA
To turn a noun into a singular possessive noun adjective, add an apostrophe followed by an S.	

Grammar Card 2.6	PNA
To turn a noun into a plural possessive noun adjective, add an S to make the noun plural and then add an apostrophe. If the noun has an irregular plural use an apostrophe followed by an S.	

1. Review the rule by reciting it and discussing the samples on the back of the card.

2. Discuss the meaning of the following phrases:

   the teacher's classes

   the helper's paper

   the girl's flowers

   Father's coats

Compare and contrast these to the plural possessive forms.

the teacher's classes	*the teachers' classes*
the helper's paper	*the helpers' papers*
the girl's flowers	*the girls' flower*
Father's coats	*Fathers' coats*

3. Direct the students to illustrate each of the eight phrases above and label them with the correct possessive form.

4. ✎ *15.8 Extra Practice: Possessives* – Complete the review activity in the workbook.

Commas in a Series

> **Grammar Card 11.1**   *Comma Rule 1*
>
> **Use commas to separate the words in a series of three or more.**

1. Review the rule by reciting it and discussing the samples on the back of the card.

2. Demonstrate on the board where to put a comma.

   A car, a truck, and a train turn.

   Mother wants bread, milk, and eggs.

   The boys run, jump, and play.

   The helpers design cards, call members, and sign letters.

3. Dictate the following sentences. Students may write them on paper or white boards.

   • The mother, father, and daughter play.

   • Sister watches cats, dogs, and ducks.

   • The boys sing, shout, and play.

   • The men drink water, read the paper, and whisper.

4. ✎ *15.9 Commas in a Series* – Complete the review activity in the workbook.

OPTIONAL PHONOGRAM ASSESSMENT & REVIEW

Phonograms

✎ *15.10 Extra Practice: Phonogram Quiz* – Dictate the following phonograms.

1. l	15. x	29. u	43. qu
2. th	16. igh	30. oi	44. i
3. a	17. c	31. or	45. ur
4. oa	18. ough	32. g	46. r
5. w	19. ea	33. er	47. j
6. oe	20. n	34. y	48. ear
7. ai	21. d	35. z	49. aw
8. ck	22. wh	36. ir	50. s
9. m	23. sh	37. au	51. ee
10. ay	24. e	38. v	52. oy
11. ng	25. kn	39. gn	53. ch
12. b	26. o	40. p	54. t
13. oo	27. ow	41. augh	55. ou
14. ar	28. tch	42. h	56. k

Optional Phonogram Practice

Practice the phonograms as needed using the following game suggestions or choose other games from *The Phonogram and Spelling Game Book*.

1. Play Speed using the Phonogram Game Cards (*The Phonogram and Spelling Game Book*, 11).

2. Play Snatch the Match (*The Phonogram and Spelling Game Book*, 24).

3. ✎ *15.11 Extra Practice: Phonogram Tic-Tac-Toe* – (*The Phonogram and Spelling Game Book*, 26).

Lesson 16

Phonograms:	ed, ew
Exploring Sounds:	Hard and Soft C and G
Spelling Rules:	1, 2, 19, 20
Grammar:	Past Tense Verbs

PART ONE

Materials Needed: Phonogram flash cards from previous lessons plus ew , ed ; Spelling Rule Cards 1 and 2; Phonogram Game Cards, two sets per group of two-four students; red pencil or highlighter.

Phonograms

New Phonogram — *ew, ed*

Show ew . */oo - ū/*

Show ed . */ed -d -t/*

Review

1. Drill the phonograms with flashcards.

2. 🖎 *16.1 Writing the Phonograms* – Write each new phonogram five times while saying the sounds aloud.

3. 🖎 *16.2 Phonogram Quiz* – Dictate the following phonograms. For extra practice, have the students read them back. Write the correct answers on the board as the students check their answers.

    1. ir
    2. ou   *toe*
    3. oe *ō ōō shoe end*
    4. wh
    5. kn

    6. ough
    7. oi *not end*
    8. au *ä author not end*
    9. augh *ä ăf taught laugh*
    10. gn

    11. ur *er hurts*
    12. oo *food took floor / ōō u ō*
    13. ear *er search*
    14. aw *ä saw*
    15. tch

    16. ow *plow snow ow - ō*
    17. oa *ō coat not end*
    18. igh *ī end of base or before T*
    19. ng *n sign begin or end*
    20. ea *ē ĕ ā*

4. Play Go Fish (*The Phonogram and Spelling Game Book*, 9).

Exploring Sounds

The Hard and Soft Sounds of C and G

What are the single-letter vowels? A, E, I, O, U, and sometimes Y.

✎ *16.3 Single-Letter vowels –* **Write the single-letter vowels in your workbook.**

✎ *16.4 Single-Letter consonants –* **Write the single-letter consonants in alphabetical order in your workbook.**
Which single-letter consonants make more than one sound? C, G, S, Y
Circle them with a red pencil.
Today we will focus on C and G.

What are the sounds of C? /k-s/
Where is the /k/ sound formed in the mouth? in the back
How would you describe the sound /k/? harsh, short, bursting
Now say the /s/ sound. Where is it formed? front
How would you describe the /s/ sound? soft, hissing, sustained
The first sound /k/ is called the hard sound. The second sound /s/ is called the soft sound.

Now say /g/. Where is it formed in the mouth? in the back
Like which sound of C? /k/
How would you describe the sound /g/? strong, nasal, short, bursting
Say the second sound of G /j/. Where is it formed in the mouth? in the front
Like what sound of C? /s/
The first sound of G /g/ is called the hard sound. The second sound /j/ is called the soft sound.

We will now learn a rule to determine when C and G will say their hard and soft sounds.

Spelling Rules

C Softens to /s/ Before an E, I, or Y

What are the two sounds of C? /k-s/

✎ *16.5 C says /k/ –* **Read the first group of words in your workbook. Hint: C will say /k/.**

cat	cop	cub	act
cap	cut	clap	picnic

What did C say in these words? /k/

✎ *16.6 C Softens to /s/ –* **Read the second group of words in your workbook. Hint: C will say /s/.**

cent	cell	cinder	cinnamon
center	cinch	citrus	cylinder

What sound do you hear in each of these words? /s/
Study the words. When does C say /s/? C softens to /s/ before an E, I, or Y.

Highlight the E, I and Y in your workbook.

Study the words. When does C say /k/? before A, O, U; before a consonant; at the end of the word

This leads us to a new rule:

Spelling Rule	1
C always softens to /s/ when followed by E, I or Y. **Otherwise C says /k/.**	

G may soften to /j/ before an E, I, or Y

✎ *16.7 G says /g/ – **Read the first group of words in your workbook. Hint: G will say /g/.***

gap	gum	green	bug
got	glad	big	rag

What sound does G say in these words? /g/

✎ *16.8 G Softens to /j/ – **Read the second group of words in your workbook. Hint: G will say /j/.***

gem	ginger	gym
general	margin	gymnast

Highlight the E, I and Y in your workbook.
What sound does G say in these words? /j/
Study the words. When does G say /j/? before an E, I, or Y
When does it say /g/? before an A, O, U; before a consonant; at the end of the word

✎ *16.9 G Says /g/ – **I will read the third group of words in your workbook. When you notice a problem, raise your hand.***

get	gift	argyle

G also says its first sound /g/ before E, I, or Y.

Highlight the E, I and Y in your workbook.
Our rule for G will be different.

Say the rule. Emphasize *may.*

Spelling Rule　　　　　　　　　　　　　　　　　　　　　　　　　2

G may soften to /j/ only when followed by E, I or Y.

Otherwise G says /g/.

Does G always soften to /j/ before an E, I or Y? No, it may.
However, when is the only time that G will say /j/? G will only say /j/ before an E, I, or Y. Otherwise it always says /g/.

Optional Spelling Rule Practice

1. Create a reference page to remember these rules. Include sample words. ©Ⓥ

2. Ask the students to teach this to another student or to a parent. ©ⓋⒶⓀ

3. Quickly review rules 1-4, 8-11, 21-22, 24, 26-28, and 30 using the Spelling Rule Cards. ⒶⓋ

4. Play Read That Word. Write a word on the board. Direct the students to read the word. Award one point for reading it correctly the first time. Award one point for identifying why the C or G say their hard or soft sounds. ⒶⓀⓋ

   - C softens to /s/ before an E – *cent, cell, cedar, cellar, censor*

   - C softens to /s/ before an I – *cinder, cinema, civic, civil, citrus, circus*

   - C softens to /s/ before a Y – *cylinder, cynic, cymbal*

   - C says /k/ before an A, O, U – *cat, call, calm, cart, cast, cash, cot, cob, cold, cord, cool, corn, cow, cost, cub, cuff, curb, curl, cut*

   - C says /k/ before a consonant – *clap, clack, clash, clam, class, claw, clear, crush, crab, crack, cram, crawl, creak, cream, crater*

   - C says /k/ at the end of the word – *arc, civic, basic, public, tonic, attic, topic*

   - G may soften to /j/ before an E – *gem, gel, general, generous, German, germ, (gear, get, gecko)*

   - G may soften to /j/ before an I - *giant, ginger, (gift, girl)*

   - G may soften to /j/ before a Y – *gym*

   - G says /g/ before A, O, U – *gap, gas, gash, gasp, gallon, gain, go, got, goat, goal, gut, gun, gull, gum*

   - G says /g/ before a consonant – *glad, glass, gleam, glint, gloss, greed, grow, grip, grant, grass, grunt, grill*

   - G says /g/ at the end of the word – *big, bag, bug, egg, wig, jog, peg, mug, frog, brag, twig*

PART TWO

Using Spelling List 16 on pages 188-189, dictate each word following the steps included on pages Intro 42 - Intro 46.

Tips for Spelling List 16

One of the difficulties with English spelling is that vowels in unaccented syllables often are pronounced as the schwa sound /ə/. In order to help the students create an auditory picture of the word, it is helpful to exaggerate the unaccented vowel.

To learn more about vowels in unaccented syllables and aiding the students in creating an auditory picture of words, see *Uncovering the Logic of English*, 121-128.

Attend

Exaggerate the vowel so that /ət tĕnd/ sounds like /ăt tĕnd/.

Lesson

Exaggerate the vowel so that /lĕs sə n/ sounds like /lĕs sŏn/.

Wonderful

Exaggerate the vowel so that /wən der fŭl/ sounds like /wŏn der fŭl/.

Excellent

Exaggerate the vowel so that /ĕx sĕl lənt/ sounds like /ĕx sĕl lĕnt/.

	Word	Practice Sentence	Say to Spell	# of Syllables	Markings
1.	**cents**	*The pencils cost fifty cents.*	sĕnts	1	cents
2.	**attend**	*You need to attend practice every day.*	ăt tĕnd	2	at tend
3.	**grow**	*He will grow to be at least six feet tall.*	grō	1	gr<u>ow</u>²
4.	**get**	*We will get a new car next week.*	gĕt	1	get
5.	**own**	*They own the store.*	ōn	1	<u>ow</u>n²
6.	**see**	*Do you see the squirrel?*	sē	1	<u>see</u>
7.	**pour**	*I will pour the drinks.*	pōr	1	p<u>ou</u>r²
8.	**water**	*Water the flowers everyday.*	wä ter	2	wä t<u>er</u>
9.	**lesson**	*Your music lesson is at six o'clock.*	lĕs sŏn	2	les son
10.	**wonderful**	*We had a wonderful time together.*	wŏn der fŭl	3	won d<u>er</u> ful
11.	**new**	*Is that a new sweater?*	noo	1	<u>new</u>
12.	**germs**	*Germs cause disease.*	jerms	1	g<u>er</u>ms
13.	**excellent**	*It is an excellent beach.*	ĕx sĕl lĕnt	3	ex cel lent
14.	**gift**	*We will buy her a gift.*	gĭft	1	gift
15.	**shoe**	*My left shoe has a hole in it.*	shoo	1	<u>shoe</u>²

Spelling Hints	Part of Speech	Vocabulary Development
1 C softens to /s/ when followed by an E, I or Y.	N	cent, centennial, centimeter, centigram
Say to spell /ăt tĕnd/. All first sounds.	V	attended, attending, attendance, attendant, attendee, nonattendance, unattended
Underline /ō/ and put a 2 over it. /ow-ō/ said its second sound.	V	grew, growing, growth, grown, grower, ingrown, outgrown, regrown, undergrowth, overgrowth, winegrower
All first sounds.	V	got, gotten, getting, getaway
Underline the /ō/ and put a 2 over it. /ow-ō/ said its second sound.	V	owned, owner, owning, ownership
Underline /ē/.	V	saw, seen, sees, oversee, overseen, seeable, unforeseen, foreseen, unforeseeable, sightseeing
Underline the /ou-ō-oo-ü/. Put a 2 over it. /ou-ō-oo-ü/ said its second sound /ō/.	V	poured, pouring, downpour, outpouring, pourable
Put two dots over the /ä/. /ă-ā-ä/ often says /ä/ after a W. Underline the /er/.	N, V, Adj	watered, watering, floodwater, headwater, seawater, rainwater, underwater, waterfall, waterlogged, waterproofed, waterspout
Say to spell: /lĕs sŏn/. All first sounds.	N	lessons
Say to spell: /wŏn der fŭl/. Underline /er/. What is the root word of wonderful? Wonder. What suffix was added? -ful. **24** -Ful is a suffix written with one L when added to another syllable.	Adj	wonderfully, wonderfulness
Underline /oo/.	Adj	news, newspaper, newborn, newly, newfound, newlywed, newscast, newscaster, newsworthy, newsroom
Underline /er/. **2** G may soften to /j/ when followed by an E, I or Y.	N	germ, germicide, germproof
Say to spell: /ĕx sĕl lĕnt/. **1** C softens to /s/ when followed by an E, I or Y.	Adj	excellently, excellency
All first sounds.	N	gifts, gifted, giftedness, giftedly, giftwrap
Underline /sh/. Underline /oo/. Put a 2 over the /oo/. /ō-oo/ said its second sound /oo/.	N, V	shoes, horseshoe, shoestring, snowshoes, shoelace, shoemaker

PART THREE

Materials Needed: Spelling Rule Cards 19, 20; green, red, and blue colored pencils; marker piece, die.

Grammar

Review

What is a noun? A noun is the name of a person, place, thing, or idea.

What is an adjective? Adjectives modify nouns and pronouns. Adjectives answer: What kind? How many? Which one? Whose?

What is an article? A, An, The. Tiny article adjectives that mark nouns and answer the question: Which?

Name the parts of a sentence. A sentence must have a capital letter, subject, verb, complete thought, and an end mark.

What is a verb? A verb shows action, links a description to the subject, or helps another verb.

What are two types of verbs we have studied so far? action verbs and transitive verbs

What are two noun jobs we have studied so far? subject noun and direct object

✎ *Spelling List 16 – Identify the parts of speech of each of the words in List 16. Mark the nouns with a red N, the verbs with a green V, and the adjectives with a blue Adj.*

Optional Spelling Cards

1. Dictate the words in Lesson 16 for the students to write on index cards. Ⓐ Ⓚ Ⓥ

2. Color a green border around the verbs, a red border around the nouns, and a blue border around the adjectives. Ⓚ Ⓥ

Past Tense

The child needs a drink.

In this sentence the child needs it now.
How would we change the sentence if this happened yesterday? The child needed a drink.
What did we add to need to make it needed? /ĕd/

The child need__ed__ a drink.

The boys start.

Today, the boys start. Yesterday the boys ____? started
What did we add? ed

The boys start__ed__.

In English the verb indicates the time when something happened. Is it happening now, did it happen in the past, or will it be in the future? Often, it is the ending of the verb that tells us if the action occurred now or in the past.

This leads to the rule:

Spelling Rule	19

To make a verb past tense, add the ending ED unless it is an irregular verb.

The Phonogram ED

Show the phonogram ed .

What does this phonogram say? /ĕd-d-t/
The phonogram /ĕd-d-t/ is the past tense ending. To make a verb past tense we add the ending ED, unless it is an irregular verb.
Like most modern languages, English has quite a few irregular verbs. These verbs show the past tense by changing in some other way.
Now we have a mystery to solve. When will ED say each of its sounds?
We will use this chart to discover the rule.

Write the following headers on the board:

/ĕd/	/d/	/t/	Irregular

I will say a word. You say the past tense. Then decide if the ed said /ĕd/, /d/, or /t/ or if it is an irregular verb. Irregular verbs do not use the suffix -ED but change in some other way to become past tense.

✎ *16.10 Past Tense –* **Write the past tense verbs in the correct column in your workbook as I say them and write them on the board.**
Start. Started. ED said /ĕd/.
Need. Needed. ED said /ĕd/.
Sign. Signed. ED said /d/.
Pick. Picked. ED said /t/.
Own. Owned. ED said /d/.
See. Saw. Irregular verb.
Shout. Shouted. ED said /ĕd/.
Help. Helped. ED said /t/.
Jump. Jumped. ED said /t/.
Sell. Sold. Irregular verb.
Water. Watered. ED said /d/.

Pour. Poured. ED said /d/.
Wait. Waited. ED said /ĕd/.
Search. Searched. ED said /t/.
Get. Got. Irregular verb.
Grow. Grew. Irregular verb.
Attend. Attended. ED said /ĕd/.

/ĕd/	/d/	/t/	Irregular
start ed	signed	picked	saw
need ed	owned	helped	sold
shout ed	watered	jumped	got
wait ed	poured	searched	grew
at tend ed			

Do you notice a pattern with the words that say /ĕd/? All the base words end in /d/ or /t/.
Could you say "start(d)" without adding the /ĕ/ sound? no
Your tongue would either trip over the t-d or d-d or you would not be able to hear it.
How many syllables is the word start? one
How about started? two
How many syllables in need? one
Needed? two

Point to the second column /d/.

How many syllables is the word sign? one
How about signed? one
How many syllables in own? one
Owned? one

Point to the third column /t/.

How many syllables is the word pick? one
How about picked? one
How many syllables in help? one
Helped? one

Say /d/ and /t/. How are they different? Touch your throat as you say them. /d/ is voiced. /t/ is unvoiced.
Do you notice a pattern with the words where ED says /d/ and /t/?
Hint: Look at the last sound. When a word ends in a voiced sound it says the voiced /d/. When it ends in an unvoiced sound it says the unvoiced /t/.

This leads to the spelling rule:

Spelling Rule	20
ED Past tense ending forms another syllable when the base word ends in /d/ or /t/. Otherwise, ED says /d/ or /t/.	

Optional Past Tense Verbs

1. ✎ *16.11 Extra Practice: Past Tense Sentences* – Rewrite each sentence in the past tense. Ⓐ Ⓚ Ⓥ

2. ✎ *16.12 Extra Practice: Irregular Past Tense* – Complete each sentence using the correct irregular past tense verb. Ⓐ Ⓚ Ⓥ

3. Say a verb. Ask the students to call out the past tense. *grow - grew, get - got, see - saw, agree - agreed, catch - caught, draw- drew, drink - drank, eat - ate, fight - fought, find - found, hear - heard, hold - held, know - knew, meet - met, read - read, sell - sold, sing - sang, sleep - slept, teach - taught, think - thought, throw- threw.* Ⓐ

4. ✎ *16.13: Extra Practice: Irregular Past Tense Game* – Provide each student with a game piece and die. The first student rolls the die and advances the number of spaces shown. As he passes each verb, he must read it aloud and state the past tense form. If the student misses one, he must remain on that space until the next turn. If a 3 is rolled, he must go back to start. Optional: The students are required to say a sentence using the past tense verb. Ⓐ Ⓚ Ⓥ

5. ✎ *16.14: Extra Practice: Irregular Past Tense* – Write the irregular past tense for each of the verbs. *grow - grew, get - got, see - saw, catch - caught, draw - drew, drink - drank, fight - fought, find - found, hear - heard, hold - held, know - knew, meet - met, read - read* Ⓚ Ⓥ

6. Past Tense Matching Game – Dictate verbs onto index cards. Direct the students to make an index card for each of the past tense forms as well. Play a memory game using the cards. Ⓐ Ⓚ Ⓥ

Identifying Parts of Speech

✎ *16.15 Identifying Parts of Speech* – **Read the phrase in your workbook. I will write it on the board. Then you will answer questions to label the parts of speech. Label each part of speech in your workbook as I write it on the board.**

Grandmother watered the flowers.

Who watered? Grandmother, subject noun
What is being said about grandmother? grandmother watered, verb
What did grandmother water? flowers, direct object
Which flowers? the, article adjective
Is there a direct object receiving the action of the verb? yes
Then what kind of verb is it? a transitive verb
Write a T next to the V to show the type of verb.

SN   TV   A   DO
Grandmother watered the flowers.

Anna's father saw a wonderful program.

Who saw? father, subject noun
Whose father? Anna's, possessive noun adjective
What is being said about father? father saw, verb
What did father see? program, direct object
What kind of program? wonderful, adjective
Which program? a, article adjective
Is there a direct object receiving the action of the verb? yes
Then what kind of verb is it? a transitive verb
Write a T next to the V to show the type of verb.

PNA SN   TV   A   Adj   DO
Anna's father saw a wonderful program.

Rebecca got a new winter coat and new shoes.

Who got? Rebecca, subject noun
What is being said about Rebecca? Rebecca got, verb
What did Rebecca get? coat, direct object
What kind of coat? new, adjective
What kind of coat? winter, adjective
What else did Rebecca get? shoes, direct object
What kind of shoes? new, adjective
What is the word "and"? conjunction
Is there a direct object receiving the action of the verb? yes
Then what kind of verb is it? a transitive verb
Write a T next to the V to show the type of verb.

SN   TV   A Adj Adj   DO   C   Adj DO
Rebecca got a new winter coat and new shoes.

Dictation

✎ *16.17 Dictation* – Read each sentence twice. Ask the students to repeat it aloud, then write it in their workbooks.

1. The children poured the water.
2. Ella got new shoes.
3. The author signed the paper.

4. The teachers attended the program.
5. Mother grew wonderful flowers.
6. The man owned an excellent boat.

Composition

Read each verb in List 16 aloud. Then use it in the past tense in a sentence.

✎ *16.18 Composition – Using the words in your workbook form sentences which include a subject, past tense verb, and direct object.*

Vocabulary Development

The Prefix un-

What is a prefix? a letter or letters added to the beginning of a word

un + opened =

What new word is formed if we add the prefix UN- to the word opened? unopened

un + opened = unopened

How is an unopened package different from an opened one? They are the opposite. An unopened package is not opened.
What is the root word of unopened? open
What prefix did we add? un
What suffix did we add? ed
Did we use the past or present tense form of the verb? past

own

What is the past tense of own? owned

un + owned

What new word is formed when the prefix UN- is added to owned? unowned

un + owned = unowned

✎ *16.19 The Prefix UN- –* **Complete the activity in your workbook.**

Answer Key: 1. unattended 2. unknown 3. unsigned 4. unmatched 5. unowned 6. uncaught 7. untaught 8. untouched 9. unneeded 10. unheard

Lesson 17

Phonograms:	ui
Exploring Sounds:	Long /ū/
Spelling Rules:	12.1, 13
Grammar:	Quotations

PART ONE

Materials Needed: Phonogram Flash Cards from previous lessons, ui and u ; Spelling Rule Cards 12.1; 2-3 Sets of 10-15 Phonogram Game Cards, 2 Wild Cards, 2 Draw Two Cards, 2 Reverse Cards.

Phonograms

New Phonogram — *ui*

Show ui . **/oo/**

> *May we use this /oo/ at the end of English words?* no
> *Why not?* English words do not end in I, U, V, or J.
> *UI is not a common spelling of the sound /oo/. It is found in only twelve base words.*

✎ *17.1 The Phonogram UI –* **Read the five words listed in your workbook. These are the most common. Underline the /oo/.**

fruit   suit   pursuit   recruit

> **Spelling Journal**   Ⓐ Ⓚ Ⓥ
>
> Enter words spelled with UI.

Review

1. Drill the phonogram sounds with flashcards.

2.   ✎   *17.2 Writing the Phonograms* – Write the new phonogram five times while saying the sound aloud.

3.   ✎   *17.3 Phonogram Practice* – Dictate the following phonograms. For extra practice, have the students read them back. Write the correct answers on the board as the students check their answers.

1. ed	6. ui	11. ur	16. oa
2. ew	7. igh	12. aw	17. ough
3. tch	8. au	13. ear	18. ea
4. augh	9. ir	14. ow	19. gn
5. ou	10. oo	15. kn	20. oe

4.   Play Last One (*The Phonogram and Spelling Game Book,* 9).

Spelling Rule

The Vowel Sound Changes Because of the E

There are nine reasons for a word to have a silent final E. Today we will learn the most common reason. This reason describes only half of words with a silent final E.

✎   *17.4 The Vowel Sound Changes Because of the E –* **Write the word I say in the first column of your workbook.**

cap

Does A say its long or short sound in cap? short
In the second column rewrite the word and add a silent final E. The silent final E makes the vowel sound long.
Read the new word. cape

cap   cape

The vowel sound changes from short to long. This is the first reason for a silent final E. Each time we have a silent final E in our spelling list, we will decide why the E is needed and mark it.

When the silent E makes the vowel long, put a line over the vowel to show that it is long and underline the E twice to show that it is silent. A double underline means a letter is silent.

cap   cāp̲e̲

Cap turning into cape illustrates the rule.

Spelling Rule	12.1
The vowel says its name because of the E.	

In the first column under cap write rip.
Does I say its long or short sound in rip? short
In the second column rewrite rip and add a silent final E.
What does it say now? ripe
Why does the I now say its long sound /ī/? The vowel sound changes because of the E.
How do we mark it? Put a line over the I to show that it is long and underline the E twice to show that it is silent.

rip   rīpe̲̲

Continue with the additional words:

not   nōte̲̲

cut   cūte̲̲

pet *   Pete̲̲ *

*If desired substitute *them* and *theme*.

The next two words do not have a matched pair. I will help you to write them correctly.
Typical. That is a typical response for him. Typical. /tĭp-ĭ-căl/
How many syllables in typical? three
Repeat the syllables. tĭp-ĭ-căl
Sound out the first syllable typ. t-ĭ-p
Use /y-ĭ-ī-ē/.
Second syllable. ĭ
Use /ĭ-ī-ē-y/.
Third syllable. c-ă-l
Use /k-s/.
Repeat the syllables to me. tĭp ĭ căl
Write typical.

Type. Type the letters on the computer. Type.
How many syllables in type? one
Sound it out. tīp
Use /y-ĭ-ī-ē/.
What do you think you will add to make the Y say its long vowel sound /ī/? a silent final E
Write type.

typical   type̲̲

What are the four sounds of Y? /y-ĭ-ī-ē/
Which sound is a consonant sound? /y/
Which sounds are vowel sounds? /ĭ-ī-ē/

What does Y say in typical? /ĭ/
Is this a long or short vowel sound? short
What does Y say in type? /ī/
Is this the long or short vowel sound? long
Why does Y say its long /ī/ sound in type? Because the vowel sound changes because of the E.

Optional Spelling Rule Practice

1. Create a reference page to remember this rule. Include sample words. ⓒⓋ

2. Ask the students to teach this to another student or to a parent. ⓒⓋⒶⓀ

3. Quickly review rules 1-4, 8-12.1, 19-22, 24, 26-28, 30 using the Spelling Rule Cards. ⒶⓋ

4. ✎ *17.5 Extra Practice: Word Search* – Dictate the following words for the students to write on the lines below the Word Search Grid: *plate, cute, date, hope, hive, plane, stone, nose, crate, ripe, cape, late, rate, tote, vote*. Direct the students to write the words, one letter per square, in the Word Search Grid. Words may go across, up, and down. Fill in the blank spaces with random letters. Have the students exchange word search puzzles and find one another's words. ⓋⒶⓀ

5. Direct the students to write words with a silent final E and illustrate them. ⓒⓋ

   - *babe, bake, bale, base, cage, cake, came, cane, care, cave, case, dare, date, ease, fade, fake, fame, game, gate, gave, grape, kale, lake, lame, lane, late, pale, pave, rage, rake, rate, rave, sale, safe, same, save, tame, vase, wade, wake, blame, blaze, drape, flake, flame, frame, glaze, grade, grave, plane, plate, quake, scale, stake, state, trade, whale, sphere, bike, bite, dike, fine, fire, five, hide, hike, hive, kite, life, lime, mile, mine, mite, pike, pile, pine, pipe, ride, site, size, tile, time, vine, wife, wipe, glide, knife, stripe, trike, twine, whine, code, coke, cone, cove, hole, hose, lone, mole, nose, note, poke, robe, role, rope, rose, rote, rove, tone, tote, vote, wove, zone, choke, chore, close, drove, prone, quote, scone, scope, shore, slope, smoke, snore, spoke, stole, store, stove, whole, wrote, cube, cute, dude, duke, fume, huge, mule, pure, rude, rule, tune, brute, fluke, byte, hype, style, type*.

6. Write silent final E words using magnetic tiles. Read the words with and without the E. ⓋⒶⓀ

Exploring Sounds

The Long /ū/ Sound

Show the phonogram ⬚u⬚. /ŭ-ū-oo-ü/

> ***What does this phonogram say?*** /ŭ-ū-oo-ü/
> ***What kind of vowel sound is /ŭ/?*** short
> ***How do we mark the short sound?*** Put a breve, or curved line, over it.

ŭ

> ***What kind of vowel sound is /ū/?*** long
> ***How do we mark the long sound?*** Write a straight line over it.

ŭ   ū

The third sound that U makes is /oo/.

>*Say /ū/ and then /oo/. What do you notice?* They both have the /oo/ sound. But the long sound starts with a /y/.

>*In many words the long /ū/ sound drops the /y/ and sounds like /oo/. These are both long sounds. We will mark the third sound /oo/ as a long sound with a line over it.*

ŭ   ū   ū

>*What is the fourth sound that U makes?* /ü/
>*How do we mark it?* Put two dots over it.

ŭ   ū   ū   ü

>*Name two places in the word that U says its long sound.* At the end of the syllable and before a silent final E.

>*We will now practice words where U says one of its long sounds /ū/ or /oo/.*

✎ *17.6 The Long /ū/ Sound – I will read a word. Before you write the word, count the syllables. Decide the reason for U saying its long sound.*
Listen to hear if the vowel is at the end of the syllable or in the middle of the syllable.
If the word follows the rule, "A E O U usually say their names at the end of the syllable," write it in the first column. If it follows the rule, "The vowel says its name because of the E," write it in the second column.

pure, student, flute, tuna, cute, human, rule, use, unit

At the End of the Syllable	Silent final E
stu dent	pure
tu na	flute
hu man	cute
u nit	rule
	use

Spelling Journal   ⒶⓀⓋ

Enter words spelled with __U and U_E.

PART TWO

Using Spelling List 17 on pages 204-205, dictate each word following the steps included on pages Intro 42 - Intro 46.

Tips for Spelling List 17

Celebrate

One of the difficulties with English spelling is that vowels in unaccented syllables often are pronounced as the schwa sound /ə/. In order to help the students create an auditory picture of the word, it is helpful to exaggerate the unaccented vowel.

Exaggerate the vowel so that /sĕl ə brāt/ sounds like /sĕl ē brāt/.

To learn more about vowels in unaccented syllables and aiding students in creating an auditory picture of words, see *Uncovering the Logic of English,* 121-128.

Say -Says - Said

Clearly each of these words is related in meaning and spelling. Both *say* and *says* use the AY phonogram. In the past tense form, *said,* the AY changes to the closely related AI phonogram.

Due to pronunciation shifts over time, the pronunciation of *says* and *said* are no longer clearly reflected in their spellings. Therefore, it is vital to show students that they have a logical relationship to one another and that the spellings are not completely random. Many auditory students also benefit from exaggerating the pronunciation of the long /ā/ sound in both *say* and *said* to create an auditory picture for spelling purposes.

PART THREE

Materials Needed: Grammar Rule Cards 11.2, 12.3 13.1, 13.2; Spelling Rule Card 13; red, blue, and green colored pencils.

Grammar

Review

What is a noun?   A noun is the name of a person, place, thing, or idea.
What is an adjective?   Adjectives modify nouns and pronouns. Adjectives answer: What kind? How many? Which one? Whose?
What is an article?   A, An, The. Tiny article adjectives that mark nouns and answer the question: Which?
Name the parts of a sentence.   A sentence must have a capital letter, subject, verb, complete thought, and an end mark.
What is a verb?   A verb shows action, links a description to the subject, or helps another verb.
What are two types of verbs we have studied so far?   action verbs and transitive verbs
What are two noun jobs we have studied so far?   subject noun and direct object

✎ *Spelling List 17 –* **Identify the parts of speech of each of the words in List 17. Mark the nouns with a red N, the verbs with a green V, and the adjectives with a blue Adj.**

Optional Spelling Cards

1.   Dictate the words in Lesson 17 for the students to write on index cards.   Ⓐ Ⓚ Ⓥ

2.   Color a green border around the verbs, a red border around the nouns, and a blue border around the adjectives.   Ⓚ Ⓥ

Review Past Tense Verbs

✎ *Spelling List 17 –* **The first 11 words can be used as verbs. Use the past tense form in a sentence aloud. Then write the past tense in the final column of your spelling list.**

Identifying Parts of Speech

✎ *17.7 Identifying Parts of Speech –* **Read the phrase in your workbook. I will write it on the board. Then you will answer questions to label the parts of speech. Label each part of speech in your workbook as I write it on the board.**

	Word	Practice Sentence	Say to Spell	# of Syllables	Markings
1.	**share**	*Share your toys.*	shār	1	<u>sh</u>ār<u>e</u>
2.	**shine**	*The lights shine brightly at night.*	shīn	1	<u>sh</u>īn<u>e</u>
3.	**learn**	*We will learn the states and capitals.*	lern	1	l<u>ea</u>rn
4.	**state**	*What state do you live in?*	stāt	1	stāt<u>e</u>
5.	**use**	*Please use a pencil on this test.*	ūz	1	ūs<u>e</u>
6.	**name**	*What is your name?*	nām	1	nām<u>e</u>
7.	**suit**	*I need to wear a suit to the meeting.*	soot	1	s<u>ui</u>t
8.	**ride**	*She will ride the bus.*	rīd	1	rīd<u>e</u>
9.	**celebrate**	*We will celebrate your birthday on Friday.*	sĕl ē brāt	3	cel ē brāt<u>e</u>
10.	**hide**	*Hide the present before he gets home.*	hīd	1	hīd<u>e</u>
11.	**say**	*I say, "That is a strange looking dog."*	sā	1	sa<u>y</u>
12.	**says**	*He says we are leaving at 5 o'clock.*	sāz	1	s<u>ay</u>s
13.	**said**	*She said, "It is time to leave."*	sād	1	s<u>ai</u>d
14.	**birthday**	*It is his birthday tomorrow.*	berth dā	2	bi<u>rth</u> da<u>y</u>
15.	**rule**	*The king and queen rule the country.*	rūl	1	rūl<u>e</u>

Spelling Hints	Part of Speech	Vocabulary Development
Underline /sh/. Put a line over /ā/. Double underline the silent final E. **12.1** The vowel says its name because of the E.	V, N	shared, sharing, plowshare, shareable, sharecrop, sharecropping, sharecropper, shareholder, shareware
Underline /sh/. Put a line over the /ī/. Double underline the silent final E. **12.1** The vowel says its name because of the E.	V	shone, shining, shiner, moonshine, sunshine, shoeshine
Underline /er/.	V	learned, learnable, learning, learnedness, learner, unlearn, relearn, overlearn
Put a line over the /ā/. Double underline the silent final E. **12.1** The vowel says its name because of the E.	N, V	states, stated, statement, downstate, interstate, overstate, understate, restate, statehood, statehouse, statesman, unstated
Put a line over /ū/. Put a 2 over the /z/. /s-z/ said its second sound /z/. Double underline the silent final E. **12.1** The vowel says its name because of the E.	V, N	used, using, usability, useful, unused, reuse, reused, useless, usable, usefully, user, usefulness, uselessness
Put a line over the /ā/. Double underline the silent final E. **12.1** The vowel says its name because of the E.	V, N	names, named, nameless, nickname, rename, surname, unnamed, namelessness
Underline the /oo/.	N, V	suits, suited, swimsuit, lawsuit, snowsuit, wetsuit, jumpsuit, suitcase, suitable, unsuitable, unsuitably
Put a line over the /ī/. Double underline the silent final E. **12.1** The vowel says its name because of the E.	V, N	rode, riding, rider, riderless, joyride , ridable
Say to spell: sĕl ē brāt/. **1** C softens to /s/ when followed by an E, I or Y. Draw a line over the /ē/. **4** A E O U usually say their names at the end of the syllable. Put a line over the /ā/. Double underline the silent final E. **12.1** The vowel says its name because of the E.	V	celebrated, celebration
Put a line over the /ī/. Double underline the silent final E. **12.1** The vowel says its name because of the E.	V	hid, hiding, hideout, cowhide, hideaway, rawhide, hidden
Underline /ā/.	V	said, saying, says, hearsay
Say to spell sāz. Notice that we add an S to "say" for subject verb agreement, but we say /sĕz /. For spelling, exaggerate the long ā to help remember it is related to the word "say." Underline /ā/. Put a 2 over the /z/. /s-z/ said its second sound.	V	
Say to spell /sād/. Notice that AY, which may be used at the end of the word, changes to AI, which may not be used at the end of the word. Underline /ā/.	V	say, unsaid
Underline the /er/. Underline /th/. Underline /ā/. **3** English words do not end in I, U, V, or J. **9** AY usually spells the sound /ā/ at the end of a base word.	N, Adj	birthdays
Put a line over the /ū/. Double underline the silent final E. **12.1** The vowel says its name because of the E.	V, N	ruled, ruling, ruler, rules, misrule

Ava got a wonderful birthday gift.

    Who got? Ava, subject noun
    What is being said about Ava? Ava got, verb
    What did Ava get? gift, direct object
    Which gift? a, article adjective
    What kind of gift? wonderful, adjective
    What kind of gift? birthday, adjective
    Is there a direct object receiving the action of the verb? yes
    Then what kind of verb is it? a transitive verb
    Write a T next to the V to show the type of verb.

  SN TV A Adj   Adj DO
Ava got a wonderful birthday gift.

The children celebrated Carter's birthday.

    Who celebrated? children, subject noun
    Which children? the, article adjective
    What is being said about children? children celebrated, verb
    What did they celebrate? birthday, direct object
    Whose birthday? Carter's, possessive noun adjective
    Is there a direct object? yes
    Then what kind of verb is it? a transitive verb
    Write a T next to the V to show the type of verb.

  A   SN   TV   PNA   DO
The children celebrated Carter's birthday.

The careful boy hid the old shoes.

    Who hid? boy, subject noun
    What is being said about boy? boy hid, verb
    Which boy? the, article adjective
    Which boy? careful, adjective
    What did he hide? shoes, direct object
    Which shoes? the, article adjective
    Which shoes? old, adjective
    Is there a direct object receiving the action of the verb? yes
    Then what kind of verb is it? a transitive verb
    Write a T next to the V to show the type of verb.

  A Adj SN TV A Adj DO
The careful boy hid the old shoes.

Quotes

When someone is speaking within a written sentence, we use a comma and quotation marks to set apart the words the person is speaking.

Quotations follow three rules:

Grammar Card 11.2	Comma Rule 2
Use a comma to separate a direct quote from the rest of the sentence.	

Grammar Card 13.1	Quotations
Use quotation marks around direct quotations.	

Grammar Card 13.2	Quotations
Place commas and periods inside the quotation marks.	

Grammar Card 12.3	Capitalization
Capitalize the first word of a direct quotation.	

Mom said, "Ella hid the books."

Notice that there is a comma after the word "said." The words that were spoken are enclosed in quotation marks.

We can also turn the sentence around and write it like this:

"Ella hid the books," Mom said.

✎ *17.8 Quotations – **Read each of the sentences in your workbook. Circle the comma and the quotation marks. Underline the capital letter.***

Vocabulary Development

Consonant Suffixes and Vowel Suffixes

What is the difference between a consonant and a vowel? A consonant is a blocked sound. It cannot be sung or shouted. A vowel is an open sound. Vowels can be sung.
What are the names of the single letter vowels in English? A, E, I , O, U, and Y
What are the names of the consonants? B, C, D, F, G, H, J, K, L, M, N, P, Qu, R, S, T, V, W, X, Y, Z

What is a suffix? A suffix is a letter or group of letters added to the end of a word that changes its meaning.

If a consonant suffix begins with a consonant, what do you think a vowel suffix begins with?
a vowel

I will write a suffix on the board. Tell me if it is a consonant or a vowel suffix.

ment	consonant suffix
er	vowel suffix
est	vowel suffix
ly	consonant suffix

✎   *17.9 Consonant and Vowel Suffixes* – ***In your workbook is a list of suffixes. Circle the vowel suffixes.***

Adding Suffixes to Silent Final E Words

Write the samples as you discuss them.

help + ful =

If we have the word "help", how do we add the suffix -ful? Just add it on to form helpful.

help + ful = helpful

laugh + ter =

How about laugh and the suffix -ter. Add the suffix to get laughter.

laugh + ter = laughter

Now we will learn how to add a suffix to a silent final E word. Watch carefully.

hide+ ing = hiding

What changed when I added the suffix? You dropped the silent final E.

I will continue to write words and suffixes. Read the base word and then read the new word that is formed. Finally, tell me if anything changed.

ride + er = rider
shine + ed = shined
name + ed = named
hope + ed = hoped
type + ist = typist

What is happening? The silent final E is disappearing.

I will write a few more words. See if you can find the pattern.

state + ment = statement

name + less = nameless

name + s = names

use + s = uses

What do you notice? The silent final E is not dropped.
Why? What is different between the two? It is dropped with a vowel suffix but not a consonant suffix.

This leads to our rule:

Spelling Rule	13
Drop the silent final E when adding a vowel suffix only if it is allowed by other spelling rules.	

✎ *17.10 Adding Suffixes to Silent Final E Words – **Complete the activity in your workbook.***

Optional Spelling Rule Practice

1. ✎ Create a reference page to remember this rule. Include sample words. ©ⓥ

2. Ask the students to teach this to another student or to a parent. ©ⓥⒶⓀ

United States

United States

Let's now look at the words United States and consider why they are spelled this way.
Why is it capitalized? It is a proper noun.
What is the root word of united? unite

unite

What does it mean to unite? to bring people together
What suffix was added to unite to form united? the past tense ending -ed

unite + ed =

How do we add the past tense ending? Drop the E because it is a vowel suffix.

unite + ed = united

> **States is the plural for state.**

state + s =

> **How do we make state plural?** add -s
> **Do we need to drop the E?** No, we are not adding a vowel suffix.

state + s = states

> **Name some of the states that are united together into one country.** Minnesota, New York…
> **United States then means a group of states that are joined together.**

✎ *17.11 Additional Spelling –* **Write United States in your workbook.**

Optional Reading Practice

✎ *17.12 Extra Practice: Reading –* Direct the students to read the sentences in the workbook aloud. Have the students read them two or three times until they can read each one fluently.

Dictation

✎ *17.13 Dictation –* Read each sentence twice. Ask the students to repeat it aloud, then write it in their workbooks.

1. The children shared the fruit.
2. The boys learned the names.
3. Father hid the birthday gift.
4. The brothers celebrate.
5. The lights shine.
6. The man owned an excellent boat.

Composition

✎ *17.14 Composition –* Read the sentences in your workbook. Add an adjective to describe the noun in bold. Rewrite each sentence by adding an adjective to describe the noun.

The boys played a **game.**

The children used the **swing.**

The girls hid the **toy**.

The woman named the **cat.**

The brothers used the **tools.**

Lesson 18

Phonograms:	wor, wr
Exploring Sounds:	wor and wr
Spelling Rules:	12.2, 12.3
Grammar:	Indirect Objects

PART ONE

Materials Needed: Phonogram Flash Cards from previous lessons, wor and wr ; Spelling Rule Cards 12.2 and 12.3; Phonogram Game Cards, slips of paper for writing phonograms, pencils, basket.

Phonograms

New Phonograms — *wor, wr*

Show wor . /wer/

> *Repeat the sound.*

Show wr . /r/

> *Repeat the sound.*

> *What do you notice about these two phonograms.* They both begin with W and have an R.

Review

1. Drill the phonograms with flashcards.

2. ✎ *18.1 Writing the Phonograms* – Write each new phonogram five times while saying the sounds aloud.

3. ✎ *18.2 Phonogram Practice* – Dictate the following phonograms. For extra practice, have the students read them back. Write the correct answers on the board as the students check their answers.

   1. oe ō oo   3. au   5. ui oo fruit   7. ear er search
   2. wor   4. tch   6. ou   8. ow ow ō
                                    ow ō oo ŭ   plow snow
                                    nouse south group
                                    country

9. igh	12. wh	15. ew	18. ir
10. gn	13. augh *ä ȧf*	16. kn	19. ough *ŏ ō ōō ow ŭf ŏf*
11. ed *ed ḋ t*	14. ur	17. wr	20. aw

4. Play Phonogram Basketball (*The Phonogram and Spelling Game Book,* 22).

Exploring Sounds

WOR and WR

✎ *18.3 WOR and WR – **Read the words in your workbook. Underline the phonograms /wr/ and /wor/. How are they limited?*** They are only used at the beginning of a baseword.

wrap	word
wrath	work
wreck	world
write	worm
wrote	worship
wring	worst
wrong	worth

There are only nine English words that use the phonogram WOR. Seven of them are in your book. Is wor **a common phonogram?** no

---

Spelling Journal   Ⓐ Ⓚ Ⓥ

Enter words spelled with WR.

Spelling Rule

English Words do not end in V or U

I will sound out each word as I write it. Raise your hand if you see a problem with how I spell the words.

hav   *liv*   *giv*   *mauv*

Is the vowel short or long in these words? short
Why? because it is in the middle of the syllable
What is wrong with these words? English words do not end in V.
To prevent them from ending in V, we add a silent final E.

Add an E to the end of each of the words.

have   live   give   mauve

Why is there a silent final E in have? English words do not end in V.
To mark it, we will underline the V to show it is the reason for the E, and underline the E twice to show it is silent.

✎ *18.4 Silent Final E – Read each of the words in your workbook and mark the reason for the silent final E.*

ha<u>ve</u>   gi<u>ve</u>   cur<u>ve</u>   wea<u>ve</u>
li<u>ve</u>   mau<u>ve</u>   oli<u>ve</u>   ser<u>ve</u>

I will sound out each word as I write it. Raise your hand if you see a problem with the way I spell the words.

clu   blu   glu   tru

What sound does the U say in these words? It says its long sound.
Why? It is at the end of the syllable.
What is wrong with these words? English words do not end in U.
How do you think we will correct these? Add an E.

clue   blue   glue   true

How do you think we will mark it? Underline the U once and the E twice.

✎ *18.5 Silent Final E –* Guide the students in reading and marking the words in their workbook.

cl<u>ue</u>   gl<u>ue</u>   arg<u>ue</u>   val<u>ue</u>
bl<u>ue</u>   tr<u>ue</u>   d<u>ue</u>   c<u>ue</u>

Show the rule and recite:

Spelling Rule	12.2
English words do not end in V or U.	

✎ *18.6 English Words Do Not End in V or U –* Dictate the following five words for the students to practice writing following the rule: English words do not end in V or U.

1. have   3. give   5. true
2. clue   4. live

The C says /s/ because of the E

I will sound out each word as I write it. Raise your hand if you see a problem with how I spell the words.

As you write each word, read it as if the E were present and the C says /s/.

fenc   voic   sauc   sinc

> **What is wrong with these words?** C softens to /s/ only before an E, I, or Y. Here it would say /k/.
> **To make the C soft we will add an E.**

> **We will mark these words by underlining the C once to show it is the reason for the E, and the E twice to show it is silent.**

fen<u>ce</u>   voi<u>ce</u>   sau<u>ce</u>   sin<u>ce</u>

✎ *18.7 Silent Final E –* **Guide the students in reading and marking the words in their workbook.**

gra<u>ce</u>   ri<u>ce</u>   voi<u>ce</u>   tra<u>ce</u>
mi<u>ce</u>   fa<u>ce</u>   sau<u>ce</u>   dan<u>ce</u>

> **I will say a word and write it on the board with a misspelling. Tell me what is wrong.** cake

cace

That would say /cāse/ because C softens to /s/ before an E.

> **How do I fix it?** Use a K.
> **Why can't I use a CK?** CK is used only after a single short vowel and here the vowel is long.

cake

The G says /j/ because of the E

> **Read the words as I write them.**

large   page   rage   huge

Why did the G say /j/? Because it is before an E.

> **We will mark these words by underlining the G once to show it is the reason for the E, and the E twice to show it is silent.**

lar<u>ge</u>   pa<u>ge</u>   ra<u>ge</u>   hu<u>ge</u>

> **This explains the third most common reason for a silent final E:**

Spelling Rule	12.3
The C says /s/ and the G says /j/ because of the E.	

> **Are there any words on the board that have a silent final E for more than one reason?**
page, rage, huge

What are the two reasons for the E in page? To make the vowel say its name and to make the G soften to /j/.

When this happens you can mark both reasons for the silent final E.

pāge̲   rāge̲   hūge̲

✎ *18.8 Silent Final E* – Guide the students in reading and marking the words in their workbook.

large̲   huge̲   orange̲   surge̲
page̲   stage̲   strange̲   age̲

✎ *18.9 The C says /s/ and the G says /j/ because of the E* – Dictate the following five words for the students to practice the rule: The C says /s/ and the G says /j/ because of the E.

1. stage   3. page   5. change
2. cage   4. large

Optional Spelling Rule Practice

1. Illustrate the spelling rule on a separate piece of paper using sample words from the board.   ©Ⓥ

2. Ask the students to teach this to another student or to a parent.   ©ⓋⒶⓀ

3. Write a word with a silent final E on the board. The students get 1 point for reading it correctly the first time, and 1 point for stating the reason the silent final E is needed.   ⓋⒶⓀ

    *   C softens to /s/ because of the E – *chance, clearance, dance, denounce, endurance, enforce, entrance, offence, notice, balance, service, voice, fence, sauce, since.*

    *   C softens to /s/ because of the E and the vowel says its name because of the E – *race, space, lace, mace, rice, grace, trace, mice, twice.*

    *   G softens to /j/ because of the E – *charge, forge, garage, merge, orange, large.*

    *   G softens to /j/ because of the E and the vowel says its name because of the E – *stage, age, average, cage, range, voyage, huge, page, rage.*

    *   English words do not end in V – *give, live, carve, move, descriptive, give, have, prove, active, instructive, relative, observe, talkative.*

    *   English words do not end in V and the vowel says its name because of the E – *live, cave, crave, cove, dive, dove, drive, hive, grave, five, grove, thrive.*

    *   English words do not end in U – *blue, clue, construe, hue, glue, sue, value, statue, true, virtue.*

    *   The vowel says its name because of the E – *bale, bake, rake, rate, late, state, bike, kite, wipe, bone, rope, stone, robe, yoke, zone, fume, prune, chute, flute.*

4. Quickly review rules 1-4, 8-12.3, 13, 19-22, 24, 26-28, 30 using the Spelling Rule Cards.   ⒶⓋ

PART TWO

Using Spelling List 18 on pages 218-219, dictate each word following the steps included on pages Intro 42 - Intro 46.

Tips for Spelling List 18

Answer

Answer has a silent W in it. In order to help auditory students create an auditory picture exaggerate the /w/ sound for spelling purposes.   /ăn swer/

Love

Notice in the word "love" that the phonogram ‎ o ‎ is pronounced as a schwa sound /ə/. Exaggerate the short /ŏ/ sound for spelling purposes.   /lŏv/

PART THREE

Materials Needed: Grammar Card 1.9; red, blue, and green colored pencils; an apple for demonstrating indirect and direct objects.

Grammar

Review

What is a noun? A noun is the name of a person, place, thing, or idea.

What is an adjective? Adjectives modify nouns and pronouns. Adjectives answer: What kind? How many? Which one? Whose?

What is an article? A, An, The. Tiny article adjectives that mark nouns and answer the question: Which?

What is a verb? A verb shows action, links a description to the subject, or helps another verb.

Name the parts of a sentence. A sentence must have a capital letter, subject, verb, complete thought, and an end mark.

What are two types of verbs we have studied so far? action verbs and transitive verbs

What are two noun jobs we have studied so far? subject noun and direct object

✎ *Spelling List 18 – **Identify the parts of speech of each of the words in List 18. Mark the nouns with a red N, the verbs with a green V, and the adjectives with a blue Adj.***

Optional Spelling Cards

1. Dictate the words in Lesson 18 for the students to write on index cards. Ⓐ Ⓚ Ⓥ

2. Color a green border around the verbs, a red border around the nouns, and a blue border around the adjectives. Ⓚ Ⓥ

Past Tense Verbs

✎ *Spelling List 18 – **The first thirteen words are verbs. Write the past tense next to each verb in your workbook.***

Indirect Objects

Bring props to act out the following sentences.

Write the sentences on the board to discuss with the students.

	Word	Practice Sentence	Say to Spell	# of Syllables	Markings
1.	**tell**	*They tell good stories.*	tĕl	1	tell
2.	**write**	*Write your name on the top of the paper.*	rīt	1	wrīte
3.	**give**	*Give me the cup.*	gĭv	1	give
4.	**bring**	*Bring lawn chairs for the picnic.*	brĭng	1	bring
5.	**make**	*I will make the birthday cake.*	māk	1	māke
6.	**take**	*Remember to take a coat with you.*	tāk	1	tāke
7.	**save**	*Save the extra paper.*	sāv	1	sāve
8.	**show**	*Did you show your parents your report card?*	shō	1	show²
9.	**answer**	*Answer the question.*	ăn swer	2	an swer
10.	**work**	*They work at the bank.*	werk	1	work
11.	**trace**	*We will trace the picture with a pencil*	trās	1	trāce
12.	**love**	*I love you.*	lŭv	1	lŏve
13.	**change**	*Change the water in the fish bowl twice a week.*	chānj	1	chānge
14.	**blue**	*Evelyn has blue eyes.*	bloo	1	blue
15.	**letter**	*Ella wrote her a long letter.*	lĕt ter	2	let ter

Spelling Hints	Part of Speech	Vocabulary Development
30 We often double F, L, and S after a single vowel at the end of a base word. Occasionally other letters also are doubled.	V	told, telling, tells
Underline /wr/. Put a line over the /ī/. Double underline the silent final E. WR is used only at the beginning of a base word. **12.1** The vowel says its name because of the E.	V	wrote, written, writer, copywriter, ghostwriter, rewrite, screenwriter, sportswriter, underwriter, typewriter
Underline the V once. Double underline the silent final E. **12.2** English words do not end in V or U.	V	gave, giving, giver, forgive, forgiven, giveaway
Underline /ng/.	V	brought, bringing, brings, upbringing
Put a line over the /ā/. Double underline the silent final E. **12.1** The vowel says its name because of the E. We cannot use C because otherwise it would say /mās/. **1** C softens to /s/ when followed by E, I, or Y.	V	made, maker, making, cabinetmaker, filmmaker, makeover, makeshift, makeup, peacemaker, rainmaker, remake
Put a line over the /ā/. Double underline the silent final E. **12.1** The vowel says its name because of the E. We cannot use C because otherwise it would say /tās/. **1** C softens to /s/ when followed by E, I, or Y.	V	took, taker, caretaker, intake, overtake, mistake, mistakes, undertake, partake, uptake, retake, takeoff, takeover
Put a line over the /ā/. Underline V. Double underline the silent final E. **12.1** The vowel says its name because of the E. **12.2** English words do not end in V or U.	V	saved, saving, saver, saves, savable
Underline /sh/. Underline /ō/ and put a 2 over it. /ow-ō/ said its second sound.	V	showed, shows, showing, reshow, shown, showmanship, showboat, showdown, showpiece, sideshow, showy
Say to spell /ăn **sw**er/. Double underline the W. W is silent. Underline the /er/.	V, N	answered, answers, answering, answerable, unanswerable
Underline /wor/. WOR is used only at the beginning of a base word. The root WORK is found in hundreds of derivatives.	V, N	worked, working, works, worker, network, handiwork, housework, homework, coworker, paperwork
Put a line over the /ā/. Underline the /s/. Double underline the silent final E. **12.1** The vowel says its name because of the E. **12.3** The C says /s/ because of the E.	V	traced, tracer, tracing, traces, traceable, retrace
Say to spell /lŏve/. Put a curve line over the O. We need to exaggerate the /ŏ/ sound. Underline the V once. Double underline the silent final E. **12.2** English words do not end in V or U.	V, N	loved, loving, lovable, beloved, lovely, loveless, lovelier, lovesick, unloved, unlovely
Underline /ch/. Put a line over /ā/. Double underline the silent final E. **12.1** The vowel says its name because of the E. Underline /j/. **12.3** The G says /j/ because of the E.	V, N	changed, changeable, changes, changeover, exchange, interchange, shortchange, unchanging, changeless
The long /ū/ sound sometimes sounds like /oo/. Underline the U once. Double underline the silent final E. **12.2** English words do not end in V or U.	Adj	bluer, bluest, bluebell, bluegrass, blueprint
Underline /er/.	N, V	letters, lettered, lettering, letterhead

The teacher gave the boy an apple.

The boy gave the teacher an apple.

How many nouns are in this sentence? three
What are they? teacher, boy, apple
Nouns have more than one job they can perform in a sentence.
What two noun jobs have we learned so far? subject and direct object
Today we will learn a third noun job, the indirect object.
Read the second sentence.

What is different between the first and second sentence? The teacher is doing the giving in the first sentence, whereas the boy is doing the giving in the second sentence. Teacher and boy switched places.

The person receiving the apple in these sentences is the indirect object. Notice that the indirect object is located between the subject and the direct object.

Grammar Card 1.9   10

The indirect object tells to whom or for whom the action is done.
The indirect object receives the direct object.
To find the indirect object, go to the verb and ask:
To whom did (the subject) _____? To what did (the subject) _____?

✎ *18.10 Identifying Parts of Speech –* **Let's identify the part of speech, or job, that each word is doing in each sentence. Mark the parts of speech in your workbook as I mark them on the board.**

The teacher gave the boy an apple.

Who gave? teacher, subject noun
Which teacher? the, article adjective describing teacher
What is being said about the teacher? teacher gave, verb
What did the teacher give? apple, direct object
Which apple? an, article adjective
To whom did the teacher give it? boy
Boy is called the indirect object.
The indirect object is always located between the verb and the direct object.
Where is the indirect object located? between the verb and the direct object
Which boy? the, article adjective
Is there a direct object receiving the action of the verb? yes
Then it is a transitive verb. Write a T next to the V to show the type of verb.

   A   SN   TV   A   IO A DO
The teacher gave the boy an apple.

The boy gave the teacher an apple.

Who gave? boy, subject noun
Which boy? the, article adjective describing boy
What is being said about the boy? boy gave, verb
What did the boy give? apple, direct object
Which apple? an, article adjective
To whom did the boy give it? teacher, indirect object
Teacher is called the indirect object.
Which teacher? the, article adjective
Where is the indirect object located? It is always located between the verb and the direct object.
Is there a direct object receiving the action of the verb? yes
Then it is a transitive verb. Write a T next to the V to show the type of verb.

A SN TV A   IO   A DO
The boy gave the teacher an apple.

Notice that by changing the position of the words teacher and boy in the sentence, their jobs change and therefore the meaning of the sentence changes.

Read the third and fourth sentences in your workbook.

The girl told the woman a secret.

Who told? girl, subject noun
Which girl? the, article adjective
What is being said about the girl? girl told, verb
What did the girl tell? secret, direct object
Which secret? a, article adjective
To whom did the girl tell it? the woman, indirect object
Which woman? the, article adjective
Is there a direct object receiving the action of the verb? yes
Then it is a transitive verb. Write a T next to the V to show the type of verb.

A SN TV A   IO   A DO
The girl told the woman a secret.

The woman told the girl a secret.

Who told? woman, subject noun

Which woman? the, article adjective

What is being said about the woman? woman told, verb

What did the woman tell? secret, direct object

Which secret? a, article adjective

To whom did the woman tell it? the girl, indirect object

Which girl? the, article adjective

Is there a direct object receiving the action of the verb? yes

Then it is a transitive verb. Write a T next to the V to show the type of verb.

A SN   TV   A   IO A DO
The woman told the girl a secret.

Optional Grammar Practice

1. ✎ *18.11 Extra Practice: Adding Suffixes to Silent Final E Words* – Review adding suffixes to silent final E words. Ⓚ Ⓥ

2. ✎ *18.12 Extra Practice: Irregular Past Tense Verbs* – Draw lines to match the present and past tense verbs. Ⓚ Ⓐ Ⓥ

3. ✎ *18.13 Extra Practice: Quotes* – Add a comma and quotation marks to each sentence.

4. Put the present tense verbs in a basket. Direct the students to choose a word, read it, then name the past tense. See how many they can get right in 30 seconds. Ⓚ Ⓥ Ⓐ

5. Put the present tense verbs in a basket. Provide each student with a lap whiteboard. The students draw a verb, read it, then write the present and past tense forms on a whiteboard. Ⓚ Ⓥ Ⓐ

6. Review Grammar Cards 1-1.5; 1.7-1.9; 2-2.6; 3-3.2; 7, 9, 11.1-11.2; 13.1-13.3. Ⓐ Ⓥ

Optional Reading Practice

✎ *18.14 Extra Practice: Reading* – Direct the students to read the sentences in the workbook aloud. Have the students read them two or three times until they can read each one fluently.

Dictation

✎ *18.15 Dictation* – Read each sentence twice. Ask the students to repeat it aloud, then write it in their workbooks.

1. The teacher told the children the answers.

2. Father showed Seth a blue car.

3. The girl wrote Grandfather a wonderful letter.

4. Mr. Larson gave the workers a ride.

5. The woman saved ten cents.

6. Mrs. Jones changed the cat's water.

Composition

Write the following simple sentence on the board. Then ask the following questions, making the sentence increasingly more complex.

The author wrote.

What did the author write? (The following answer is an example. Write what the students suggest on the board.)

The author wrote a book.

How many books?

The author wrote three books.

What kind of author?

The new author wrote three books.

What kind of books?

The new author wrote three excellent books.

✎ *18.16 Composition* – Direct the students to write a simple sentence in their workbooks. Then direct them to ask and answer four questions to expand the sentence, rewriting the sentence each time.

Vocabulary Development

Adding Prefixes

What is a prefix? A group of letters than can be added to the beginning of a word to change its meaning.
Adding a prefix changes the meaning of the word. Knowing the meaning of common prefixes will help you to understand new vocabulary words.

For example:

re + take =

> **What new word is formed with re and take?** retake
> **What does re- mean?** do it again.
>
> **Today we will learn three new prefixes. I will write a prefix and word on the board. Tell me the new word that is formed. Then I will write it. Define the word and use it in a sentence. When you know what the prefix means, raise your hand.**

mis + take = mistake

> A **mistake** means to do something wrong. "I made a mistake on the math test."

mis + count = miscount

> **Miscount** means to count something wrong. "She miscounted the books."
>
> **Mis-** means to do something wrong.

under + paid = underpaid

> **Underpaid** means to be paid too little. "I was underpaid for that job."

under + shot = undershot

> **Undershot** means to not shoot far enough. "The player undershot the ball and missed the basket."
>
> **Under-** means to do too little.

over + paid = overpaid

> **Overpaid** means to be paid too much. "The man overpaid me for mowing the lawn."

over + feed = overfeed

> **Overfeed** means to feed too much. "It is important not to overfeed the dog."
>
> **Over-** means too much.

✎ *18.17 Adding Prefixes –* **Complete the activity in your workbook.**

Lesson 19

Phonograms:	ph
Exploring Sounds:	The /l/ Sound
Spelling Rules:	12.4, 12.5
Grammar:	Subject and Predicate

PART ONE

Materials Needed: Phonogram Flash Cards from previous lessons and ph ; Spelling Rule Cards 12.4 and 12.5, 1 set of Phonogram Game Cards.

Phonograms

New Phonogram — ph

Show ph . /f/

All of the words which use this phonogram are based upon Greek. This phonogram is not very common.

✎ *19.1 The Phonogram PH –* **Read the words in your workbook. Underline the PH.**

graph	phrase	phone
photo	pharmacist	telephone
photograph	phonogram	

Review

1. Drill the phonograms with flashcards.

2. ✎ *19.2 Writing the Phonograms* – Write the new phonogram five times while saying the sound aloud.

3. ✎ *19.3 Phonogram Practice* – Dictate the following phonograms. For extra practice, have the students read them back. Write the correct answers on the board as the students check their answers.

1. oe *ō oo*
2. wor
3. au *2 letter ä not at end*
4. tch *3 letter ch used only after a single vowel that is*
5. ui *no + long*
6. ou *ow ō oo ŭ not at end*
7. ear *er of search*
8. ow *ow ō may use at end*
9. igh *3 letter ī used only at end/before t*
10. gn *2 letter n beg or end*
11. ed *ed d t*
12. wh *used only at beg.*
13. augh *ä äf*
14. ur *er of hurt*
15. ew *oo ū end*
16. kn *2 letter n -beg*
17. wr *2 letter /r/ -beg.*
18. ir *The er of bird*
19. ough *ŏ ō oo ow ŭff ŏff*
20. aw *2 letter ä that may be used at end*

4. Play Phonogram Snatch (*The Phonogram and Spelling Game Book*, 8).

Exploring Sounds

The Consonant L

> *Say the sound /l/.*
> *Is it a consonant or a vowel?* consonant
> *Why?* Because the sound is blocked by the tongue. Vowels are open sounds without anything blocking the sound.
> *Can you sustain or hold it?* yes
> *Can you make it louder and softer?* yes
> *Even though the tongue is blocking the sound, /l/ is similar to a vowel because it can be sustained.*

Spelling Rules

Every syllable must have a written vowel

> *I will say a word. Repeat the word, tell me how many syllables are in the word, then sound out each syllable as I write it.*
>
> *Table.* table, 2 syllables
> *First syllable?* /tā/
> *Second syllable?* /bl/

ta bl

> *In English every syllable must have a written vowel. What is the vowel in the first syllable /tā/?* A
> *What is the vowel in the second syllable /bl/?* There isn't one.
> *Sometimes the sound /l/ tries to act like a vowel at the end of the word. When this happens we need to add a silent final E.*

ta ble

> *Why do we have a silent final E in table?* Every syllable must have a written vowel.
> *This is the fourth reason for a silent final E.*

Spelling Rule	12.4

Every syllable must have a written vowel.

We will mark this reason for the silent final E by underlining the L once to show it is acting a bit like a vowel and underlining the E twice to show it is silent.

ta b<u>l<u>e</u></u>

✎ *19.4 Every Syllable Needs a Vowel* – **Read the words in your workbook. Underline the final syllable in each word.**

dou<u>ble</u>	mid<u>dle</u>	buc<u>kle</u>	ti<u>tle</u>
trou<u>ble</u>	snif<u>fle</u>	pic<u>kle</u>	set<u>tle</u>
un<u>cle</u>	waf<u>fle</u>	ap<u>ple</u>	puz<u>zle</u>
can<u>dle</u>	wig<u>gle</u>	ma<u>ple</u>	siz<u>zle</u>
cra<u>dle</u>	ea<u>gle</u>	has<u>sle</u>	

Read each word. What are the possible last syllables that need a silent final E so that the syllable has a vowel? ble, cle, dle, fle, gle, kle<, ple, sle, tle, zle

< **Teacher Tip:** *Buckle and pickle divide the syllable between the C and the K. This closes the first syllable to make the vowel sound short.*

✎ *19.5. Final Syllable* – **Write these syllables in your workbook.**

Answer Key: ble, cle, dle, fle, gle, kle, ple, sle, tle, zle

Exploring Sounds

Syllable Breaks and Vowels

When reading and spelling words, it is important to know where the syllables break.

When a word ends with an L followed by a silent final E, it is easy to figure out where the syllable breaks.

✎ *19.6 Syllables and Vowels* – **Say each of the words in your workbook. Put your hand under your chin. Remember, your mouth will drop open with each syllable. Draw a slash between the syllables.**

ta/ble	waf/fle	ma/ple
bub/ble	wig/gle	has/sle
un/cle	ea/gle	ti/tle
cra/dle	twin/kle	puz/zle
mid/dle	ap/ple	

What is the pattern for where the syllable breaks in each of these words? The syllable breaks three letters from the end of the word.

Which rule tells us what the vowel will say at the end of the syllable? A E O U usually say their names at the end of the syllable.

How does knowing where the syllable breaks help you know how the vowel is pronounced in these words? When a single vowel is at the end of the first syllable it says its long sound. When a consonant is at the end of the first syllable the vowel says its short sound.

How does knowing where the syllable breaks, tell you how to spell the words? When there is a long vowel sound, there is only one consonant before the L. When there is a short vowel sound, there are two consonants before the L. This means in words like *middle, waffle, wiggle,* and *puzzle,* the consonant is doubled. Syllables break between double consonants.

Spelling Rules

Add an E to keep singular words that end in S from looking plural.

✎ *19.7 Silent Final E –* **Read the words in your workbook. Each of these words follows a new reason for a silent final E.**

house	*horse*	*promise*
mouse	*goose*	*license*
spouse	*moose*	*cause*

Tell me if you can figure out why the E is needed. All the words end in S.
Are these words singular or plural? singular
What do we add to make a word plural? S
Many singular words that end in S add a silent final E to keep them from looking plural. This does not occur with all singular words ending in S.
This leads to the rule:

Spelling Rule	12.5
We often add an E to keep singular words that end in S from looking plural.	

Mark this reason for the silent final E by underlining the S once to show it is the reason for the E and underlining the E twice to show it is silent.

hou<u>se</u>	*hor<u>se</u>*	*promi<u>se</u>*
mou<u>se</u>	*goo<u>se</u>*	*licen<u>se</u>*
spou<u>se</u>	*moo<u>se</u>*	*cau<u>se</u>*

Optional Spelling Rule Practice

1. Create a reference page to remember these rules. Include sample words.   ©Ⓥ

2. Ask the students to teach the rules to another student or to a parent.   ©ⓋⒶⓀ

3. Write one of the following syllables on the board: *ble, cle, dle, fle, gle, kle, ple, tle, zle*. See how many words each student or team of students can write that end in the syllable. ⒶⓋⓀ

    *   **-ble** *babble, bobble, bramble, bubble, bumble, cable, cobble, dribble, fable, feeble, fumble, grumble, humble, mumble, noble, stable, tremble, wobble*

    *   **-cle** *article, bicycle, chronicle, circle, cycle, icicle, miracle, oracle, particle, tricycle, vehicle*

    *   **-dle** *bridle, bundle, candle, cradle, cuddle, curdle, dawdle, doodle, dwindle, fiddle, griddle, handle, hurdle, kindle, middle, needle, noodle, riddle, saddle, straddle, swaddle*

    *   **-fle** *baffle, muffle, raffle, ruffle, scuffle, shuffle, sniffle, waffle*

    *   **-gle** *angle, beagle, boggle, bugle, bungle, dangle, eagle, gargle, giggle, google, haggle, jingle, juggle, mingle, single, smuggle, straggle, struggle, triangle, wiggle*

    *   **-kle** *ankle, buckle, chuckle, crinkle, heckle, knuckle, pickle, shackle, speckle, suckle, tickle, trickle, twinkle, wrinkle*

    *   **-ple** *ample, apple, couple, cripple, crumple, dimple, example, maple, multiple, people, pimple, purple, ripple, rumple, sample, simple, temple, trample, triple*

    *   **-tle** *battle, beetle, bottle, brittle, bustle, castle, chortle, hurtle, kettle, mantle, nestle, nettle, prattle, rattle, settle, title, trestle, whistle, whittle*

    *   **-zle** *dazzle, drizzle, frazzle, guzzle, muzzle, nuzzle, puzzle, sizzle*

4. Play picture dictionary using the words above. Write the words on index cards. Place them in a basket. One student draws a picture representing the word on a whiteboard. The others try to guess the word by writing the word on their own whiteboard. Whoever guesses correctly illustrates the next word.   ⒶⓋⓀ

5. Dictate some of the words from Option 3 for the students to write on a white board or spell with magnetic letters.   ⒶⓋⓀ

PART TWO

Using Spelling List 19 on pages 232-233, dictate each word following the steps included on pages Intro 42 - Intro 46.

Tips for Spelling List 19

Photograph

One of the difficulties with English spelling is that vowels in unaccented syllables often are pronounced as the schwa sound /ə/. In order to help the students create an auditory picture of the word, it is helpful to exaggerate the unaccented vowel.

Exaggerate the vowel so that /fō tə grăf/ sounds like /fō tō grăf/.

To learn more about vowels in unaccented syllables and aiding students in creating an auditory picture of words, see *Uncovering the Logic of English,* 121-128.

PART THREE

Materials Needed: Spelling Rule Card 13; red, blue, and green colored pencils.

Grammar

Review

What is a noun? A noun is the name of a person, place, thing, or idea.
What are the three noun jobs? Subject noun, direct object, indirect object
What is an adjective? Adjectives modify nouns and pronouns. Adjectives answer: What kind? How many? Which one? Whose?
What is an article? A, An, The. Tiny article adjectives that mark nouns and answer the question: Which?
What is a verb? A verb shows action, links a description to the subject, or helps another verb.
✎ *Spelling List 19 –* **Identify the parts of speech of each of the words in List 19. Mark them in your workbook. Mark the nouns with a red N, the verbs with a green V, and the adjectives with a blue Adj.**

✎ *Spelling List 19 –* **Write the past tense of each verb, and the plural for each noun.**

Optional Spelling Cards

1. Dictate the words in Lesson 19 for the students to write on index cards. Ⓐ Ⓚ Ⓥ

2. Color a green border around the verbs, a red border around the nouns, and a blue border around the adjectives. Ⓚ Ⓥ

Subject and Predicate

Name the parts of a sentence. A sentence must have a capital letter, subject, verb, complete thought, and an end mark.
What two types of words does a sentence always need? subject and verb

subject

verb — predicate

Another name for the verb is the predicate.
How long can the shortest sentence be? two words
A sentence needs two words: a subject and a verb. The verb is also called the predicate.

◁ Teacher Tip: *Some commands have an implied subject of "you." For example in the sentence: "Stop!" the implied subject is you and the verb is stop. Though it is written with only one word it still has a subject. The sentence could be written, "You stop."*

Word	Practice Sentence	Say to Spell	# of Syllables	Markings
1. **juice**	*Would you like a glass of juice?*	joos	1	ju͟i͟c͟e
2. **photograph**	*I took a photograph of the beautiful waterfall.*	fō tō grăf	3	p͟h͟ō tō gra͟p͟h
3. **table**	*Put the cup on the table.*	tā bl	2	tā b͟l͟e
4. **apple**	*An apple a day keeps the doctor away.*	ăp pl	2	ap p͟l͟e
5. **little**	*The little baby is cute.*	lĭt tl	2	lit t͟l͟e
6. **house**	*We live in the white house.*	hows	1	h͟o͟u͟s͟e
7. **large**	*That is a large bouquet of flowers.*	larj	1	la͟r͟g͟e
8. **word**	*This word is easy to spell.*	werd	1	w͟o͟r͟d
9. **spell**	*How do you spell your name?*	spĕl	1	spell
10. **fruit**	*Fresh fruit is a healthy breakfast.*	froot	1	fr͟u͟it
11. **move**	*Let's move the table over here.*	möv	1	möv͟e
12. **horse**	*Shannon rode the black horse.*	hōrs	1	h͟o͟r͟s͟e
13. **phone**	*The phone is ringing.*	fōn	1	p͟h͟ō͟n͟e
14. **like**	*They like to swim.*	līk	1	līk͟e
15. **offer**	*I will offer you twenty dollars for the job.*	ŏf fer	2	of f͟e͟r

Spelling Hints	Part of Speech	Vocabulary Development
Underline the /oo/. Underline the /s/. Double underline the E. **12.3** The C says /s/ because of the E.	N, V	juices, juicy, juicier, juiciness, juicing, juicer, juiceless
Greek root. Uses PH to spell /f/. Underline the /f/. Put a line above the O. **4** A E O U usually say their names at the end of the syllable. Put a line above the O. **4** A E O U usually say their names at the end of the syllable. Underline the /f/.	N, V	photographer, photography, photographed, photographs, rephotograph
Put a line above the A. **4** A E O U usually say their names at the end of the syllable. Underline the /l/. Double underline the silent final E. **12.4** Every syllable must have a vowel.	N, V	tables, tablespoon, tablespoonful, tabletop
Underline the /l/. Double underline the silent final E. **12.4** Every syllable must have a vowel.	N	apples, applecart, applejack, applesauce, pineapple
Underline the /l/. Double underline the silent final E. **12.4** Every syllable must have a vowel.	Adj	littler, littlest, belittle, littleness
Underline the /ow/. Underline the /s/. Double underline the silent final E. **12.5** Add an E to keep singular words that end in S from looking plural.	N	houses, birdhouse, doghouse, farmhouse, housekeeper, houseplant, housetop, poorhouse, lighthouse, townhouse
Underline /ar/. Underline the /j/. Double underline the E. **3** The G says /j/ because of the E.	Adj	larger, largest, enlarge, enlargement, largely, largeness, overlarge
Underline /wer/.	N	wording, worded, words, afterword, buzzword, foreword, password, reword, wordless, wordsmith, wordy
30 We often double F, L, and S after a single vowel at the end of a base word. Occasionally other letters also are doubled.	V	spelled, spelling, speller, misspell, misspelling, respell, spellbound
Underline the /oo/.	N	fruits, fruity, fruitcake, fruitful, fruitfulness, fruitless, fruitlessly, grapefruit, kiwifruit, unfruitful, unfruitfulness
/ŏ-ō-ö/ said its third sound. Put two dots over it. Underline the /v/. Double underline the silent final E. **12.2** English words do not end in V or U.	V, N	moved, moving, mover, moves, movable, countermove, movement, immovable, irremovable, movie, remove, unmoving
Underline the /or/. Underline the /s/. Double underline the silent final E. **12.5** Add an E to keep singular words that end in S from looking plural.	N	horses, horseman, horsemanship, horseshoe, racehorse, sawhorse, workhorse, horseradish, horseless
Underline /f/. Put a line over the /ō/. Double underline the silent final E. **12.1** The vowel says its name because of the E.	N, V	phoned, phones, telephone, cellphone, megaphone, microphone, phonetic, saxophone, earphone, homophone
C says /s/ before E, I, or Y, therefore the K must be used. Put a line over /ī/. Double underline the silent final E. **12.1** The vowel says its name because of the E.	V, N	likeable, liking, likes, liked, childlike, childlikeness, likewise, lifelike, likely, unlikely, businesslike, misliked
Underline /er/.	V, N	offered, offering, offertory, offertories

Tell me some sentences with only a subject and a verb and I will write them on the board.

Write the phrases the students come up with on the board.

Mother worked.   Boys read.

Girls played.   Children sang.

Sometimes when we are writing, it is important to know which words belong to the subject and which words belong to the predicate. Knowing this information will help when you are writing long sentences to make sure that the sentence can be clearly understood.

When a sentence only has a subject and a verb, it is called a simple sentence. We can easily divide the subject and the predicate in these sentences.

Mother / worked.   Boys / read.

Girls / played.   Children / sang.

Now we will look at a few longer sentences.
The complete subject includes the simple subject and all the words that modify it.
The complete predicate includes the verb and all the words which modify the verb.

The horse ate an apple.

What is the subject of the sentence? horse
What is being said about the horse? horse ate, verb
Predicate is another word for verb. Therefore the simple predicate is ate.
The simple sentence that this longer sentence is based upon is:

Horse ate.

Ate what? an apple
An apple is modifying ate, so it is part of the predicate.
We divide the subject and the predicate by drawing a line between horse and ate.

The horse / ate an apple.

The children spelled the words.

Who spelled? children, subject
What is being said about the children? spelled, verb or predicate
What is the simple sentence?

Children spelled.

Where do we divide the subject from the predicate? between children and spelled

The children / spelled the words.

✎ *19.8 Simple Subject and Simple Predicate – **Read the sentences. Write the simple subject and simple predicate.***

Identifying the Parts of Speech

✎ *19.9 Identifying Parts of Speech – **We will now read four sentences, identify the parts of speech, and divide the subject from the predicate.***

> *The large horse pulled the hay wagon.*
>
> **Who pulled?** horse, subject noun
> **Which horse?** the, article adjective
> **What kind of horse?** large, adjective
>
> A   Adj   SN
> *The large horse pulled the hay wagon.*
>
> **What is being said about the horse?** horse pulled, verb
> **What did the horse pull?** wagon, direct object
> **Which wagon?** the, article adjective
> **What kind of wagon?** hay, adjective
> **Is there a direct object receiving the action of the verb?** yes
> **Then it is a transitive verb. Write a T next to the V to show the type of verb.**
>
> A   Adj   SN   TV   A   Adj   DO
> *The large horse pulled the hay wagon.*
>
> **What is the subject of the sentence?** horse
> **What is the predicate or the verb?** pulled
> **The simple sentence would be:**
>
> *Horse pulled.*
>
> **The complete subject and complete predicate are divided right between horse and pulled. Put a slash between them.**
>
> *The large horse /pulled the hay wagon.*
>
> **What is the complete subject of the sentence?** the large horse
> **What is the complete predicate?** pulled the hay wagon

The kind teacher offered the children apple juice.

    Who offered? teacher, subject noun
    Which teacher? the, article adjective
    What kind of teacher? kind, adjective
    What is being said about the teacher? teacher offered, verb
    What did the teacher offer? juice, direct object
    What kind of juice? apple, adjective
    To whom did the teacher offer it? children, indirect object
    Which children? the, article adjective
    Is there a direct object receiving the action of the verb? yes
    Then it is a transitive verb. Write a T next to the V to show the type of verb.

   A   Adj   SN   TV   A   IO   Adj   DO
The kind teacher offered the children apple juice.

    What is the subject of the sentence? teacher
    What is the predicate or the verb? offered
    The simple sentence would be:

Teacher offered.

    Divide the complete subject from the complete predicate.

The kind teacher /offered the children apple juice.

    What is the complete subject of the sentence? the kind teacher
    What is the complete predicate? offered the children apple juice

---

The photographer moved six little tables.

    Who moved? photographer, subject noun
    Which photographer? the, article adjective
    What is being said about the photographer? photographer moved, verb
    What did the photographer move? tables, direct object
    What kind of tables? little, adjective
    How many tables? six, adjective
    Is there a direct object receiving the action of the verb? yes
    Then it is a transitive verb. Write a T next to the V to show the type of verb.

   A   SN   TV   Adj Adj DO
The photographer moved six little tables.

> *What is the subject of the sentence?* photographer
> *What is the predicate or the verb?* moved
> *The simple sentence would be:*
>
> *Photographer moved.* **Divide the complete subject from the complete predicate.**
>
> *The photographer/moved six little tables.*
>
> *What is the complete subject of the sentence?* the photographer
> *What is the complete predicate?* moved six little tables

Optional Grammar Practice

1. ✎ *19.10 Extra Practice: Articles* – Review when to use "a" and "an." Complete the review in the workbook. Ⓚ Ⓥ Ⓐ

2. ✎ *19.11 Extra Practice: Titles of Respect* – Review the meanings of Mr., Mrs., Ms., and Dr. Dictate them for your students to write in their student workbooks.

3. ✎ *19.12 Extra Practice: Reading* – Direct the students to read the sentences in the workbook aloud. Have the students read them two or three times until they can read each one fluently.

4. Read the sentences for *19.12 Reading*. Write a slash to divide the subject from the predicate.

Vocabulary Development

The Suffix -able

What does this say? able

work + able =

What word is formed when we add work and able? workable

work + able = workable

save + able =

What new word is formed with save and -able? savable
What do you need to know about the word save before adding the suffix -able? That it ends with a silent final E.
Why is the E needed? To make the A say its name, and because English words do not end in V.
Can we drop the E when adding the suffix -able? yes
Why? Drop the silent final E when adding a vowel suffix only if it is allowed by other spelling rules.

save + able = savable

charge + able =

> ***What do we get if we add charge and -able?*** chargeable
> ***What do you need to know about the word charge before adding the suffix -able?*** That it ends with a silent final E.
> ***Why is the E needed?*** to soften the G to /j/
> ***Can we drop the E when adding the suffix -able?*** no
> ***Why not?*** G may soften to /j/ before E, I, and Y. The G would no longer say /j/.

charge + able = chargeable

trace + able =

> ***What do we get if we add trace and able?*** traceable
> ***What do you need to know about the word trace before adding the suffix -able?*** That it ends with a silent final E.
> ***Why is the E needed?*** To soften the C to /s/, and to make the A say /ā/.
> ***Can we drop the E when adding the suffix -able?*** no
> ***Why not?*** Otherwise, it would say /trakable/.

trace + able = traceable

> ***The rule to drop an E says "only if it is allowed by other spelling rules."***
> ***Which rules do you think this refers to?*** C softens to /s/ before E, I, and Y, and G may soften to /j/ before an E, I, or Y.

Spelling Rule	13

Drop the silent final E when adding a vowel suffix only if it is allowed by other spelling rules.

> **C softens to /s/ when followed by an E, I, or Y.**
> **G may soften to /j/ before E, I, or Y.**

✎ *19.13 Adding the Suffix -able –* **Complete the practice activities in your workbook.**

workable   *chargeable*
changeable   *agreeable*
valuable
reachable
solvable
enjoyable
traceable
savable

Challenge

Two words in our spelling list are based upon Greek roots. Do you know which ones? Hint: they both use the Greek spelling of /f/. phone and photograph

phone

What other words can you think of that have the word phone in them?

telephone, phonogram, microphone, saxophone, cellphone, megaphone

Each of these words share the Greek root phone. What do you think phone means?

Allow discussion and guessing.

Phone means sound.

Photograph is made of two Greek roots. What do you think they are?

photo   graph

Photo is the Greek word for light. It appears in more than 350 English words. What other words include the word photo?

photography, photographer, photosynthesis, telephoto...

Can you think of other words that include the word graph?

graphics, biography, autograph, calligraphy, choreograph, telegraph...

What do you think graph means?
Graph in Greek means a picture or something written. What does photograph mean? a light picture

This is how a camera works. The light enters the camera. When cameras used film, the light formed a picture on the film. Therefore, a photograph is a picture formed by light.

Many words are built from Latin and Greek roots. Phone and photograph are two examples. We will learn more roots as we continue.

Dictation

✎ *19.14 Dictation* – Read each sentence twice. Ask the students to repeat it aloud, then write it in their workbooks.

1. The boy spelled the words.
2. The children drink juice and eat apples.
3. Father took the boy's photograph.
4. Mother liked the little house.
5. The girls noticed the large horse.
6. The helpers moved the tables.

Composition

Write the following simple sentence on the board. Then ask the following questions, making the sentence increasingly more complex. Encourage the students to use any word they think is most interesting.

The girls liked.

> **What do the girls like?** (The following answer is an example. Write what the students suggest on the board.)

The girls liked the horse.

> **How many girls?**

The three girls liked the horse.

> **What kind of girls?**

The three enjoyable girls liked the horse.

> **What kind of horse?**

The three enjoyable girls liked the black horse.

> **How many horses?**

The three enjoyable girls liked the three black horses.

> **Whose horses?**

The three enjoyable girls liked Emma's three black horses.

✎ *19.15 Composition* – Direct the students to write a simple sentence in their workbooks. Then direct them to ask and answer four questions to expand the sentence, rewriting the sentence each time.

Lesson 20 — Assessment & Review

SPELLING ASSESSMENT

Materials Needed: Red and blue colored pencils.

1. ✎ *20.1 Assessment* – Dictate the sentences to the students while they write them in their workbook.

   1. Mother gave the girl a birthday gift.
   2. Grandmother said, "The man takes wonderful photographs."
   3. The little boys liked the apples, fruit, and juice.
   4. Father loves the large horse.
   5. A woman showed the man an excellent house.

   6. The owner mailed the letters.
   7. The girls traced the trees.
   8. The worker answered the phone.
   9. Ella poured the water.
   10. The teacher said, "The man moved the table."

2. Direct the students to read the sentences aloud while you write them on the board. Sound out each word and model the thought process. The students should mark corrections in red. Encourage the students to discuss what they missed. Create an atmosphere where it is acceptable to make errors. Model the attitude and strategies to move forward in practice.

3. Recheck the students' work. Note the words and concepts which need further practice.

4. Did the students:

   _____ *use -ED to form the regular past tense?*
   _____ *spell the irregular past tense verbs correctly?*
   _____ *capitalize the first letter in the sentence?*
   _____ *end each sentence with a period?*
   _____ *add a silent E to make the vowel sound long?*
   _____ *add a silent final E to soften a C to /s/ or a G to /j/?*
   _____ *add a silent final E if the syllable needed a vowel?*
   _____ *add a silent final E to keep a singular word from ending in -S?*
   _____ *drop the silent final E when adding a vowel suffix?*
   _____ *add an -S or -ES to make words plural?*
   _____ *add an -S or -ES to form the singular verb?*
   _____ *use quotation marks to show someone is speaking?*
   _____ *use a comma to set off a quotation?*

5. ✎ *20.2 Reading* – Ask the students to read the following words, phrases, and sentences. Note the words they did not read fluently.

   1. The boys attended class and learned useful new words.

   2. The sun shines.
   3. Mother and Father celebrated.

4. The girls saw the blue shoes.

5. Bring the suit and shoes.

6. the horse's new name

7. The boy grew three inches.

8. Father said, "Write the letter."

9. say, says, said

10. Mother said, "Save the change."

11. Bring a coat, shoes, and warm socks.

12. ten cents

13. Get a ride.

14. Share the toys.

15. bad germs

16. The children hide.

17. The girls traced the trees.

18. Spell the words.

19. United States, Canada, and the United Kingdom

20. the children's lessons

6. ✎ *20.3 Words to Practice* – Ask the students to read the words in the list and mark which ones they would like to practice further.

7. ✎ Using the assessment and your knowledge as a teacher, identify words to dictate onto Spelling Word Cards.

1. _____ answer	21. _____ large	41. _____ say
2. _____ apple	22. _____ learn	42. _____ says
3. _____ attend	23. _____ lesson	43. _____ see
4. _____ birthday	24. _____ letter	44. _____ share
5. _____ blue	25. _____ like	45. _____ shine
6. _____ bring	26. _____ little	46. _____ shoe
7. _____ celebrate	27. _____ love	47. _____ show
8. _____ cents	28. _____ make	48. _____ spell
9. _____ change	29. _____ move	49. _____ state
10. _____ excellent	30. _____ name	50. _____ suit
11. _____ fruit	31. _____ new	51. _____ table
12. _____ germs	32. _____ offer	52. _____ take
13. _____ get	33. _____ own	53. _____ tell
14. _____ gift	34. _____ phone	54. _____ trace
15. _____ give	35. _____ photograph	55. _____ use
16. _____ grow	36. _____ pour	56. _____ water
17. _____ hide	37. _____ ride	57. _____ wonderful
18. _____ horse	38. _____ rule	58. _____ word
19. _____ house	39. _____ said	59. _____ work
20. _____ juice	40. _____ save	60. _____ write

SPELLING WORD REVIEW

1. Dictate the missed words onto Spelling Word Cards or index cards. Have the students highlight the part of the word that was difficult.

2. Choose from the review activities below or use another activity found in *The Phonogram and Spelling Game Book.*

Optional Spelling Word Practice

1. ✎ *20.4 Extra Practice: Sink & Spell –* (*The Phonogram and Spelling Game Book,* 52)

2. Practice the words with Sky Writing (*The Phonogram and Spelling Game Book,* 45).

3. Practice the words by typing them on a computer.

OPTIONAL SPELLING RULE REVIEW

Use the following mini-lessons to review the concepts as needed.

Spelling Rule 12.1

Spelling Rule	12.1
The vowel says its name because of the E.	

1. Review the rule by reciting it and discussing the samples on the back of the card.

2. Write words on the board for the students to practice reading. Ask them to pronounce the word with and without the silent final E.

- *babe, bake, bale, base, cage, cake, came, cane, care, case, cave, dare, date, ease, fade, fake, fame, game, gate, gave, kale, lake, lame, lane, late, pale, pave, rage, rake, rate, rave, safe, sale, same, save, tame, vase, wade, wake, blame, blaze, drape, flake, flame, frame, glaze, grade, grape, grave, plane, plate, quake, scale, stake, state, trade, whale, sphere, bike, bite, dike, fine, fire, five, hide, hike, hive, kite, life, lime, mile, mine, mite, pike, pile, pine, pipe, ride, site, size, tile, time, vine, wife, wipe, glide, knife, stripe, trike, twine, whine, code, coke, cone, cove, hole, hose, lone, mole, nose, note, poke, robe, role, rope, rose, rote, rove, tone, tote, vote, wove, zone, choke, chore, close, drove, prone, quote, scone, scope, shore, slope, smoke, snore, spoke, stole, store, stove, whole, wrote, cube, cute, dude, duke, fume, huge, mule, pure, rude, rule, tune, brute, fluke, byte, hype, style, type.*

3. Dictate word from the list above for the students to write on white boards or with magnetic letters.

4. Write _a_e on the board. See how many new words the students can make. Then write _i_e; _o_e; _u_e. (Do not use _e_e. It is not a common spelling of the long E sound.) For variation: set a timer and ask the students to write as many words as possible in one minute. Each word spelled correctly is worth one point.

Spelling Rule 12.2

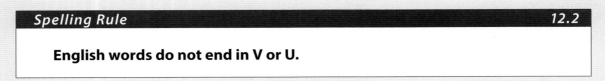

Spelling Rule	*12.2*
English words do not end in V or U.	

1. Review the rule by reciting it and discussing the samples on the back of the card.

2. Write the following words on the board. Ask the students to find the spelling error and correct it.

   dov   *hav*   *clu*

   eav   *valu*   *hu*

3. Dictate 5-10 of the following words for the students to write on white boards or with magnetic letters.

   - **-ve** *above, active, alive, approve, arrive, carve, cave, chive, clove, cove, crave, creative, cursive, curve, dive, dove, drive, drove, eve, forgive, gave, give, glove, grave, grove, halve, have, hive, groove, improve, involve, live, love, mauve, native, nerve, olive, pave, prove, rave, survive, swerve, twelve, valve, wave*

   - **-ue** *avenue, blue, continue, cue, due, glue, hue, overdue, pursue, rescue, sue, true, value*

4. Challenge students to think of as many words as possible that end in /v/. Write them on the board and notice that they all end in VE.

Spelling Rule 12.3

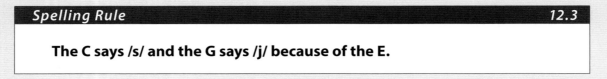

Spelling Rule	*12.3*
The C says /s/ and the G says /j/ because of the E.	

1. Review the rule by reciting it and discussing the samples on the back of the card.

2. Write words on the board for the students to practice reading. Ask them to pronounce the word with and without the silent final E.

   - **-ce** *ace, dice, face, ice, lace, lice, mice, nice, pace, race, rice, vice, brace, dance, fence, force, grace, juice, mince, ounce, peace, place, pounce, price, sauce, since, slice, space, spice, trace, truce, twice, voice, wince, advice, bounce, chance, choice, fleece, glance, notice, palace, police, prince, reduce, scarce, source, stance*

   - **-ge** *age, cage, huge, page, rage, urge, wage, hinge, image, large, stage, usage, forge, purge, range, change, lounge, orange, plunge, sponge, voyage*

3. Dictate 5-10 of the words for the students to write on white boards or with magnetic letters.

Spelling Rule 12.4

Spelling Rule	12.4
Every syllable must have a written vowel.	

1. Review the rule by reciting it and discussing the samples on the back of the card.

2. Reteach:

    - If the first vowel sound is long, the consonant is not doubled: *cable, fable, noble, stable, title.*

    - If the first vowel sound is short, the following consonant is doubled if there is only one consonant sound before the /l/: *babble, cobble, dribble, riddle, saddle, duffle, muffle, shuffle, giggle, juggle, smuggle, ripple, brittle, nettle, dazzle, muzzle, puzzle.* (pp. 227-228)

3. Dictate 5-10 of the following words for the students to write on white boards or with magnetic letters.

    - **-ble** *babble, bobble, bramble, bubble, bumble, cable, cobble, dribble, fable, feeble, fumble, grumble, humble, mumble, noble, stable, tremble, wobble*

    - **-cle** *article, bicycle, chronicle, circle, cycle, icicle, miracle, oracle, particle, tricycle, vehicle*

    - **-dle** *bridle, bundle, candle, cradle, cuddle, curdle, dawdle, doodle, dwindle, fiddle, griddle, handle, hurdle, kindle, middle, needle, noodle, riddle, saddle, straddle, swaddle*

    - **-fle** *baffle, muffle, raffle, ruffle, scuffle, shuffle, sniffle, waffle*

    - **-gle** *angle, beagle, boggle, bugle, bungle, dangle, eagle, gargle, google, giggle, haggle, jingle, juggle, mingle, single, smuggle, straggle, struggle, triangle, wiggle*

    - **-kle** *ankle, buckle, chuckle, crinkle, heckle, knuckle, pickle, shackle, speckle, suckle, tickle, trickle, twinkle, wrinkle*

    - **-ple** *ample, apple, couple, cripple, crumple, dimple, example, maple, multiple, people, pimple, purple, ripple, rumple, sample, simple, temple, trample, triple*

    - **-tle** *battle, beetle, bottle, brittle, bustle, castle, chortle, hurtle, kettle, mantle, nestle, nettle, prattle, rattle, settle, title, trestle, whistle, whittle*

    - **-zle** *dazzle, drizzle, frazzle, guzzle, muzzle, nuzzle, puzzle, sizzle*

4. Set a timer for one minute. Call out a word from the list above. Direct the students to write as many words that rhyme as they can before the timer beeps. Give one point for each word that rhymes and is spelled correctly. Play to 30 points.

Silent Final E Review

✎ *20.5 Extra Practice: Silent Final E Game* – Write 20-30 silent final E words from the activities above on index cards. Provide each student with a marker for the game board. Ask the student to draw a card. Students move forward one space for reading the word correctly, and one space for identifying the reason for the silent final E.

Past Tense Verbs

Spelling Rule	19
To make a verb past tense, add the ending -ED unless it is an irregular verb.	

Spelling Rule	20
ED, past tense ending, forms another syllable when the base word ends in /d/ or /t/. Otherwise, ED says /d/ or /t/.	

1. Review the rules by reciting them and discussing the samples on the back of the cards.

2. ✎ *20.6 Extra Practice: ED Past Tense Ending* – Explain that each of the following words will use -ED past tense ending. Read the word aloud. Ask the students to write the word in the column that shows the sound that -ED is saying.

   • /ed/ – *needed, attended, gifted, started, waited*

   • /d/ – *called, answered, learned, owned, showed, destroyed, enjoyed, opened, played, pulled*

   • /t/ – *walked, talked, worked, matched, helped, jumped, pushed, reached, searched*

3. ✎ *20.7 Extra Practice: Irregular Verbs* – Match the present tense verbs to the past tense irregular verbs.

4. Play charades using the irregular verbs in the workbook. To guess the answer, the students must write both the present and past tense of the word on a white board.

OPTIONAL GRAMMAR REVIEW

Re-teach or practice the rules as needed using the activities below.

Grammar Card 11.2   **Comma Rule 2**

Use a comma to separate a direct quote from the rest of the sentence.

Grammar Card 13.1   **Quotations**

Put quotation marks around direct quotations.

Grammar Card 13.2   **Quotations**

Place commas and periods inside the quotation marks.

Grammar Card 12.3   **Capitalization**

Capitalize the first word of a direct quotation.

---

1. Review the rule by reciting it and discussing the samples on the back of the card.

2. Ask the students to create sentences that include quotes. Write them on a white board with the correct punctuation. For example:

   Mother said, "Bring a coat."

Once several sentences are written on the board, ask the students to close their eyes. Erase the quotation marks and commas. Ask the students to make corrections.

OPTIONAL PHONOGRAM ASSESSMENT & REVIEW

Phonograms

20.8 Extra Practice: Phonogram Quiz – Dictate the following phonograms by reading the sounds and spelling aids.

1. a	5. r	9. s	13. c
2. ou	6. ck	10. qu	14. ow
3. z	7. b	11. p	15. d
4. th	8. gn	12. ph	16. aw

17. e	29. ir	41. ough	53. ea
18. oi	30. oo	42. ay	54. w
19. oy	31. g	43. m	55. wor
20. ch	32. wr	44. ear	56. er
21. t	33. u	45. ai	57. k
22. igh	34. au	46. x	58. augh
23. wh	35. ar	47. tch	59. ee
24. o	36. h	48. ed	60. y
25. ur	37. oe	49. sh	61. ui
26. f	38. v	50. j	62. ng
27. kn	39. oa	51. or	63. ew
28. n	40. i	52. l	

Optional Phonogram Practice

Practice the phonograms as needed using the following game suggestions or choose other games from *The Phonogram and Spelling Game Book.*

1. Play Dragon (*The Phonogram and Spelling Game Book,* 10).

2. ✎ *20.9 Extra Practice: Phonogram Flip* (*The Phonogram and Spelling Game Book,* 27).

3. Play Eraser Race (*The Phonogram and Spelling Game Book,* 28).

Lesson 21

Phonograms:	ei, ey eigh
Exploring Sounds:	Usage of EI, EY, and EIGH
Spelling Rules:	
Grammar:	Subject Pronouns

PART ONE

Materials Needed: Phonogram Flash Cards from previous lessons, and ei , ey , and eigh ; Phonogram Game Cards

Phonograms

New Phonograms — *ei, ey, eigh*

Today we will learn three new phonograms that are related.

Show ei . /ā-ē-ī/

Can you use this at the end of the word? no
Why not? English words do not end in I, U, V, or J.

Show ey . /ā-ē/

Can you use this at the end of the word? yes

Show eigh . /ā-ī/

Where will this phonogram be used? only before a T or at the end of the base word

Show ei /ā-ē-ī/ and ey /ā-ē/.

How are these two related? They both begin with an E. They both say /ā-ē/. One ends in a Y and may be used at the end of English words. The other ends in I and may not be used at the end of English words.

Show ⬚ei /ā-ē-ī/ and ⬚eigh /ā-ī/.

> ***How are these two related?*** They both begin with an EI. They both say /ā-ī/.
> ***How are they different?*** One ends in GH. EI says an additional sound /ē/.

Exploring Sounds

Usage of EI, EY, and EIGH

Show ⬚ei .

> ***What does this say?*** /ā-ē-ī/
> ✏ *21.1 Reading Words with EI –* **Read the words in your workbook aloud. Underline the /ā-ē-ī/.**

/ā/	/ē/	/ī/
their	weird	(either)<
reign	either	(neither)<
rein	neither	seismic
veil	leisure	kaleidoscope
vein	protein	rottweiler
heir	seize	Einstein
skein	caffeine	feisty
surveillance	sheik	

> < Teacher Tip: *Some people pronounce* either *and* neither *with a long /ī/.*

> **The EI phonogram is not commonly used. These are the most common words. EI says the long /ī/ sound in German words.**

Spelling Journal   Ⓐ Ⓚ Ⓥ

Add words that use EI to spell /ā/, /ē/, and /ī/.

Show ⬚ey .

> ***What does this say?*** /ā-ē/
> ✏ *21.2 Reading Words with EY –* **Read the words in your workbook aloud. Underline the /ā-ē/.**

> < Teacher Tip: *"key" is the only one-syllable word where EY says /ē/.*

/ā/	/ē/	
they	honey	turkey
hey	hockey	valley
obey	alley	volley
convey	money	chimney
prey	kidney	donkey
whey	pulley	monkey
	parsley	jersey

The EY phonogram is not commonly used. These are the most common words.
Where does EY say the long /ē/ sound? at the end of a multi-syllable word

---

Spelling Journal   Ⓐ Ⓚ Ⓥ

Add words that use EY to spell /ā/ and /ē/.

Show eigh .

What does this say? /ā-ī/

✎ *21.3 Reading Words with EIGH – **Read the words in your workbook aloud. Underline the /ā-ī/.***

/ā/	/ī/
eight	height
freight	sleight
sleigh	
weigh	
neigh	
neighbor	

These are all the words that use EIGH.
Are these phonograms you should write in lots of words? no
Rather, when you learn a word that has one of these three phonograms, it needs extra attention because it is not as common of a spelling.

What spelling rule limits the use of EIGH? Phonograms ending in GH are used only at the end of a base word or before the letter T.

There is one exception to the rule: Phonograms ending in GH are used only at the end of a base word or before a letter T in this list. Can you find it? Neighbor. The EIGH is followed by a B.

This is the only known exception to this rule.

Spelling Journal   Ⓐ Ⓚ Ⓥ

Add words which use EIGH to spell /ā/ and /ī/.

Optional: Review Spellings of Long /ā/

EI, EY, and EIGH all say the long /ā/ sound.
Are these common spellings of the long /ā/ sound? no
What is the most common spelling of long /ā/ at the end of the syllable. single-vowel A
Give me a few examples.

a
bā ker
pā per
flā vor
mā jor

What is the most common spelling of long /ā/ at the end of the words? ay
Give me a few examples.

a	ay
bā ker	d*ay*
pā per	cl*ay*
flā vor	pl*ay*
mā jor	tr*ay*

What is the most common spelling of long /ā/ in the middle of the syllable? ai
Give me a few examples.

a	ay	ai
bā ker	d*ay*	j*ai*l
pā per	cl*ay*	n*ai*l
flā vor	pl*ay*	p*ai*n
mā jor	tr*ay*	st*ai*rs

What is the final spelling of long /ā/ that we have learned? ea
Where is EA used? in the middle of the syllable
Is it very common? No, it is only found in seven common base words.
Name a few examples.

a	ay	ai	ea	
bā ker	d<u>ay</u>	j<u>ai</u>l	steak	wear
pā per	cl<u>ay</u>	n<u>ai</u>l	great	tear
flā vor	pl<u>ay</u>	p<u>ai</u>n	bear	pear
mā jor	tr<u>ay</u>	st<u>ai</u>rs	break	

Phonograms

Review

1. Drill the phonograms with flash cards.   *[handwritten: Show phonogram and have her say the sound(s)]*

2. ✎ *21.4 Writing the Phonograms* – Write each new phonogram five times while saying the sounds aloud.

3. ✎ *21.5 Phonogram Practice* – Dictate the following phonograms. For extra practice, have the students read them back. Write the correct answers on the board as the students check their answers.

1. eigh   *[handwritten: ā ī eight height]*
2. ear
3. kn
4. wor
5. wr
6. gn
7. ur
8. tch   *[handwritten: ch k sh]*
9. ei   *[handwritten: ā ē ī their protein feisty]*
10. ou   *[handwritten: ow ō oo ŭ house soul group]*
11. au
12. ey   *[handwritten: ā ē they key]*
13. ew
14. ir
15. ow
16. ph
17. ough
18. augh
19. aw
20. oa   *[handwritten: ō coat]*

4. Play Phonogram Snatch using the Phonogram Game Cards (*The Phonogram and Spelling Game Book*, 8).

Spelling Rules

Review: Reasons for a Silent Final E.

What are the five reasons we have learned for adding a silent final E? To make the vowel say its name; English words do not end in V or U; to make the C say /s/ and the G say /j/; every syllable must have a vowel; to keep singular words that end in S from looking plural.

I will write a word with a silent final E. Read the word and tell me why the E is needed.

give	English words do not end in V or U.
table	Every syllable must have a vowel.
large	The G softens to /j/ because of the E.
race	The A says its name because of the E. The C softens to /s/ because of the E.
house	House is singular. The E is needed to keep the S from making it look plural.

pole	The O says its name because of the E.
mauve	English words do not end in V or U.
age	The A says its name because of the E. The G softens to /j/ because of the E.
mouse	Mouse is singular. The E is needed to keep the S from making it look plural.
title	Every syllable must have a vowel.

Optional Spelling Rule Practice

1. Quickly review rules 1-4, 8-12.5, 13, 19-22, 24, 26-28, 30 using the Spelling Rule Cards. Ⓐ Ⓥ

2. *21.6 Extra Practice: Silent Final E Game* - Cut out the cards. Place them face down on the table. Students choose a card, read it, and identify the reason(s) for the silent final E.

   - If the student reads the word correctly and identifies all the reasons for the silent E, the student keeps the card.

   - If the student cannot read the word or misses one of the reasons, the card is returned to the pile.

   - If the student draws one of the additional cards, he should follow the directions on the card. These cards are not returned to the pile once they are used, but set aside.

   - Play ends when all the cards are drawn.

   Award points as follows:

   - one point for reading the word correctly

   - one point for identifying each reason for the silent final E

   - one point for each card in the student's possession at the end of the game

   The person with the most points wins.

PART TWO

Using Spelling List 21 on pages 256-257, dictate each word following the steps included on pages Intro 42 - Intro 46.

Tips for Spelling List 21

I, You

The words *I* and *you* are true exceptions to the rule, "English words do not end in I, U, V, or J." Help students to memorize these with the phrase, "You and I are very special!" Also remember to tell students that *I* is always written with a capital letter.

Breakfast

Notice that *breakfast* is a compound word formed with the words *break* and *fast*. *Breakfast* refers to breaking the fast from eating during the night. Point out to students how the phonogram EA shifts its pronunciation from /ā/ in *break* to /ĕ/ in *breakfast*.

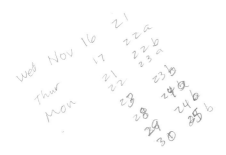

	Word	Practice Sentence	Say to Spell	# of Syllables	Markings
1.	**I**	*I like you.*	ī	1	ī
2.	**you**	*You are my friend.*	yoo	1	you[3]
3.	**they**	*They went to the movie.*	THā	1	they[2]
4.	**eight**	*There are eight pencils on the table.*	āt	1	eight
5.	**wild**	*The tiger lives out in the wild.*	wīld	1	wīld
6.	**weigh**	*The letters weigh four ounces each.*	wā	1	weigh
7.	**height**	*What is his height?*	hīt	1	height[2]
8.	**type**	*Everyone should learn how to type.*	tīp	1	tȳpe
9.	**ask**	*May I ask for a glass of water?*	ăsk	1	ask
10.	**breakfast**	*We are having pancakes for breakfast.*	brĕk făst	2	break[2] fast
11.	**lunch**	*Come over for lunch.*	lŭnch	1	lunch
12.	**dinner**	*Dinner will be at 6 o'clock.*	dĭn ner	2	din ner
13.	**practice**	*To become a strong reader and speller, practice everyday.*	prăc tĭs	2	prac tice
14.	**add**	*Add the numbers together.*	ăd	1	add
15.	**number**	*Count the number of cards in the stack.*	nŭm ber	2	num ber

excellent

Spelling Hints	Part of Speech	Vocabulary Development
Capitalize the I. **3** English words do not end in I, U, V, or J. This is a true exception. Memorization tip: "You and I are very special!"	Pro	
Underline /oo/. Put a 3 over it. /ow-ō-oo-ŭ/ says its third sound. **3** English words do not end in I, U, V, or J. This is a true exception. Memorization tip: "You and I are very special!"	Pro	your
Underline /TH/ and put a 2 over it. /th-TH/ says its second sound. Underline /ā-ē/.	Pro	their
Underline /ā-ī/. **28** Phonograms ending in GH are used only at the end of a base word or before the letter T. The GH is either silent or pronounced /f/.	Adj, N	eights, eighteen, eighty, eighteenth, eighties, eightieth
Put a line over the I. **8** I and O may say /ī/ and /ō/ before two consonants.	Adj	wilder, wildest, wildflower, wildcat, wildebeest, wilderness, wildfire, wildlands, wildlife, wildly, wildness, wildwoods
Underline /ā-ī/. **28** Phonograms ending in GH are used only at the end of a base word or before the letter T. The GH is either silent or pronounced /f/.	V	weight, weights, weighed, weighty, counterweight, overweight, underweight, weighted, weightlessness, deadweight
Underline /ā-ī/ and put a 2 over it. /ā-ī/ says its second sound. **28** Phonograms ending in GH are used only at the end of a base word or before the letter T. The GH is either silent or pronounced /f/.	N	heights, heighten, heightening
Put a line over the /ī/. Y is saying its long vowel sound /ī/. Double underline the silent final E. **12.1** The vowel says its name because of the E.	N, V	typing, typed, typist, archetype, genotype, prototype, stereotype, typify, typical, typeset, typewritten, typewriter, typo
All first sounds.	V	asked, asking, asker
Underline /ĕ/ and put a 2 over it. /ē-ĕ-ā/ says its second sound. Discuss the meaning that breakfast is a compound word using *break* and *fast*. *Fast* means to go without food. At breakfast we break our fast.	N, V	breakfasts, breakfasting, breakfasted
Underline the /ch/.	N, V	lunches, lunchroom, luncheon
Underline the /er/.	N	dinners, dinnerless, dinnerware
Underline the /s/, double underline the E. **12.3** The C says /s/ because of the E.	V, N	practiced, practicing, practices
30 We often double F, L, and S after a single vowel at the end of a base word. Occasionally other letters also are doubled.	V	added, adding, addition, additional, additive
Underline the /er/.	N	numbers, numbered, numbering, numeral, innumerable

PART THREE

Materials Needed: Grammar Rule Cards 6, 6.1; red, pink, green and blue colored pencils; whiteboards, markers, erasers.

Grammar

Review

What is a noun? A noun is the name of a person, place, thing, or idea.
What are the three noun jobs we have learned so far? subject noun, direct object, indirect object
What is an adjective? Adjectives modify nouns and pronouns. Adjectives answer: What kind? How many? Which one? Whose?
What is an article? A, An, The. Tiny article adjectives that mark nouns and answer the question: Which?
Name the parts of a sentence. A sentence must have a capital letter, subject, verb, complete thought, and an end mark.
What is a verb? A verb shows action, links a description to the subject, or helps another verb.
What are the two types of verbs we have learned about so far? action verbs and transitive verbs

✎ *Spelling List 21 – Identify the parts of speech for words 4-15 in List 21. Mark the nouns with a red N, the verbs with a green V, and the adjectives with a blue Adj.*

✎ *Spelling List 21 – Write the past tense of each verb and the plural for each noun.*

Subject Pronouns

Today we will learn a new part of speech: the pronoun.

I will read you a story. I want you to tell me if you hear something that doesn't sound right.

John went to the store. John bought a saw. After John brought it home, John took a piece of wood and John used the saw to cut it. When John was finished, John hung the saw in his garage.

The story keeps using the word "John" again and again.

How could we change the story so that it sounds better? Use the word "he" instead of John.
We could change the story by saying: John went to the store. He bought a saw. After he brought it home, he took a piece of wood, and he used the saw to cut it. When he was finished, he hung the saw in his garage.

Rather than saying John again and again, what word did I use? he
He is a pronoun. The word "he" replaces the word "John" in the sentence. A pronoun takes the place of a noun.

Grammar Card 6   **Pro**

A pronoun takes the place of a noun.

Write the following sentences on the board:

Grandmother coughed.	*She coughed.*
Father slept.	*He slept*
The dog played.	*It played*
Mother and Father ate popcorn.	*They ate popcorn.*

Instead of "Grandmother coughed," we could say, "She coughed."
What would we say instead of "Father slept?" He slept.
The dog played? It played.
Mother and Father ate popcorn? They ate popcorn.

Have the students help you list the subject pronouns as you write them on the board:

Subject Pronouns

I

you

he

she

it

we

they

Read the definition of a Subject Pronoun together and discuss the samples on the back.

Grammar Card 6.1   **SP**

A subject pronoun takes the place of a subject noun.
I, you, he, she, it, we, they

Make up a sentence using each of the subject pronouns.
✎ *21.7 Subject Pronouns - Write the subject pronouns in your workbook.*

✎ *Mark the pronouns in List 21 with a pink Pro.*

Identifying the Parts of Speech

✎ *21.8 Identifying Parts of Speech – **We will now read five sentences, identify the parts of speech, and divide the subject from the predicate.***

We ate breakfast.

Who ate? we, subject
Since "we" is a pronoun and the subject of the sentence, we will call it the subject pronoun.
What is being said about we? we ate, verb
What did we eat? breakfast, direct object
Is there a direct object receiving the action of the verb? yes
Then it is a transitive verb. Write a T next to the V to show the type of verb.
What is the subject of the sentence? we
What is the predicate? ate breakfast
Put a slash between the subject and the predicate.

SP   TV   DO
We / ate breakfast.

She practiced the difficult music.

Who practiced? she, subject pronoun
What is being said about she? she practiced, verb
What did she practice? music, direct object
What kind of music? difficult, adjective
Which music? the, article adjective
Is there a direct object receiving the action of the verb? yes
Then it is a transitive verb. Write a T next to the V to show the type of verb.
Put a slash between the subject and the predicate.

SP   TV   A   Adj   DO
She / practiced the difficult music.

He added the large numbers.

Who added? he, subject pronoun
What is being said about he? he added, verb
What did he add? numbers, direct object
What kind of numbers? large, adjective
Which numbers? the, article adjective
Is there a direct object receiving the action of the verb? yes
Then it is a transitive verb. Write a T next to the V to show the type of verb.
Put a slash between the subject and the predicate.

SP   TV   A   Adj   DO
He / added the large numbers.

They weighed the apples and the oranges.

Who weighed? they, subject pronoun
What is being said about they? they weighed, verb
What did they weigh? apples, direct object
What else did they weigh? oranges, direct object
How many direct objects are in this sentences? two
Which word is joining them together? and, conjunction
Which apples? the, article adjective
Which oranges? the, article adjective
Is there a direct object receiving the action of the verb? yes
Then it is a transitive verb. Write a T next to the V to show the type of verb.
Put a slash between the subject and the predicate.

SP   TV   A   DO   C   A   DO
They / weighed the apples and the oranges.

I read the little boy a good book.

Who read? I, subject pronoun
What is being said about I? I read, verb
What did I read? book, direct object
What kind of book? good, adjective
Which book? a, article adjective
To whom did I read it? boy, indirect object
What kind of boy? little, adjective
Which boy? the, article adjective
Is there a direct object receiving the action of the verb? yes
Then it is a transitive verb. Write a T next to the V to show the type of verb.
What is the subject of the sentence? I
What is the predicate? read the little boy a good book
Put a slash between the subject and the predicate.

SP   TV   A   Adj   IO   A   Adj   DO
I / read the little boy a good book.

1st, 2nd, and 3rd Person

Every sentence and every story is written from the perspective of a person. Before we write, we need to first consider who we want to tell the story.

If I am telling the story about myself, it will sound like this:
Yesterday, I walked to the store. When I arrived, I saw my friend Sam who was buying paint. I said, "Hello."

When the story is told using the pronoun I, it is called first person.

Tell me a short story using first person.   Answers will vary.

If I were telling the story about you, it would sound like this:
Yesterday you went to the park. While you were there you saw a small black dog. You took the dog home."

When we tell a story about you *it is called second person. It is not very common to write in second person.*

Tell me a short story using second person.   Answers will vary.

If I am telling the story about Jack it may sound like this:
Last night Jack stayed up too late reading a good book. This morning he could not stay awake in class. He kept falling asleep. He even began to snore loudly during math.

When the pronouns he, she, *and* it *are used, they are called third person.*

Tell me a short story using third person.   Answers will vary.

If I tell a story about two girls who are gymnasts, it may sound like this:

On Saturday two girls competed at the gymnastics meet. They worked hard. They focused on each event. They both received good scores.

Do you think this is first, second, or third person? third
Why? It is a story about someone else.

I will tell another story. Tell me if you think this story is first, second, or third person.

Dad and I went fishing. When we got to the lake we took out our fishing poles. We dropped our lines in the water. Immediately we both felt a tug. When we reeled in the lines we discovered we had caught each other."

Since I am telling the story about something I did, it is first person, even though there is someone else with me.

✎ *21.9 Matching the Pronouns to the Person – Match the pronouns to the person.*

✎ *21.10 First, Second, or Third Person – Read the short stories. Decide they are written in first, second, or third person. Circle the answer.*

> 1. Third   3. Second
> 2. First

Grammar Challenge

Direct the students to find two books or stories that are told in first person and two books or stories that are told in third person.

Optional Grammar Practice

1. ✎ *21.11 Extra Practice: Subject Pronouns* - Rewrite each sentence by replacing the subject with a pronoun.   Ⓚ Ⓥ Ⓐ

2. ✎ *21.12 Extra Practice: Articles* - Review when to use "a" and "an." Complete the review activity in the workbook about using the articles "a" and "an."   Ⓚ Ⓥ Ⓐ

3. ✎ *21.13 Extra Practice: Titles of Respect* - Review the meanings of Mr., Mrs., Ms., and Dr. Direct the students to complete the activity about titles of respect in their workbook. Ⓚ Ⓥ Ⓐ

4. Practice reciting the subject pronouns. Write them on the board. Recite the list. Erase one pronoun and recite the list again. Erase another pronoun and recite. Continue in this manner until all the pronouns have been erased and students are reciting from memory. Ⓚ Ⓥ Ⓐ

5. Challenge students to list the subject pronouns on paper. Time them to see how fast they can write them. Optional: Time students to see how fast they can say the subject pronouns.   Ⓚ Ⓥ Ⓐ

6. Ask students to tell about a certain event in first, second, or third person. For example: describe making a sandwich, waking up in the morning, going to the zoo...   Ⓒ Ⓐ

Optional Reading Practice

1. ✎ *21.14 Extra Practice: Reading* – Direct the students to read the sentences in the workbook aloud. Have the students read them two or three times until they can read each one fluently.

2. *Optional* – Reread the sentences. Divide the subject and the predicate.

Optional Spelling Cards

1. Dictate the words in Lesson 21 for the students to write on index cards. Ⓐ Ⓚ Ⓥ

2. Color a green border around the verbs, a red border around the nouns, a pink border around the pronouns, and a blue border around the adjectives. Ⓚ Ⓥ

3. Dictate all of the subject pronouns onto index cards. Ⓚ Ⓥ Ⓐ

4. Direct students to arrange the cards into sentences using a noun, verb, and if needed direct and indirect object. Demonstrate how the subject noun can be replaced with a pronoun by laying the correct pronoun over the subject. Ⓚ Ⓥ Ⓐ

Dictation

✎ *21.15 Dictation* – Read each sentence twice. Ask the students to repeat it aloud, then write it in their workbooks.

1. She weighed eight apples.

2. He practiced the music.

3. We named the wild dog.

4. I added the numbers.

5. You ate breakfast, lunch, and dinner.

6. They asked the workers.

Composition

Today we will write sentences in first, second, and third person.
Which pronouns could I use to tell a story in first person? I or we
Let's write the sentence beginning with the pronoun I.

I

What is being said about me? Answers will vary. For example: I rode.

I rode.

What did I ride? I rode a bike.

I rode a bike.

What kind of bike? I rode a large bike.

I rode a large bike.

Now let's write a sentence in the second person. What pronoun will I use? you

You

What is being said about you? Answers will vary. For example: You ate.

You ate.

Continue by asking two or three questions to flesh out the sentence, while writing it on the board.

Now let's write a sentence in the third person. Which pronouns can we use? he, she, it, they
Let's use they.
What is being said about them? Answers will vary.

Continue by asking two or three questions to flesh out the sentence, while writing it on the board.

✎ *21.16 Composition – **Write three sentences in your workbook using first, second, and third person.***

Vocabulary Development

Provide each student with a small whiteboard. Read the word. They will write it and then use it in two sentences to demonstrate the multiple ways the words may be used.

Many words have more than one meaning. These are called homographs.

homograph

Homo means one or the same.
Do you remember what graph means? to write or something that is written

A homograph is a word that has two meanings but both words are written in the same way. Sometimes the words are also pronounced differently.

I will say a word. Write it. Then use the word in two sentences that show its meanings.

rock

1) a stone; 2) to move something back and forth.
Examples: 1) Pick the rocks out of the grass before you mow. 2) I will rock the baby to sleep.

duck

1) a type of water bird; 2) to move away from a moving object.
Examples: 1) The duck quacked. 2) She ducked out of the way of the flying rock.

plain

1) simple, not decorated; 2) flat land without trees.
Examples: 1) Wear the plain shirt with those pants. 2) Buffalo live on the open plains.

long

1) length; 2) a strong desire for something.
Examples: 1) How long is the table? 2) I long to go to the beach.

sharp

1) something that cuts well; 2) someone who is smart.
Examples: 1) The knife is sharp. 2) She has a sharp mind.

yard

1) a measurement equal to three feet; 2) the land around a house.
Examples: 1) He ran 100 yards. 2) Go play in the yard.

stamp

1) a postage stamp; 2) a mark you put on paper using a stamp; 3) a device for putting a mark on paper; 4) to pound your feet.
Examples: 1) Put a stamp on the envelope. 2) This document has an official stamp. 3) Use the star stamp to make a card. 4) That horse stamps his feet when he is angry.

pound

1) a measurement of weight equal to sixteen ounces; 2) to hit something hard.
Examples: 1) The dog weighs 10 pounds. 2) Pound the nail into the wall.

change

1) to make something different; 2) money in the form of coins.
Examples: 1) Change your clothes before we go. 2) I have $5 worth of change in my purse.

charge

1) to move ahead quickly and with force; 2) to pay for a purchase with a credit card.
Examples: 1) The players charged onto the soccer field. 2) I will charge the purchase on my credit card.

sign

1) to write your name or signature; 2) written directions or ads; 3) an indication; 4) hand motions.
Examples: 1) Sign you name on the bottom of this page. 2) That is a stop sign. 3) He showed signs of a fever. 4) She signed him to hurry up.

saw

1) the past tense of **see**; 2) to cut wood; 3) a tool used to cut.
Examples: 1) She saw you at the park. 2) They will saw the logs into the correct size. 3) This saw is sharp.

Lesson 22

Phonograms:	
Exploring Sounds:	Voiced and Unvoiced Pairs
Spelling Rules:	12.6, 12.7, 12.8, 12.9
Grammar:	Object Pronouns

PART ONE

Materials Needed: Phonogram Flash Cards from previous lessons; Spelling Rule Cards 12.6, 12.7, 12.8, and 12.9; slips of paper, and baskets for phonogram basketball,

Phonograms

Review

1. Drill the phonograms with flash cards.

2. ✎ *22.1 Phonogram Practice* – Dictate the following phonograms. For extra practice, have the students read them back. Write the correct answers on the board as the students check their answers.

   1. ir   *bird*
   2. ew   *oo ū*   *plew few*
   3. ow   *ow ō*
   4. ur   *hurt*
   5. oo   *oo ŭ ō*   *food took floor*
   6. kn   *n*
   7. ear   *search*
   8. au   *ä not used a end*
   9. wor
   10. ph
   11. ei   *ā ē ī*
   12. aw   *ä used @ end*
   13. gn
   14. ey   *ā ē*
   15. wr
   16. ou   *ow ō oo ŭ*
   17. eigh   *ā ī*   *ĭ height*
   18. ough
   19. augh
   20. igh

3. Play Phonogram Basketball (*The Phonogram and Spelling Game Book*, 22).

Exploring Sounds

Voiced and Unvoiced Pairs

What is the rule for making a noun plural? To make a noun plural add the ending -S unless the word hisses or changes, then add -ES. Occasional nouns have no change or an irregular spelling.

Today we will focus on words that change:

wife

> **What is the plural of wife?** wives
> **What sound did the /f/ in wife change to in wives?** /v/
> **What do we need to add to make it plural?** -ES
>
> **What kind of word is wife?** a silent final E word
> **How do we add a suffix to a silent final E word?** Drop the silent final E when adding a vowel suffix only if it is allowed by other spelling rules.
> **Can we drop the E?** yes

wives

> **Say /f/ and /v/. How are these sounds related?** They are made in the same part of the mouth. /f/ is unvoiced. /v/ is voiced.
> **Sometimes voiced and unvoiced pairs will substitute for one another within words.**
> **Can you find any other voiced/unvoiced pairs?** /th-TH/, /t-d/, /s-z/, /p-b/, /k-g/, /ch-j/.
>
> **I will write some pairs of words on the board. Tell me how the words are related, and how the sounds changed between the forms.**

life	*lives*	Lives is the plural of life. The unvoiced /f/ turns into a voiced /v/.
knife	*knives*	Knives is the plural of knife. The unvoiced /f/ turns into a voiced /v/.
cloth	*clothes*	Cloth is used to make clothes. The TH becomes voiced.
breath	*breathe*	I take a breath when I breathe. The TH becomes voiced.

Spelling Rules

Rule 12.6

> **Today we will learn four more reasons for a silent final E. These are not as common as the first five reasons we learned.**
>
> **Before we begin, what are the five reasons for adding a silent final E that we have learned so far?**
> 1) to make the vowel say its name;
> 2) English words do not end in V or U;
> 3) to make the C says /s/ and the G say /j/;
> 4) every syllable must have a vowel;
> 5) to keep a singular word from looking plural.
>
> ✎ *22.2 Silent Final E – **Read the words in your workbook. Double underline the silent final E.***
> **Can you guess why each of these words has a silent final E?** answer may vary

These words have a silent final E to make them longer. Some two and three letter words have a silent final E to add length to the word.

are	axe	rye
awe	dye	bye

These words follow the rule:

Spelling Rule	12.6
Add an E to make the word look bigger.	

< Teacher Tip: *The following is a complete list of two letter words in English: ah, am, an, as, at, ax (or axe), be, by, do, ho, if, in, is, it, ma, me, my, no, of, oh, on, or, ow, ox, pa, pi, to, up, us, we.*

Rule 12.7

✎ *22.3 Silent Final E –* **Read the words in your workbook. Double underline the silent final E. How do these words change when we add a silent final E?** The /th-TH/ changes from unvoiced to voiced. In bathe, clothe, and breathe the vowels changes from short to long.

bath bathe		breath breathe
cloth clothe		teeth teethe

This leads to our new rule for a silent final E:

Spelling Rule	12.7
TH says its voiced sound /TH/ because of the E.	

This reason for a silent final E is not very common.

Rule 12.8

✎ *22.4 Silent Final E –***Read the pairs of words in your workbook. Double underline the silent final E. After you read each pair, compare the meaning of each word.**

brows browse		laps	lapse
teas tease		or	ore

What do you notice about these words? They are pronounced the same but they have different meanings.
Use each one in a sentence.

This leads to our eighth reason for a silent final E.

Spelling Rule	12.8
Add an E to clarify meaning.	

Rule 12.9

The final reason for a silent final E is:

Spelling Rule	12.9
Unseen reason.	

There are a few word where we can no longer see the reason for the silent final E. At one time the E may have been pronounced. I will write a few examples on the board.

come   some   done   were

What sound does the O make in come, some, and done? /ə/
When we spell these words we will say /cŏm/, /sŏm/ and /dŏn/. We will exaggerate the short /ŏ/ sound to help us remember how to spell them.

Optional Spelling Rule Practice

1. Quickly review rules 1-4, 8-13, 19-22, 24, 26-28, 30 using the Spelling Rule Cards.   Ⓐⓥ

2. *22.5 Extra Practice: Silent Final E Game* - Cut out the cards. Place them face down on the table. Students choose a card, read it and identify the reason(s) for the silent final E.

   - If the student reads the word correctly and identifies all the reasons for the silent E, the student keeps the card.

   - If the student cannot read the word or misses one of the reasons, the card is returned to the pile.

   - If the student draws one of the additional cards, he should follow the directions on the card. These cards are not returned to the pile once they are used, but set aside.

   - Play ends when all the cards are drawn.

   Award points as follows:

   - one point for reading the word correctly

   - one point for identifying each reason for the silent final E

   - one point for each card in the student's possession at the end of the game

   The person with the most points wins.

PART TWO

Using Spelling List 22 on pages 272-273, dictate each word following the steps included on pages Intro 42 - Intro 46.

Tips for Spelling List 22

Some, Come

Exaggerate the /ŏ/ sound to aid students in creating an auditory picture.

	Word	Practice Sentence	Say to Spell	# of Syllables	Markings
1.	**her**	*The teacher picked her.*	her	1	h<u>er</u>
2.	**us**	*The teacher picked us.*	ŭs	1	us
3.	**them**	*The teacher picked them.*	THĕm	1	<u>th</u>em²
4.	**simple**	*We will try a simple problem first.*	sĭmpl	2	sim pl<u>e</u>
5.	**key**	*I need the key to the car.*	kē	1	k<u>ey</u>
6.	**price**	*Put a price on each item.*	prīs	1	prī<u>ce</u>
7.	**some**	*Please give Hannah some paper.*	sŏm	1	som<u>e</u>
8.	**whole**	*The whole pie is in the refrigerator.*	whōl	1	<u>wh</u>ōl<u>e</u>
9.	**home**	*It is time to go home.*	hōm	1	hōm<u>e</u>
10.	**clothes**	*Change your clothes before you work outside.*	clōTHz	1	clō<u>th</u>es²
11.	**white**	*You will need to wear a white shirt for the concert.*	whīt	1	<u>wh</u>īt<u>e</u>
12.	**knife**	*Be careful with the knife.*	nīf	1	<u>kn</u>īf<u>e</u>
13.	**rescue**	*The boys will rescue the dog.*	rĕs cū	2	res c<u>ue</u>
14.	**come**	*They will come home at 8 o'clock.*	cŏm	1	com<u>e</u>
15.	**yellow**	*The yellow rose is beautiful.*	yĕl lō	2	yel l<u>ow</u>²

Spelling Hints	Part of Speech	Vocabulary Development
Underline /er/.	Pro	herself
All first sounds.	Pro	
Underline /TH/. Put a 2 over it. /th-TH/ said its second sound.	Pro	themselves
Underline the L and double underline the silent final E. **12.4** Every syllable must have a vowel.	Adj	simpler, simplest, oversimple, simplify, simpleton, simpleminded
Underline /ē/.	N, Adj	keys, keyboard, keyboarding, keyed, keyhole, keyless, keynote, keypad, keypunch, keystone, keystroke, keyword
Draw a line over the /ī/, underline the C, double underline the E. **12.1** The vowel says its name because of the E. **12.3** The C says /s/ because of the E.	V, N	priceless, priced, pricing, overpriced, underpriced, reprice, pricier, pricey
Say to spell sŏme. Double underline the silent final E. At one time the E was pronounced. **12.9** Unseen reason.	Adj	someone, somewhere, something, burdensome, handsome, awesome, irksome, lonesome, worrisome
Underline the /wh/. Draw a line over the /ō/. Double underline the silent E. **12.1** The vowel says its name because of the E.	Adj	wholeness, wholesome, wholesomely, wholesomeness, wholehearted, wholesale, wholesaler
Draw a line over the /ō/. Double underline the silent E. **12.1** The vowel says its name because of the E.	N	homes, homely, homeless, homemaker, homework, homeopathic, homeroom, homesick, homestead, homespun
Draw a line over the /ō/. Underline /TH/. Put a 2 over it. /th-TH/ said its second sound. Double underline the silent E. **12.1** The vowel says its name because of the E.	N	clothe, clothing, cloth, bedclothes, nightclothes, underclothes, clothesline, clothespin, dishcloth, washcloth, plainclothes, tablecloth
Underline the /wh/. Draw a line over the I. Double underline the silent final E. **12.1** The vowel says its name because of the E.	Adj	whites, whiter, whitest, nonwhite, whiteboard, whiten, whitened, whitener, whitening, whiteness, whitetail, whitewash
Underline /n/. Used only at the beginning of a base word. Draw a line over the /ī/ and double underline the silent final E. **12.1** The vowel says its name because of the E.	N	knives, knifed, penknife, pocketknife, jackknife, penknives, pocketknives, jackknives
Underline U. Double underline the silent final E. **12.2** English words do not end in V or U.	V	rescued, rescuer, rescuing, rescues
Say to spell cŏme. Double underline the silent final E. **12.9** Unseen reason.	V	came, comeback, income, incomes, latecomer, become, newcomer, outcome, overcome, welcome, welcoming
Underline the /ō/. Put a 2 over it. /ow-ō/ said its second sound.	Adj	yellows, yellower, yellowness, yellowish

PART THREE

Materials Needed: Grammar Rule Card 6.2; pink, red, green, and blue colored pencils.

Grammar

Review

What is a noun? A noun is the name of a person, place, thing, or idea.

What are the three noun jobs we have learned so far? subject noun, direct object, indirect object

What is an adjective? Adjectives modify nouns and pronouns. Adjectives answer: What kind? How many? Which one? Whose?

What is an article? A, An, The. Tiny article adjectives that mark nouns and answer the question: Which?

Name the parts of a sentence. A sentence must have a capital letter, subject, verb, complete thought, and an end mark.

What is a verb? A verb shows action, links a description to the subject, or helps another verb.

What are the two types of verbs we have learned about so far? action verbs and transitive verbs

✎ *Spelling List 22 –* **Identify the parts of speech for words 4-15 in List 22. Mark the nouns with a red N, the verbs with a green V, and the adjectives with a blue Adj.**

✎ *Spelling List 22 –* **Write the past tense of each verb and the plural for each noun.**

Object Pronouns

Yesterday we learned the subject pronouns. I will write them on the board as you list them.

Subject	Object
I	
You	
He	
She	
It	
We	
They	

Make up a sentence using each of these pronouns.

Today, we will learn the object pronouns.

We will use this practice sentence to discover them:

The teacher called _____.

> **We do not say, "The teacher called I." What word do we use instead?** me
> **Say the whole sentence.** The teacher called me.

Point to *you*.

> **What will we say here? The teacher called ___.** you

Elicit student responses to fill in the rest of the chart.

Subject	Object
I	me
you	you
he	him
she	her
it	it
we	us
they	them

Recite the definition and discuss the samples on the back of Grammar Card 6.2.

Grammar Card 6.2

An object pronoun takes the place of an object noun.
me, you, him, her, it, us, them

✎ *22.6 Object Pronouns* – **Write the subject and object pronouns in your workbook.**

✎ *Spelling List 22* – **Mark the pronouns in List 22 with a pink Pro.**

Identifying Parts of Speech

✎ *22.7 Identifying Parts of Speech* – Label the parts of speech in your workbook, while I label them on the board.

We fought it.

Who fought? we, subject pronoun
What is being said about we? we fought, verb
What did we fight? it, direct object
Is there a direct object receiving the action of the verb? yes
Then it is a transitive verb. Write a T next to the V to show the type of verb.
Divide the subject and the predicate.

SP   TV   DO
We / fought it.

They saw him.

Who saw? they, subject pronoun
What is being said about they? they saw, verb
Whom did they see? him, direct object
Is there a direct object receiving the action of the verb? yes
Then it is a transitive verb. Write a T next to the V to show the type of verb.
Divide the subject and the predicate.

SP   TV DO
They / saw him.

The firemen rescued her.

Who rescued? firemen, subject noun
Which firemen? the, article adjective
What is being said about firemen? Firemen rescued, verb.
Whom did they rescue? her, direct object
Is there a direct object receiving the action of the verb? yes
Then it is a transitive verb. Write a T next to the V to show the type of verb.
Divide the subject and the predicate.

A   SN   TV   DO
The firemen / rescued her.

Indirect objects also use the object pronouns.

I gave him the ball.

Who gave? I, subject pronoun
What is being said about I? I gave, verb.
What did I give? ball, direct object
Which ball? the, article adjective
To whom did I give the ball? him, indirect object
Is there a direct object receiving the action of the verb? yes
Then it is a transitive verb. Write a T next to the V to show the type of verb.
Divide the subject and the predicate.

SP   TV   IO   A   DO
I / gave him the ball.

She sold them three books.

Who sold? she, subject pronoun
What is being said about she? She sold, verb.
What did she sell? books, direct object
How many books? three, adjective
To whom did she sell the books? them, indirect object
Is there a direct object receiving the action of the verb? yes
Then it is a transitive verb. Write a T next to the V to show the type of verb.
Divide the subject and the predicate.

SP   TV   IO   Adj   DO
She / sold them three books.

Optional Grammar Practice

1. Direct students to make up a sentence using one of the following verbs and an object pronoun. *liked, saw, fought, rescued, needed, wanted.* ⒶⒸ

2. ✎ *22.8 Extra Practice: Pronouns* – Complete the activity in the workbook. Choose a pronoun that completes each sentence. Some sentences have more than one correct answer. ⓋⒶⓀ

3. ✎ *22.9 Extra Practice: Sentences and Fragments* – Review sentences and sentence fragments. Complete the activity in the workbook. ⓋⒶⓀ

4. ✎ *22.10 Extra Practice: Person* – Review first, second, and third person in the workbook. ⓋⒶⓀ

5. Ask the students to tell a short story in first person, then change it to second person, then third person. ⓋⒶⒸ

6. ✎ *22.11 Extra Practice: Editing* – Each of the sentences has three mistakes. Rewrite the sentences without errors. ⓋⒶⓀ

7. Practice reciting the subject and object pronouns. Write them on the board. Recite the list. Erase one pronoun and recite the list again. Erase another pronoun and recite. Continue in this manner until all the pronouns have been erased and students are reciting from memory. ⓀⓋⒶ

8. Challenge students to list the subject and object pronouns on paper. Time them to see how fast they can write them. Optional: Time students to see how fast they can say the subject and object pronouns. ⓀⓋⒶ

9. Ask students to tell about a certain event in first, second, or third person. For example: describe receiving a gift, going to the park, running a race... ⒸⒶ

Optional Reading Practice

✎ *22.12 Extra Practice: Reading* – Direct the students to read the sentences in the workbook aloud. Have the students read them two or three times until they can read each one fluently. *Optional:* Reread the sentences. Divide the subject and the predicate.

Optional Spelling Cards

1. Dictate the words in Lesson 22 for the students to write on index cards.   Ⓐ Ⓚ Ⓥ

2. Color a green border around the verbs, a red border around the nouns, a pink border around the pronouns, and a blue border around the adjectives.   Ⓚ Ⓥ

3. Dictate all of the object pronouns onto index cards.   Ⓐ Ⓚ Ⓥ

4. Direct students to arrange the cards into sentences using a noun, verb, and if needed, direct and indirect object. Demonstrate how the subject noun and object nouns can be replaced with a pronoun by laying the correct pronoun over the noun that it is representing.   Ⓐ Ⓚ Ⓥ Ⓒ

Composition

✎ *22.13 Composition* – **In your student workbook write sentences using a subject pronoun, past tense verb, and an object pronoun.**

Dictation

✎ *22.14 Dictation* – Read each sentence twice. Ask the students to repeat it aloud, then write it in their workbooks.

1. He likes me.
2. They found Mr. Hill's keys.
3. Mrs. White rescued them.

4. Grandmother loves us.
5. I gave her the whole apple.
6. She took all the yellow clothes.

Vocabulary Development

What is a compound word? two words combined together to form a new word

✎ *22.15 Compound Words* – **Turn to your workbook. Combine the words to form ten new compound words.**

Answer Key: *homesick, homework, homeroom, keyboard, keypad, whiteboard, pocketknife, wildcat, wildfire, comeback, applesauce, password, farmhouse, birdhouse, lighthouse*

Lesson 23

Phonograms:	bu, gu
Exploring Sounds:	Consonant and Vowel Sounds of Y
Spelling Rules:	6, 7, 15, 16
Grammar:	Possessive Pronouns

PART ONE

Materials Needed: Phonogram Flash Cards from previous lessons, and ⬛ bu ⬛, ⬛ gu ⬛, and ⬛ y ⬛; Spelling Rule Cards 6 and 7.

Phonograms

New Phonograms — *bu, gu*

> *Today we will learn two phonograms which are related. I want you to tell me how they are related.*

Show ⬛ bu ⬛. /b/ Make sure to pronounce this /b/ not /bŭ/.

Show ⬛ gu ⬛. /g/ Make sure to pronounce this /g/ not /gŭ/.

> *How are these phonograms related?* They both have a silent U.
> *Can they be used at the end of the word?* no
> *Why?* English words do not end in I, U, V, or J.
>
> *Words spelled with these phonograms are not very common.*

✎ *23.1 Phonograms BU and GU* – **Read the words in your workbook. Underline the BU and the GU.**

build

built

buy

buoyant

guilt

guide

guard

guitar

guy

guarantee

guess

guest

tongue

Spelling Journal   Ⓐ Ⓚ Ⓥ

Enter words spelled with BU and GU.

Review

1. Drill the phonograms with flash cards.

2. ✎ *23.2 Writing the Phonograms* – Write each new phonogram five times while saying the sounds aloud.

3. ✎ *23.3 Phonogram Blitz* – Dictate the following phonograms onto the Phonogram Blitz game board in the student workbook.

1. th	10. ch	19. ou	28. ed
2. ck	11. oo	20. ow	29. ew
3. ng	12. oa	21. ough	30. ui
4. er	13. oe	22. tch	31. wor
5. ea	14. igh	23. gn	32. wr
6. sh	15. wh	24. kn	33. ph
7. ai	16. au	25. ir	34. ei
8. ay	17. aw	26. ur	35. ey
9. oy	18. augh	27. ear	36. eigh

4. Play Phonogram Blitz (*The Phonogram and Spelling Game Book*, 29).

Exploring Sounds

Consonant and Vowel Sounds of Y

Show the students the phonogram $\boxed{\text{y}}$.

> **What sounds does this phonogram make?** /y-ĭ-ī-ē/
> **Which sound is a consonant sound?** /y/
> **Why is this a consonant sound?** The teeth and tongue are blocking the sound. It cannot be sung.
> **Which sounds are vowel sounds?** /ĭ-ī-ē/
> ✎ *23.4 The Sounds of Y* – **Write the three vowels sounds of Y in your workbook.**

Spelling Rules

> **Today we will learn which vowel sound Y makes at the end of the word.**
> **What are the vowel sounds of Y?** /ĭ-ī-ē/

Write the following chart on the board:

/ĭ/	/ī/	/ē/

> **I will say a word that ends in Y.**
> **Listen to which sound of Y it is making.**
> ✎ *23.5 Y at the End of the Word* – **Then tell me which column to write it in based upon which sound it is making. Write the words in your workbook as I write them on the board.**

baby	lady	story	copy
cry	study	my	fly
try	heavy	dry	why

/ĭ/	/ī/	/ē/
	cry	baby
	try	lady
	my	study
	dry	heavy
	fly	story
	why	copy

> **What do you notice about these words?** There are no words where Y says /ĭ/ at the end.
> **When does Y say long /ī/?** at the end of a one syllable word
> **When does Y say long /ē/?** at the end of a multi-syllable word

This leads to our new spelling rules:

Spelling Rule	6

When a one syllable word ends in a single vowel Y, it says /ī/.

Spelling Rule	7

Y says long /ē/ only at the end of a multi-syllable word. I says long /ē/ only at the end of a syllable that is followed by a vowel.

Does Y always say /ī/ at the end of a one syllable word? yes
Does Y always say /ē/ at the end of a multi-syllable word? no
Notice that the rule says: Y says long /ē/ only at the end of a multi-syllable word. That means it does not say long /ē/ anyplace else in the word. But look at these words:

apply   *simplify*   *reply*

What does it say in each of these words? /ī/
Usually, Y says long /ē/ at the end of a multi-syllable word but it may say /ī/.
It is true though that Y usually says the long /ē/ sound at the end of a multi-syllable word.
Also, Y is the most common spelling of the long /ē/ sound at the end of a multi-syllable word.

Why don't we spell "cry" like this?

cri

English words do not end in I, U, V, or J.
What letter do we use instead of I to say the long /ī/ sound? Y

cry

I and Y have a special relationship in English. Often the Y stands in for the I at the end of the word.

< **Teacher Tip:** *We will cover the second part of Rule 7, which discusses where I says the long /ē/ sound, in Lesson 38.*

Spelling Journal

Add words which use a single-vowel Y to spell the long /ī/ sound and the long /ē/ sound at the end of the word.

Optional Spelling Rule Practice

1. Quickly review rules 1-4, 6-13, 19-22, 24, 26-28, 30 using the Spelling Rule Cards.   Ⓐ Ⓥ

2. Create notebook pages to remember these rules, using sample words from the board.   Ⓒ Ⓥ

3. Ask the students to teach this to another student or to a parent.   Ⓒ Ⓥ Ⓐ Ⓚ

4. Direct the students to write words ending in Y and illustrate them.   Ⓒ Ⓥ   *baby, lady, story, copy, cry, dry, fly, my*

5. Dictate the following words for students to write on whiteboards. Notice that words ending in the long /ī/ sound are usually spelled with Y, and multi-syllable words ending in the long /ē/ sound are usually spelled with Y.   Ⓐ Ⓚ Ⓥ

   - *by, my, buy, guy, cry, fly, fry, pry, sky, shy, sly, spy, try, why, wry*

   - *baby, lady, army, easy, pony, tiny, ugly, tidy, ebony*

PART TWO

Using Spelling List 23 on pages 286-287, dictate each word following the steps included on pages Intro 42 - Intro 46.

Tips for Spelling List 23

Your

Notice the relationship in the spelling between *you* and *your*. Though the pronunciation of the phonogram OU shifts, the word retains the same root for spelling purposes.

Their

Notice the relationship between *they* and *their*. The phonogram EY changes to EI when it is no longer at the end of the word.

Word	Practice Sentence	Say to Spell	# of Syllables	Markings
1. **my**	*That is my book.*	mī	1	my
2. **your**	*That is your book.*	yōr	1	y<u>ou</u>r ²
3. **its**	*The dog destroyed its toy.*	ĭts	1	its
4. **our**	*That is our book.*	our	1	<u>our</u>
5. **their**	*That is their book.*	THār	1	<u>their</u> ²
6. **happy**	*I feel happy today.*	hăp pē	2	hap py
7. **baby**	*The baby is crying.*	bā bē	2	bā by
8. **guess**	*Guess how old I am.*	gĕs	1	<u>g</u>uess
9. **study**	*It is important to study for the test.*	stŭd ē	2	stud y
10. **student**	*The student read the book.*	stū dĕnt	2	stū dent
11. **build**	*They will build a new bridge.*	bĭld	1	<u>bu</u>ild
12. **cry**	*Do not cry over spilled milk.*	crī	1	cry
13. **hungry**	*The hungry boys ate five bowls of soup.*	hŭn grē	2	hun gry
14. **buy**	*I need to buy new running shoes.*	bī	1	<u>bu</u>y
15. **visit**	*Let's go visit her in the hospital.*	vĭz ĭt	2	vis it ²

Spelling Hints	Part of Speech	Vocabulary Development
6 When a one-syllable word ends in single vowel Y, it says /ī/.	Pro	myself
Underline /ō/. Write a 2 over it. /ow-ō-oo-ū/ said its second sound.	Pro	yours, yourself, yourselves
All first sounds.	Pro	itself
Underline the /ow/.	Pro	ourself, ourselves
Underline /TH/ and put a 2 over it. /th-TH/ says its second sound. Underline /ā/.	Pro	theirs
7 Y says long /ē/ only at the end of a multi-syllable word. I says long /ē/ only at the end of a syllable that is followed by a vowel.	Adj	unhappy, happier, happiest, happiness, happily, unhappier, unhappiness, unhappily
Put a line over the /ā/. **4** A E O U usually say their names at the end of the syllable. **7** Y says long /ē/ only at the end of a multi-syllable word. I says long /ē/ only at the end of a syllable that is followed by a vowel.	N, V	babies, babied, babyhood, babyish, babysitter, crybaby
Underline /g/.	V, N	guesses, guessing, guessed, guesswork, outguess
7 Y says long /ē/ only at the end of a multi-syllable word. I says long /ē/ only at the end of a syllable that is followed by a vowel.	V, N	studied, studying, understudy, restudy, studiedness, studio, studious, studiousness
Put a line over the /ū/. U said the sound /oo/. **4** A E O U usually say their names at the end of the syllable.	N	students, nonstudent
Underline /b/.	V	building, built, builder, bodybuilder, buildable, buildup, outbuilding, overbuild, rebuild, shipbuilder
6 When a one-syllable word ends in single vowel Y, it says /ī/.	V, N	crying, cried, crier, crybaby
7 Y says long /ē/ only at the end of a multi-syllable word. I says long /ē/ only at the end of a syllable that is followed by a vowel.	Adj	hungrier, hungriest, hungrily, hungriness
Underline /b/ **6** When a one-syllable word ends in single vowel Y, it says /ī/. Exception when adding suffixes to Y changing to I.	V, N	buying, bought, buyable, buyback, buyer, buyout, overbuy, underbuy
Put a 2 over the /z/. /s-z/ said its second sound.	V, N	visitor, visited, visiting, revisit, revisited, revisiting, visitation, visits

PART THREE

Materials Needed: Grammar Rule Card 6.3; Spelling Rule Cards 15, 16, and 21; pink, red, green, and blue colored pencils.

Grammar

Review

What is a noun? A noun is the name of a person, place, thing, or idea.

What are the three noun jobs we have learned? subject noun, direct object, indirect object

What is an adjective? Adjectives modify nouns and pronouns. Adjectives answer: What kind? How many? Which one? Whose?

What is an article? A, An, The. Tiny article adjectives that mark nouns and answer the question: Which?

Name the parts of a sentence. A sentence must have a capital letter, subject, verb, complete thought, and an end mark.

What is a verb? A verb shows action, links a description to the subject, or helps another verb.

✎ *Spelling List 23 –* **Identify the parts of speech for words 6-15 in List 23. Mark the nouns with a red N, the verbs with a green V, and the adjectives with a blue Adj.**

✎ *Spelling List 23 –* **Write the past tense of each verb and the plural for each noun.**

Possessive Pronouns.

What is a pronoun? A pronoun takes the place of a noun.

Say the subject pronouns as I write them on the board. I, you, he, she, it, we, they

Subject Pronoun	Object Pronoun	Possessive Pronoun Adjective
I		
you		
he		
she		
it		
we		
they		

✎ *23.6 Pronouns–* **Write the subject pronouns in your workbook.**
Say the object pronouns as I write them on the board.
Hint: She saw ____. me, you, him, her, it, us, them

Subject Pronoun	Object Pronoun	Possessive Pronoun Adjective
I	me	
you	you	
he	him	
she	her	
it	it	
we	us	
they	them	

✎ *23.6 Pronouns – **Write the object pronouns in your workbook.*** ***Today, we will learn the possessive pronouns.***

uncle's boat

> ***What pronoun in our list could we use in place of "uncle's"?*** his

uncle's boat – his boat

> ***This answers the question: Whose boat?*** his
> ***His is describing the boat. Therefore, it is a possessive pronoun adjective.***

possessive pronoun adjective

> ***What does it mean to possess something?*** to own it
> ***What is a pronoun?*** a word that takes the place of a noun
> ***Do you see the word noun in pronoun? This is because they share the same root.***
> ***What is an adjective?*** A word that modifies a noun or a pronoun and answers the questions: What kind? How many? Which one? Whose?
> ***We could also say:***

The boat is his.

aunt's car

> ***Which word in our spelling list can replace aunt?*** her

aunt's car – her car

> ***Whose car?*** her
> ***Her is a possessive pronoun adjective describing car.***
> ***We could also say:***

The car is hers.

> ***Notice that we added an -s to hers.***

Help me to fill in the rest of the chart. Using the phrases:

_____ car   The car is _____.

Subject Pronoun	Object Pronoun	Possessive Pronoun Adjective	
I	me	my	mine
You	you	your	yours
He	him	his	his
She	her	her	hers
It	it	its	its
We	us	our	ours
They	them	their	theirs

Recite the definition and discuss the samples on the back of Grammar Card 6.3.

Grammar Card 6.3	PPA

Possessive pronoun adjectives take the place of possessive noun adjectives.
my, mine, your, yours, his, her, hers, its, our, ours, their, theirs

✎ *23.6 Pronouns – **Write the possessive pronoun adjectives in your workbook.
Make up sentences aloud using each of the possessive pronoun adjectives.***

Identifying Parts of Speech

✎ *23.7 Identifying Parts of Speech – **Label the parts of speech in your workbook, while I label them on the board.***

We bought his car.

Who bought? we, subject pronoun
What is being said about we? we bought, verb
What did we buy? car, direct object
Whose car? his, possessive pronoun adjective
We will mark possessive pronoun adjectives with a PPA.
Is there a direct object receiving the action of the verb? yes
Then it is a transitive verb. Write a T next to the V to show the type of verb.
Divide the subject and the predicate.

SP   TV   PPA DO
We / bought his car.

Our students built the rocket.

Who built? students, subject noun
Whose students? our, possessive pronoun adjective
What is being said about students? students built, verb
What did they build? rocket, direct object
Which rocket? the, article adjective
Is there a direct object receiving the action of the verb? yes
Then it is a transitive verb. Write a T next to the V to show the type of verb.
Divide the subject and the predicate.

PPA SN   TV   A   DO
Our students / built the rocket.

My brother visited your school.

Who visited? brother, subject noun
Whose brother? my, possessive pronoun adjective
What is being said about brother? he visited, verb
What did he visit? school, direct object
Whose school? your, possessive pronoun adjective
Is there a direct object receiving the action of the verb? yes
Then it is a transitive verb. Write a T next to the V to show the type of verb.
Divide the subject and the predicate.

PPA SN   TV   PPA   DO
My brother / visited your school.

Their workers guessed the problem.

Who guessed? workers, subject noun
Whose workers? their, possessive pronoun adjective
What is being said about workers? workers guessed, verb
What did they guess? problem, direct object
Which problem? the, article adjective
Is there a direct object receiving the action of the verb? yes
Then it is a transitive verb. Write a T next to the V to show the type of verb.
Divide the subject and the predicate.

PPA SN   TV   A   DO
Their workers / guessed the problem.

Optional Spelling Cards

1. Dictate the words in Lesson 23 for the students to write on index cards. ⓚⓥ

2. Color a pink border around the pronouns, a red border around the nouns, a green border around the verbs, and a blue border around the adjectives. ⓚⓥ

3. Dictate the possessive pronoun adjectives for students to write on index cards. ⓐⓚⓥ

4. Direct students to arrange the possessive pronoun adjectives and nouns into short possessive phrases. For example: her house, his watch, etc. ⓐⓚⓥⓒ

5. Use the cards to form sentences using the possessive pronoun adjectives. ⓐⓚⓥⓒ

Optional Grammar Practice

1. ✎ *23.8 Extra Practice: Pronouns 1* – Complete the activity in the workbook. Replace each word written in bold with the correct pronoun. ⓥⓐⓚ

2. ✎ *23.9 Extra Practice: Pronouns 2* – Complete the activity in the workbook. Choose a pronoun that completes each sentence. Some sentences have more than one correct answer. ⓥⓐⓚ

3. ✎ *23.10 Extra Practice: Editing* – Correct the sentences in the workbook. Each one has four errors. ⓚⓥⓐ

4. Practice reciting the possessive pronoun adjectives. Write them on the board. Recite the list. Erase one pronoun and recite the list again. Erase another pronoun and recite. Continue in this manner until all the pronouns have been erased and students are reciting from memory. ⓚⓥⓐ

5. Challenge students to list the subject, object and possessive pronouns on paper. Time them to see how fast they can they write them. Optional: time students to see how fast they can say the subject, object, and possessive pronouns. ⓚⓥⓐ

Vocabulary Development

How is the Y in these words different?

dry   toy

The Y in dry is a single vowel Y. The Y in toy is part of the phonogram OY which says /oi/.
How do we make toy plural? just add -s

toys

Today we will learn how to add a suffix to words that end in a single vowel Y.

I will write some words on the board. Then I will add a suffix. Read each word, then read it with the suffix. Raise your hand when you see the pattern that explains how to add a suffix to words ending in a single vowel Y.

dry + ed = dried

happy + er = happier

happy + ness = happiness

hungry + ly = hungrily

study + ed = studied

fry + ing = frying

dry + ing = drying

study + ing = studying

baby + ish = babyish

The Y is changed to I when adding suffixes that start with vowels and consonants but not with suffixes that start with I.

Our new spelling rules says:

Spelling Rule	15
Single vowel Y changes to I when adding any ending, unless the ending begins with I.	

Look again at frying and babyish. Notice that we kept the Y.
Why? because the suffix begins with I
This is because:

Spelling Rule	16
Two I's cannot be next to one another in English words.	

baby

Which two rules will I need to consider, if I want to write the word babies?

Show the cards as you discuss the rules:

Spelling Rule	15

Single vowel Y changes to I when adding any ending, unless the ending begins with I.

Spelling Rule	21

To make a noun plural, add the ending -S, unless the word hisses or changes, then add -ES. Occasional nouns have no change or an irregular spelling.

Will the Y change to I? yes
Do I add -S or -ES? ES
Why? because the Y changed to an I

baby + es = babies

lady

How do we write ladies? Change Y to I and add ES.

lady + es = ladies

story

How do we write stories? Change the Y to I and add ES.
Why? Story ends in a single vowel Y. When a word ends in a single vowel Y, the Y changes to I when adding any ending, unless the ending begins with I. To make a word that changes plural we add ES.

story + es = stories

boy

How do we write boys? Just add S.
Why don't we add ES? Boy ends in the phonogram OY. It does not end in a single vowel Y.

boy + s = boys

day

How do we write days? Just add S.
Why don't we add ES? Day ends in the phonogram AY. It does not end in a single vowel Y.

day + s = days

The same thing happens with verbs.
Read the sentence.

The birds fly.

How will we change fly if it is only one bird? We need to change the Y to I and add -ES.

The bird flies.

Sam _____ the dishes.

How would I spell dries? Change the Y to I and add -ES.

Sam dries the dishes.

What if we want to make this sentence past tense? How would we write dried? Change the I to Y and add -ED

Why? To make a verb past tense, add the ending -ED unless it is an irregular verb. And single vowel Y changes to I when adding any ending, unless the ending begins with I.

Sam dried the dishes.

✎ *23.11 Adding Suffixes to Single Vowel Y Words* – **Complete the activity in your workbook**

Optional Vocabulary Practice

1. ✎ *23.12 Extra Practice: Plurals* – Complete the activity in the workbook. Write the plural form of each word. Ⓥ Ⓐ Ⓚ

2. ✎ *23.13 Extra Practice: Adding Suffixes Flow Chart* – Introduce the adding suffixes flow chart. Discuss how it is important to know if the word ends in a silent final E or a single vowel Y before adding a suffix. Ⓐ Ⓚ Ⓥ

3. **Adding suffixes game** - Provide students with a whiteboard, marker, and eraser. Read a root word. Direct students to write it on the whiteboard. Award one point if it is spelled correctly. Read the word again, this time with an added suffix. Students should change the word on the whiteboard by adding the suffix and, if needed, dropping the E or changing the Y to I. Ⓐ Ⓚ Ⓥ

   - **Just add the suffix** – *boyish, asked, adding, answered, attended, grower, learning, owner, payment, worker, destroyed, enjoyable*

   - **Drop the E before a vowel suffix** – *rescued, priced, typing, practicing, giver, likable, lovable, maker, mover, ruler, savable*

   - **Retain the E before a consonant suffix** – *wholeness, priceless, largely, nameless, statement*

   - **Retain the E to keep the C or G soft** – *changeable, traceable*

   - **Change the Y to I** – *happiness, babies, hungrily, ladies, studied, drier*

   - **Retain the Y before a suffix beginning in I** – *studying, babyish*

   - Variation - In a classroom, award the point to the first student to hold up the whiteboard with the correct spelling. Play until one student earns 5 or 10 points, or for an allotted time.

Spelling Challenge

There are a number of exceptions to Spelling Rule 15. All of the exceptions are single-syllable words ending in Y when adding the suffixes *-able, -ness, -er, -est,* and *-ly.*

If desired provide students with a copy of the chart below or help them to create one on blank paper as a reference. Draw attention to the pattern. **Single-syllable words ending in a single-vowel Y do not change the I to Y when adding the suffixes -able, -ness, -er, -est, and -ly.** Point out that some words, according to The Oxford Dictionary, have two acceptable spellings. *Crier,* however, is always spelled with an I. Note the spellings of *buys* and *buyer*.

Spelling Challenge Continued

Y Changes to I	Y Does not Change	Y Changes to I	Y Does not Change
	buyable	shied	
	buys <	shies	
	buyer		shyer
cries			shyly
cried		shiest	shyest
crier			shyness
	dryness		slyer
drier	dryer		slyest
driest	dryest		slyness
drily	dryly	slily	slyly
dries	drys		spryly
	flyable		spryness
flier	flyer	sprier	spryer
flies		spriest	spryest
frier	fryer	tries	
fries		tried	
fried			wryness
pried			wryly
pries		wrier	wryer
skies		wriest	wryest

< **Teacher Tip:** *Note that buys is the only word that retains the Y with the suffix -S.*

Spelling Challenge Continued

1. Direct students to write the words above in columns grouped by their suffix.

    -able   *-ness*   *-ly*   *-er*   *-est*

2. Together with the students, write a rule which explains these words. For example: **Single-syllable words ending in Y do not change the I to Y when adding the suffixes -able, -ness, -er, -est, and -ly.**

3. Practice the words above by dictating them for students to write on a whiteboard.

Optional Reading

✎ *23.14 Extra Practice: Reading* – Direct the students to read the sentences in the workbook aloud. Have the students read them two or three times until they can read each one fluently.

Optional - Reread the sentences. Divide the subject and the predicate.

Dictation

✎ *23.15 Dictation* – Read each sentence twice. Ask the students to repeat it aloud, then write it in their workbooks.

1. I visited your sisters.
2. We celebrated his birthday.
3. Mr. Smith built the house.
4. The hungry boys ate all their dinner.
5. I told her our whole story.
6. They guessed my answer.

Composition

I will write two sentences on the board. Read them, then we will replace some of the nouns with pronouns.

Tom ate Tom's breakfast. Tom had eggs, toast, and juice.

Which words could we replace with a pronoun to make these sentences flow better? Replace Tom's with his, and replace Tom with he.

Tom ate his breakfast. He had eggs, toast, and juice.

Let's do one more.

Emma bought Emma's father a gift. Emma's father liked the gift.

Which words could we replace with pronouns? Replace Emma's with her, Emma's father with he, and gift with it.

Emma bought her father a gift. He liked it.

✎ *23.16 Composition –* **Rewrite the sentences in the workbook using pronouns.**

✎ *23.17 Composition –* **Write a sentence using at least two possessive pronouns.**

Lesson 24

Phonograms:	
Exploring Sounds:	The Relationship of I and Y
Spelling Rules:	5
Grammar:	Adverbs

PART ONE

Materials Needed: Phonogram Flash Cards from previous lessons. Set aside i , y , ai , ay , oi , oy , ei , and ey ; Spelling Rule Card 5; Phonogram Game Cards and a cloth bag.

Phonograms

Review

1. Drill the phonograms with flash cards.

2. ✎ *24.1 Phonogram Practice* – Dictate the following phonograms. For extra practice, have the students read them back. Write the correct answers on the board as the students check their answers.

1. bu	6. ph	11. ir	16. ou
2. gu	7. wor	12. ur	17. ow
3. ei	8. wr	13. ear	18. ough
4. ey	9. ui	14. kn	19. au
5. eigh	10. ew	15. gn	20. aw

3. Play Rotten Egg using the Phonogram Game Cards (*The Phonogram and Spelling Game Book*, 13).

Exploring Sounds

Show the students the phonograms | i | and | y | .

> *What do these phonograms have in common?* They both say /ĭ-ī-ē-y/.
> *We have begun to learn more about the relationship between these two phonograms. What are some of the ways they are related?* They both say /ĭ-ī-ē-y/; Y changes to I when adding a vowel suffix; when we hear the long /ī/ sound at the end of the word, it is written with a Y.
>
> *What happens to the Y when we add a suffix to words such as happy?*

happy + er =

> The Y changes to I.

happy + er = happier

> *What is one of the most common spellings for a word that ends with the long /ī/ sound?* Y

cry

try

> *What do these phonogram pairs demonstrate about the relationship between I and Y?*

ai	*ay*
oi	*oy*
ei	*ey*

> English words do not end in I so the Y stands in for the I at the end of the word.

Spelling Rules

I and Y at the End of the Syllable

Show the phonogram | i | .

> *What are the sounds of I?* /ĭ-ī-ē-y/.
> *What sound does I make at the end of the word?* English words do not end in I.
> *What does I say in the middle of the syllable?* /ĭ/
> *Today we will learn what I says at the end of the syllable.*

Divide the board into the following columns:

/ĭ/	/ī/	/y/

I will say a word. Listen for which sound of I is used at the end of the syllable. Tell me which column to write it under.

pilot, clinic, quiet, terrible, family, title, silent, divide

/ĭ/	/ī/	/y/
cli nic	pi lot	
ter ri ble	qui et	
fam i ly	ti tle	
di vide	si lent	

What sounds does I say at the end of the syllable? /ĭ/ and /ī/.

Show the phonogram ⌷ y ⌷.

What are the sounds of y? /y-ĭ-ī-ē/.
What sounds does Y make at the end of the word? /ī/ and /ē/.
What does Y say in the middle of the syllable? /ĭ/
Now we will learn what Y says at the end of the syllable.

I will say a word. Listen for which sound of Y is used at the end of the syllable. Tell me which column to write it under.

physical, typo, typical, cry

/ĭ/	/ī/
phy si cal	ty po
ty pi cal	cry

What sounds does Y say at the end of the syllable? /ĭ/ and /ī/.
This leads to our new spelling rule:

Spelling Rule	5
I and Y may say /ĭ/ or /ī/ at the end of a syllable.	

Spelling Journal   Ⓐ Ⓚ Ⓥ

Add words spelled with I and Y at the end of the syllable saying /ĭ/ and /ī/.

Optional Spelling Rule Practice

1. Quickly review rules 1-13, 15-16, 19-22, 24, 26-28, 30 using the Spelling Rule Cards.   Ⓐ Ⓥ

2. Create a reference page to remember this rule. Include sample words.   Ⓒ Ⓥ

3. Ask the students to teach this to another student or to a parent.   Ⓒ Ⓥ Ⓐ Ⓚ

4. **Adding suffixes game** - Provide students with a whiteboard, marker, and eraser. Read a root word. Direct students to write it on the whiteboard. Award one point if it is spelled correctly. Read the word again this time with an added suffix. Students should change the word on the whiteboard by adding the suffix and, if needed, dropping the E or changing the Y to I.

   - **Just add the suffix** – *learned, learner, suitable, bringing, workable, excellently, owned*

   - **Drop the E before a vowel suffix** – *sharing, shined, named, celebrated, ruler, likable*

   - **Retain the E before a consonant suffix** – *nameless, changeless, loveless*

   - **Retain the E to keep the C or G soft** – *changeable, traceable*

   - **Change the Y to I** – *happiness, babies, hungrily, ladies, studied, drier*

   - **Retain the Y before a suffix beginning in I** – *studying, babyish*

PART TWO

Using Spelling List 24 on pages 304-305, dictate each word following the steps included on pages Intro 42 - Intro 46.

Tips for Spelling List 24

Often

Clearly enunciate the /t/ for spelling purposes. /ŏf tĕn/

Sometimes

Exaggerate the /ŏ/ to aid students in creating an auditory picture of the word. /sŏm tīmz/. Point out to students this is a compound word formed by combining the words *some* and *times*.

	Word	Practice Sentence	Say to Spell	# of Syllables	Markings
1.	**often**	*We often go swimming on Saturday.*	ŏf tĕn	2	of ten
2.	**never**	*Never lie.*	nĕv er	2	nev <u>er</u>
3.	**slowly**	*The turtle crawled slowly across the garden.*	slō lē	2	sl<u>ow</u>² ly
4.	**yesterday**	*Liam got a perfect score yesterday.*	yĕs ter dā	3	yes <u>ter</u> <u>day</u>
5.	**today**	*She is swimming today.*	tö dā	2	tö d<u>ay</u>
6.	**sometimes**	*Sometimes I like to sleep late.*	sŏm tīmz	2	som<u>e</u> tīm<u>e</u>s²
7.	**accident**	*The train accident was late at night.*	ăk sĭ dĕnt	3	ac ci dent
8.	**family**	*We are a family.*	făm ĭ lē	3	fam i ly
9.	**careful**	*Be careful where you step.*	kār fŭl	2	cār<u>e</u> ful
10.	**listen**	*Listen carefully to the instructions.*	lĭs tĕn	2	lis ten
11.	**copy**	*Copy the words neatly.*	kŏp ē	2	cop y
12.	**beautiful**	*What a beautiful day!*	bē ū tĭ fŭl	4	b<u>ea</u> ū ti ful
13.	**animal**	*What kind of animal is that?*	ăn ĭ măl	3	an i mal
14.	**story**	*I will tell you a story*	stōr ē	2	st<u>or</u> y
15.	**heavy**	*That is a heavy book.*	hĕv ē	2	h<u>ea</u>² y

Spelling Hints	Part of Speech	Vocabulary Development
Say to spell /ŏf tĕn/. All first sounds.	Adv	oftener, oftenest, oftentimes
Underline /er/.	Adv	nevermore, nevertheless
Underline /ō/. Put a 2 over it. /ow-ō/ said its second sound. **7** Y says long /ē/ only at the end of a multi-syllable word. I says long /ē/ only at the end of a syllable that is followed by a vowel.	Adv	slow, slowed, slowdown, slowness, slowpoke
Underline /er/. Underline /ā/.	Adv	
Put two dots over the /ö/. /ŏ-ō-ö/ said its third sound. Underline /ā/.	Adv	
What two words form sometimes? *some* and *times*. Double underline the silent final E in *some*. **12.9** Unseen reason. Draw a line over the /ī/ and double underline the silent final E. **12.1** The vowel says its name because of the E. Put a 2 over /s-z/.	Adv	something, someone
1 C softens to /s/ when followed by an E, I, or Y. Otherwise, C says /k/. **5** I and Y may say /ĭ/ or /ī/ at the end of the syllable.	N	accidents, accidental, accidentally
5 I and Y may say /ĭ/ or /ī/ at the end of the syllable. **7** Y says long /ē/ only at the end of a multi-syllable word.	N	families, familial, familiar, familiarize, familiarities, familiarization, familiarly, unfamiliar, unfamiliarly, unfamiliarity
Base word = care. Suffix = ful. Put a line over the /ā/. Double underline the silent final E. **12.1** The vowel says its name because of the E. **24** -Ful is a suffix written with one L when added to another syllable.	Adj	caring, cared, careful, careless, carefully, carelessly, caregiver, caretaker, medicare, carefree, caress
Say to spell /lĭs tĕn/.	V	listened, listener, listening, listenership, listenable
7 Y says long /ē/ only at the end of a multi-syllable word. I says long /ē/ only at the end of a syllable that is followed by a vowel.	V, N	copying, copied, copier, copybook, copycat, copyright, copyrighted, copyreader, recopy, photocopy, copywriter
Underline /ē/. Put a line over the /ū/. **4** A E O U usually say their names at the end of the syllable **5** I and Y may say /ĭ/ or /ī/ at the end of the syllable. **24** -Ful is a suffix written with one L when added to another syllable.	Adj	beauty, beautician, beautify, beauties, beautification, beautified, beautifier, unbeautiful
5 I and Y may say /ĭ/ or /ī/ at the end of the syllable.	N	animals, animalism, animalistic
Underline /or/. **7** Y says long /ē/ only at the end of a multi-syllable word. I says long /ē/ only at the end of a syllable that is followed by a vowel.	N	stories, storybook, storyteller, storyboard
Underline /ĕ/. Put a 2 over it. /ē-ĕ-ā/ said its second sound. **7** Y says long /ē/ only at the end of a multi-syllable word. I says long /ē/ only at the end of a syllable that is followed by a vowel.	Adj	heavier, heaviest, heaviness, heavyhearted, heavyheartedness, heavyset, heavyweight, heave, heaved

PART THREE

Materials Needed: Grammar Rule Card 4; yellow, red, green, and blue colored pencils.

Grammar

Review

> ***What is a noun?*** A noun is the name of a person, place, thing, or idea.
>
> ***What is a pronoun?*** A pronoun takes the place of a noun.
>
> ***What are the three noun jobs we have learned so far?*** subject noun, direct object, indirect object
>
> ***What is an adjective?*** Adjectives modify nouns and pronouns. Adjectives answer: What kind? How many? Which one? Whose?
>
> ***What is an article?*** A, An, The. Tiny article adjectives that mark nouns and answer the question: Which?
>
> ***Name the parts of a sentence.*** A sentence must have a capital letter, subject, verb, complete thought, and an end mark.
>
> ***What is a verb?*** A verb shows action, links a description to the subject, or helps another verb.
>
> ***What are the two types of verbs we have learned about?*** action verb and transitive verb

Adverbs

> ***I will write a sentence on the board. We will then ask questions to help us understand the sentence and to make it more interesting.***

The people listened.

> ***Who listened?*** people, subject noun
>
> ***Which people?*** the, article adjective
>
> ***What is being said about people?*** they listened, verb

   A   SN   V
The people listened.

> ***This is a simple sentence. To add interest to this sentence we could add an adjective.***
>
> ***What questions do adjectives answer?*** What kind? How many? Which one? Whose?
>
> ***Think of some adjectives to add to describe people.***

For example:

The hungry people listened.

Three people listened.

> ***Another way to add information to the sentence is an adverb.***

Grammar Card 4	Adv

An adverb modifies a verb, adjective, or another adverb.

An adverb answers: How? When? Where? To what extent?

What are some words that would answer, how did the people listen? silently, happily, carefully…

What are some words that would answer, when did the people listen? yesterday, today, tomorrow, often, never…

What are some words that would answer, where did the people listen? at home, at work, at school…

verb   adverb

What do you notice about the words verb and adverb? They both have verb in them.

An adverb modifies verbs. To find the adverb we go to the verb and ask: How? When? Where? or To what extent?

Identifying Parts of Speech

✎ *24.2 Identifying Parts of Speech* – Label the parts of speech in your workbook while I label them on the board.

The children read silently.

> *Who read?* children, subject noun
> *Which children?* the, article adjective
> *What is being said about children?* children read, verb
> *How did they read?* silently, adverb
> *Is there a direct object receiving the action of the verb?* no
> *Divide the complete subject from the complete predicate.*

A   SN   V   Adv
The children / read silently.

> *Notice that we can also say:*

The children silently read.

Silently the children read.

My brother slowly ate the apple.

> **Who ate?** brother, subject noun
> **Whose brother?** my, possessive pronoun adjective
> **What is being said about brother?** brother ate, verb
> **What did he eat?** apple, direct object
> **Which apple?** the, article adjective
> **How did he eat?** slowly, adverb
> **Is there a direct object receiving the action of the verb?** yes
> **Then it is a transitive verb. Write a T next to the V to show the type of verb.**
> **Divide the complete subject from the complete predicate.**

PPA SN   Adv   TV A DO
My brother / slowly ate the apple.

> **How else could we say this sentence?**

Slowly my brother ate the apple.

My brother ate the apple slowly.

Yesterday their family built a tree house.

> **Who built?** family, subject noun
> **Whose family?** their, possessive pronoun adjective
> **What is being said about family?** family built, verb
> **What did they build?** house, direct object
> **Which house?** a, article adjective
> **What kind of house?** tree house, adjective
> **When did they build it?** yesterday, adverb
> **Is there a direct object receiving the action of the verb?** yes
> **Then it is a transitive verb. Write a T next to the V to show the type of verb.**
> **Divide the complete subject from the complete predicate.**

Adv   PPA SN   TV A Adj   DO
Yesterday their family / built a tree house.

> **Is there a word modifying the predicate that is found in the subject part of the sentence?** Yes. "Yesterday" modifies "built." It answers the question, when did they build it?
> **As we have seen adverbs can move around in the sentence. When an adverb is found in the subject part of the sentence, underline it twice.**

Adv   PPA SN   TV A Adj   DO
<u>Yesterday</u> their family / built a tree house.

> **How else could we say this sentence?**

Their family built a tree house yesterday.

Parts of Speech

✎ *Spelling List 24* – Direct students to label the parts of speech for each word in Spelling List 24.

Label the adverbs with a yellow Adv. To find the adverbs ask: How? When? Where? To what extent?

Label the nouns with a red N. To find the nouns ask: Is it a person, place, thing, or idea? Does it make sense with the word "the ___."

Label the verbs with a green V. To find the verbs ask: Can I ___?

Label the adjectives with a blue Adj. To find the adjectives ask: What kind? How many? Which one? Whose?

✎ *Spelling List 24* – Write the plural form of each noun and the past tense of each verb for Spelling List 24.

Optional Spelling Cards

1. Dictate the words in Lesson 24 for the students to write on index cards. Ⓚ Ⓥ Ⓐ

2. Ask the students to color a green border around the verbs, a red border around the nouns, a blue border around the adjectives, and a yellow border around the adverbs. If a word can be used as more than one part of speech, color two borders. Ⓚ Ⓥ

3. Direct students to arrange the cards into sentences which include all the parts of speech. Practice reading the sentences aloud. Ⓚ Ⓥ Ⓒ Ⓐ

Optional Grammar Practice

1. ✎ *24.3 Extra Practice: Editing* – Correct the sentences in the workbook. Each one has three errors. Ⓚ Ⓥ Ⓐ

2. ✎ *24.4 Extra Practice: Pronouns* – Write a pronoun in each blank that completes the sentence. In some sentences there is more than one choice that is grammatically correct. Ⓚ Ⓥ Ⓐ

Vocabulary Development

The Suffix -LY

Many adjectives can be changed into adverbs by adding the suffix -ly .

slow + ly

How do we add the suffix -ly to slow? just add the ending *slow + ly = slowly*

> **Use slow in a sentence.**   Ex. The slow turtle walked.
> **Now use slowly in a sentence.**   Ex. The turtle walked slowly.

loud + ly

> **How do we add the suffix -ly to loud?** just add the ending

loud + ly = loudly

> **Use loud in a sentence.**   Ex. The train is loud.
> **Now use loudly in a sentence.**   Ex. The crowd shouted loudly.

happy + ly

> **How do we add the suffix -ly to happy?**   Change the Y to I and add the ending.
> **What is the rule?**   Single vowel Y changes to I when adding any ending, unless the ending begins with I.

happy + ly = happily

hungry + ly

> **How do we add the suffix -ly to hungry?**   Change the Y to I and add the ending.

hungry + ly = hungrily

love + ly

> **How do we add the suffix -ly to love?**   Keep the E and add -ly.
> **Why?**   Drop the silent final E only when adding a vowel suffix.

love + ly = lovely

careful + ly

> **How will we add the suffix -ly to careful?**   Just add the suffix.

careful + ly = carefully

> **What is the root word of carefully?** care
> **How many suffixes have we added?** two, -ful and -ly

    ✎   *24.5. The Suffix -LY –* **Complete the activity in the workbook.**

‹ Teacher Tip: *There is one exception to retaining the E before a consonant suffix. Simple + ly = simply*

‹ Teacher Tip: *Single-syllable words ending in Y do not always change to I when adding the suffix -LY. Shyly is always spelled with a Y. However, drily-dryly, slily-slyly, and wrily-wryly may be spelled with either a Y or an I. See Lesson 23 page 296 to learn more about the exceptions to this rule.*

Spelling Challenge

shy + ly =

What happens when we add the suffix -ly to shy? We need to keep the Y.

shy + ly = shyly

Which one syllable words ending in Y may be written with either an I or a Y when adding the suffix -LY? drily-dryly, slily-slyly, wrily-wryly.

Direct students to practice writing shyly, drily-dryly, slily-slyly, and wrily-wryly by using each of them in a sentence.

Optional Reading

✎ *24.6 Extra Practice: Reading* – Direct the students to read the sentences in the workbook aloud. Have the students read them two or three times until they can read each one fluently.

Optional - Reread the sentences. Divide the subject and the predicate.

Dictation

✎ *24.7 Dictation* – Read each sentence twice. Ask the students to repeat it aloud, then write it in their workbooks.

1. The boat sailed slowly.
2. The children listened carefully.
3. The hungry children ate lunch happily.
4. He often rides the bus.
5. The happy students talked loudly.
6. The beautiful wild animals slept.

Composition

✎ *24.8 Composition* – Direct the students to compose five sentences including a subject, verb, and adverb using the words in the workbook.

Lesson 25 — Assessment & Review

Materials Needed: red colored pencil.

1. ✎ *25.1 Assessment* – Dictate the sentences to the students while they write them in their workbook.

   1. Yesterday we visited the wild animals.
   2. Our family built a beautiful new house.
   3. The students guessed the right answer.
   4. My sister never practiced her music.
   5. They came home today.
   6. We carefully made eight copies.
   7. Sometimes you buy white clothes.
   8. The babies cried.
   9. We ate our whole breakfast.
   10. My brother lost his keys.

2. Direct the students to read the sentences aloud while you write them on the board. Sound out each word and model the thought process. The students should mark corrections in red. Encourage the students to discuss what they missed.

3. Recheck the students' work. Note the words and concepts which need further practice.

4. Did the students:

   ____ **use silent final E's correctly?**
   ____ **change the Y to I correctly?**
   ____ **add an ED to form the past tense?**
   ____ **spell the irregular past tense verbs correctly?**
   ____ **spell the suffix -ful with one L?**
   ____ **add -ly to form the adverb?**

5. ✎ *25.2 Reading* – Ask the students to read the following sentences. Note the words they did not read fluently.

   1. The man accidentally hurt his finger.
   2. Add the numbers three and four.
   3. The teacher asked.
   4. The students answered.
   5. The worker hauled a heavy load.
   6. The man weighed too much for his height.
   7. I told the happy children simple stories.
   8. Use the sharp knife.
   9. The hungry workers ate lunch.
   10. I often study late at night.
   11. We rescued their ducks.
   12. She slowly and carefully practiced the music.
   13. I have some.
   14. We gave them a present.
   15. I saw a beautiful yellow coat.
   16. We celebrated your birthday.
   17. The helpers listened carefully.

6.   ✎ *25.3 Words to Practice* – Ask the students to read the words in the list and mark which ones they would like to practice further.

7.   Using the assessment and your knowledge as a teacher, identify words to dictate onto index cards.

1. _____ accident	21. _____ height	41. _____ some
2. _____ add	22. _____ her	42. _____ sometimes
3. _____ animal	23. _____ home	43. _____ story
4. _____ ask	24. _____ hungry	44. _____ student
5. _____ baby	25. _____ I	45. _____ study
6. _____ beautiful	26. _____ its	46. _____ their
7. _____ breakfast	27. _____ key	47. _____ them
8. _____ build	28. _____ knife	48. _____ they
9. _____ buy	29. _____ listen	49. _____ today
10. _____ careful	30. _____ lunch	50. _____ type
11. _____ clothes	31. _____ my	51. _____ us
12. _____ come	32. _____ never	52. _____ visit
13. _____ copy	33. _____ number	53. _____ weigh
14. _____ cry	34. _____ often	54. _____ white
15. _____ dinner	35. _____ our	55. _____ whole
16. _____ eight	36. _____ practice	56. _____ wild
17. _____ family	37. _____ price	57. _____ yellow
18. _____ guess	38. _____ rescue	58. _____ yesterday
19. _____ happy	39. _____ simple	59. _____ you
20. _____ heavy	40. _____ slowly	60. _____ your

SPELLING WORD REVIEW

Materials Needed: Index cards, highlighter; slips of paper, pencils, basket; recorder.

1.   Dictate the missed words onto index cards. Have the students highlight the part of the word that was difficult.

2.   Choose from the review activities below or use an activity found in the *The Phonogram and Spelling Game Book.*

1. Play Spelling Basketball (*The Phonogram and Spelling Game Book,* 43).

2. ✎ *25.4 Extra Practice: Crossword Maze* – Create a Crossword Maze (*The Phonogram and Spelling Game Book,* 53).

3. Direct the students to read the words and record them in order to create a personalized spelling quiz. Students then listen to the recording and write each word.

OPTIONAL SPELLING RULE REVIEW

Materials Needed: Spelling Rule Cards 6-7, 12.1-12.9, 13, 15, 19, 20; whiteboard, marker, eraser, timer.

Use the following mini-lesson to review the concepts as needed.

Silent Final E's

Spelling Rule	12.1-12.9

The vowel says its name because of the E.

English words do not end in V or U.

The C says /s/ and the G says /j/ because of the E.

Every syllable must have a written vowel.

We often add an E to keep singular words that end in the letter -S from looking plural.

Add an E to make the word look bigger.

TH says its voiced sound /TH/ because of the E.

Add an E to clarify meaning.

Unseen reason.

1. Review the rules by reciting them and discussing the samples on the back of the cards.

2. Direct the students to write 15-25 words with silent final E's on index cards. Then have them sort the cards into piles based upon the reason for the silent final E.

3. ✎ *25.5 Extra Practice: Sort the E's* – Dictate the words to the students. Direct them to write the word under the reason for the E. *live, give, sponge, date, goose, have, dance, hinge, mouse, puzzle, teethe, blue, moose, bathe, stake, glue, love, wiggle, choice, due, true, hose, fine, cable, voice, title, juice, house, clothe*

Silent Final E Word Lists

- **The vowels sound changes because of the E** – *babe, bake, bale, base, cage, cake, came, cane, care, case, cave, dare, date, fade, fake, fame, game, gate, gave, kale, lake, lame, lane, late, pale, pave, rage, rake, rate, rave, safe, sale, same, save, tame, vase, wade, wake, blame, blaze, drape, flake, flame, frame, glaze, grade, grape grave, plane, plate, quake, scale, stake, state, trade, whale, sphere, bike, bite, dike, fine, fire, five, hide, hike, hive, kite, life, lime, mile, mine, mite, pike, pile, pine, pipe, ride, site, size, tile, time, vine, wife, wipe, glide, knife, stripe, trike, twine, whine, code, coke, cone, cove, hole, hose, lone, mole, nose, note, poke, robe, role, rope, rose, rote, rove, tone, tote, vote, wove, zone, choke, chore, close, drove, prone, quote, scone, scope, shore, slope, smoke, snore, spoke, stole, store, stove, whole, wrote, cube, cute, dude, duke, fume, huge, mule, pure, rude, rule, tune, brute, fluke, byte, hype, style, type*

- **English words do not end in V or U** – **-ve** *above, active, alive, approve, arrive, carve, cave, chive, clove, cove, crave, creative, cursive, curve, dive, dove, drive, drove, eve, forgive, gave, give, glove, grave, grove, halve, have, hive, groove, improve, involve, live, love, mauve, native, nerve, olive, pave, prove, rave, survive, swerve, twelve, valve, wave*   **-ue** *avenue, blue, continue, cue, due, glue, hue, overdue, pursue, rescue, sue, true, value*

- **The C says /s/ and the G says /j/ because of the E** – **-ce** *ace, dice, face, ice, lace, lice, mice, nice, pace, race, rice, vice, brace, dance, fence, force, grace, juice, mince, ounce, peace, place, pounce, price, sauce, since, slice, space, spice, trace, truce, twice, voice, wince, advice, bounce, chance, choice, fleece, glance, notice, palace, police, prince, reduce, scarce, source, stance*   **-ge** *age, cage, huge, page, rage, urge, wage, forge, hinge, image, large, purge, stage, range, usage, change, lounge, orange, plunge, sponge, voyage*

- **Every syllable must have a vowel** – **-ble** *babble, bobble, bramble, bubble, bumble, cable, cobble, dribble, fable, feeble, fumble, grumble, humble, mumble, noble, stable, tremble, wobble*   **-cle** *article, bicycle, chronicle, circle, cycle, icicle, miracle, oracle, particle, tricycle, vehicle*   **-dle** *bridle, bundle, candle, cradle, cuddle, curdle, dawdle, doodle, dwindle, fiddle, griddle, handle, hurdle, kindle, middle, needle, noodle, riddle, saddle, straddle, swaddle*   **-fle** *baffle, duffle, muffle, raffle, ruffle, scuffle, shuffle, sniffle, waffle*   **-gle** *angle, beagle, boggle, bugle, bungle, dangle, eagle, gargle, google, giggle, haggle, jingle, juggle, mingle, single, smuggle, straggle, struggle, triangle, wiggle*   **-kle** *ankle, buckle, chuckle, crinkle, heckle, knuckle, pickle, shackle, speckle, suckle, tickle, trickle, twinkle, wrinkle*   **-ple** *ample, apple, couple, cripple, crumple, dimple, example, maple, multiple, people, pimple, purple, ripple, rumple, sample, simple, temple, trample, triple*   **-tle** *battle, beetle, bottle, brittle, bustle, castle, chortle, hurtle, kettle, mantle, nestle, nettle, prattle, rattle, settle, title, trestle, whistle, whittle*   **-zle** *dazzle, drizzle, frazzle, guzzle, muzzle, nuzzle, puzzle, sizzle*

- **To keep singular words that end in S from looking plural** – *house, mouse, spouse, horse, goose, moose, promise, license, cause*

- **To make the word look bigger** – *are, awe, axe, dye, rye, bye*

- **To make TH say its voiced sound** – *bathe, clothe, breathe, teethe*

- **To distinguish homophones** – *browse, tease, lapse, ore*

- **Unseen reason** – *come, some, done, were*

> ### Spelling Rule   13
>
> **Drop the silent final E when adding a vowel suffix only if it is allowed by other spelling rules.**

1. Review the rule by reciting it and discussing the samples on the back of the card.

2. On the board practice adding the following suffixes to silent final E words: *-s, -er, -able, -ed, -less, -ment* using words from the list on page 316.

3. **Silent Final E Olympics** - Explain to students they will earn points in four events: Reading, Dictation, E Identification, Adding Suffixes. Students may work individually or in teams. The student or team with the most points wins.

   - ✎ *25.6 Extra Practice: Silent E Reading* Lists A and B – Set the timer for 1 or 2 minutes. Direct students to turn to the Silent Final E word list in their workbook. When you say, "go," the students are to begin reading the words in the list as quickly as possible. Stop when the timer beeps. Put a mark next to words that were not read correctly. Award 1 point for each word that was read correctly. (Students may work in pairs in a larger class, with one student checking the other's reading.)

   - *Dictation* - Set the timer for 3-5 minutes. Dictate silent final E words from the Silent Final E Word list on page 316. When the timer beeps, count how many words each student spelled correctly. Award students 5 points for each word spelled correctly.

   - *E Identification* - Choose 15-25 words. Explain that you will write a word on the board. The students are awarded one point for correctly identifying each reason for the silent final E. (In a larger class direct students to work in pairs using Silent E Reading Lists A and B. Set a time limit of 2 minutes.)

   - ✎ *25.7 Extra Practice: Adding Suffixes* – Complete the activity in the workbook. Award one point for each correct answer.

Words Ending in Single Vowel Y

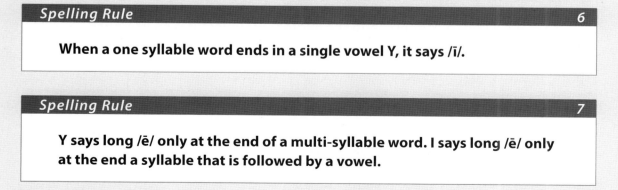

> ### Spelling Rule   6
>
> **When a one syllable word ends in a single vowel Y, it says /ī/.**

> ### Spelling Rule   7
>
> **Y says long /ē/ only at the end of a multi-syllable word. I says long /ē/ only at the end a syllable that is followed by a vowel.**

1. Review the rule by reciting it and discussing the samples on the back of the card.

2. Remind the students that English words do not end in I. Therefore when the long I sound is heard at the end, Y stands in.

3. Dictate 5-10 of the following words: *cry, try, fry, why, my, buy, guy, simplify, baby, study, lady, buggy, puppy, happy, slowly, copy.*

Spelling Rule   15

Single Vowel Y changes to I when adding any ending, unless the ending begins with I.

---

1. Review the rule by reciting it and discussing the samples on the back of the card.

2. Practice adding suffixes using the following words: *baby + ed = babied, baby + ish = babyish, copy + er = copier, happy + ness = happiness, try + es = tries, puppy + es = puppies, study + ed = studied, study + ing = studying, cry + ed = cried, cry + ing = crying.*

3. ✎ *25.8 Extra Practice: Adding Suffixes to Single Vowel Y Words* – Practice adding suffixes using words in the workbook.

Adding the Suffix -LY to any word

1. Review Rules 13 and 15.

2. Using the Adding Suffix flow chart, practice adding the suffix -ly to words.

3. ✎ *25.9 Extra Practice: Adding Suffixes Chart* – Practice adding the suffix -ly using the Adding Suffixes Chart. Demonstrate the examples on the board. Encourage the students to ask the questions and direct the steps. *accidentally, carefully, heavily, hungrily, beautifully, cheaply, excellently, happily, humanly, largely, lightly, motherly, fatherly, namely, openly, perfectly, plainly, quickly, rightly, secretly, sharply, sisterly*

4. ✎ *25.10 Extra Practice: The Suffix -LY* – Complete the activity in the workbook.

Past Tense

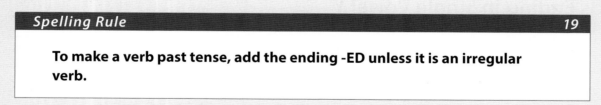

Spelling Rule   19

To make a verb past tense, add the ending -ED unless it is an irregular verb.

Spelling Rule   20

ED, past tense ending, forms another syllable when the base word ends in /d/ or /t/. Otherwise, ED says /d/ or /t/.

---

1. Review the rules by reciting them and discussing the samples on the back of the card.

2. ✎ *25.11 Extra Practice: ED Past Tense Ending* – Explain that each of the following words will use ED past tense ending. Read the word aloud. Ask the students to write the word in the column that shows

the sound that ED is saying. Encourage students to consider the root word and if the root ends in a silent E or a single vowel Y. *added, asked, babied, copied, cried, guessed, listened, practiced, rescued, studied, typed, visited.*

3. ✎ *25.12 Extra Practice: Irregular Verbs* – Match the present tense verbs to the past tense irregular verbs.

OPTIONAL PHONOGRAM ASSESSMENT & REVIEW

Phonograms

✎ *25.13 Extra Practice: Phonogram Quiz* – Dictate the phonograms.

1. ei	18. aw	35. g	52. x
2. gu	19. e	36. wr	53. tch
3. ou	20. oi	37. u	54. sh
4. a	21. oy	38. au	55. j
5. z	22. ew	39. ar	56. or
6. th	23. ch	40. h	57. l
7. r	24. t	41. oe	58. ea
8. ck	25. igh	42. eigh	59. w
9. b	26. wh	43. bu	60. wor
10. gn	27. ey	44. v	61. er
11. s	28. o	45. oa	62. k
12. qu	29. ur	46. i	63. augh
13. p	30. f	47. ough	64. ee
14. ph	31. kn	48. ay	65. y
15. c	32. n	49. m	66. ed
16. ow	33. ir	50. ear	67. ui
17. d	34. oo	51. ai	68. ng

Optional Phonogram Practice

Practice the phonograms as needed using the following game suggestions or choose other games from *The Phonogram and Spelling Game Book.*

1. Play Team Up using the Phonogram Game Cards (*The Phonogram and Spelling Game Book,* 14).

2. Play Teacher Trouble (*The Phonogram and Spelling Game Book,* 29).

3. Practice the phonograms with Back Writing (*The Phonogram and Spelling Game Book,* 24).

Lesson 26

Phonograms:	dge
Exploring Sounds:	DGE and GE
Spelling Rules:	25
Grammar:	Commands, Nouns of Direct Address

PART ONE

Materials Needed: Phonogram Flash Cards from previous lessons and dge ; Spelling Rule Card 25.

Phonograms

New Phonogram — *dge*

Show dge . /j/

> **What do you notice about this phonogram?** The G says /j/ because of the E. The D is silent.

Review

1. Drill the phonograms with flash cards.

2. ✎ *26.1 Writing the Phonograms* – Write the new phonogram five times while saying the sound aloud.

3. ✎ *26.2 Phonogram Practice* – Dictate the following phonograms. For extra practice, have the students read them back. Write the correct answers on the board as the students check their answers.

1. bu	6. ed	11. ey	16. ir
2. ei	7. gn	12. ph	17. ur
3. kn	8. ou	13. ew	18. ear
4. wr	9. ow	14. eigh	19. tch
5. ui	10. gu	15. wor	20. au

4. ✎ *26.3 Phonogram Tic-Tac-Toe* - Play Phonogram Tic-Tac-Toe. Each student has six game boards in their workbook. (For directions see *The Phonogram and Spelling Game Book*, 26.)

Spelling Rules

Words Ending in -dge

✎ *26.4 DGE – Read the words using three letter /j/ in your workbook. Underline three letter /j/.*

badge	drudge	judge	porridge
bridge	edge	ledge	ridge
budge	fidget	lodge	sledge
budget	fridge	midget	sludge
cartridge	fudge	nudge	smidgen
dodge	grudge	partridge	trudge
dredge	hedge	pledge	wedge

Where does three letter /j/ most commonly spell /j/? at the end of a base word
Is three letter /j/ preceded by a single or multi-letter vowel? single letter vowel
What type of vowel, long, short, or broad, comes before three letter /j/? short
This leads to the rule:

Spelling Rule	25
DGE is used only after a single vowel which says its short (first) sound.	

What rule does this remind us of? CK is used only after a single vowel which says its short sound.
What are some words that follow the CK rule? duck, luck, truck, block, clock, quick, black

Are words ending in DGE silent final E words?
How do we add a suffix to a silent final E word? Drop the silent final E when adding a vowel suffix only if it is allowed by other spelling rules.
Let's explore a few words and see how the DGE behaves.

Write:

judge + ed = judged
judge + ing = judging
dodge + ed = dodged
dodge + ing = dodging

What is occurring in these words? We drop the E when adding a vowel suffix.

knowledge

> ***What root word do you see?*** know
> ***Sound out this word.*** /nō lĕj/
> ***We say /nŏ lĕj/.***
> ***What does knowledge mean?*** information that we know
>
> ***What ending do we need to add to turn this word into knowledgeable?*** -able

knowledge + able =

> ***Will we drop the silent final E in "knowledge" to form "knowledgeable?"*** no
>
> ***Why?*** G may say /j/ only before an E, I, or Y. It would be before an A and therefore the G would say /g/.

Spelling Journal   Ⓐ Ⓚ Ⓥ

Add words which use the phonogram DGE to spell /j/.

Optional Spelling Rule Practice

1. Quickly review rules 1-13, 15-16, 19-22, 24, 25-28, 30 using the Spelling Rule Cards.   Ⓐ Ⓥ

2. Create a reference page to remember this rule. Include sample words.   Ⓒ Ⓥ

3. Ask the students to teach this to another student or to a parent.   Ⓒ Ⓥ Ⓐ Ⓚ

4. Practice writing words which end in the phonogram -DGE. Use the words listed on the previous page. Students may use magnetic letters or whiteboards.   Ⓥ Ⓐ Ⓚ

Exploring Sounds

DGE and GE

Write the following words on the board.

> ***Read each of the words as I write them on the board.***

stage	badge	page	pledge
fringe	fridge	large	ledge

How does the rule: English words do not end in I, U, V or J apply to these words? They all end in the /j/ sound. But /j/ cannot be spelled with a J at the end of the word.

What are the two options for spelling /j/ at the end of the word? the phonogram DGE and G followed by a silent final E.

I will read each of these pairs. Close your eyes and listen to the last sound in each word. If you can hear a difference in the last sound in each pair of words, raise your hand. Not everyone will be able to hear the difference. It is subtle. The first sound GE is softer than the second sound DGE which is harder or harsher.

Next read each word aloud. Compare the words ending in DGE with the words ending in GE. This time see if you can feel a difference in your mouth. With DGE the tongue touches the roof of the mouth as if it is saying the /d/ sound before the /j/.

If you are unable to hear this sound, do not worry. This will be a point of memorization. If you are able to hear the sounds, this will help you to know when to use DGE.

PART TWO

Using Spelling List 26 on pages 326-327, dictate each word following the steps included on pages Intro 42 - Intro 46.

Tips for Spelling List 26

Person

For spelling purposes, exaggerate the vowel so that / per sən/ sounds like /per sŏn/.

People

The ⬚o⬚ in *people* causes many students difficulty. It is not pronounced. Though it may be more accurate to say that *people* includes the phonogram ⬚eo⬚ which says the long /ē/ sound, many students find it easier to recall the spelling by adding an extra syllable. In this case the ⬚o⬚ will say the long /ō/ sound at the end of the syllable. Though this is obviously not how the word is pronounced, creating an auditory picture which follows the rules is often helpful for internalizing the correct spelling. /pe ō pl/

The only other known words which include the phonogram ⬚eo⬚ are: *jeopardy, leopard, luncheon, surgeon, sturgeon, dungeon, pigeon*. The ⬚eo⬚ phonogram is used only before a ⬚p⬚ and ⬚n⬚. In all the other words which have an ⬚e⬚ followed by an ⬚o⬚ both phonograms are clearly pronounced. For example: *deodorize, geology, stereo…*

Important

For spelling purposes exaggerate the vowel so that /ĭm pōr tənt/ sounds like /ĭm pōr tănt/.

To learn more about vowels in unaccented syllables and aiding students in creating an auditory picture of words, see *Uncovering the Logic of English,* 121-128.

	Word	Practice Sentence	Say to Spell	# of Syllables	Markings
1.	**here**	*What time will you be here?*	hĕr	1	h<u>ē</u>r<u>e</u>
2.	**there**	*Put the tables over there.*	THĕr	1	<u>the</u>r<u>e</u>
3.	**judge**	*The judge declared him guilty.*	jŭj	1	ju<u>dge</u>
4.	**person**	*Treat every person with respect.*	per sŏn	2	p<u>er</u> son
5.	**people**	*How many people are coming to the party?*	pē **ō** pl	2	pē ō p<u>le</u>
6.	**fly**	*We will fly to Arizona.*	flī	1	fly
7.	**important**	*She has important news to tell us.*	ĭm pōr tănt	3	im p<u>or</u> tant
8.	**each**	*Take one of each.*	ēch	1	<u>ea</u>ch
9.	**circle**	*Circle the first word on the page.*	ser kl	2	c<u>ir</u> c<u>le</u>
10.	**solve**	*Can you solve this puzzle?*	sŏlv	1	solv<u>e</u>
11.	**carry**	*I will carry the bags.*	kăr rē	2	căr ry
12.	**example**	*Please give me an example.*	ĕx ăm pl	3	ex am p<u>le</u>
13.	**please**	*Please give me an example.*	plēz	1	pl<u>ea</u>s<u>e</u>
14.	**airplane**	*It was his first time on an airplane.*	ār plān	2	<u>air</u> plān<u>e</u>
15.	**center**	*Center the picture on the wall.*	sĕn ter	2	cen t<u>er</u>

Spelling Hints	Part of Speech	Vocabulary Development
Draw line over the /ē/. Double underline the silent final E. **12.1** The vowel says its name because of the E.	Adv	hereto, heretofore, hereinabove, hereinafter, hereinbefore, hereinbelow, hereof, hereafter, hereby, hereabout
Put a 2 over the /th-TH/. Double underline the silent final E. **12.9** Unseen reason.	Adv	therefore, therein, thereafter, thereabout, therefrom, thereof, thereon, thereto, thereupon, therewith, therewithal
Underline /j/. **25** DGE used only after a single vowel which says its short sound. **3** English words do not end in I, U, V, or J.	N, V	judges, judgement, judged, judging
Say to spell /per **sŏ**n/. Underline /er/.	N	people, personal, impersonal, depersonalize, personality, persona, anchorperson, businessperson, chairperson
Say to spell /pē **ō** pl/. Put a line over the /ē/. E said the sound /ē/. Put a line over the /ō/. O said the sound /ō/. **4** A E O U usually say their names at the end of the syllable. Underline the L. Double underline the silent final E. **12.4** Every syllable must have a vowel.	N	peopled, salespeople, tradespeople, businesspeople
5 I and Y may say /ĭ/ or /ī/ at the end of the syllable.	N, V	flier, flew, flies, butterfly, deerfly, dragonfly, firefly, flyable, flyaway, flycatcher, flyby, flywheel, horsefly, housefly
Say to spell /ĭm **pōr tă**nt /. Underline /or/.	Adj	importantly, unimportant
Underline /ē/. Underline /ch/.	Adj	
Underline /er/. Underline the L. Double underline the silent final E. **12.4** Every syllable must have a vowel.	V, N	circled, circling, circles, encircle, semicircle, circus, circulate, circulation, circumscribe, recirculate, semicircular
Underline V. Double underline the silent final E. **12.2** English words do not end in V or U.	V	solved, solving, solvable, absolve, dissolve, resolve, irresolvable, solvency, solvent, solver, unsolved
7 Y says long /ē/ only at the end of a multi-syllable word. I says long /ē/ only at the end of a syllable that is followed by a vowel.	V	carrying, carried, carrier, carries, carriage, carryback, carryforward, carryover, miscarry
Underline the L. Double underline the silent final E. **12.4** Every syllable must have a vowel.	N	examples, counterexample
Underline the /ē/. Double underline the silent final E. **12.5** Add an E to keep singular words that end in S from looking plural. This also occurs with verbs. (S is added to singular verbs. No ending is used for plural verbs.)	Adv, V	pleased, displeased, displeases, pleaser, pleases
Underline two letter /ā/. Put a line over the single-vowel /ā/. Double underline the silent final E. **12.1** The vowel says its name because of the E.	N	airplanes
Underline /er/. **1** C softens to /s/ when followed by an E, I or Y.	V, N	centered, centering, centerboard, self-centeredness, centerpiece

PART THREE

Materials Needed: Grammar Rule Cards 1.12, 9.7, 9.8, 11.3; green, red, blue, and yellow colored pencils.

Grammar

Review

What is a noun?   A noun is the name of a person, place, thing, or idea.

What are the three noun jobs we have learned so far? subject noun, direct object, indirect object

What is an adjective? Adjectives modify nouns and pronouns. Adjectives answer: What kind? How many? Which one? Whose?

What is an article? A, An, The. Tiny article adjectives that mark nouns and answer the question: Which?

Name the parts of a sentence.   A sentence must have a capital letter, subject, verb, complete thought, and an end mark.

What is a verb? A verb shows action, links a description to the subject, or helps another verb.

What are the two types of verbs we have learned? action verb and transitive verb

What is an adverb? An adverb modifies a verb, adjective, or another adverb. An adverb answers: How? When? Where? To what extent?

✎ *Spelling List 26 – Label the adverbs with a yellow Adv. Label the nouns with a red N. Label the verbs with a green V. Label the adjectives with a blue Adj.*

✎ *Spelling List 26 – Write the plural of each noun and the past tense of each verb.*

Optional Spelling Cards

1. Dictate the words in Lesson 26 for the students to write on index cards. Ⓚ Ⓥ Ⓐ

2. Ask the students to color a green border around the verbs, a red border around the nouns, a blue border around the adjectives, and a yellow border around the adverbs. If a word can be used as more than one part of speech, color two borders. Ⓚ Ⓥ

Types of sentences

There are four types of sentences in English. So far we have focused on statements. A statement provides us with information and ends with a period. For example:

I found my watch.

> ### Grammar Card 9.7
>
> **A statement ends with a period.**

Today we will learn about a second type of sentence, a command.
I will write a command on the board. Read it and then do it.

Speak loudly.

Stand up slowly.

Come here quickly.

What sort of punctuation is at the end of each of these sentences? a period

Change the period into an exclamation point.

Speak loudly!

Stand up slowly!

Come here quickly!

How did I change the sentences? You added an exclamation point.
How does this change the meaning of the sentence? The exclamation point makes the command more forceful or more urgent.

> ### Grammar Card 9.8
>
> **A command ends with a period or an exclamation point.**

How do all these sentences begin? with a verb

What is the subject of the sentence? Hint: who am I talking to? you
I could say:

You, speak loudly.

You, stand up slowly.

You, come here quickly.

Though we could say it this way, it sounds rude. We usually either leave off the "you" or we say the person's name. This is called a noun of direct address.

✎ *26.5 Commands – **Read the first three commands in your workbook.***

Peter, tell me your brother's name.

Grace, show me the book.

Zander, close the door.

What did I write after the noun of direct address? a comma
Underline the noun of direct address and circle the comma in your workbook for the first three commands.
Where are the nouns of direct address located in these sentences? at the beginning of the sentence

Grammar Card 1.12	NDA
A noun of direct address identifies to whom the sentence is directed. Separate a noun of direct address from the rest of the sentence with a comma.	

Read the second group of commands in your workbook. Underline the nouns of direct address and circle the commas.
Where are the nouns of direct address located in these sentences? at the end of the sentence

Open the trunk, Kayla.

Catch the frog, Austin.

Watch the ball, Jordan.

To make the sentence more polite, we often add the word please.

Read the third group of commands in your workbook. Underline the nouns of direct address and circle the commas. Put a box around "please." In these sentences "please" is an adverb answering the question, "how."

Peter, please bring me the newspaper.

Please talk quietly, girls.

Please, Rachel, throw this away.

In sentences with nouns of direct address, the comma tells us that this is the person to whom we are directing the command. It is very important to write the comma in order to prevent confusion. Read the following sentences as I write them on the board. Tell me what is wrong.

Come and eat, Grandma.

Read the sentence on the board. What does it mean? This sentence means that we are to eat Grandma.
How would I change it to mean I am calling Grandma to come and eat? Add a comma before Grandma.

LESSON 26   //   331

Come and eat, Grandma.

Now what does it mean? It means you are calling Grandma to come and eat.

Kick Jim.

What does this sentence mean? It is a command to kick Jim.
How would I change it to be a command for Jim to follow? Add a comma before Jim.

Kick, Jim.

Grammar Card 11.3	**Comma Rule 3**
Use a comma to separate a Noun of Direct Address from the rest of the sentence.	

Whenever you give a command and include a person's name, you must write a comma to set it apart from the rest of the sentence. This is one of the most common reasons for adding a comma to a sentence. The comma demonstrates that the noun of direct address is not the subject noun.

< **Teacher Tip:** *Statements are sometimes called declarative sentences. If you prefer to teach the term declarative, tie it to the root "declare." Demonstrate to students how these sentences declare information to the reader.*

< **Teacher Tip:** *Commands are sometimes called imperative sentences. If you prefer to teach the term imperative, tie it to the meaning of "imperative." Somthing that is imperative is very important and must be done.*

Identifying Parts of Speech

✎ *26.6 Identifying Parts of Speech* – **Label the parts of speech in your workbook, while I label them on the board.**

> *Read the book quietly.*
>
> **Who read?** you, subject pronoun
> **Since "you" is not written in the sentence but implied, we will write it in parenthesis at the beginning of the sentence.**
> **What is being said about you?** you read, verb
> **Read what?** book, direct object
> **Which book?** the, article adjective
> **Read how?** quietly, adverb
> **Is there a direct object receiving the action of the verb?** Yes. So, it is a transitive verb.
> **Divide the complete subject from the complete predicate.**
>
> ```
>   SP      TV   A   DO   Adv
> (You) / Read the book quietly.
> ```

Solve the six problems carefully.

Who solves? you, subject pronoun
Since "you" is not written in the sentence but implied, we will write it in parenthesis at the beginning of the sentence.
What is being said about you? you solve, verb
Solve what? problems, direct object
How many problems? six, adjective
Which problems? the, article adjective
Solve them how? carefully, adverb
Is there a direct object receiving the action of the verb? Yes. So, it is a transitive verb.
Divide the complete subject from the complete predicate.

```
      SP      TV     A  Adj   DO      Adv
(You) / Solve the six problems carefully.
```

Jacob, circle the first example.

Who circles? you, subject pronoun
Though you might think that Jacob is the subject, we need to remember that the person saying this sentence is speaking directly to Jacob. In that case they mean, "Jacob, you circle the first example." "You" is the implied subject of the sentence. Therefore, we will write it in parenthesis.
What is being said about you? you circle, verb
Circle what? example, direct object
Which example? first, adjective
Which example? the, article adjective
Is there a direct object receiving the action of the verb? Yes. So, it is a transitive verb.
That leaves one word in the sentence that has not been identified. It is Jacob. Jacob is the noun of direct address. We will mark it NDA for noun of direct address.
A noun of direct address is always separated by a comma from the rest of the sentence.
Divide the complete subject from the complete predicate.

```
  NDA      SP      TV    A  Adj  DO
Jacob, (you) / circle the first example.
```

Come here quickly, Samantha.

Who comes? you, implied subject pronoun
What is being said about you? you come, verb
Come where? here, adverb
Come how? quickly, adverb
What is the word "Samantha?" a noun of direct address
A noun of direct address is separated with a comma from the rest of the sentence.
Is there a direct object receiving the action of the verb? no
Divide the complete subject from the complete predicate.

```
  SP     V   Adv   Adv      NDA
(You) / Come here quickly, Samantha.
```

Lily, please carry the red bag.

Who carries? you, subject pronoun
Since "you" is not written in the sentence but implied, we will write it in parenthesis at the beginning of the sentence.
What is being said about you? you carry, verb
Carry what? bag, direct object
What kind of bag? red, adjective
Which bag? the, article adjective
Carry it how? please, adverb
What is the word "Lily?" a noun of direct address
Is there a direct object receiving the action of the verb? Yes. So, it is a transitive verb.
Divide the complete subject from the complete predicate.

```
 NDA SP     Adv  TV  A Adj DO
Lily, (you) / please carry the red bag.
```

The Importance of Punctuation

Grammar Challenge 1

How many ways can you arrange the words in this sentence? "Samantha, please drink your milk."
I will write them on the board as you list them.

Samantha, please drink your milk.

Please drink your milk, Samantha.

Samantha, drink your milk, please.

Please, Samantha, drink your milk.

Drink your milk, please, Samantha.

What do you notice? Samantha is always set off by a comma(s). When please is at the end of the sentence it is also set off by a comma.

What word does please modify? It is an adverb modifying drink. It answer the question drink how?

When the adverb is next to the verb it is modifying, the comma is not needed. When it is separated from the verb it is modifying, a comma is used to set it apart from the rest of the sentence.

Grammar Challenge 2

Direct students to compare the sentence with and without the comma by identifying the parts of speech.

Come and eat Grandma.

Who comes? you, subject pronoun
What is being said about you? you come, verb
What is being said about you? you eat, verb
And is a conjunction joining come and eat.
Eat what? Grandma, direct object

SP   V   C   V   DO
(You) Come and eat Grandma.

Come and eat, Grandma.

Who comes? you, subject pronoun
What is being said about you? you come, verb
What is being said about you? you eat, verb
And is a conjunction joining come and eat.
Eat what? it doesn't say
What is Grandma? It is set off by a comma. Therefore it is a noun of direct address.

SP   V   C   V   NDA
(You) Come and eat, Grandma.

Kick Jim.

Who kicks? you, subject pronoun
What is being said about you? you kick, verb
Kick what? Jim, direct object

SP   V   DO
(You) Kick Jim.

Kick, Jim.

Who kicks? you, subject pronoun
What is being said about you? you kick, verb
Kick what? The sentence doesn't say what to kick.
What is Jim? A noun of direct address because it is set off by a comma.

SP   V   NDA
(You) Kick, Jim.

Optional Grammar Practice

1. Have the students take turns giving commands verbally to one another. For example: *Stand up. Close the door...* Direct them to practice giving commands starting with a verb. Then practice giving commands which include a noun of direct address. Ⓐ Ⓚ Ⓥ

2. ✎ *26.7 Extra Practice: Statement or Command?* – Direct students to write *State.* by the statements and *Com.* next to the commands. Ⓚ Ⓥ

3. ✎ *26.8 Extra Practice: Nouns of Direct Address* – Practice using commas with the nouns of direct address. Ⓚ Ⓥ

4. ✎ *26.9 Extra Practice: Editing* – Correct the sentences in the workbook. Each one has three errors. Ⓥ Ⓐ

5. ✎ *26.10 Reading* – Direct the students to read the sentences in the workbook aloud. Have the students read them two or three times until they can read each one fluently.

6. *Optional* – Reread the sentences. Divide the subject and the predicate.

Vocabulary

homophone

> **What word do you recognize within the word homophone?** phone
> **What does the root phone mean?** sound
> **Homo is the Latin root for "same". Therefore homophone means same sound.**

their

there

> **Read these words.**
> **These two words are sometimes mixed up in English because they are homophones. They have the same sound.**
>
> **Do you see any way to tell them apart?** answers will vary

their – they

there – here

> **How do these words help to clarify the meaning?** "They" and "their" are related. They are both pronouns. "They" ends with two letter /ā/ that may be used at the end of English words. "Their" has a two letter /ā/ that may not be used at the end of English words. The meaning of "there" and "here" are also related. "Here" and "there" both refer to location. If you add a T to "here" it spells "there."

th__ei__r – th__ey__

t__here__ – __here__

That is _____ car.   *We went _____.*

Which one should I use in each of these sentences?

That is__their__ car.   *We went__there__.*

✎ *26.11 Their and There –***Complete the activity in the workbook.**

Dictation

✎ *26.12 Dictation –* Read the sentence two times. Ask the students to repeat it aloud, then write it in their student workbooks.

1. Jack, carry the knife carefully.

2. Ten people knew the answer.

3. Please give me an example.

4. Circle each person's name.

5. Fly the airplanes here.

6. Morgan, solve problem number three.

Composition

Direct the students to practice forming commands aloud. Write their examples on the board.

✎ *26.13 Composition –* Using the words in the workbook, direct the students to write five commands.

Challenge

Direct students to write step-by-step instructions. For example: How to make a fried egg. How to make a glass of chocolate milk. How to make a bed. How to plant a seed. How to take care of a dog.

Lesson 27

Phonograms:	ie
Exploring Sounds:	The Long /ē/ Sound
Spelling Rules:	23
Grammar:	Linking Verbs, Predicate Nouns, Predicate Adjectives

PART ONE

Materials Needed: Phonogram Flash Cards from previous lessons and ie ; Spelling Rule Card 23; Game pieces for Bingo

Phonograms

New Phonogram — *ie*

Show ie . /ē/

✎ *27.1 The Phonogram IE –Read the words in your workbook and underline the IE.*

field	yield	grieve	relieve
piece	brief	shield	shriek
fierce	chief	thief	priest
wield	grief	believe	

Spelling Journal Ⓐ Ⓚ Ⓥ

Enter words which use IE to spell the long /ē/ sound.

Review

1. Drill the phonograms with flash cards.

2. ✎ *27.2 Writing the Phonogram* – Write the new phonogram five times while saying the sound aloud.

3. ✎ *27.3 Phonogram Practice* – Dictate the following phonograms. For extra practice, have the students read them back. Write the correct answers on the board as the students check their answers.

1. gu *g gw*	6. ur *hurt*	11. ei *ā ē ī* / *their protein fiesty*	16. gn *2 letter n beg or end*
2. ie *ē*	7. bu *2 letter b buy*	12. ey *ā ē*	17. kn *2 n beg*
3. ou *ow ŏ oo ŭ*	8. ir *bird*	13. eigh *ā ī*	18. ai *ā*
4. aw	9. ui *oo fruit*	14. augh *ă ăf*	19. ar *är*
5. igh	10. dge	15. ew *oo ū*	20. oy *oi*

4. ✎ *27.4 Phonogram Bingo* (*The Phonogram and Spelling Game Book*, 26).

Exploring Sounds

The Long /ē/ Sound

List the phonograms that say the long /ē/ sound. e, ea, ee, ei, ey, ie, y, i

e   ea   ee   ei   ey   ie   y   i

✎ *27.5 Spellings of Long /ē/* – **Write the spellings of long /ē/ in your workbook.**

How many ways are there to spell the long /ē/ sound? eight

This is one of the most difficult sounds to spell in English. Nevertheless, we can eliminate some of our options by considering where the long /ē/ sound is heard in the word.

Optional – Direct students to reference the words in their Spelling Journals as they answer the questions.

✎ *27.6 Spellings of the Long /ē/* – Fill in the spellings of long /ē/ on the chart on the board, while students write them in their workbook.

End of the Syllable	Middle of the Syllable	End of a One-Syllable Word	End of a Multi-Syllable Word

Which spelling of long /ē/ is most common at the end of the syllable? e

Which spellings of /ē/ are most common in the middle of the syllable? ea, ee, ie

Which spellings of long /ē/ do we find at the end of a one-syllable word? e, ee, (ea)

Which spelling of /ē/ is the most common at the end of a multi-syllable word? y

Which other spelling do we find at the end of a multi-syllable word? ey

Which spelling of /ē/ is not very common? ei

Where is ei used? In the middle of the syllable.

I will write it in parenthesis to show it is not very common.

We will learn where I says the long /ē/ sound in a later lesson.

End of the Syllable	Middle of the Syllable	End of a One-Syllable Word	End of a Multi-Syllable Word
e, i	ea, ee, ie, (ei)	e, ee, ea	y, ey

Optional Exploring Sounds

1. ✎ *27.7 Extra Practice: Reading Words with the Long /ē/ Sound* – Read the words spelled with long /ē/. Underline the phonogram saying the long /ē/ sound. ⒶⓀⓋ

2. Practice dictating some of the IE words in exercise *27.1 The Phonogram IE* while students write them on a whiteboard. ⒶⓀⓋ

3. Practice spelling words from previous lists and their derivatives with the long /ē/ sound. Dictate words while students write them on a whiteboard. If desired, turn it into a game by awarding points for a correct spelling. ⒶⓀⓋ

   - **EE in the middle of the syllable** – *street, green, wheel, meet, need*

   - **EE at the end of the word** – *three, tree, see*

   - **EA in the middle of the syllable** – *clean, wheat, teach, cheap, read, reach, ear, hear, each, please*

   - **E at the end of the syllable** – *hero, secret, design, remember, celebrate, he, she, me*

   - **I at the end of the syllable** – *radio, stadium*

   - **Y at the end of a multi-syllable word** – *happy, hungry, baby, study, slowly, family, copy, story, heavy, carry, strongly, stringy, quickly, cleanly, poorly, sharply, cheaply, rightly, simply, homely, happily, hungrily, carefully, heavily, importantly*

   - **E Consonant Silent Final E** – *here*

   - **EY at the end of the word** – *key*

4. Direct students to add words from the exercise above to their Spelling Journals. ⒶⓀⓋ

Spelling Rules

Rule 23

Listen as I say the following words. What do you hear that is the same among them: always, also, almost.

They all begin with /äl/.

I will say a word. Sound it out as I write it on the board:

always   *also*   *almost*   *although*

What is the same between each of these words? The /äl/ is spelled al.

This leads to the rule:

Spelling Rule	23
AL- is a prefix written with one L when preceding another syllable.	

Optional Spelling Rule Practice

1. Quickly review rules 1-13, 15-16, 19-28, 30 using the Spelling Rule Cards. ⒶⓋ

2. Create a reference page to remember this rule. Include sample words. ©Ⓥ

3. Ask the students to teach this to another student or to a parent. ©ⓋⒶⓀ

PART TWO

Using Spelling List 27 on pages 342-343, dictate each word following the steps included on pages Intro 42 - Intro 46.

Tips for Spelling List 27

Was

Words within English sentences receive various amounts of stress or accent. Many of the common grammatical words are not stressed and therefore the vowel sound degenerates to a schwa sound. In order to aid students in forming an auditory picture of the word, exaggerate the vowel sound for spelling purposes. In this case /wəz/ becomes /wăz/.

Husband

Exaggerate the vowel sound for spelling purposes. Say to spell /hŭz bănd/.

	Word	Practice Sentence	Say to Spell	# of Syllables	Markings
1.	**be**	*Please be on time.*	bē	1	bē
2.	**is**	*She is a good friend.*	ĭz	1	is²
3.	**are**	*You are working tonight.*	är	1	a͟r͟e
4.	**was**	*He was there.*	wăz	1	wä²s
5.	**were**	*They were at the party with us.*	wer	1	we͟r͟e
6.	**always**	*We always watch a movie on Friday night.*	äl wāz	2	äl wa͟ys²
7.	**field**	*Let's run through the field.*	fēld	1	fi͟eld
8.	**almost**	*Dinner is almost ready.*	äl mōst	2	äl mōst
9.	**niece**	*She is my niece.*	nēs	1	ni͟e͟ce
10.	**cousin**	*Our cousin lives in Africa.*	kŭz ĭn	2	co͟u͟⁴²s in
11.	**husband**	*Her husband will be here soon.*	hŭz bănd	2	hus² band
12.	**wife**	*His wife will be here soon.*	wīf	1	wi͟f͟e
13.	**uncle**	*My uncle is coming tomorrow.*	ŭn kl	2	un cl͟e
14.	**nephew**	*He is my nephew.*	nĕf ū	2	nep͟h e͟w²
15.	**ready**	*We are ready.*	rĕd ē	2	re͟a²d y

Spelling Hints	Part of Speech	Vocabulary Development
Draw a line over the /ē/. **4** A E O U usually say their names at the end of the syllable.	V	maybe
Put a 2 over the /z/. /s-z/ said its second sound.	V	
Underline /ar/. Double underline the silent final E. **12.6** Add an E to make the word look bigger.	V	
Say to spell / wäz/. Put two dots over the /ä/. /ă-ā-ä/ said its third sound. Put a 2 over the /z/. /s-z/ said its second sound.	V	
Underline the /er/. Double underline the silent final E. **12.9** Unseen reason.	V	
Put two dots over the /ä/. /ă-ā-ä/ said its third sound. Notice it said its third sound before an L. Underline two letter /ā/. Put a 2 over the /z/. /s-z/ said its second sound. **23** Al- is a prefix written with one L when preceding another syllable.	Adv	
Underline the /ē/.	N, (V)	fields, backfield, airfield, battlefield, fieldwork, grainfield, infield, outfield, midfield
Put two dots over the /ä/. /ă-ā-ä/ said its third sound. A said /ä/ before an L. Put a line over the /ō/. **8** I and O may say /ī/ and /ō/ before two consonants.	Adv	
Underline /ē/. Underline /s/. Double underline the silent final E. **12.3** The C says /s/ and the G says /j/ because of the E.	N	nieces, grandniece
Underline the /ŭ/. Put a 4 over /ow-ō-oo-ŭ/. It said its fourth sound. Put a 2 over the /s-z/. /s-z/ said its second sound.	N	cousins
Say to spell /huzbănd/. Put a 2 over the /z/. /s-z/ said its second sound.	N	husbands, husbandry
Put a line over /ī/. Double underline the silent final E. **12.1** The vowel says its name because of the E.	N	wives, housewife, wifely, midwife, midwifery
Underline the /l/. Double underline the silent final E. **12.4** Every syllable must have a vowel.	N	uncles
Underline /f/. Underline /ū/. Put a 2 over it. /oo-ū/ said its second sound.	N	nephews, grandnephew
Underline /ĕ/ and put a 2 over it. /ē-ĕ-ā/ said its second sound.	Adj	readiness, unready

PART THREE

Materials Needed: Grammar Rule Cards 1.11, 2.7, 3.3, 14.1; green, red, yellow, and blue colored pencils.

Grammar

Review

What is a noun? A noun is the name of a person, place, thing, or idea.

What is a pronoun? A pronoun takes the place of a noun.

What are the four noun jobs we have learned so far? subject noun, direct object, indirect object, noun of direct address

What is an adjective? Adjectives modify nouns and pronouns. Adjectives answer: What kind? How many? Which one? Whose?

What is an article? A, An, The. Tiny article adjectives that mark nouns and answer the question: Which?

Name the parts of a sentence. A sentence must have a capital letter, subject, verb, complete thought, and an end mark.

What is a verb? A verb shows action, links a description to the subject, or helps another verb.

What are the two types of verbs we have learned so far? action verbs and transitive verbs

✓ *What is an adverb?* An adverb modifies a verb, adjective, or another adverb. An adverb answers: How? When? Where? To what extent?

✎ *Spelling List 27 –* **Explain to students that the first five words in List 27 are verbs. Direct them to label them with a green V. Direct students to label words 6-15 as they have in previous lists. Label the Adverbs with a yellow Adv. Label the nouns with a red N. Label the adjectives with a blue Adj.**

✎ *Spelling List 27 –* **Direct students to write the plural form of each of the nouns in List 27 .**

Present Tense State of Being Verbs

Today we will learn the forms of the verb "to be." The "to be" verbs are irregular. This means we do not simply add an -S to form the third person singular.

English is not alone. In most languages the "be" verb is irregular.

We will begin by writing the subject pronouns on the board. Tell me the subject pronouns while I write them.

Subject Pronouns	To Be Verbs Present Tense	To Be Verbs Past Tense
I		
you		

he
she
it
we
they

To discover the forms of "be," let's use the following sentence.

I _____ happy.

What word is missing in this sentence? am

Subject Pronouns	To Be Verbs Present Tense	To Be Verbs Past Tense
I	am	

Now we will change it to:

You _____ happy.

Which form of the verb "be" would I use? are

Subject Pronouns	To Be Verbs Present Tense	To Be Verbs Past Tense
I	am	
you	are	

Continue in this manner until all the "Present Tense To Be Verbs" are filled in.

Subject Pronouns	To Be Verbs Present Tense	To Be Verbs Past Tense
I	am	
you	are	
he	is	
she	is	
it	is	
we	are	
they	are	

Make up sentences orally using each of the subject pronouns and "to be" verbs. I am a student. You are a teacher…

Past Tense Be Verbs

Now we will discover how the "to be" verb changes in the past tense.
We will use the following sentence to help us.

Yesterday I _____ happy.

What word is missing in this sentence? was

Subject Pronouns	To Be Verbs Present Tense	To Be Verbs Past Tense
I	am	was

Yesterday you _____ happy.

What word is missing in this sentence? were

Subject Pronouns	To Be Verbs Present Tense	To Be Verbs Past Tense
I	am	was
you	are	were

Continue in this manner until all the "Past Tense To Be Verbs" are filled in.

Subject Pronouns	To Be Verbs Present Tense	To Be Verbs Past Tense
I	am	was
you	are	were
he	is	was
she	is	was
it	is	was
we	are	were
they	are	were

What is similar between the words are and were? They both end in -*re*. They are both used with *you, we,* and *they.*

What is similar between is and was? They both end in S. They are both used with *he, she,* and *it.*

< Teacher Tip: *Words changing based upon the person, tense, or case is called inflection. English has less inflection than many modern languages. When learning a language it is important to understand that endings can change based upon the grammar of the sentence. It is also important to know that the "be" verbs are irregular in most languages.*

✎ *27.8 Be Verbs –* **Fill in the chart in your workbook. First write the subject pronouns, then write the present and past tense "be" verbs.**

Predicate Nouns and Predicate Adjectives

What kind of verbs have we studied so far? action verbs and transitive verbs
What is an action verb? An action verb shows an action like run, shout, think, write, read…
What is a transitive verb? A transitive verb transfers the action of the verb to a direct object.

Do the words am, is, are, was, and were show actions? no

The forms of "be" have multiple jobs in a sentence. One job is to show a state of being.

I am.

She is.

What do these very simple sentences tell us? They tell us that "I exist" and that "she exists."

Commonly these verbs tell us something more about the state of the subject than simply that it exists. Forms of the "be" verb do this by linking the subject to another noun or a pronoun that describes the subject.

Read the sentences as I write them on the board.

My dog is black.

What does this sentence tell us about my dog? It is black.
What part of speech is black? adjective
"Black" is an adjective describing dog.
In the sentence, "My dog is black," the word "is" links the subject noun dog with the adjective black.
I could write:

black dog

The airplane is damaged.

What does this sentence tell us about the airplane? It is damaged.
What part of speech is damaged? adjective
"Damaged" is an adjective describing the airplane.
In the sentence, "The airplane is damaged," the word "is" links the subject noun airplane with the adjective damaged.
I could write:

the damaged airplane

In these sentences, black and damaged are called predicate adjectives, because they are adjectives found in the predicate part of the sentence.

Grammar Card 2.7	PA
Predicate adjectives describe the subject and are linked to the subject with a linking verb.	

My uncle is an engineer.

What does this sentence tell us about my uncle? He is an engineer.
What part of speech is engineer? noun
Hint: we can see it is a noun because it has the noun marker "an" before it.
In the sentence, "My uncle is an engineer," the word "is" links the subject noun uncle with the noun engineer.

uncle = engineer

That building is the capitol.

What does this sentence tell us about the building? It is the capitol.
What part of speech is capitol? noun
Hint: we can see that it is a noun because it has the noun marker "the" before it.
In the sentence, "That building is the capitol," the word "is" links the subject noun building with the noun capitol.

building = capitol

In these sentences engineer and capitol are both predicate nouns, because they are nouns found in the predicate.

Grammar Card 1.11	PN
Predicate nouns rename the subject and are linked to the subject with a linking verb.	

This leads to the definition of a linking verb:

Grammar Card 3.3	LV
A **linking verb** connects the subject to additional information about the subject. It may link a noun, pronoun, or an adjective to the subject.	

Identifying Parts of Speech

✎ *27.9 Identifying Parts of Speech –* **Label the parts of speech in your workbook while I label them on the board.**

James is happy.

> ***Who is happy?*** James, subject noun
> ***What is being said about James?*** James is, verb
> ***What is James?*** happy
> ***What kind of word is happy?*** an adjective

SN V A
James is happy.

> **Happy is an adjective describing James. Therefore in this sentence "is" is a linking verb. Add an L before the V.**
> **When the subject noun is joined to an adjective with a linking verb, the adjective is called a predicate adjective. Mark it with a PA.**

> **The predicate is the part of the sentence following the verb.**
> **Divide the subject and the predicate.**

SN LV PA
James / is happy.

> **"Happy" is describing James. What word is linking "James" and "happy"?** is
> **In this sentence "is" links the adjective "happy" to the subject "James."**

The house is yellow.

> ***What is?*** house, subject noun
> ***Which house?*** the, article adjective
> ***What is being said about the house?*** the house is, linking verb
> ***What is the house?*** yellow, predicate adjective
> ***Divide the subject and the predicate.***

A SN LV PA
The house / is yellow.

> **"Yellow" is an adjective in the predicate describing the house.**
> **What word is linking "house" and "yellow?"** is
> **In this sentence "is" links the adjective "yellow" to the subject "house."**

She is my niece.

What is? she, subject pronoun
What is being said about she? she is, linking verb
What is she? niece
Is niece a noun or an adjective? predicate noun
A linking verb can link an adjective or a noun to the subject.
Niece is a predicate noun describing who "she" is. We will mark predicate nouns PN.
Whose niece? my, possessive pronoun adjective
Divide the subject and the predicate.

SP   LV PPA PN
She / is my niece.

"Niece" is a noun in the predicate describing "she".
What word is linking "she" and "niece?" is
In this sentence "is" links the noun "niece" to the subject "she."

They are bluebirds.

What are? they, subject pronoun
What is being said about them? they are, linking verb
What are they? bluebirds
Is bluebird a noun or an adjective? noun
Therefore it is a predicate noun. Write a PN above "bluebirds."
The word "are" is linking the words "they" and "bluebirds."
Divide the subject and the predicate.

SP   LV   PN
They / are bluebirds.

"Bluebirds" is a noun in the predicate describing "they".
What word is linking "they" and "bluebirds?" are
In this sentence "are" is linking the noun "bluebirds" to the subject "they."

Optional Spelling Cards

1. Dictate the words in List 27 for the students to write on index cards. ⓀⓥⒶ

2. Ask the students to color a green border around the verbs, a red border around the nouns, a yellow border around the adverbs, and a blue border around the adjectives. If a word can be used as more than one part of speech color two borders. Ⓚⓥ

3. Using the Spelling Cards, instruct students to arrange the cards into sentences using nouns, adjectives, articles, and "be" verbs. ⓀⓥⒸ

Optional Grammar Practice

1. ✎ *27.10 Extra Practice "Be" Verbs* – Complete the sentences in the workbook with the correct form of the "Be" verb. Ⓥⓚ

2. ✎ *27.11 Extra Practice: Linking Verbs* – Read the sentences in your workbook. Together we will underline the subject, circle the linking verb, divide the subject from the predicate, underline the predicate adjective or noun that is describing the subject, and draw an arrow back to the subject. ⓋⒶⓚ

3. ✎ *27.12 Extra Practice: There or Their* – Review the use of *there* and *their*. ⓋⒶ

4. ✎ *27.13 Extra Practice: Editing* – Correct the sentences in the workbook. Each one has three errors. ⓚⓋⒶ

5. Direct students to say the "be" verbs aloud while you write them on the board. Begin to erase one verb at a time. Each time one is erased ask the students to recite the list of "be" verbs. ⓋⒶ

6. *"Be" Verb Race* – Direct students to write the "be" verbs as quickly as possible on a whiteboard. Time them with a stop watch. Have them erase the list and write them again trying to beat their previous time. Repeat until they have a best time. ⓋⒶⓚ

Challenge

Other verbs also fulfill the role of a linking verb. For example:

> *The flowers smell wonderful.*
>
> *The bread tastes good.*
>
> *The music sounds harsh.*
>
> *The students appear tired.*

Smell, taste, sound, and *appear* are all linking the subjects with an adjective that describes the subject. Write the parts of speech over each of the words as you discuss them.

> ```
> A   SN   LV    PA
> ```
> *The flowers smell wonderful.*

> ```
> A   SN   LV    PA
> ```
> *The bread tastes good.*

> ```
> A   SN   LV    PA
> ```
> *The music sounds harsh.*

> ```
> A   SN    LV    PA
> ```
> *The students appear tired.*

Vocabulary Development

Contractions

I am sad.

> **Rather than saying, "I am sad," how do we often shorten, "I am?"** I'm
> **What sound do we leave out when we say I'm?** ă
>
> **In writing, the sound that is left out is replaced with an apostrophe.**

I am = I'm

Grammar Card 14.1	Apostrophe
Use an apostrophe to denote the sound(s) omitted from a contraction.	

> **This is called a contraction. Can you hear the word contract in contraction?**
> **What does it mean to contract?** to make something smaller or shorter
> **A contraction, therefore, is a shortened form.**

you are =

> **What is the contraction for you are?** you're
> **Use it in a sentence.** Answers vary. For example: You're kind.
> **What sound is left out?** ä
> **How does the /oo/ sound change?** It changes to /ō/.
> **Is this one of the sounds of /ou-ō-oo-ŭ/?** yes
> **How would we write the contraction for you are?** put an apostrophe for the ä

you are = you're

> **Does this sound like another word?** your

your

> **Use your in a sentence.** Answers vary. For example: That is your book.
> **How are these different?** "Your" shows possession.
> **Which one means you are?** The one with the apostrophe.
> **To keep these from being mixed up, you need to ask yourself if "you are" makes sense in this sentence.**

_____ a great student.   *That is _____ coat.*

> **Which one would we use in the first sentence?** you're
> **How do we know?** "You are a great student," makes sense.
> **Which one would we use in the second sentence?** your
> **Why?** "That is "you are" coat," doesn't make sense.

You're a great student.   *That is your coat.*

he is =

> **What is the contraction for he is?** he's
> **Which sound is replaced with an apostrophe?** ĭ

he is = he's

she is =

> **What is the contraction for she is?** she's
> **Which sound is replaced with an apostrophe?** ĭ

she is = she's

it is =

> **What is the contraction for it is?** it's
> **Which sound is replaced with an apostrophe?** ĭ
> **What word have we learned recently that sounds the same as it's?** its

its

> **What is the difference between it's and its?** "It's" with an apostrophe means it is. "Its" without an apostrophe means something that belongs to it.
> **One way to test which one you need is to see if "it is" makes sense. If it does, spell "it's" with an apostrophe.**

_____ a rainy day.   *The dog spilled ___ water.*

> **Which one would we use in the first sentence?** it's
> **How do we know?** "It is a rainy day," makes sense.
> **Which one would we use in the second sentence?** its
> **Why?** "The dog spilled "it is" water," doesn't make sense.

It's a rainy day.   *The dog spilled its water.*

we are =

> **What is the contraction for we are?** we're
> **Which sound is replaced with an apostrophe?** ä

we are = we're

they are =

> **What is the contraction for they are?** they're
> **Which sound is replaced with an apostrophe?** ä

they are = they're

that is =

What is the contraction for that is? that's
Which sound is replaced with an apostrophe? ĭ

that is = that's

✎ *27.14 Contractions –* **Write the contractions in your workbook.**

Optional Vocabulary Practice

1. *Family Members Guessing Game –* One student completes the sentence: "I am thinking of my _____." Other students guess the answer.

For example: "I am thinking of someone who is my mother's daughter." Answer: your sister. ⒸⒶ

2. *Contractions –* One student calls out a pronoun and its corresponding "be" verb. Other students write the contraction on whiteboards. Reverse the process. One student calls out a contraction, the other students write the corresponding pronoun and verb. ⒸⒶⓀⓋ

3. Dictate the following pronouns and forms of "be" for students to write on index cards. *I, you, he, she, it, we, they, that; am, are, is, are.* Dictate the following contractions: I'm, you're, he's, she's, it's, we're, they're, that's. Direct students to match the pronoun and verb pairs with the contractions. ⒶⓀⓋ

4. Direct students to tell a story from first, second, or third person. Instruct them to use contractions in their story. For example, tell about: Washing the car, walking the dog, meeting a friend for dinner...

Dictation

✎ *27.15 Dictation –* Read each sentence twice. Ask the students to repeat it aloud, then write it in their workbooks.

1. She's always a good example.
2. He is her husband.
3. It was the girl's birthday party.
4. They are our nieces and nephews.
5. We're almost ready.
6. We're cousins.

Composition

✎ *27.16 Composition –* **Direct the students to write six sentences using the sample words in their workbook. They may use contractions if they desire.**

28

Lesson 28

Phonograms:	
Exploring Sounds:	Spellings of /ow/
Spelling Rules:	
Grammar:	Numbers, hyphenating numbers, ordinal numbers

PART ONE

Materials Needed: Phonogram Flash Cards from previous lessons; 3 decks of Phonogram Game Cards, including 3 Slap cards.

Phonograms

Review

1. Drill the phonograms with flash cards.

2. 🖎 *28.1 Phonogram Practice* – Dictate the following phonograms. For extra practice, have the students read them back. Write the correct answers on the board as the students check their answers.

   1. gu *g gw*
   2. ie *ē field / the ē of �*
   3. ou *ow ō oo ŭ*
   4. aw *ä saw / 2 letter ä end*
   5. wr *2 letter r used only at beg*
   6. ur *hurt*
   7. bu *2 letter b*
   8. ir *bird*
   9. ui *oo fruit / 2 letter oo not at end*
   10. dge *edge / hard j used only after single short vowel*
   11. ei *ā ē ī fiesty / their protein*
   12. ey *ā ē / they key*
   13. eigh *ā ī / height*
   14. augh *ä äf / only at end - before t*
   15. ew *oo ū / grew few*
   16. gn *2 letter n beg or end*
   17. kn *2 letter n beg*
   18. wor *wer worship*
   19. ar *ar*
   20. oy *oi end*

3. Play Phonogram Slap (*The Phonogram and Spelling Game Book*, 10).

Spelling Rules

Adding Suffixes

What do we need to consider when we add a suffix to a word? Does it end in E or Y?
What rule applies if the word ends in a silent final E? Drop the E when adding a vowel suffix only if it is allowed by other spelling rules.

What rule applies if the word ends in Y? Single vowel Y changes to I when adding any ending unless the ending begins with I.

✎ *28.2 Adding Suffixes Flow Chart –* **Let's look at the Adding Suffixes Flow Chart in your workbook. This chart will help you to add a suffix to words.**

Read through the chart. Discuss the various questions together.

I will write a word and a suffix on the board. Using the questions on the Flow Chart, tell me how to write the derivative. Then I will write it on the board.

1. ready + ness = readiness

"Ready" ends in single vowel Y. The suffix begins with a consonant. Therefore, we change the Y to I and add the suffix.

2. solve + able = solvable

"Solve" ends in a silent final E. The suffix begins with a vowel. Dropping the E is allowed by other spelling rules. Therefore, drop the E and add the suffix.

3. carry + ing = carrying

"Carry" ends in single vowel Y. The suffix begins with an I. Therefore, do not change the Y to I. Just add the ending.

4. example + s = examples

"Example" ends in a silent final E. The suffix begins with a consonant. Therefore, just add the suffix.

5. story + es = stories

"Story" ends in single vowel Y. The suffix begins with an E. Therefore, we change the Y to I and add the suffix.

6. recharge + able = rechargeable

"Recharge" ends in a silent final E. The suffix begins with a vowel. Dropping the E is not allowed by other spelling rules. G may soften to /j/ only before an E, I or Y. Therefore, retain the E and add the suffix.

7. please + ing = pleasing

"Please" ends in a silent final E. The suffix begins with a vowel. Dropping the E is allowed by other spelling rules. Therefore, drop the E and add the suffix.

8. center + ed = centered

"Center" does not end in a silent final E or in a single vowel Y. Therefore, just add the suffix.

✏️ *28.3 Adding Suffixes –* **I will say a word that has a suffix added. Write the word in your workbook.**

1. *pleased*

2. *copies*

3. *days*

4. *heaviness*

5. *uncles*

6. *visits*

7. *chargeable*

8. *circling*

Optional Spelling Rule Practice

1. Quickly review rules 1-13, 15-16, 19-28, 30 using the Spelling Rule Cards. Ⓐ Ⓥ

Exploring Sounds

Spellings of /ow/

What are the spellings of the sound /ow/ that we have learned?

ou, ow, ough

✏️ *28.4 Phonograms that say /ow/ –* **Write them in your workbook.**

Which spelling is not very common? ough
OUGH says /ow/ in only three words.

bough   *drought*   *plough*

Which spelling cannot be used at the end of the word? ou

If you hear /ow/ at the end of the word and it is not bough or plough, how will it be spelled? OW

✏️ *28.5 Words Ending with OW –* **Read the words in your workbook. Underline the /ow/ as you read them. What do you notice about words that end in the sound /ow/?** They are all very short. They are all spelled with OW.

bow	*cow*	*plow*	*vow*
brow	*how*	*prow*	*wow*
chow	*now*	*sow*	

What is the difference between a bough and a bow?   A bough is a branch of a tree, to bow is to bend over.
Plough is the British spelling and plow is the American spelling for the same word.

✎ *28.6 Words Spelled with OW in the Middle of the Syllable* – **In your workbook is a list of some of the most common base words where OW is found in the middle of the syllable. Read the words aloud. Underline the /ow/. What do you notice?**   OW commonly spells /ow/ in the middle of the word before an N, L and ER.

down	drown	vowel	glower
brown	gown	power	browse
town	growl	tower	
clown	yowl	powder	
crown	fowl	shower	

✎ *28.7 Words Spelled with OU in the Middle of the Syllable* – **In your workbook is a list of some of the most common base words where OU is found in the middle of the syllable. Read the words aloud. Underline the /ow/.**

couch	compound	devout	dour
vouch	account	scout	sour
cloud	noun	route	flour
loud	foul	snout	house
proud	doubt	stout	blouse
shroud	mount	trout	grouse
bound	about	mouth	joust
hound	out	scour	mouse
found	spout	devour	ounce

Spelling Journal   Ⓐ Ⓚ Ⓥ

Enter words spelled with OU, OW, and OUGH in your Spelling Journal.

PART TWO

Using Spelling List 28 on pages 360-361, dictate each word following the steps included on pages Intro 42 - Intro 46.

Tips for Spelling List 28

Alone

One of the difficulties with English spelling is that vowels in unaccented syllables often are pronounced as the schwa sound /ə/. In order to help students create an auditory picture of the word, it is helpful to exaggerate the unaccented vowel. Therefore, exaggerate the vowel so that /ə lōn/ sounds like /ā lōn/.

To learn more about vowels in unaccented syllables and aiding students in creating an auditory picture of words, see *Uncovering the Logic of English,* 121-128.

One

Most exceptions to the rules presented in *Uncovering the Logic of English* occur in the most common words within the language. The pronunciation of these words has shifted over time. Nevertheless, a logic or reason for their spelling can often be found. The spelling of the number *one* is a classic example. Before teaching how to spell *one*, teach students to spell: *lone, alone,* and *only*. Point out that the root /ōn/ means *one* in each of these words. When you are alone, there is one person in the room. A lone deer in a field means there is one deer. Then teach the number *one* saying to spell /ōn/. This will create a strong auditory picture of the word as well as connect it to its roots.

Two

The spelling of the number *two* can also be connected to its roots. Consider the words: *twin, twice, twelve,* and *twenty*. Each of these words refers to the number *two* in some way. Say to spell /twö/ pronouncing the /w/ to create a strong auditory picture. This will also aid students in not mixing up the homophones *two, to,* and *too*.

Four, Forty

Draw students' attention to the shift in spelling for the sound /ōr/ between four and forty.

Word	Practice Sentence	Say to Spell	# of Syllables	Markings
1. **lone**	*A lone bird flew overhead.*	lōn	1	lōn̲e̲
2. **alone**	*Work on your problems alone.*	ā lōn	2	ā lōn̲e̲
3. **only**	*There is only one answer.*	ōn lē	2	ōn ly
4. **one**	*One dog is barking.*	ōn	1	ōn̲e̲
5. **twin**	*Twins are two babies born at the same time.*	twĭn	1	twin
6. **twelve**	*He is twelve years old.*	twĕlv	1	twel̲v̲e̲
7. **twice**	*We looked for it twice.*	twīs	1	twī̲c̲e̲
8. **twenty**	*Twenty copies will be plenty.*	twĕn tē	2	twen ty
9. **two**	*She is two years old.*	twö	1	twö
10. **four**	*They have four daughters.*	fōr	1	fou̲r²
11. **forty**	*In forty days we will travel to Egypt.*	fōr tē	2	fo̲r̲ ty
12. **five**	*There are five days in a work week.*	fīv	1	fī̲v̲e̲
13. **fifty**	*It costs fifty dollars.*	fĭf tē	2	fif ty
14. **hundred**	*The tickets cost one hundred dollars.*	hŭn drĕd	2	hun dred
15. **thousand**	*The car is worth five thousand dollars.*	thou zănd	2	tho̲u̲² sand

Spelling Hints	Part of Speech	Vocabulary Development
Draw a line above the /ō/. Double underline the silent final E. **12.1** The vowel says its name because of the E.	Adj	lonely, loneliness, lonelier, loneliest, lonesome, lonesomeness, loner, alone
Say to spell /ā lōn/. Draw a line above the /ā/. **4** A E O U usually say their names at the end of the syllable. Draw a line above the /ō/. Double underline the silent final E. **12.1** The vowel says its name because of the E.	Adv, Adj	aloneness
Draw a line above the /ō/. There is no visible reason for the O to say its long sound.	Adj, Adv	
Say to spell /ōn/. Ask: How are lone, alone, only, and one related? They all mean 1. Draw a line above the /ō/. Underline the E twice. **12.1** The vowel says its name because of the E.	Adj, N	
All first sounds.	N	twins, twinning, twinned
Underline the V once and double underline the Silent Final E. **12.2** English words do not end in V or U.	Adj, N	twelves
Draw a line over the /ī/. Underline the C once and double underline the silent final E. The E is needed for two reasons. **12.1** The vowel says its name because of the E. **12.3** The C says /s/ because of the E.	Adv	
7 Y says long /ē/ only at the end of a multi-syllable word. I says long /ē/ only at the end of a syllable that is followed by a vowel.	Adj, N	twentieth
Say to spell /twö/. Ask: What is the same between twin, twelve, twice, twenty, and two. They all have TW and mean 2. Put two dots over the O. /ŏ-ō-ö/ said its third sound.	Adj, N	twofold, twopence, twopenny, twosome
Underline the /ō/ and put a 2 over it. /ow-ō/ said its second sound.	Adj, N	fours, fourth, fourths, fourthly, fourteen, fourteenth, fourfold, foursome, foursquare
Underline the /ōr/. **7** Y says long /ē/ only at the end of a multi-syllable word. I says long /ē/ only at the end of a syllable that is followed by a vowel.	Adj, N	fortieth
Draw a line over the /ī/. Underline the V once and double underline the silent final E. The E is needed for two reasons. **12.1** The vowel says its name because of the E. **12.2** English words do not end in V or U.	Adj, N	fives, fivefold
7 Y says long /ē/ only at the end of a multi-syllable word. I says long /ē/ only at the end of a syllable that is followed by a vowel.	Adj, N	fiftieth
All first sounds.	Adj, N	hundreds, hundredth. hundredfold
Underline /th/. Underline /ow/. Put a 2 above the /z/. /s-z/ said its second sound /z/.	Adj, N	thousands, thousandth, thousandfold

PART THREE

Materials Needed: Grammar Rule Cards 15.1, 15.2, 15.3, 15.8; red, blue, and yellow colored pencils; highlighter for vocabulary section.

Grammar

Review

What is a noun?   A noun is the name of a person, place, thing, or idea.

What is a pronoun?   A pronoun takes the place of a noun.

What are the five noun jobs we have learned?   subject noun, direct object, indirect object, predicate noun, noun of direct address

What is an adjective?   Adjectives modify nouns and pronouns. Adjectives answer: What kind? How many? Which one? Whose?

What is an article?   A, An, The. Tiny article adjectives that mark nouns and answer the question: Which?

Name the parts of a sentence.   A sentence must have a capital letter, subject, verb, complete thought, and an end mark.

What is a verb?   A verb shows action, links a description to the subject, or helps another verb.

What are the three types of verbs we have learned?   action verbs, transitive verbs, and linking verbs

What is an adverb?   An adverb modifies a verb, adjective, or another adverb. An adverb answers: How? When? Where? To what extent?

✎ *Spelling List 28 –* **Label the nouns, adjectives, and adverbs.**
Write the plural of twin.

What is the theme of today's words?   They are all related to numbers.

Optional Spelling Cards

1. Dictate the words in Lesson 28 for the students to write on index cards. ⓀⓋⒶ

2. Ask the students to color a red border around the nouns, a yellow border around the adverbs, and a blue border around the adjectives. If a word can be used as more than one part of speech, color two borders. ⓀⓋ

Numbers

When writing numbers you must follow two sets of rules. The first set of rules tells us when to hyphenate a number. The second set tells us when we must write the number in words and when we can use the numeral.

Grammar Card 15.1	Numbers

Hyphenate numbers twenty-one through ninety-nine.

Grammar Card 15.2	Numbers

Hyphenate fractions.

A hyphen is a small line written at the halfway point between the baseline and the top line. A hyphen joins two words together into a compound word.

Which numbers do we hyphenate? twenty-one through ninety-nine and fractions

Grammar Card 15.3	Numbers

Spell out numbers zero through one hundred. Use numerals for numbers greater than 100.

Which numbers do we need to spell out? zero—one hundred

Grammar Card 15.8	Numbers

Spell out times on the hour.
Use numerals for exact times that include minutes.
Use the lower-case for a.m. and p.m.

What times do we need to spell out in words? times on the hour

What times may we use numerals for? exact times that include minutes

✎ *28.8 Numbers – I will say a number. Write it in your workbook. Then I will write it on the board.*

eighty-eight   four o'clock a.m.
forty-six   5:36 p.m.
three-fourths   twenty-seven
1,346   one-third
156

Optional Grammar Practice

1. ✎ *28.9 Extra Practice: Number Reference Chart* – Create a number reference chart in your workbook. Ⓥ Ⓐ

2. ✎ *28.10 Numbers* – Fill in the correct form of the number in each sentence. Ⓥ Ⓐ Ⓚ

3. *Numbers Game* - Write some numbers and times on index cards. Direct one student to take a card and read the number. The other students need to write the number on a whiteboard. Each number written correctly is awarded one point. This includes, spelling, hyphenation, and if it should be spelled out in words or written in numerals. The first person to reach fifteen points wins. Ⓚ Ⓥ Ⓐ

Identifying Parts of Speech

✎ *28.11 Identifying Parts of Speech* – **Label the parts of speech in your workbook while I label them on the board.**

Her nephews are twins.

What are? nephews, subject noun
Whose nephews? her, possessive pronoun adjective
What is being said about nephews? nephews are, linking verb
Are what? twins
Is twins a noun or an adjective? noun
Therefore, "twins" is a predicate noun.
Divide the subject and the predicate.

PPA SN   LV PN
Her nephews / are twins.

Four fields are almost dry.

What are? fields, subject noun
How many fields? four, adjective
What is being said about the fields? fields are, linking verb
What are they? dry, predicate adjective
Dry to what extent? almost, adverb
Divide the subject and the predicate.

Adj SN   LV Adv PA
Four fields / are almost dry.

The judge is important.

> ***What is?*** judge, subject noun
> ***Which judge?*** the, article adjective
> ***What is being said about the judge?*** judge is, linking verb
> ***What is he?*** important, predicate adjective
> ***Divide the subject and the predicate.***

A   SN   LV PA
The judge / is important.

She is always alone.

> ***What is?*** she, subject pronoun
> ***What is being said about her?*** she is, linking verb
> ***What is she?*** alone, predicate adjective
> ***When is she alone?*** always, adverb
> ***Divide the subject and the predicate.***

SP   LV Adv   PA
She / is always alone.

Vocabulary

Ordinal Numbers

In English we count using the numerals one, two, three, four…
When people, places, or things are placed in a particular order though, we count them using ordinal numbers: first, second, third, fourth …

Count aloud using the ordinal numbers to thirty. first, second, third, fourth …

✎ *28.12 Ordinal Numbers – In your workbook you have a list of the ordinal numbers to fiftieth. I want you to study the list. First find the pattern. How are the ordinal numbers formed?* first, second, and third are unique. Starting with fourth, -th is added to the end of the word. The numbers twenty-first… are hyphenated.

What happens to the /v/ in five and twelve? It turns into the unvoiced /f/.
Highlight these with a colored pencil.

There are four numbers in the list that do not add only -th. What are they? twentieth, thirtieth, fortieth, fiftieth.
What is added? -eth
Highlight the numbers which add -eth.

Why? Does it remind you of any other rules? Change the Y to I when adding any ending, unless the ending begins with I. Add an -S to make a word plural, unless the word hisses or changes then add -ES. Here we are adding TH to make the ordinal, but when the Y changes to I we add an E as well.

Which ordinal numbers does not follow the rule: drop the silent final E when adding a vowel suffix? ninth, twelfth

Why is it strange that the E is dropped? because TH is not a vowel suffix

Highlight "ninth" and "twelfth:" these are exceptions.

eight + th =

What do you notice about eighth? the t is not doubled

first	*eighteenth*	*thirty-fifth*
second	*nineteenth*	*thirty-sixth*
third	*twentieth*	*thirty-seventh*
fourth	*twenty-first*	*thirty-eighth*
fifth	*twenty-second*	*thirty-ninth*
sixth	*twenty-third*	*fortieth*
seventh	*twenty-fourth*	*forty-first*
eighth	*twenty-fifth*	*forty-second*
ninth	*twenty-sixth*	*forty-third*
tenth	*twenty-seventh*	*forty-fourth*
eleventh	*twenty-eighth*	*forty-fifth*
twelfth	*twenty-ninth*	*forty-sixth*
thirteenth	*thirtieth*	*forty-seventh*
fourteenth	*thirty-first*	*forty-eighth*
fifteenth	*thirty-second*	*forty-ninth*
sixteenth	*thirty-third*	*fiftieth*
seventeenth	*thirty-fourth*	

The ordinal numbers first through one hundredth are also spelled out in writing.

Optional Vocabulary Practice

1. ✎ *28.13 Extra Practice: Ordinal Numbers* – Create an ordinal number reference chart in your workbook. Ⓥ Ⓐ Ⓚ

2. ✎ *28.14 Extra Practice: Ordinal Numbers in Sentences* – Fill in the correct form of the number in each sentence. Ⓥ Ⓐ Ⓚ

3. ✎ *28.15 Extra Practice: Checks* – Teach the students how to write checks. Use the blank checks in the workbook. Practice filling them out using the sales information provided.

4. Play I'm Thinking of a Number. One student thinks of a number between one and one hundred and writes it on a piece of paper. The other students take turns guessing the number by writing it on a whiteboard. The student who thought of the number says, "higher," "lower," or "that is it." The student who guesses correctly takes the next turn thinking of a number. Ⓚ Ⓥ Ⓐ

Dictation

✎ *28.16 Dictation* – Read each sentence twice. Ask the students to repeat it aloud, then write it in their workbooks.

1. There are only twenty-five students here.

2. The teacher said, "I need only two people."

3. I bought fifty-four eggs, forty-two loaves of bread, and only one apple.

4. "I do not like to be alone!" shouted the crying boy.

5. There are two sets of twins.

6. We will leave at one o'clock.

Composition

Today we will write a sentence with a list of things we bought at the store. I want you to list the number of each item you bought as I write it on the board.

For example:

Today I bought six knives, two tables, thirty-three apples, sixty-one pencils...

✎ *28.17 Composition* – **Write a sentence which includes a list of six items to buy at the store, including the quantities. You must use at least three hyphenated numbers.**

Lesson 29

Phonograms:	ti, ci, si
Exploring Sounds:	Spellings of /sh/
Spelling Rules:	17, 18
Grammar:	Exclamations, Interjections

PART ONE

Materials Needed: Phonogram Flash Cards from previous lessons and ti , ci , si ; Spelling Rule Cards 17 and 18; 2-3 decks of Phonogram Game Cards.

Phonograms

New Phonograms — *ti, ci, si*

Show ti . /sh/

Show ci . /sh/

Show si . /sh-ZH/

> *What is the difference between the sounds /sh/ and /ZH/?* /sh/ is unvoiced, /ZH/ is voiced.

> *What is similar between each of these phonograms?* They all say /sh/. They all end in I.

> *How are the sounds /sh-ZH/ related?* They are formed in the same way in the mouth.

Show ti and ci .

> *To be able to tell these apart, we will call* ti *tall /sh/*
> *And we will call* ci *short /sh/.*
> *Why do you suppose we would call the TI tall /sh/ and CI short /sh/?* Because T is a taller letter than C.

> *TI, CI, and SI are found in Latin roots. We will call them the Latin spellings of /sh/. The Latin spellings of /sh/ are very common in multi-syllable words because 90% of multi-syllable words in English come from Latin.*

Review

1. Drill the phonograms with flash cards.

2. ✎ *29.1 Writing the Phonograms* – Write each new phonogram five times while saying the sounds aloud.

3. ✎ *29.2 Phonogram Practice* – Dictate the following phonograms. For extra practice, have the students read them back. Write the correct answers on the board as the students check their answers.

1. gu	6. ur	11. ei	16. gn
2. ie	7. bu	12. aw	17. ui
3. ti	8. augh	13. eigh	18. th
4. ey	9. kn	14. ir	19. ci
5. igh	10. dge	15. ew	20. si

4. Play Speed (*The Phonogram and Spelling Game Book*, 11).

Spelling Rules

Uses of TI, SI, CI and SH

Which other phonograms do we know that say /sh/? SH and CH
Today we will focus on words that use SH and the Latin spellings of /sh/, TI, CI, and SI.

‹ Teacher Tip: *Words where the CH phonogram says /sh/ are all French based words. For example: chef, Chicago, chandelier, champagne, brochure, machine, parachute…*

✎ *29.3 Latin Spellings of /sh/* – **Read each of the words in your workbook. Underline the phonograms that say /sh/.**

action	discussion	shining	share
ship	partial	finish	fishing
expression	publish	social	famish
physician	accomplish	tension	confession

✎ *29.4 The Spellings of /sh/* – **Write each word under the column based upon which spelling of /sh/ is used. As you write each word, break it into syllables.**

SH	TI, CI, SI
ship	ac tion
pub lish	ex pres sion
ac com plish	phy si cian
shin ing	dis cus sion
fin ish	par tial
share	so cial
fish ing	ten sion
fam ish	con fes sion

What are the the limits to the SH phonogram? SH is used only at the beginning of a word and the end of a syllable.

When are the Latin spellings of /sh/ used? They are used only at the beginning of a syllable in the middle of the word.

Introduce the rules: Note we have not talked about the ending -ship yet.

This leads to the new spelling rules:

Spelling Rule	17
TI, CI, and SI are used only at the beginning of any syllable after the first one.	

Spelling Rule	18
SH spells /sh/ at the beginning of a base word and at the end of a syllable. SH never spells /sh/ at the beginning of any syllable after the first one, except for the ending -ship.	

The rule stated that there is one time that the phonogram SH is used at the beginning of a syllable after the first one. What is it? with the ending -ship

Exploring Sounds

The Latin Spellings of /sh/

Write the words on the board and discuss the spellings of /sh/.

action

> **What is the root word of action?** act
> **Why do you think we used TI instead of SI, or CI in "action?"** Act ends in T.

discussion

> **What is the root word of discussion?** discuss
> **Why do you think we used SI rather than TI, or CI in discussion?** Discuss ends in S.

physician

> **What is the root word of physician?** physic
> **Why do you think we use CI instead of TI or SI in physician?** Physic ends in C.

> **What is a good strategy for determining which Latin spelling of /sh/ will be used?** Look to the root.
> **This does not work with all the words. However, it does work with many of them.**
> **For example:**

social

> **Here the Latin root is not an English root. So we will not be able to know which spelling of the sound /sh/ to use.**

> **How do we know if we will need a Latin spelling of /sh/ in a word?** If /sh/ is heard at the beginning of a syllable in the middle of the word, it is a Latin spelling of /sh/.

Show si .

> **What does this say?** /sh-ZH/

> **Read the pairs of words as I write them on the board. Raise your hand when you notice a pattern.**

divide   *division*

explode   *explosion*

conclude   *conclusion*

> **The base words end in the sound /d/ and the derivative has a /ZH/ sound and is spelled with SI.**

> **Is /d/ voiced or unvoiced?** voiced
> **Is /ZH/ voiced or unvoiced?** voiced
> **When a word ends in the sound /d/, the derivatives with Latin spellings of /sh/ will be spelled SI and say /ZH/.**

Spelling Journal

Ⓐ Ⓚ Ⓥ

Enter words spelled with SH, TI, CI, and SI.

Optional Spelling Rule Practice

1. ✎ *29.5 Extra Practice: Latin Roots* – Direct students to match the root to the derivative. Then underline the letter which determines which spelling of /sh/ is used in the derivative.

2. Create a reference page to remember these rules. Include sample words. Ⓒ Ⓥ

3. Ask the students to teach this rule to another student or to a parent. Ⓒ Ⓥ Ⓐ Ⓚ

4. Quickly review rules 1-13, 15-28, 30 using the Spelling Rule Cards. Ⓐ Ⓥ

5. *Latin Spellings of /sh/ Matching Game* – Write words which use the Latin spellings of /sh/ from the activity above on index cards. Write the roots on another set of index cards. Provide students with both sets of cards. Ask them to read the words aloud then match the root with the derivative. Ⓐ Ⓥ Ⓚ

6. *Spellings of /sh/ Game* – Dictate words with the spellings of /sh/ for students to write on whiteboards. Say a word from the list below aloud. Ask student to raise their hand and identify which spelling of /sh/ is used and why. Notice that the Latin spellings of /sh/ can all be determined by the English root. Ⓐ Ⓥ Ⓚ

   - **TI** – *action, intimidation, mitigation, motivation, adoption, deletion, creation, dilution, Egyptian, ignition, addiction, education, vibration, violation, direction, invention*

   - **SI** – *depression, discussion, impression, profession, compression, confession, expression, obsession, regression, transgression, confusion, tension*

   - **CI** – *racial, physician, clinician, mathematician, politician, technician, musician, facial, spacial*

   - **SH at the end of the word** – *fish, fresh, ash, blush, brash, bush, brush, clash, cherish, dash, crush, dish, foolish, gash, wash, push, rush, finish, slush, slash, leash, wish, marsh*

   - **SH at the beginning of the word** – *shadow, shade, shack, shaft, shady, shake, shall, shallow, shamble, shame, shampoo, shape, share, shark, sheriff, sharp, shawl, sheep, sheet, shell, shift, ship, shirt, shoe, shop, shore, shower, show, shrimp, shrink, shrub, shut, shuffle, shy, shuttle*

Optional Spelling Rule Practice Continued

7. *Latin Spellings of /sh/ Game* – Dictate words with the Latin spellings of /sh/ for students to write on whiteboards. Each of the Latin spellings can be determined from the root. Students should write the root, then write the derivative. Award one point for the correct root, one point for the correct spelling of /sh/, one point for spelling the root correctly, and one point for spelling the derivative correctly. Ⓐ Ⓥ Ⓚ

   - **TI** – *action, intimidation, mitigation, motivation, adoption, deletion, creation, dilution, Egyptian, ignition, addiction, education, vibration, violation, direction, invention*

   - **SI** – *depression, discussion, impression, profession, compression, confession, expression, obsession, regression, transgression, confusion, tension*

   - **CI** – *racial, physician, clinician, mathematician, politician, technician, musician, facial, spacial*

PART TWO

Using Spelling List 29 on pages 376-377, dictate each word following the steps included on pages Intro 42 - Intro 46.

Tips for Spelling List 29

Action, Official, Invention, Expression, Direction

With each of these words, remind students to look to the English roots (*act, office, invent, express, direct*) in order to determine which Latin spelling of /sh/ is used.

In each of these words the final syllable is unstressed and pronounced with a schwa /ə/ sound. Exaggerate the final vowel sound for spelling purposes. /ăc shŏns/, /ŏf fĭ shăl/, /ĭn věn shŏn/, /ěx prě shŏn/, /dī rěc shŏns/

PART THREE

Materials Needed: Grammar Cards 8, 8.1, and 9.10; Spelling Rule Card 18; green, red, blue, yellow, and pink colored pencils.

Grammar

Review

What is a noun? A noun is the name of a person, place, thing, or idea.

What is a pronoun? A pronoun takes the place of a noun.

What are the five noun jobs we have learned? subject noun, direct object, indirect object, predicate noun, noun of direct address

What is an adjective? Adjectives modify nouns and pronouns. Adjectives answer: What kind? How many? Which one? Whose?

What is an article? A, An, The. Tiny article adjectives that mark nouns and answer the question: Which?

Name the parts of a sentence. A sentence must have a capital letter, subject, verb, complete thought, and an end mark.

What is a verb? A verb shows action, links a description to the subject, or helps another verb.

What are the three types of verbs we have learned? action verbs, transitive verbs, and linking verbs

What is an adverb? An adverb modifies a verb, adjective, or another adverb. An adverb answers: How? When? Where? To what extent?

✎ *Spelling List 29 –* **The final four words in the spelling list: "this", "that," "these," "those" are pronouns. Label them with a pink PRO.**

> ### Grammar Card 6.4
>
> **Demonstrative pronouns represent a noun. There are four demonstrative pronouns: this, that, these, those.**

✎ *Spelling List 29 –* **Label the nouns, verbs, and adjectives.**

✎ *Spelling List 29 –* **Write the plural of each noun and the past tense of each verb.**

Optional Spelling Cards

1. Dictate the words in Lesson 29 for the students to write on index cards. Ⓚ Ⓥ Ⓐ

2. Ask the students to color a green border around the verbs, a red border around the nouns, a blue border around the adjectives, and a pink border around the pronouns. If a word can be used as more than one part of speech, color two borders. Ⓚ Ⓥ

	Word	Practice Sentence	Say to Spell	# of Syllables	Markings
1.	**actions**	*Actions speak louder than words.*	ăc shŏns	2	ac tions
2.	**office**	*The office building is for sale.*	ŏf fĭs	2	of fice
3.	**official**	*You will need to ask the official.*	ŏf fĭ shăl	3	of fi cial
4.	**invention**	*What a wonderful invention.*	ĭn vĕn shŏn	3	in ven tion
5.	**high**	*Look at the bird sitting high in the tree.*	hī	1	high
6.	**expression**	*She has a funny expression on her face.*	ĕx prĕ shŏn	3	ex pres sion
7.	**strange**	*It has been a strange night.*	strānj	1	strānge
8.	**rise**	*The balloons will rise into the sky.*	rīz	1	rīse
9.	**directions**	*Please write down the directions to your house.*	dī rĕc shŏns	3	dī rec tions
10.	**bridge**	*The car drove over the bridge*	brĭj	1	bridge
11.	**party**	*The birthday party was a lot of fun.*	pär tē	2	par ty
12.	**this**	*This is my home.*	THĭs	1	this
13.	**that**	*Is that your house?*	THăt	1	that
14.	**these**	*These are delicious grapes.*	THēz	1	these
15.	**those**	*Those papers need to be filed.*	THōz	1	those

Spelling Hints	Part of Speech	Vocabulary Development
Say to spell: /ăc shŏns/. Underline /sh/. **17** TI, CI, and SI are used only at the beginning of any syllable after the first one.	N	action, actionable, reaction, interaction, inaction, retroaction, transaction
Underline the /s/. Double underline the silent final E. **1** C softens to /s/ when followed by an E, I, or Y. Otherwise, C says /k/.	N	officer, officeholder, offices
Say to spell: /ŏf fĭ shăl/. Underline /sh/. **17** TI, CI, and SI are used only at the beginning of any syllable after the first one.	N, Adj	nonofficial, officialdom, unofficial, officially
Say to spell: /ĭn věn shŏn/. Underline /sh/. **17** TI, CI, and SI are used only at the beginning of any syllable after the first one.	N	inventions, invent, invented, inventor, inventing, inventory, reinvent, coinvent, reinventions
Underline /ī/. **28** Phonograms ending in GH are used only at the end of a base word or before the letter T. The GH is either silent or pronounced /f/.	Adj	higher, highest, highball, highborn, highchair, highlight, highness, highway, highroad, highland
Say to spell: /ĕx prĕ shŏn/. Underline /sh/. **17** TI, CI, and SI are used only at the beginning of any syllable after the first one.	N	express, expressed, expressive, expressly, inexpressible, inexpressibility, unexpressive, expressions, expressionless, expressionlessly
Put a line over the /ā/. Underline the /j/ and double underline the silent final E. **12.1** The vowel says its name because of the E. **12.3** The G says /j/ because of the E.	Adj	stranger, strangely, strangeness, estrange, estrangement, estranging
Put a line over the /ī/. Double underline the silent final E. **12.1** The vowel says its name because of the E. Put a 2 over the /z/. /s-z/ said its second sound.	V	rose, rising, risen, arise, arises, uprise
Say to spell: /dī rĕc shŏns/. The root is direct. Since "direct" ends in T, use TI to spell /sh/. Put a line over the /ī/. Underline /sh/.	N	direct, director
Underline /j/. **25** DGE is used only after a single vowel which says its short sound. **3** English words do not end in I, U, V, or J.	N, V	bridges, abridge, abridged, unabridged, bridgeable, bridgework, drawbridge, footbridge
Underline /ar/. **7** Y says long /ē/ only at the end of a multi-syllable word. I says long /ē/ only at the end of a syllable that is followed by a vowel.	N, V	parties, partying, partied
Underline the /TH/. Put a 2 over it. /th-TH/ said its second sound.	Pro	
Underline the /TH/. Put a 2 over it. /th-TH/ said its second sound.	Pro	
Underline the /TH/. Put a 2 over it. /th-TH/ said its second sound. Put a line over the /ē/. Double underline the silent final E. **12.1** The vowel says its name because of the E. Put a 2 over the /z/. /s-z/ said its second sound.	Pro	
Underline the /TH/. Put a 2 over it. /th-TH/ said its second sound. Put a line over the /ō/. Double underline the silent final E. **12.1** The vowel says its name because of the E. Put a 2 over the /z/. /s-z/ said its second sound.	Pro	

Contractions

Today we will learn a new contraction. I will write the words on the board. Tell me how you think it will be written.

that is =

Replace the I with an apostrophe.

that + is = that's

Optional Grammar Practice

✎ *29.6 Extra Practice: Contractions* – Review the contractions with the activity in the workbook. Ⓚ Ⓐ Ⓥ

Exclamations, Interjections

So far we have learned two types of sentences: statements and commands. Today we will learn how to write exclamations.

It's alive!

He tricked me!

That hurts!

What do you notice about these sentences? They all end in an exclamation mark. They all show strong emotion.

Grammar Card 9.10	Exclamation
An exclamation shows strong emotion and ends with an exclamation point.	

I will now add to each of the sentences. Read them aloud.

Wow! It's alive!

Hey! He tricked me!

Ouch! That hurts!

Notice that the first word in the sentence expresses emotion. It is called an interjection.

What do you notice about the interjection? It is capitalized. There is an exclamation mark after it. The next word is capitalized. The sentence makes sense without it.

Notice that I can also write these words alone and they communicate a thought or feeling to the reader. An interjection can stand alone.

Wow!

Hey!

Ouch!

Grammar Card 8   I

Interjections show strong emotion. They can stand alone.

✎ *29.7 Interjections – Read the sentences in your workbook. Write I over the interjections. Circle the punctuation. What do you notice?* When the emotion is not as strong, a comma follows the interjection. In this case the next word is not capitalized.

Grammar Card 8.1   I

Separate an interjection from the rest of the sentence with a comma or an exclamation point. If using an exclamation point, capitalize the next word in the sentence.

Identifying Parts of Speech

✎ *29.8 Identifying Parts of Speech* – Label the parts of speech in your workbook while I label them on the board.

Yikes! That is a strange expression!

What is? "that," subject pronoun
What is being said about that? that is, linking verb
What is "that?" expression, predicate noun
What kind of expression? strange, adjective
Which expression? a, article adjective
What is the word "yikes?" interjection
Write an I over "yikes."
Divide the subject and the predicate.

   I   SP   LV A   Adj   PN
Yikes! That / is a strange expression.

Good job! Those are the right answers.

What are? those, subject pronoun
What is being said about those? those are, linking verb
What are they? answers, predicate noun
What kind of answers? right, adjective
Which answer? the, article adjective
What is "Good job!" interjection
Divide the subject and the predicate.

   I   SP   LV A Adj PN
Good job! Those / are the right answers.

The officials quietly gave me the directions.

Who gave? officials, subject noun
Which officials? the, article adjective
What is being said about the officials? they gave, verb
Gave what? directions, direct object
Which directions? the, article adjective
To whom did the officials give them? me, indirect object
How did they give them? quietly, adverb
Is there a direct object receiving the action of the verb? Yes. So, it is a transitive verb.
Divide the complete subject from the complete predicate.

 A   SN   Adv TV IO A   DO
The officials / quietly gave me the directions.

My two uncles quickly solved the difficult problem.

Who solved? uncles, subject noun
How many uncles? two, adjective
Which uncles? my, possessive pronoun adjective
What is being said about uncles? uncles solved, verb
What did they solve? problem, direct object
What kind of problem? difficult, adjective
Which problem? the, article adjective
How did they solve it? quickly, adverb
Is there a direct object receiving the action of the verb? Yes. So, it is a transitive verb.
Divide the complete subject from the complete predicate.

PPA Adj SN   Adv TV A Adj   DO
My two uncles / quickly solved the difficult problem.

Optional Grammar Practice

1. ✎ *29.9 Extra Practice: Their and There* – Review the use of *their* and *there*. ⓀⒶⓋ

2. ✎ *29.10 Extra Practice: Homophones* – Circle the correct spelling. ⓀⒶⓋ

3. ✎ *29.11 Extra Practice: Editing* – Find the three mistakes in each sentence. Rewrite the sentences correctly ⓀⒶⓋ

4. Encourage students to list as many interjections as possible as you write them on the board. For example: *ah, aha, brr, bummer, congratulations, duh, eh, gee, good job, hello, help, hey, hi, hmm, hurray, oh, oh-oh, oops, ouch, ow, sh, thanks, ugh, uh-uh, whoops, wow, yeah, yes, yikes, yuck…* ⒶⓋⒸ

5. Direct students to form sentences orally which include an interjection. ⒶⒸ

Optional Spelling Cards

Dictate interjections for students to write on index cards. Using the interjections and other spelling cards, direct students to form sentences. ⒶⓀⓋⒸ

Vocabulary Development

The Ending -ship

Let's say the rule again about the phonogram SH.

Spelling Rule	18

SH spells /sh/ at the beginning of a base word and at the end of a syllable. SH never spells /sh/ at the beginning of any syllable after the first one, except for the ending -ship.

There is one suffix that begins with SH. It is the ending -ship.
Can you think of any words that end in -ship?

Write the words on the board as the students list them aloud.

friendship   readership
relationship   ownership
showmanship   leadership
workmanship   sportsmanship
horsemanship   worship

Are these words nouns, adjectives, verbs, or adverbs?
Hint: can you use "the" with them?

They are all nouns.

Use each of the words in a sentence.

Whenever you hear "ship" at the end of the word, it is spelled with SH.

Adding the endings: -ion, -tion, -ation, -ition, -sion

act + _____ = action

What suffix has been added to act to form action? -ion

act + ion = action

Now I will write two sentence on the board. Read them as I write them.

He acted bravely and won an award.

His brave actions led to the award.

How are "act" and "action" related? Act is a verb, showing what he did. Action is a noun describing what he did.

express + _____ = expression

What suffix has been added to express to form expression? -ion

express + ion = expression

She expressed her joy about winning the prize.

Her expression showed joy about winning the prize.

How are "express" and "expression" related? Express is the action, expression is a noun describing what she expressed.

Write the suffixes on the board:

-ion, -tion, -ation, -ition, -sion

These five suffixes are all related. Latin suffixes changed based upon the rules of Latin. These spellings have carried over into English. As we showed earlier, many times we can determine which Latin spelling of /sh/ will be found in a word. Sometimes though, the Latin spelling of /sh/ is part of an ending. Begin by looking to the root. If that does not tell you which Latin spelling to use, then it is important to know that TI is the most common Latin spelling of /sh/.

imagine + _____ = imagination

Which suffix was added to form imagination? -ation

imagine + ation = imagination

define + _____ = definition

Which suffix was added to form definition? -ition

define + ition = definition

✎ *29.12 Vocabulary Development –* **Write the words in your workbook formed by adding the suffixes.**

Optional Vocabulary Practice

1. ✎ *29.13 Extra Practice: Numbers –* Fill in the correct form of the number in each sentence.

2. Play "I'm Thinking of a Number." One student thinks of a number between one and one hundred and writes it on a piece of paper. The other students take turns guessing the number by writing it on a whiteboard. The student who thought of the number says, "higher," "lower," or "that is it." The student who guesses correctly takes the next turn thinking of a number. Ⓚ Ⓥ Ⓐ

Challenge

The word "act" is found in hundreds of derivatives. The list below is not comprehensive, but meant to demonstrate the enormous number of words derived from the single root "act."

1. Challenge the students to think of derivatives of "act" while you write them on the board. Encourage the students to explain how the prefix and/or suffix changes the meaning and to use each word in a sentence.

2. Challenge the students to find as many derivatives as possible on their own. See who can create the longest list.

act	activator	enacting	radioactivity
acted	activation	hyperactive	react
acting	actor	hyperactivity	reacted
action	actors	inactive	reacting
actions	actress	inaction	reaction
active	actresses	interacted	transact
activity	deactivate	interacting	transacted
activities	deactivated	interaction	transaction
actively	deactivating	overreact	underact
activate	deactivation	overreaction	underactive
activated	enact	proactive	
activating	enacted	radioactive	

Dictation

✎ *29.14 Dictation* – Read each sentence twice. Ask the students to repeat it aloud, then write it in their workbooks.

1. "The program starts at twelve o'clock," said the official.

2. The child said, "I invented it!"

3. The teacher said, "That's a great expression."

4. That is a high bridge.

5. Mother said, "I need those directions."

6. "Those are strange animals!" shouted the students.

Composition

Write the sentence starters on the board.

Direct the students to finish each sentence as you write it on the board.

It is _____

The official gave _____

The inventor _____

✎ *29.15 Composition* – Direct the students to complete the sentences in their workbooks.

Lesson 30 — Assessment & Review

SPELLING ASSESSMENT

Materials Needed: red colored pencil and highlighter.

1. ✎ *30.1 Assessment* – Dictate the sentences to the students while they write them in their workbook.

   1. The careless official's actions hurt her.
   2. Please judge all fifty-two examples.
   3. My cousin needs those directions.
   4. Her niece threw her a birthday party.
   5. The high bridge is five thousand feet long.
   6. That's a strange expression.
   7. We're always here.
   8. I know only one person there.
   9. It's an important invention.
   10. Twelve airplanes are almost ready.

2. Direct the students to read the sentences aloud while you write them on the board. Sound out each word and model the thought process. The students should mark corrections in red. Encourage the students to discuss what they missed.

3. Recheck the students' work. Note the words and concepts which need further practice.

4. Did the students:

   _____ *use DGE correctly?*
   _____ *use silent final E's correctly?*
   _____ *use Y to spell the long /ē/ sound at the end of a multi-syllable word?*
   _____ *use the correct form of here/hear, their/there?*
   _____ *write numbers correctly?*
   _____ *use the correct Latin spelling of the sound /sh/: TI, CI, or SI?*
   _____ *write contractions correctly?*

5. ✎ *30.2 Reading* – Ask the students to read the following sentences, phrases and words. Note the words they did not read fluently.

   1. The teacher wrote the directions and examples on the board.
   2. I feel alone.
   3. He carried five watches and two phones.
   4. Center the photograph on the wall.
   5. Circle each example.
   6. The corn in the large field is ripe.
   7. The pilots flew the airplanes in formation.
   8. My uncle gave his son one hundred dollars.
   9. The husband and wife waited.
   10. The lone bird flew over the lake.
   11. Our nieces and nephews are beautiful people.
   12. I need the right tools.
   13. We will solve the problem.
   14. Forty people signed up for class.
   15. We were there twice this year.
   16. His wife turned twenty-nine yesterday.
   17. My cousins are twins.

6. ✎ *30.3 Words to Practice* – Ask the students to read the words in the list and mark which ones they would like to practice further.

7. Using the assessment and your knowledge as a teacher, identify words to dictate onto Spelling Word Cards.

1. _____ actions	21. _____ forty	41. _____ please
2. _____ airplane	22. _____ four	42. _____ ready
3. _____ almost	23. _____ here	43. _____ rise
4. _____ alone	24. _____ high	44. _____ solve
5. _____ always	25. _____ hundred	45. _____ strange
6. _____ are	26. _____ husband	46. _____ that
7. _____ be	27. _____ important	47. _____ there
8. _____ bridge	28. _____ invention	48. _____ these
9. _____ carry	29. _____ is	49. _____ this
10. _____ center	30. _____ judge	50. _____ those
11. _____ circle	31. _____ lone	51. _____ thousand
12. _____ cousin	32. _____ nephew	52. _____ twelve
13. _____ directions	33. _____ niece	53. _____ twenty
14. _____ each	34. _____ office	54. _____ twice
15. _____ example	35. _____ official	55. _____ twin
16. _____ expression	36. _____ one	56. _____ two
17. _____ field	37. _____ only	57. _____ uncle
18. _____ fifty	38. _____ party	58. _____ was
19. _____ five	39. _____ people	59. _____ were
20. _____ fly	40. _____ person	60. _____ wife

SPELLING WORD REVIEW

Materials Needed: Index cards, highlighter, timer, whiteboard, markers, eraser.

1. Dictate the missed words onto index cards. Have the students highlight the part of the word that was difficult.

2. Choose from the review activities below or use an activity found in the *The Phonogram and Spelling Game Book*.

1. Practice the words with Speed Writing (*The Phonogram and Spelling Game Book*, 37).

2. Play Spelling I-Spy (*The Phonogram and Spelling Game Book*, 54).

3. Practice the words with Blind Writing (*The Phonogram and Spelling Game Book*, 42).

OPTIONAL SPELLING RULE REVIEW

Spelling Rule 25

Use the following mini-lessons to review the concepts as needed.

Spelling Rule	25
DGE is used only after a single vowel which says its short sound.	

1. Review the rule by reciting it and discussing the examples on the back of the card.

2. Dictate the following words. Write them on paper using blind writing, or with magnetic tiles. These are the most common words spelled with the phonogram DGE. *badge, bridge, budge, budget, cartridge, dodge, dredge, drudge, edge, fidget, fledge, fridge, fudge, gadget, grudge, hedge, hodgepodge, judge, ledge, ledger, lodge, nudge, partridge, pledge, porridge, ridge, sledge, sludge, smidgen, trudge, wedge, widget.*

3. Using the The Logic of English™ Phonogram Game Cards, direct students to lay out the phonogram cards A and DGE. Challenge them to find phonograms which complete the word. Continue with IDGE, EDGE, ODGE, and UDGE.

Spelling Rule 23

Spelling Rule	23
AL- is a prefix written with one L when preceding another syllable.	

1. Review the rule by reciting it and discussing the examples on the back of the card.

2. Dictate the following words while students write them on a whiteboard or a piece of paper: *also, almost, always, although*

Spelling Rule 17 and 18

Spelling Rule	17

TI, CI, and SI are used only at the beginning of any syllable after the first one.

Spelling Rule	18

SH spells /sh/ at the beginning of a base word and at the end of a syllable. SH never spells /sh/ at the beginning of any syllable after the first one, except for the ending -ship.

1. Review the rules by reciting them and discussing the examples on the back of the card.

2. Demonstrate how words that end in a voiced /d/ or /z/ sound will be spelled with the voiced /ZH/ spelled SI. *divide - division, explode - explosion, conclude - conclusion, delude - delusion*

3. Look to the Roots Game – Provide each student with a small whiteboard. Explain that you will call out a word. They are to write the correct Latin spelling of /sh/ that will be used. Remind the students to consider the roots. Award one point for each correct answer. *physician, partial, facial, confession, recession, commercial, Egyptian, clinician, exception, recession, election, confidential, infectious, racial, official, discussion, progression, tension*

4. ✎ *30.4 Extra Practice: The Spellings of /sh/* – Direct students attention to the four columns in their student workbook. Explain that you will dictate a word. They are to write it in the correct column. Award one point for identifying the correct spelling of /sh/ and one point for spelling the word correctly.

    - **TI** - *action, intimidation, mitigation, motivation, adoption, deletion, creation, dilution, Egyptian, ignition, addiction, education, vibration, violation, direction, invention*

    - **SI** - *depression, discussion, impression, profession, compression, confession, expression, obsession, regression, transgression, confusion, tension*

    - **CI** – *racial, physician, clinician, mathematician, politician, technician, musician, facial, spacial*

    - **SH at the end of the word** – *fish, fresh, ash, blush, brash, bush, brush, clash, cherish, dash, crush, dish, foolish, gash, wash, push, rush, finish, slush, slash, leash, wish, marsh*

    - **SH at the beginning of the word** – *shadow, shade, shack, shaft, shady, shake, shall, shallow, shamble, shame, shampoo, shape, share, shark, sheriff, sharp, shawl, sheep, sheet, shell, shift, ship, shirt, shoe, shop, shore, shower, show, shrimp, shrink, shrub, shut, shuffle, shy, shuttle*

    - **Words that use the ending -ship** – *battleship, citizenship, authorship, relationship, horsemanship, readership, worship, warship, workmanship*

Adding a Suffix to Any Word

1.   *30.5 Extra Practice: Adding Suffixes Flow Chart* – Read through the chart. Discuss the various questions together.

   I will write a word and a suffix on the board. Using the questions on the Flow Chart, tell me how to write the derivative. Then I will write it on the board.

   1. *cloudy + ness = cloudiness*

      "Cloudy" ends in single vowel Y. The suffix begins with the consonant N. Therefore, we change the Y to I and add the suffix.

   2. *drive + able = drivable*

      "Drive" ends in a silent final E. The suffix begins with a vowel. Dropping the E is allowed by other spelling rules. Therefore, drop the E and add the suffix.

   3. *study + ing = studying*

      "Study" ends in single vowel Y. The suffix begins with an I. Therefore, do not change the Y to I. Just add the ending.

   4. *table + s = tables*

      "Table" ends in a silent final E. The suffix begins with a consonant. Therefore, just add the suffix.

   5. *army + es = armies*

      "Army" ends in single vowel Y. The suffix begins with an E. Therefore, we change the Y to I and add the suffix.

   6. *service + able = serviceable*

      "Service" ends in a silent final E. The suffix begins with a vowel. Dropping the E is not allowed by other spelling rules. C softens to /s/ only before an E, I or Y. Therefore, retain the E and add the suffix.

   7. *strange + er = stranger*

      "Strange" ends in a silent final E. The suffix begins with a vowel. Dropping the E is allowed by other spelling rules. The G will still say /j/. Therefore, drop the E and add the suffix.

   8. *act + ed = acted*

      "Act" does not end in a silent final E or in a single vowel Y. Therefore, just add the suffix.

✎ *30.6 Extra Practice: Adding Suffixes –* **I will say a word that has a suffix added. Write the word in your workbook.**

1. *rising*	9. *readiness*
2. *parties*	10. *flying*
3. *invented*	11. *flier*
4. *offices*	12. *circling*
5. *acting*	13. *examples*
6. *lonely*	14. *pleasing*
7. *loneliness*	15. *airplanes*
8. *cousins*	16. *copier*

OPTIONAL GRAMMAR REVIEW

Homophones

1. Review the homophones *hear* and *here*; *they're, there* and *their*; *its* and *it's*; *you're* and *your*.

homophone

> **What are homophones? Words that sound the same but have different meanings.**

hear

here

> **Read these words.**
> **How can we tell them apart?** Hear means to hear something with your ears. It has the same spelling as "ear" within it. "Here" refers to location. The spelling is reflected in the word "there."

Come _____.   I _____ a noise.

> **Which one should I use in each of these sentences?**

Come _here_ .   I _hear_ a noise.

their

there

they're

> **Read these words.**
> **How can we tell them apart?** "They" and "their" are related. They are both pronouns. "They" ends with two letter /ā/ that may be used at the end of English words. "Their" has a two letter /ā/ that may not be used at the end of English words. The meaning of "there" and "here" are also

related. "Here" and "there" both refer location. If you add a T to "here," it spells "there." They're is a contraction that means "they are."

their - they

there - here

That is _____ house.   She went _____.   _____ at home.

Which one should I use in each of these sentences?

That is their house.   *She went there .*   *They're at home.*

your

you're

Read these words.
How can we tell them apart? You're is a contraction that means, you are. This is clear because the apostrophe is replacing a sound. Your is a possessive noun adjective. To keep these from being mixed up, you need to ask yourself if "you are" makes sense in this sentence.

_____ a great helper.   *_____ jacket is in the closet.*

Which one should I use in each of these sentences?

You're a great helper.   *Your jacket is in the closet.*

its

it's

Read these words.
How can we tell them apart? "It's" with an apostrophe means it is. "Its" without an apostrophe means something that belongs to it. One way to test which one you need is to see if "it is" makes sense. If it does, spell "it's" with an apostrophe.

_____ cold outside.   *The dog chased _____ tail.*

Which one should I use in each of these sentences?

It's cold outside.   *The dog chased its tail.*

✎ *30.7 Extra Practice: Homophones –* **Circle the correct form of the word in your workbook.**

Numbers

Grammar Card 15.1	Numbers 1
Hyphenate numbers twenty-one through ninety-nine.	

Grammar Card 15.2	Numbers 2
Hyphenate fractions.	

Grammar Card 15.3	Numbers 3
Spell out numbers zero through one hundred. Use numerals for numbers greater than 100.	

Grammar Card 15.8	Numbers 3
Spell out times on the hour. **Use numerals for exact times that include minutes.** **Use the lower-case for a.m. and p.m.**	

1. Review the rules by reciting them and discussing the samples on the back of the cards.

2. Play "I'm Thinking of a Number." One student thinks of a number between one and one hundred and writes it on a piece of paper. The other students take turns guessing the number by writing it on a whiteboard. The student who thought of the number says, "higher," "lower," or "that is it." The student who guesses correctly takes the next turn thinking of a number. Ⓚ Ⓥ Ⓐ

3. ✎ *30.8 Extra Practice: Numbers* – Write the numbers in words your workbook.

4. ✎ *30.9 Extra Practice: Checks* – Practice writing checks. Sample checks are provided in the workbook.

Contractions

Grammar Card 14.1	Apostrophe
Use an apostrophe to denote the sound(s) omitted from a contraction.	

Review how to form contractions demonstrating that the apostrophe replaces the sound that is omitted.

I + am = I'm

that + is = that's

they + are = they're

it + is = it's

✏ *30.10 Extra Practice: Contractions* – **Write the contraction.**

✏ *30.11 Extra Practice: Contractions* – **Write the words that form the contraction.**

OPTIONAL PHONOGRAM ASSESSMENT & REVIEW

Phonograms

✏ *30.12 Extra Practice: Phonogram Quiz* – Dictate the phonograms.

1. sh	19. o	37. t	55. ou
2. or	20. gn	38. ed	56. j
3. th	21. ir	39. g	57. augh
4. ai	22. c	40. oo	58. x
5. z	23. wh	41. u	59. ti
6. ough	24. p	42. gu	60. dge
7. ck	25. igh	43. ei	61. ie
8. ear	26. d	44. ow	62. oi
9. m	27. ur	45. h	63. k
10. tch	28. qu	46. ew	64. si
11. ng	29. e	47. ar	65. ay
12. a	30. oe	48. oa	66. l
13. ee	31. r	49. v	67. eigh
14. n	32. oy	50. aw	68. ph
15. er	33. f	51. i	69. bu
16. kn	34. au	52. ey	
17. b	35. s	53. w	
18. ea	36. ch	54. ci	

Optional Phonogram Practice

Practice the phonograms as needed using the following game suggestions, or choose other games from *The Phonogram and Spelling Game Book.*

1. ✎ *30.13 Extra Practice: Speed Bingo* – Play Speed Bingo (*The Phonogram and Spelling Game Book,* 26).

2. Play Beat the Clock (*The Phonogram and Spelling Game Book,* 27).

3. Practice the phonograms with Sky Writing (*The Phonogram and Spelling Game Book,* 23).

Lesson 31

Phonograms:	cei
Exploring Sounds:	Accented Syllables
Spelling Rules:	29
Grammar:	Prepositions

PART ONE

Materials Needed: Phonogram Flash Cards from previous lessons and cei ; Phonogram Game Cards, two sets per group of two-four students.

Phonograms

New Phonogram — *cei*

Show the phonogram cei . /sē/

> **What do you notice about this phonogram?** C says /s/ because it is before an E. EI is a phonogram that says /ē/.
>
> **Many people have learned the rule: Use I before E except after C and when it says /ā/. Have any of you learned this rule?**
>
> **The I before E rule has too many exceptions to be considered a good spelling rule.**
>
> **Rather than learning this rule, it is helpful to learn that CEI is a phonogram which includes the two phonograms C and EI.**

✎ *31.1 The CEI Phonogram – Read each of the words which use CEI in your workbook. Underline the CEI. There are only eight base words which use this phonogram.*

ceiling	receipt	deceit	conceive
receive	deceive	conceit	perceive

Optional Spelling Journal   Ⓐ Ⓚ Ⓥ

Enter words spelled with CEI.

Review

1. Drill the phonograms with flash cards.

2. ✎ *31.2 Writing the Phonogram* – Write the new phonogram five times while saying the sound aloud.

3. ✎ *31.3 Phonogram Practice* – Dictate the following phonograms. For extra practice, have the students read them back. Write the correct answers on the board as the students check their answers.

1. cei	8. ie	15. ew
2. ti	9. dge	16. ir
3. ph	10. bu	17. ur
4. si	11. wr	18. ear
5. gu	12. ei	19. er
6. wor	13. ey	20. oo
7. ci	14. eigh	

4. Play Go Fish (*The Phonogram and Spelling Game Book*, 9).

Exploring Sounds

Accented Syllables

English is a rhythmic language.
What do we call the beats in words? syllables
How do you count the syllables in English? Put your hand under your chin. The mouth opens for each syllable. Or hum the word. Then count how many hums.
How many vowel sounds are in a syllable? one
How many consonants? zero or more

I will say a word. Repeat the word, then count the syllables.

table	2	*musician*	3	*photograph*	3
garage	2	*pumpkin*	2	*family*	3
school	1	*elevator*	4		

The beats in words mean we can write chants, songs, and poems with rhythm.
Let's say the words again and clap the syllables as we say them.

Sometimes it is difficult to clap words with more than two syllables because, like in music, there are strong beats and weak beats. The stronger beats in words are called accent. Some people are able to hear the accent. Listen as I say the following words. Tell me if you hear a syllable which is said more strongly. That is the accented syllable.

ta' ble	*les' son*	*e quip'*	*ti' mer*
ti' tle	*a bout'*	*qui' et*	*a round'*

Many people struggle to hear accent. Some people feel it better. To feel the accent, put your hand under your chin. Your mouth will drop open farther on the accented syllable.

I will say the words. Repeat each word. Try to feel the accent.

ta' ble	*les' son*	*e quip'*	*ti' mer*
ti' tle	*a bout'*	*qui' et*	*a round'*

Do not worry if it is difficult for you. Finding the accent takes practice for most people.

Spelling Rule

Rule 29

What two phonograms say /z/? S and Z
Read the words as I write them on the board.

zipper	*zebra*	*zone*	*zero*
zoo	*zigzag*	*zap*	*zesty*

Which spelling of /z/ will I use at the beginning of the word? Z
This leads to the rule:

Spelling Rule	29
Z, never S, spells /z/ at the beginning of a base word.	

Optional Spelling Rule Practice

1. Review rules 1-13, 15-30 using the Spelling Rule Flash Cards. Ⓥ Ⓐ

2. Direct students to create a sentence(s) which includes all the CEI word. For example: "The conceited boy perceived the receipt he received was on the ceiling and he had been deceived by someone conceiving clever deceit." Ⓚ Ⓥ Ⓒ Ⓐ

3. Make a Crossword Puzzle with the CEI words (*Phonogram and Spelling Game Book*, 54). Ⓚ Ⓥ Ⓒ Ⓐ

4. Dictate words starting with Z for students to write on paper. *zip, zipper, zone, zoo, zebra, zero, zap, zinger, zesty, zigzag*

5. ✎ *31.4 Accent* – Read the words in your workbook. Mark the accented syllable. *rock′ et, la′ zy, a bout′, lum′ ber, be tween′, lit′ tle, chick′ en, mar′ble, liz′ ard, po lice′, to day′, un der stand′, for get′ ful, tel′ e phone, cam′ er a, mu′ si cal.* Ⓚ Ⓥ Ⓐ

PART TWO

Using Spelling List 31 on pages 400-401, dictate each word following the steps included on pages Intro 42 - Intro 46.

Tips for Spelling List 31

Above

One of the difficulties with English spelling is that vowels in unaccented syllables often are pronounced as the schwa sound /ə/. In order to help students create an auditory picture of the word, it is helpful to exaggerate the unaccented vowel. Therefore exaggerate the vowel so that /ə bəv/ sounds like /ā bŏv/.

To learn more about vowels in unaccented syllables and aiding students in creating an auditory picture of words, see *Uncovering the Logic of English*, 121-128.

Hospital

In order to help students create an auditory picture of the word, it is helpful to exaggerate the unaccented vowel. Therefore exaggerate the vowel so that /hŏs pĭ tə l/ sounds like /hŏs pĭ tăl/.

Mountain

In order to help students create an auditory picture of the word, it is helpful to exaggerate the unaccented vowel. Therefore exaggerate the vowel so that /moun tə n/ sounds like /moun tān/.

PART THREE

Materials Needed: Grammar Cards 1.10 and 5; green, red, and black colored pencils.

Grammar

Review

> ***What is a noun?*** A noun is the name of a person, place, thing, or idea.
>
> ***What is a pronoun?*** A pronoun takes the place of a noun.
>
> ***What are the five noun jobs we have learned?*** subject noun, direct object, indirect object, predicate noun, noun of direct address
>
> ***What is an adjective?*** Adjectives modify nouns and pronouns. Adjectives answer: What kind? How many? Which one? Whose?
>
> ***What is an article?*** A, An, The. Tiny article adjectives that mark nouns and answer the question: Which?
>
> ***Name the parts of a sentence.*** A sentence must have a capital letter, subject, verb, complete thought, and an end mark.
>
> ***What is a verb?*** A verb shows action, links a description to the subject, or helps another verb.
>
> ***What are the three types of verbs we have learned?*** action verbs, transitive verbs, and linking verbs
>
> ***What is an adverb?*** An adverb modifies a verb, adjective, or another adverb. An adverb answers: How? When? Where? To what extent?

Prepositions

> *Today we will learn one of the most commonly used parts of speech: the preposition. A preposition links a noun or a pronoun to the rest of the sentence. It may speak of location, direction, possession, or time.*
>
> *I will write a sentence on the board. Read the sentence, then act out the sentence using your pencil and desk. I will write the prepositional phrase in a different color so that it stands out.*

The pencil is on the desk.

The pencil is under the desk.

The pencil is above the desk.

The pencil is by the desk.

The pencil is below the desk.

> ***What are the nouns in each of these sentences?*** pencil and desk
>
> ***Each of these sentences includes a preposition. The preposition in these sentences shows the relationship between the pencil and the desk.***
>
> ***What are the prepositions?*** on, under, above, by, below

	Word	Practice Sentence	Say to Spell	# of Syllables	Markings
1.	**by**	*The dog is by the box.*	bī	1	by
2.	**over**	*The dog is over the box.*	ō ver	2	ō v<u>er</u>
3.	**under**	*The dog is under the box.*	un der	2	un d<u>er</u>
4.	**between**	*The dog is between the boxes.*	bē twēn	2	bē tw<u>ee</u>n
5.	**above**	*The dog is above the box.*	ā bŏv	2	ā bov<u>e</u>
6.	**below**	*The dog is below the box.*	bē lō	2	bē l<u>ow</u>²
7.	**near**	*My house is near the park.*	nēr	1	n<u>ear</u>
8.	**ceiling**	*This room has a high ceiling.*	cē ling	2	c<u>ei</u> li<u>ng</u>
9.	**sea**	*We went to the sea for a vacation.*	sē	1	s<u>ea</u>
10.	**window**	*Place the plant near a window.*	wĭn dō	2	win d<u>ow</u>²
11.	**store**	*Which store do you want to go to?*	stōr	1	st<u>ōr</u><u>e</u>
12.	**medicine**	*Take this medicine twice a day.*	mĕd ĭ sĭn	3	med i cin<u>e</u>
13.	**look**	*Look at me.*	lük	1	l<u>oo</u>²k
14.	**hospital**	*He took Steve to the hospital.*	hŏs pĭ tăl	3	hos pi tal
15.	**mountain**	*The highest mountain in the United States is in Alaska.*	moun tān	2	m<u>ou</u>n t<u>ai</u>n

Spelling Hints	Part of Speech	Vocabulary Development
5 I and Y may say /ĭ/ or /ī/ at the end of the syllable.	P	standby, passerby, byline, bygone, bystander, bypass, bypassed, byroad, byway
Put a line over the /ō/. O said the sound /ō/. **4** A E O U usually say their names at the end of the syllable. Underline /er/.	P	carryover, overstatement, overreact, makeover, overachiever, overabundant, overactive, overbake, overcome
Underline /er/.	P	underneath, understand, underactive, underachieve, underarm, undercurrent, undercut, underdone, underrate, underlie
Put a line over the /ē/. E said the sound /ē/. **4** A E O U usually say their names at the end of the syllable. Underline the /ē/ double /ē/.	P	
Say to spell / **ā** bŏv/. Put a line over the /ā/. A said the sound /ā/. **4** A E O U usually say their names at the end of the syllable. Underline the V once. Double underline the silent final E. **12.2** English words do not end in V or U.	P	
Put a line over the /ē/. E said the sound /ē/. **4** A E O U usually say their names at the end of the syllable. Underline /ō/. Put a 2 over /ow-ō/. It said its second sound.	P	
Underline the /ē/.	P	nearby, nearly, nearer, nearest, nearsighted, nearsightedness, nearness
Underline /ē/. Underline /ng/.	N	ceilings
Underline the /ē/.	N	seacraft, seafarer, seafaring, seacoast, seabird, seabed, seaworthy
Underline /ō/. Put a 2 over /ow-ō/. It said its second sound.	N	windows, windowless, windowpane, windowsill, windowsills
Put a line over the /ō/. Double underline the silent final E. **12.1** The vowel says its name because of the E.	N, V	stored, storing, bookstore, drugstore, storefront, storehouse, storekeeper, storeroom, storewide, superstore, restore
5 I and Y may say /ĭ/ or /ī/ at the end of the syllable. **1** C softens to /s/ when followed by an E, I or Y. Otherwise C says /k/. Double underline the silent final E. **12.9** Unseen reason.	N	medicines
Underline the /ü/ and put a 2 over it. /oo-ü-ō/ said its second sound.	V, N	looked, looking, looker, looks, lookup, onlooker, outlook, overlook
Say to spell: /hŏs pĭ **tăl**/. **5** I and Y may say /ĭ/ or /ī/ at the end of the syllable.	N	hospitals, hospitalize, hospitalization, rehospitalization, rehospitalize, hospitality
Say to spell: /moun **tān**/. Underline /ow/. Underline /ā/.	N	mountains, mountaineer, mountaineering, mountainous, mountainside, mountaintop

Write a P over the prepositions as the students list them.

                    P
The pencil is on the desk.

                      P
The pencil is under the desk.

                      P
The pencil is above the desk.

                    P
The pencil is by the desk.

                    P
The pencil is below the desk.

> **The noun that follows is called the object of the preposition.**
> **We can find the object of the preposition by going to the preposition and asking:**

_____ *what?*

_____ *whom?*

> **On what?** on the desk
> **Desk is the object of the preposition. We will mark it with an OP.**

             P   *OP*
The pencil is on the desk.

> **Under what?** under the desk
> **Desk is the object of the preposition. We will mark it with an OP.**

             P   *OP*
The pencil is under the desk.

> **What is the object of the preposition in all of these sentences?**   desk
> **Mark the object of the preposition with an OP.**

             P   *OP*
The pencil is above the desk.

             P   *OP*
The pencil is by the desk.

             P   *OP*
The pencil is below the desk.

> **This leads to two new grammar rules:**

Grammar Card 5	P

A preposition links a noun or a pronoun to the rest of the sentence.

Grammar Card 1.10	OP

The object of the preposition is the noun or pronoun which follows the preposition. To find the object of the preposition, go to the preposition and ask: _____ what? _____ whom?

Help me to create a list of prepositions that could be used in the following sentence:

The boy is _____ the car.

I will write the prepositions of location on the board as you identify them.

in	by	beside	underneath
on	over	near	in front of
between	across from	on top of	
under	around	inside	
next to	behind	past	

These are prepositions that describe the location of one noun related to another noun.

✎ *31.5 Prepositions –* **List the prepositions of location that complete the sentence: The cat is _____ the box(es).**

✎ *Spelling List 31 –* **Label the nouns red, the verbs green, and the prepositions black.**

✎ *Spelling List 31 –* **Write the plural of each noun and the past tense of each verb.**

Optional Spelling Cards

1. Dictate the words in Lesson 31 for the students to write on index cards. Ⓚ Ⓥ Ⓐ

2. Ask the students to color a green border around the verbs, a red border around the nouns, and a black border around the prepositions. If a word can be used as more than one part of speech, color two borders. Ⓚ Ⓥ

Identifying Parts of Speech

✎ *31.6 Identifying Parts of Speech –* **We will now identify the parts of speech using the sentences in your workbook. Label each part of speech in your workbook, while I write it on the board.**

The new airplane is on the runway.

> **What "is?"** airplane is, subject noun
> **Which airplane?** the, article adjective
> **What kind of airplane?** new, adjective
> **What is being said about the airplane?** airplane is, verb
> **What is the word "on?"** preposition
> **On what?** runway, object of the preposition
> **Which runway?** the, article adjective

> A   Adj   SN   V P A   OP
> *The new airplane is on the runway.*

> **"On the runway" is a prepositional phrase. This phrase is modifying airplane. It answers the question, which airplane? The airplane on the runway.**
> **This means the word "is" is a linking verb connecting "airplane" to the prepositional phrase "on the runway." Write an L before the verb to show it is a linking verb.**
> **We will put parentheses around the prepositional phrase.**
> **Divide the complete subject from the complete predicate.**

> A   Adj   SN   LV P A   OP
> *The new airplane / is (on the runway.)*

The storm clouds are over the mountains.

> **What "are?"** clouds are, subject noun
> **Which clouds?** the, article adjective
> **What kind of clouds?** storm, adjective
> **What is being said about clouds?** clouds are, verb
> **What is the word "over?"** preposition
> **Over what?** mountains, object of the preposition
> **Which mountains?** the, article adjective

> A   Adj   SN   V   P A   OP
> *The storm clouds are over the mountains.*

> **"Over the mountains" is a prepositional phrase. This phrase is modifying clouds.**
> **It answers the question, which clouds?**
> **This means the word "are" is a linking verb connecting "clouds" to the prepositional phrase "over the mountains." Write an L before the verb to show it is a linking verb.**
> **Put parentheses around the prepositional phrase.**
> **Divide the complete subject from the complete predicate.**

> A   Adj   SN   LV P A   OP
> *The storm clouds / are (over the mountains.)*

She looked under the window.

Who looked? she, subject pronoun
What is being said about she? she looked, verb
What is the word "under?" preposition
Under what? window, object of the preposition
Which window? the, article adjective

SP   V   P   A   OP
She looked under the window.

"Under the window" is a prepositional phrase. This phrase is modifying the verb, looked. It answers the question, where did she look?
Is looked modifying the subject? no
Then it is not a linking verb.
Is there a direct object receiving the action of the verb? no
Then it is not a transitive verb.
We will put parentheses around the prepositional phrase.
Divide the complete subject from the complete predicate.

SP   V   P   A   OP
She / looked (under the window.)

I hear a strange noise in the ceiling.

Who hears? I, subject pronoun
What is being said about "I?" I hear, verb
What do I hear? noise, direct object
What kind of noise? strange, adjective
Which noise? a, article adjective
What is the word "in?" preposition
In what? ceiling, object of the preposition
Which ceiling? the, article adjective
Is there a direct object receiving the action of the verb? yes
Then it is a transitive verb.

SP TV A Adj   DO   P   A   OP
I hear a strange noise in the ceiling.

"In the ceiling" is a prepositional phrase.
What is the prepositional phrase "in the ceiling" modifying? noise
It answers the questions, which noise?
We will put parentheses around the prepositional phrase.
Divide the complete subject from the complete predicate.

SP TV A Adj   DO   P   A   OP
I / hear a strange noise (in the ceiling.)

Optional Grammar Activities

1. ✎ *31.7 Extra Practice: Prepositional Phrases* – Direct the students to read the sentences. Instruct the students to write a P over the preposition and put parentheses around the prepositional phrase. Ask the students to draw a picture of each sentence. Ⓚ Ⓥ Ⓒ

2. Play Simon Says with prepositional phrases. Have the students give commands about where to put an object. Ⓚ Ⓥ Ⓒ Ⓐ

3. Create prepositional phrases using the Spelling Cards. Build prepositional phrases using a black preposition card + an article + a noun. Ⓚ Ⓥ Ⓒ Ⓐ

Dictation

✎ *31.8 Dictation* – Read each sentence twice. Ask the students to repeat it aloud, then write it in their student workbooks.

1. The party store is near the hospital.

2. The directions are under the window.

3. Two hundred people waited by the sea.

4. The high bridge is over the river.

5. Beautiful flowers grow in that field.

6. The fly is on the ceiling.

Composition

Write the sentence on the board. Lead the students in completing it aloud using prepositional phrases.

The photographs are _____.

✎ *31.9 Composition* – Complete each sentence in your workbook with a prepositional phrase.

Vocabulary Development

The Prefixes over- and under-

over-   *under-*

Many prepositions also act as prefixes.
Can you think of any words that begin with over-? Answers will vary.
What are some words that begin with under-? Answers will vary.

overpriced   *underpriced*

Read each word. How have the prefixes over- and under- changed the meaning? Something that is overpriced is priced too high. Something that is underpriced is priced too low.

Use them in a sentence. Answers will vary. For example: I found a new shirt that costs $200. It was overpriced. The store is having a sale. Everything is underpriced.

overworked   underworked

What do each of these words mean? Overworked refers to someone who works too much. Underworked means not enough work.

Use them in a sentence. Answers will vary. For example: My father has been working fifteen hours a day. He is overworked. My teacher does not give us any assignments. We are underworked.

✎ *31.10 Vocabulary Development –* **Complete the activity in the workbook.**

Challenge: CEI Words

Which words use the phonogram cei?

receive   receipt   deceive   deceit
conceit   conceive   perceive   ceiling

What do you notice about these words? Four of them have the root "ceive." Two have the root "ceit." One is similar with "ceipt."

ceit   ceipt   ceive

These are all related. The root ceit/ceipt/ceive means to take or to catch in Latin.

What does receive mean? to be given, or to get
Use it in a sentence. I received a letter from Grandpa.
The prefix re- means again or back. So receive literally means to take again or take back.

What is a receipt? a piece of paper to show you received something
Use it in a sentence. The cashier handed me a receipt for my purchase.

What does it mean to deceive? to lie
Use it in a sentence. The children deceived their teacher into thinking that Evan was at home sick.
The prefix de- means down. So deceive literally means to take down.

What does deceit mean? a lie
Use it in a sentence. With much secrecy and deceit, the boy snuck the puppy into his room.

What is conceit? pride, arrogance
Use it in a sentence. The conceited boy tossed his head in the air and ran away.

What does it mean to conceive? to form an idea
Use it in a sentence. Thomas Edison conceived the idea of a phonograph in 1877.
The prefix con- means to do something intensely. "To conceive literally means to take something intensely.

What does it mean to perceive? to know or sense something
Use it in a sentence.   His mother perceived he was deceiving her and searched his room.
The prefix per- means to do something thoroughly. So to perceive literally means to take it in or to understand thoroughly.

✎ *31.11 CEI Words –* **Complete the exercise using each of these words in your workbook**

Lesson 32

Phonograms:	
Exploring Sounds:	Single and Double Consonants
Spelling Rules:	14
Grammar:	Prepositions, Paragraphs

PART ONE

Materials Needed: Phonogram Flash Cards from previous lessons; Spelling Rule Card 14.

Phonograms

Review

1. Drill the phonograms with flash cards.

2. ✎ *32.1 Phonogram Practice* – Dictate the following phonograms. For extra practice, have the students read them back. Write the correct answers on the board as the students check their answers.

1. bu	8. ey	15. ou
2. ie	9. eigh	16. ph
3. wr	10. gu	17. wor
4. ui	11. ew	18. ough
5. cei	12. kn	19. aw
6. dge	13. ti	20. wh
7. si	14. ei	

3. Play Phonogram Basketball (*The Phonogram and Spelling Game Book*, 22).

Exploring Sounds

Single and Double Consonants in the Middle of the Word

✎ *32.2 Double Consonants –* **Read the words in your workbook. Mark the vowel long or short.**

di ner din ner   bab ble ba by

pa per hap py   fun nel fu ner al

What spelling rule is illustrated by "diner," "paper," "baby," and "funeral"? A E O U usually say their names at the end of the syllable.
When there is one consonant, the syllable is left open so that the vowel sound is long.
When the vowel sound is short, what do you notice? There is often a double consonant.
The double consonant closes the syllable.

✎ *32.3 Double Consonants –* **Read the words. Draw a line between the syllables.**

forget   whisper   enjoy

Where does the syllable divide in these words? between the consonants

for/get   whis/per   en/joy

When you hear a word with only one consonant sound in the middle of the word, you must consider if the vowel sound before it is long or short.
If the vowel is long, do not double the consonant. If the vowel sound is short, then the consonant is usually doubled.

✎ *32.4 Practice Words –* **Write the words in your notebook as I say them.**

1. below   3. cubby   5. robber   7. super

2. bellow   4. cubic   6. robot   8. supper

Spelling Rule

Adding a Suffix to a Word Ending in One Vowel and One Consonant (Rule 14)

✎ *32.5 Words Ending in One Vowel and One Consonant –* **Read the words in your workbook.**

1. run   4. slip   7. ship   10. cup

2. bag   5. win   8. drop

3. stop   6. swim   9. plan

Are these words difficult to spell? no
What is the same between each of these words? They all end in a single vowel followed by a single consonant.

Today we will discover the rule for adding a suffix to words ending in one vowel followed by one consonant.

Write the following suffixes on the board.

-ed, -er, -ing, -ful, -ment

Which suffixes can we add to run? -er, -ing

run + er = runner

What changed when I added the suffix -er? You added another N.
How many syllables is "run?" one
How many syllables is "runner?" two
What would it say if we did not add the N? rū ner

run + ing = running

What did we do to add the suffix -ing? doubled the N
How many syllables in "run?" one
How many in "running?" two
What would it say if we did not add the N? rū ning

Which suffixes can we add to "bag?" -ed, -er, -ing, -ful
Let's begin with -ed.

bag + ed = bagged

What did we do before we added the suffix? doubled the G

Now we will consider:

bag + ful = bagful

Did we double the G? no
What was different? We added a consonant suffix.

Which suffixes can we add to "ship?" -er, -ing, -ment
Let's begin with -ment.

ship + ment = shipment

Did we double the P? no
Why? because we added a consonant suffix

What do you think the rule is for adding a suffix to words ending in one vowel followed by one consonant? Answers will vary.

The rule is:

Spelling Rule	14

> **Double the last consonant when adding a vowel suffix to words ending in one vowel followed by one consonant, only if the syllable before the suffix is accented.**

The second part of this rule deals with accent. We will learn more about accent in the next lesson when we apply this rule to two syllable base words.

stick +er =

How do we add the suffix -er to "stick"? Just add the ending.
Why don't we double the last consonant? "Stick" ends in two consonants. The rule only applies to words ending in one consonant.

stick + er = sticker

sleep + ing =

How do we add the suffix -ing to "sleep?" Just add the suffix.
Why don't we double the P? Because "sleep" has two vowels and the rule only applies to words with a single vowel.

sleep + ing = sleeping

The next word has something special going on. I will write it on the board. Then we will talk about it.

fix +ed =

How do we add the suffix -ed to "fix?" Answers vary.
I will show you.

fix +ed = fixed

Do you have any idea why you do not double the last consonant?
How many sounds do you hear with the letter X at the end? two: /k/ and /s/
We do not double the last consonant because it ends in two consonant sounds.

✎ *32.6 Adding Suffixes – **Complete the activity in your workbooks.***

Answers: shipping, shipment; madden, madly; puppy, pups; snuggest, snugly; sadden, sadly; bigger, bigness; hotter, hotly; buggy, bugs; wetter, wetness.

Reading Words

Words with Single and Double Consonants

When reading and spelling, many people confuse pairs of words such as:

hopping hoping

Read each of the words.
How can we tell them apart? When there is only one consonant in the middle of the word, the first vowel is long. When there are two consonants in the middle of the word, the vowel is short.

Point to hopping.

What is the root of this word? hop

hop

How do we add a suffix to hop? "Hop" ends in one vowel followed by one consonant so we double the last consonant before adding a vowel suffix.

Point to hoping.

What is the root of this word? hope

hope

How do we add a suffix to hope? "Hope" ends in a silent final E. We drop the E before adding a vowel suffix.

✏️ *32.7 Reading Words –* **Read each of the words in your workbook.**

hopping	*cutter*	*robbed*	*pinning*
hoping	*cuter*	*robed*	*pining*

Point to cutter.
What is the root of this word? cut
How do we add a suffix to cut? "Cut" ends in one vowel followed by one consonant so we double the last consonant before adding a vowel suffix.

Point to cuter.
What is the root of this word? cute
How do we add a suffix to cute? "Cute" ends in a silent final E. We drop the E before adding a vowel suffix.

✏️ *32.8 Pairs of Words –* **I will say a word. Circle it in your workbook.**

robed   *pinning*

hopping   *cuter*

✎ *32.9 Writing Words – **I will say a word. Write it in your workbook. Make sure to consider the root first and whether it ends in a Silent Final E or in one vowel followed by one consonant.***

1. twinned	3. hopped	5. cutter
2. twined	4. hoped	6. cuter

Optional Spelling Rule Practice

1. Create a reference page to remember this rule. Include sample words. ©Ⓥ

2. Ask the students to teach this to another student or to a parent. ©ⓋⒶⓀ

3. Review rules 1-30 using the Spelling Rule Flash Cards. ⓋⒶ

4. Using magnetic letter tiles, practice adding the suffixes to the following words. Direct students to explain why the final consonant doubled or not. ⓀⓋⒶ

   - **Ending in one vowel and one consonant** – *big+est = biggest; fat + est = fattest; flip + er = flipper; mop + ed = mopped; pop + er = popper; hop + ed = hopped; stop + ed = stopped*

   - **Ending in two consonants** – *bold + est = boldest; cold + est = coldest; dark + est = darkest; long + est = longest; camp + er = camper; help + er = helper*

   - **Two vowels** – *cool + est = coolest; beep + er = beeper, feed + er = feeder; seed + ed = seeded; heat + ed = heated*

5. Adding Suffixes Game – Provide each student with a whiteboard, marker, and eraser. Call out a word and suffix using the list above. Direct students to write the word on the whiteboard. Award one point for spelling it correctly and one point for identifying the correct reason the final consonant is or is not doubled. ⓀⓋ©Ⓐ

6. ✎ *32.10 Extra Practice: Accent –* Read the words in your workbook. Mark the accented syllable. *in' to, de sign', ser' vice, a' ble, in stead', suc cess', ma' jor, a ward', a mount', des pite', a lone', ac cept', re view', o' pen, un less'* ⓀⓋⒶ

PART TWO

Using Spelling List 32 on pages 416-417, dictate each word following the steps included on pages Intro 42 - Intro 46.

Tips for Spelling List 32

Around

One of the difficulties with English spelling is that vowels in unaccented syllables often are pronounced as the schwa sound /ə/. In order to help students create an auditory picture of the word, it is helpful to exaggerate the unaccented vowel. Therefore exaggerate the vowel so that /ə rownd/ sounds like /ā rownd/.

To learn more about vowels in unaccented syllables and aiding students in creating an auditory picture of words, see *Uncovering the Logic of English,* 121-128.

Of

Though "of" is a true exception, there is still a logic behind its spelling. First, the O is pronounced with a schwa sound /ə/ because the word "of" is a grammatical word which is not accented within the sentence (*Uncovering the Logic of English,* 126). Second, because "of" is the only known word where the phonogram F says /v/, it is likely the pronunciation shifted over time. Notice that /f/ and /v/ are a voiced and unvoiced pair. Point out to students this relationship between the sounds. Some students may want to say to spell /ŏf/ others may simply remember how to spell the word "of" by rote.

Across

Exaggerate the vowel so that /ə crŏs/ sounds like /ā crŏs/.

Winner

Encourage students to consider the root "win" before spelling "winner." Ask them what suffix is being added and which rule governs adding a suffix to a word ending in one vowel followed by one consonant.

Stopped

Encourage students to consider the root "stop" before spelling "stopped." Ask them what suffix is being added and which rule governs adding a suffix to a word ending in one vowel followed by one consonant.

	Word	Practice Sentence	Say to Spell	# of Syllables	Markings
1.	**to**	*The dog ran to the car.*	tö	1	tö
2.	**around**	*The dog ran around the car.*	ā rownd	2	ā <u>ro</u>und
3.	**beside**	*The dog sat beside the car.*	bē sīd	2	bē sī<u>de</u>
4.	**toward**	*The dog ran toward the car.*	tō ärd	2	<u>tow</u>² <u>ar</u>d
5.	**off**	*The dog jumped off the car.*	ŏf	1	off
6.	**out**	*The dog jumped out of the car.*	owt	1	<u>out</u>
7.	**through**	*The dog ran through the car.*	throo	1	<u>through</u>³
8.	**of**	*The dog jumped out of the car.*	ə v	1	of
9.	**down**	*The dog ran down the street.*	down	1	<u>down</u>
10.	**across**	*The dog ran across the street.*	ā crŏs	1	ā cross
11.	**race**	*The children race around the track.*	rās	1	rā<u>ce</u>
12.	**winner**	*You are the winner!*	wĭn ner	2	win n<u>er</u>
13.	**stopped**	*He stopped at home to get his back-pack.*	stŏpt	2	stopp<u>ed</u>³
14.	**surprise**	*It is a surprise.*	ser prīz	2	<u>sur</u> pri<u>se</u>²
15.	**suddenly**	*She suddenly jumped out at me.*	sŭd dĕn lē	3	sud den ly

Spelling Hints	Part of Speech	Vocabulary Development
Put two dots over the /ö/. /ŏ-ō-ö/ said its third sound.	P	into, onto
Say to spell /ā round/. Put a line over the /ā/. **4** A E O U usually say their names at the end of the syllable. Underline /ou/.	P	runaround, turnaround, wraparound
Put a line over the /ē/. **4** A E O U usually say their names at the end of the syllable. Put a line over the /ī/. Double underline the silent final E. **12.1** The vowel says its name because of the E.	P	besides
Underline the /ō/ and put a 2 over it. /ow-ō/ said its second sound. Underline the /är/	P	
30 We often double F, L, and S after a single vowel at the end of a base word. Occasionally other letters also are doubled.	P	offset, cutoffs, handoff, kickoff, layoff, castoff, payoff, offprint, offshoot, playoff, offside, turnoff
Underline the /ow/.	P	outside, outer, outage, outback, outdated, outbound, burnout, tryout, cookout, outcome, outfit, outguess, outlook
Underline the /th/. Underline the /oo/ and put a 3 over it. /ŏ-ō-oo-ow-ŭf-ŏf/ said its third sound.	P	breakthrough, throughout, throughway
This word is a true exception. Discuss how /ə/ replaces the /ŏ/ because this word is not accented in the sentence. Note that /f/ and /v/ are a voice and unvoiced pair and how pronunciation shifted over time.	P	
Underline /ow/.	P	downer, breakdown, clampdown, downbeat, downpour, downspout, downsize, slowdown, downtime, downward
Say to spell /ā crŏs/. Put a line over the /ā/. **4** A E O U usually say their names at the end of the syllable. **30** We often double F, L, and S after a single vowel at the end of a base word. Occasionally other letters also are doubled.	P	
Put a line over the /ā/. Underline the C. Double underline the silent final E. **12.1** The vowel says its name because of the E. **12.3** The C says /s/ and the G says /j/ because of the E.	V, N	racing, raced, racer, racecourse, racehorse, racetrack
Win + er. Underline the /er/. **14** Double the last consonant when adding a vowel suffix to words ending in one vowel followed by one consonant.	N	winning, won, breadwinner, prizewinning, prizewinner
Stop + ed. Underline the /t/ and put a 3 over it. /ed-d-t/ said its third sound. **14** Double the last consonant when adding a vowel suffix to words ending in one vowel followed by one consonant.	V	stop, stopper, stoppable, backstop, doorstop, shortstop, stopgap, stoplight, stoppage, unstoppable
Underline /er/. Put a 2 over the /z/. /s-z/ said its second sound. Double underline the silent final E. **12.5** Add an E to keep singular words that end in S from looking plural.	V, N	surprised, surprising
7 Y says long /ē/ only at the end of a multi-syllable word. I says long /ē/ only at the end of a syllable that is followed by a vowel.	Adv	sudden, suddenness

PART THREE

Materials Needed: Grammar Cards 16, 16.1; toy dog, toy car; red, green, yellow, black colored pencils.

Grammar

Review

What is a noun? A noun is the name of a person, place, thing, or idea.

What is a pronoun? A pronoun takes the place of a noun.

What are the six noun jobs we have learned? subject noun, direct object, indirect object, predicate noun, noun of direct address, object of the preposition

What is an adjective? Adjectives modify nouns and pronouns. Adjectives answer: What kind? How many? Which one? Whose?

What is an article? A, An, The. Tiny article adjectives that mark nouns and answer the question: Which?

Name the parts of a sentence. A sentence must have a capital letter, subject, verb, complete thought, and an end mark.

What is a verb? A verb shows action, links a description to the subject, or helps another verb.

What are the three types of verbs we have learned? action verbs, transitive verbs, and linking verbs

What is an adverb? An adverb modifies a verb, adjective, or another adverb. An adverb answers: How? When? Where? To what extent?

What is a preposition? A preposition links a noun or a pronoun to the rest of the sentence.

Prepositions

If possible, bring a toy dog and car to act out the following sentences.

Today we will learn prepositions that show direction.

What is a preposition? A preposition connects a noun or a pronoun to the rest of the sentence.

I will read a sentence. Call out the preposition in each sentence.

The dog ran past the car. past
The dog ran to the car. to
The dog ran around the car. around
The dog sat beside the car. beside
The dog jumped into the car. into
The dog ran toward the car. toward

The dog jumped onto the car. onto
The dog jumped off the car. off
The dog jumped out of the car. out of
The dog ran through the car. through
The dog ran down the street. down
The dog ran across the street. across

✎ *32.11 Prepositions – **In your workbook you have a list of action verbs and prepositions. Use these words to make up sentences aloud that include a prepositional phrase.***

Action verbs			Prepositions		
tiptoe	drive	throw	past	to	toward
march	jump	climb	onto	up	off
stamp	skate	talk	into	around	out
run	walk	swim	upon	beside	through
kneel	stomp	bike	down	across	of

✏ *Spelling List 32* – **Identify the parts of speech for each word in List 32.**

✏ *Spelling List 32* – **Write the plural of each noun and the past tense of each verb.**

Optional Spelling Cards

1. Dictate the words in Lesson 32 for the students to write on index cards. ⓀⓋⒶ

2. Ask the students to color a black border around the prepositions, a green border around the verbs, a yellow border around the adverbs, and a red border around the nouns. If a word can be used as more than one part of speech color two borders. ⓀⓋ

Identifying Parts of Speech in Sentences

✏ *32.12 Identifying Parts of Speech* – **We will now identify the parts of speech using the sentences in your workbook. Label each part of speech in your workbook while I write it on the board.**

The happy winners ran around their school.

Who ran? winners, subject noun
Which winners? the, article adjective
What kind of winners? happy, adjective
What is being said about the winners? winners ran, verb
What is the word "around?" preposition
Around what? school, object of the preposition
Whose school? their, possessive pronoun adjective

A Adj SN V P PPA OP
The happy winners ran around their school.

What is the prepositional phrase? around their school
What is the prepositional phrase "around their school" modifying? ran
Put parentheses around the prepositional phrase.

A Adj SN V P PPA OP
The happy winners ran (around their school.)

My cousins raced across the yard, down the street, and to the hospital.

Who raced? cousins, subject noun
Whose cousins? my, possessive pronoun adjective
What is being said about the cousins? cousins raced, verb
What is the word "across?" preposition
Across what? yard, object of the preposition
Which yard? the, article adjective
What is the word "down?" preposition
Down what? street, object of the preposition
Which street? the, article adjective
What is "and?" conjunction
What is the word "to?" preposition
To what? hospital, object of the preposition
Which hospital? the, article adjective

PPA SN   V   P   A   OP   P   A   OP   C   P   A   OP
My cousins raced across the yard, down the street, and to the hospital.

Put parentheses around the prepositional phrases.

PPA SN   V   P   A   OP   P   A   OP   C   P   A   OP
My cousins raced (across the yard,) (down the street), and (to the hospital.)

The brown squirrel suddenly ran up the tree.

Who ran? squirrel, subject noun
What kind of squirrel? brown, adjective
Which squirrel? the, article adjective
What is being said about the squirrel? squirrel ran, verb
How did it run? suddenly, adverb
What is the word "up?" preposition
Up what? tree, object of the preposition
Which tree? the, article adjective

 A   Adj   SN   Adv   V   P   A   OP
The brown squirrel suddenly ran up the tree.

Put parentheses around the prepositional phrase.

 A   Adj   SN   Adv   V   P   A   OP
The brown squirrel suddenly ran (up the tree.)

Optional Grammar Activities

1. ✎ *32.13 Extra Practice: Practicing Prepositions* – Direct the students to read the sentences. Instruct the students to write a P over the preposition and put parentheses around the prepositional phrase. Ask the students to draw a picture of each sentence. Ⓚ︎Ⓥ︎Ⓒ︎

2. Play Simon Says with prepositional phrases. Direct students to command each other to move around the room using prepositional phrases. Ⓚ︎Ⓥ︎Ⓒ︎Ⓐ︎

3. Create prepositional phrases using the Spelling Cards. Build prepositional phrases using a black preposition card + an article + a noun. Ⓚ︎Ⓥ︎Ⓒ︎Ⓐ︎

Challenge - Misplaced Modifiers

I will write two sentences on the board. Read the sentence then tell me what is different between them.

The child threw the book on the table.
The child on the table threw the book.

The first sentence means that the child threw the book on the table. The second sentence means the child was on the table.

The prepositional phrase modifies the noun that it is directly before it.
The place of the prepositional phrase in the sentence is very important.

The child threw the book on the table.

Which book? the book on the table
Circle the word book, and draw a line with an arrow to show that the phrase "on the table" is modifying book.

The child threw the (book) on the table.

The child on the table threw the book.

Which child? the child on the table

The (child) on the table threw the book.

My uncle forgot his (medicine) in the hospital.

Which medicine? the medicine in the hospital

My (uncle) in the hospital forgot his medicine.

Which uncle? my uncle in the hospital

Paragraphs

Sentences that are grouped together to tell a story or explain a topic are written in paragraph form. Paragraphs begin with an indent.

Grammar Card 16	Paragraph
A paragraph is a closely related group of sentences about a unified topic.	

Grammar Card 16.1	Paragraph
Paragraphs begin with an indent.	

✎ *32.14 Paragraphs – Read the paragraphs in your workbook aloud. Put a line under the indent. Circle the capital letters and the end marks.*

Emma and I raced through the house, down the street, across the park, around the corner, and to our grandmother's house. We knocked on her door and waited. Our sweet grandmother opened the door and invited us inside. Grandma made us lunch. I sat beside Emma. Grandma sat across from me. Grandma told us stories. We had a wonderful time.

A young girl ran the fastest time. She was the winner at the school race. After the race, she stood on a platform and received a gold medal. As she waved at the people, a photographer took her picture for the newspaper. Her teacher gave her one yellow flower. She felt happy.

My aunt and uncle hiked in the mountains. They walked through thick forests and saw beautiful trees. One night they camped by a river. A bear tried to eat their food. Thankfully it was tied high up in a tree. They enjoyed their trip.

Two people walked toward the house. They stopped. They looked around the yard. Slowly they opened the door and slipped inside. Then they shouted, "Surprise! Happy Birthday!"

Dictation

✎ *32.15 Dictation – Today for your dictation, you will write a paragraph.*

How does a paragraph begin? with an indent
Each sentence will then be written directly after the previous sentence.
I will read one sentence at a time.
When we have finished dictating the paragraph, I want you to read it back to me aloud.

My grandmother was in the hospital. I stopped by her room and surprised her. We walked around the paths. We ate lunch together. I sat beside her bed and talked to her. It was a wonderful visit.

Composition

Simple Sentences

A simple sentence includes only a subject and a verb.

For Example:

Boys run.

Girl swims.

They play.

If we only wrote and spoke in simple sentences it would be boring and choppy.

To make writing more interesting, writers use a variety of tools. We have learned three tools to add information to a sentence: adjectives, adverbs, and prepositional phrases. These words add more information and interest to the sentence.

Writing Game

I will write a simple sentence on the board. I will point to a student. That student needs to call out either "adjective," "adverb," or "prepositional phrase." The next student needs to add that part of speech to the sentence to make it more interesting.

For example:

Children play.

Adjective — *Happy children play.*

Prepositional phrase — *Happy children play in the park.*

Adverb — *Happy children play noisily in the park.*

Prepositional phrase — *Happy children play noisily in the park on First Street.*

Adjective — *Happy children play noisily in the large park on First Street.*

Prepositional phrase — *Happy children play noisily on the swings in the large park on First Street.*

Girls swim.

Children walk.

Boys bike.

Squirrels climb.

Dogs howl.

✎ *32.16 Composition* – Beginning with the sentence in your workbook, modify it according to the suggestions. Rewrite the sentence each time.

Challenge - Misplaced Modifiers

Write a sentence which includes a direct object and an indirect object.

The children gave the man some water.

Add a prepositional phrase.

The children gave the man in the car some water.

Move the prepositional phrase to change the meaning of the sentence.

The children gave the man some water in the car.
The children in the car gave the man some water.

Vocabulary

Derivatives of Down

There are more than 125 words which are derived from the word "down." This activity will challenge students to think of as many as possible.

Decide if the students will work as individuals or groups. Decide if a prize will be offered and what the standard is to receive the prize. Prizes may go to students who collect fifty, seventy-five, or one hundred words. Or a prize may be awarded to the student who finds the most derivatives.

> **Some words generate a lot of derivatives.**
> **Guess how many words include the word "down?"**
> **I have a list of 127 words that include the word "down."**
> **Let's think of five examples. I will write them on the board as you say them.**

Write the words on the board as students list them.

✎ *32.17 Vocabulary Development* – **Find as many words as you can that include the word "down." Write them in your workbook. You may use a dictionary to aid your search and check the spelling, but you may not use the internet.**

Plurals are considered derivatives.

breakdown	downing	downstaters	markdown
breakdowns	downlink	downstream	markdowns
clampdown	downlinks	downstroke	meltdown
clampdowns	download	downstrokes	meltdowns
comedown	downloadable	downswing	pushdown
comedowns	downloaded	downswings	pushdowns
countdown	downloading	downtick	rubdown
countdowns	downloads	downticks	rubdowns
crackdown	downplay	downtime	rundown
crackdowns	downpour	downtimes	rundowns
down	downpours	downtown	shakedown
downbeat	downrange	downtowns	shakedowns
downbeats	downright	downtrend	showdown
downcast	downs	downtrodden	showdowns
downdraft	downscale	downturn	shutdown
downdrafts	downshift	downturns	shutdowns
downed	downshifted	downward	slowdown
downer	downshifting	downwardly	slowdowns
downers	downshifts	downwardness	splashdown
downfall	downside	downwards	splashdowns
downfallen	downsides	downwind	sundown
downfalls	downsize	downy	sundowns
downgrade	downsized	eiderdown	swansdown
downgraded	downsizes	eiderdowns	thistledown
downgrades	downsizing	facedown	touchdown
downgrading	downspout	hoedown	touchdowns
downhearted	downspouts	hoedowns	tumbledown
downheartedly	downstage	knockdown	turndown
downheartedness	downstages	knockdowns	turndowns
downhill	downstairs	letdown	
downier	downstate	letdowns	
downiest	downstater	lowdown	

Lesson 33

Phonograms:	
Exploring Sounds:	Accented Syllables
Spelling Rules:	14
Grammar:	Helping Verbs Present Continuous Tense

PART ONE

Materials Needed: Phonogram Flash Cards from previous lessons; Spelling Rule Card 14; Phonogram Game Cards.

Phonograms

Review

1. Drill the phonograms with flash cards.

2. ✎ *33.1 Phonogram Practice* – Dictate the following phonograms. For extra practice, have the students read them back. Write the correct answers on the board as the students check their answers.

1. ir	8. augh	15. gu
2. ur	9. si	16. ei
3. ear	10. ti	17. ey
4. er	11. ci	18. eigh
5. cei	12. sh	19. kn
6. au	13. ie	20. gn
7. aw	14. bu	

3. Play Last One! using the game cards (*The Phonogram and Spelling Game Book,* 12).

Exploring Sounds

Accented Syllables

Today we will practice finding the accent within a word.
What are some strategies we can use to find the accent? Listen for the strongest beat. Put your hand under your chin and feel for the syllable where the mouth drops open the furthest.

I will write a word on the board. Read the word. Count the syllables. Then tell me which syllable is accented.

forget

/for gĕt/. Two syllables. The second syllable is accented.

for get'

limit

/lĭm ĭt/. Two syllables. The first syllable is accented.

lim' it

prefer

/prē fer/. Two syllables. The second syllable is accented.

pre fer'

control

/kŏn trōl/. Two syllables. The second syllable is accented.

con trol'

open

/ō pĕn/. Two syllables. The first syllable is accented.

o' pen

> **Teacher Tip:** *Another way to find the accent is to listen for the syllable which has a clearly pronounced vowel sound. Often, though not always, the vowel will sound like the schwa sound /ə/ in the unaccented syllable.*

Spelling Rules

Adding Suffixes to Words Ending in One Vowel & One Consonant

get

How do we add the suffix -ing to the word "get?" Double the last consonant, then add the -ing.
Why? What rule is this following? Double the last consonant when adding a vowel suffix to words ending in one vowel followed by one consonant.

getting

> *Where is the accent in the word "getting?"* on the first syllable

get' ting

> *Lets read the whole rule:*

Spelling Rule   14

Double the last consonant when adding a vowel suffix to words ending in one vowel followed by one consonant, only if the syllable before the suffix is accented.

> *Where should the accent be if we are to double the last consonant?* on the syllable before the suffix
> *Is the syllable before the suffix accented in the word "getting?"* yes

forget + ing

> *What do we need to consider before we add the suffix -ing to "forget?"* Does it end in one vowel followed by one consonant? Are we adding a vowel suffix? And where is the accent in the derivative "forgetting?"*
> *Does "forget" end in one vowel followed by one consonant?* yes
> *Are we adding a vowel suffix?* yes
> *Where is the accent in "forgetting?"* on the second syllable - get
> *Is this the syllable before the suffix?* yes
> *Therefore we double the last consonant before adding the vowel suffix -ing.*

forget + ing = for get' ting

begin + er

> *What do we need to consider before we add the suffix -er to "begin?"* Does it end in one vowel followed by one consonant? Are we adding a vowel suffix? And where is the accent in the derivative "beginner?"*
> *Does "begin" end in one vowel followed by one consonant?* yes
> *Are we adding a vowel suffix?* yes
> *Where is the accent in "beginner?"* on the second syllable - gin
> *Is this the syllable before the suffix?* yes
> *Therefore we double the last consonant before adding the vowel suffix -er.*

begin + er = be gin' ner

open + er

What do we need to consider before we add the suffix -er to "open?" Does it end in one vowel followed by one consonant? Are we adding a vowel suffix? And where is the accent in the derivative "opener?"

Does "open" end in one vowel followed by one consonant? yes

Are we adding a vowel suffix? yes

Where is the accent in "opener?" on the first syllable - o

Is this the syllable before the suffix? no

Should we double the last consonant? no

Why? The syllable before the suffix is not accented.

open + er = o´ pen er

occur + ed

What do we need to consider before we add the suffix -ed to "occur?" Does it end in one vowel followed by one consonant? Are we adding a vowel suffix? And where is the accent in the derivative "occur?"

Does "occur" end in one vowel followed by one consonant? yes

The R controlled phonograms ER, IR, UR are all one vowel followed by one consonant even if you cannot hear the vowel sound clearly.

Are we adding a vowel suffix? yes

Where is the accent in "occurred?" on the second syllable - cur

Is this the syllable before the suffix? yes

Therefore we double the last consonant before adding the vowel suffix -ed.

occur + ed = oc cur´ red

limit + ing

What do we need to consider before we add the suffix -ing to "limit?" Does it end in one vowel followed by one consonant? Are we adding a vowel suffix? And where is the accent in the derivative "limiting?"

Does "limit" end in one vowel followed by one consonant? yes

Are we adding a vowel suffix? yes

Where is the accent in "limiting?" on the first syllable lim-

Is this the syllable before the suffix? no

Should we double the last consonant? no

Why? The syllable before the suffix is not accented.

limit + ing = lim´ it ing

equip + ment =

What do we need to consider before we add the suffix -ment to "equip?" Does it end in one vowel followed by one consonant? Are we adding a vowel suffix? And where is the accent in the derivative, "equipment?"

Does "equip" end in one vowel followed by one consonant? answers will vary

Is the U a vowel in the phonogram QU? no

Why? Q always needs a U. U is not a vowel here. Therefore, equip ends in one vowel followed by one consonant.

Are we adding a vowel suffix? no
Should we double the last consonant? no
Why? -ment is a consonant suffix.

equip + ment = e quip' ment

quiz + ed =

Does "quiz" end in one vowel followed by one consonant? yes
Are we adding a vowel suffix? yes
Where is the accent in "quizzed?" on the first syllable quiz-
Is this the syllable before the suffix? yes
Should we double the last consonant? yes

quiz + ed = quiz' zed

Look back over the derivatives on the board. Is the suffix ever accented? no
When listening for the accented syllable, remember the accent will never be on the suffix.

✎ *33.2 Adding Suffixes –* **Add suffixes to the words in your workbook. Write the word in the correct column. Divide it into syllables and write an accent mark on the accented syllable.**

Answer Key

	Double the last consonant	Do not double the last consonant
limit + ing		lim' it ing
control + ed	con trol' led	
forget + ful		for get' ful
equip + ing	e quip' ping	
medal + ist		med' al ist
begin + er	be gin' ner	
forget + able	for get' table	
forget + ing	for get' ting	
prefer + ed	pre fer' red	
prefer + ence		pref' er ence

Optional Spelling Rule Practice

1. Create a notebook page to remember these rules using sample words from the board. ©Ⓥ

2. Ask the students to teach this to another student or to a parent. ©ⓋⒶⓀ

3. Review rules 1-30 using the Spelling Rule Flash Cards. ⓋⒶ

4. ✎ *33.3 Extra Practice: Accent* – Read the words in your workbook. Mark the accented syllable. *prob' lem, re turn', be hind', lev' el, a go', in deed', bod' y, per' son, of' fice, her self', fath' er, stud' y, ac count'* ⓀⓋⒶ

5. Adding Suffixes Game – Provide each student with a whiteboard, marker, and eraser. Call out a word and suffix using the list below. Direct students to write the word on the whiteboard. Award one point for spelling it correctly and one point for identifying the correct reason the final consonant is or is not doubled. ⓀⓋ©Ⓐ

   - **Ending in one vowel and one consonant, the accent is on the syllable before the suffix** – *let + ing = letting, commit + ing = committing, split + ing = splitting, benefit + ed = benefitted, sled + ed = sledded, prod + ed = prodded, shred + ed = shredded, stir + ed = stirred, fur + y = furry, blur + y = blurry, occur + ed = occurred, begin + er = beginner, red + ish = reddish*

   - **Ending in one vowel and one consonant, the accent is NOT on the syllable before the suffix** – *medal + ist = medalist, fasten + er = fastener, soften + er = softener, garden + er = gardener, level + ed = leveled, travel + ed = traveled*

   - **Ending in two consonants** – *charm + er = charmer, paint + er = painter, vent + ed = vented, farm + er = farmer, blast + ed = blasted, fast + en = fasten, list + ed = listed*

   - **Two vowels** – *train + er = trainer, feel + ing = feeling, heal + ed = healed, sail + ed = sailed, fail + ed = failed, mail + er = mailer, trail + er = trailer*

PART TWO

Using Spelling List 33 on pages 434-435, dictate each word following the steps included on pages Intro 42 - Intro 46.

Tips for Spelling List 33

Beginner

Encourage students to consider the root "begin" before spelling "beginner." Ask them what suffix is being added and which rule governs adding a suffix to a word ending in one vowel followed by one consonant.

Prefer

One of the difficulties with English spelling is that vowels in unaccented syllables often are pronounced as the schwa sound /ə/. In order to help students create an auditory picture of the word, it is helpful to exaggerate the unaccented vowel. Therefore, exaggerate the vowel so that /prə fer/ sounds like /prē fer/.

To learn more about vowels in unaccented syllables and aiding students in creating an auditory picture of words, see *Uncovering the Logic of English,* 121-128.

Vacation

Exaggerate the vowel so that /və kā shən/ sounds like /vā kā shŏn/.

Any

This is a true exception. The A is saying the short /ĕ/ sound. Many students will find it helpful to exaggerate the vowel so that /ĕn ē/ sounds like /ăn ē/ for spelling purposes.

Many

This is a true exception. The A is saying the short /ĕ/ sound. Many students will find it helpful to exaggerate the vowel so that /mĕn ē/ sounds like /mån ē/ for spelling purposes.

Forgetting

Encourage students to consider the root "forget" before spelling "forgetting." Ask them what suffix is being added and which rule governs adding a suffix to a word ending in one vowel followed by one consonant.

Several

Exaggerate the vowels so that /sĕv er əl/ sounds like /sĕv er ăl/.

From

Exaggerate the vowel so that /frəm/ sounds like /frŏm/. The O is pronounced with a schwa sound /ə/ because the word "from" is a grammatical word which is not accented within the sentence (*Uncovering the Logic of English,* 126).

	Word	Practice Sentence	Say to Spell	# of Syllables	Markings
1.	**beginner**	*She is a beginner.*	bē gĭn ner	3	bē gin n<u>er</u>
2.	**prefer**	*I prefer the brown dress.*	prē fer	2	prē f<u>er</u>
3.	**receive**	*We will receive four packages today.*	rē cēv	2	rē c<u>ei</u>v<u>e</u>
4.	**fix**	*The plumber will fix the sink.*	fĭx	1	fix
5.	**team**	*Our team won the soccer game.*	tēm	1	t<u>ea</u>m
6.	**noise**	*The noise is loud.*	noiz	1	n<u>oi</u>s<u>e</u>²
7.	**vacation**	*Next week we will leave for vacation.*	vā kā shŏn	3	vā cā <u>tion</u>
8.	**took**	*I took pictures.*	tük	1	t<u>oo</u>²k
9.	**any**	*Do you have any paper?*	ăn ē	2	an y
10.	**many**	*There are many types of butterflies in the garden.*	mănē	2	man y
11.	**forgetting**	*I keep forgetting to bring warm clothes.*	fōr gĕt ting	3	f<u>or</u> get ting
12.	**several**	*We need several volunteers.*	sĕv er ăl	3	sev <u>er</u> al
13.	**present**	*Mother bought her a present.* *They will present the awards tonight.*	prĕz ĕnt *prē zent	2	pres² ent *prē sent²
14.	**for**	*This gift is for Karen.*	fōr	1	f<u>or</u>
15.	**from**	*The gift is from her grandfather.*	frŏm	1	from

Spelling Hints	Part of Speech	Vocabulary Development
Put a line over the /ē/. **4** A E O U usually say their names at the end of the syllable. **14** Double the last consonant when adding a vowel suffix to words ending in one vowel followed by one consonant, only if the syllable before the suffix is accented. Underline /er/.	N	begin, beginning, begins, began
Say to spell /prē fer/. Put a line over the /ē/. **4** A E O U usually say their names at the end of the syllable. Underline /er/.	V	prefers, preferred, preferable, preferably, preferences, preferential
Put a line over the /ē/. **4** A E O U usually say their names at the end of the syllable. Underline /sē/. Underline the /v/ once and the silent final E twice. **12.2** English words do not end in V or U.	V	received, receiver, receiving, receives
All first sounds.	V, N	fixed, fixing, fixer, fixable, fixture, affix, prefix, suffix, transfix, transfixed
Underline /ē/.	N, V	teams, teaming, teamed, teammate, teamster, teamwork
Underline the /oi/. Put a 2 over the /z/. /s-z/ said its second sound. Double underline the silent final E. **12.5** Add an E to keep singular words that end in S from looking plural.	N	noises, noisy, noiseless, noiselessly, noisemaker, noisemakers
Say to spell /vā kā shŏn/. Root: Vacate. Put a line over the /ā/. Put a line over the /ā/. **4** A E O U usually say their names at the end of the syllable. Underline /sh/. **17** TI, CI, and SI are used only at the beginning of any syllable after the first one.	N	vacations, vacationed, vacationer, vacationing, vacationland, vacate, vacant
Underline the /ü/. Put a 2 over it. /oo-ü-ō/ said its second sound.	V	take, taken, mistook, overtook, retook, undertook, caretaker, undertaker, partake, overtake, takeaway, takeout, takeover
Say to spell /ăn ē /. **7** Y says long /ē/ only at the end of a multi-syllable word. I says long /ē/ only at the end of a syllable that is followed by a vowel.	Adj	anyone, anywhere, anytime, anything, anyway
Say to spell / măn ē/. **7** Y says long /ē/ only at the end of a multi-syllable word. I says long /ē/ only at the end of a syllable that is followed by a vowel.	Adj	manyfold
Underline /or/.	V	forget, forgot, forgotten, forgetting, forgetful, forgetfully, forgetfulness, forgettable, unforgettable, unforgettably
Say to spell / sĕv er ăl/. Underline /er/.	Adj	severalfold, severally
Put a 2 over the /z/. /s-z/ said its second sound. *Homonym: Put a line over the /ē/. **4** A E O U usually say their names at the end of the syllable. Put a 2 over the /z/. /s-z/ said its second sound.	N *V	presents, presented, presenter, presentable, presentation
Underline /or/.	P	
Say to spell /frŏm/.	P	

PART THREE

Materials Needed: Grammar Card 3.4; green, red, blue, and black colored pencils.

Grammar

Review

What is a noun? A noun is the name of a person, place, thing, or idea.

What is a pronoun? A pronoun takes the place of a noun.

What are the six noun jobs we have learned? subject noun, direct object, indirect object, predicate noun, noun of direct address, object of the preposition

What is an adjective? Adjectives modify nouns and pronouns. Adjectives answer: What kind? How many? Which one? Whose?

What is an article? A, An, The. Tiny article adjectives that mark nouns and answer the question: Which?

Name the parts of a sentence. A sentence must have a capital letter, subject, verb, complete thought, and an end mark.

What is a verb? A verb shows action, links a description to the subject, or helps another verb.

What are the three types of verbs we have learned? action verbs, transitive verbs, and linking verbs

What is an adverb? An adverb modifies a verb, adjective, or another adverb. An adverb answers: How? When? Where? To what extent?

What is a preposition? A preposition links a noun or a pronoun to the rest of the sentence.

✎ *Spelling List 33 – In your workbook, label the nouns with a red N, the verbs with a green V, and the adjectives with a blue Adj. Label words 14 and 15, "for" and "from," with black as prepositions.*

✎ *Spelling List 33 – Write the plural of each noun and the past tense of each verb.*

Optional Spelling Cards

1. Dictate the words in Lesson 33 for the students to write on index cards. Ⓚ Ⓥ Ⓐ

2. Ask the students to color a black border around the prepositions, a green border around the verbs, a red border around the nouns, and a blue border around the adjectives. If a word can be used as more than one part of speech, color two borders. Ⓚ Ⓥ

Present Continuous Tense

Write the following sentences in two columns on the board.

Read the sentences as I write them. What do you notice?

I brush my teeth.   I am brushing my teeth.

Dad fixes the car in our driveway.   Dad is fixing the car in our
                                             driveway.

We study math in school.   We are studying math in school.

What is the difference between each of the sentences in the two columns? The verb has the suffix -ing added to one column and a form of the "to be" verb added. One means we do it usually, the other means now.

usually

Looking at the sentences, which sentences can we add the word "usually" to?

I usually brush my teeth.

Dad usually fixes the car in the driveway.

We usually study math in school.

now

Which sentences can we add the word "now" to?

I am brushing my teeth now.

Now Dad is fixing the car in the driveway.

We are now studying math in school.

The sentences in the first column are written in the simple present tense. The sentences written in the second column are written in present continuous tense. When we tell a story using present continuous tense it is as if someone is giving us a play by play of the action as it is happening.

Point to the sentence, "I am brushing my teeth."

How many verbs do you see in this sentence? two - am, brushing

-ing

We can add -ing to the verb when we want to show that something is happening now.

Can I say, "I brushing?" No, you need to say, "I am brushing."
Can you say, "Dad fixing?" No, you need to say, "Dad is fixing."
When we use the -ing form of the verb, we need to add a form of the "to be" verb to help make it a complete verb. The "to be" verb is called a helping verb. It is helping to make the verb complete and to show when an action is occurring. This is called tense. Tense refers to the time that the sentence takes place.

Grammar Card 3.4	HV
Helping verbs help the main verb by expressing tense, mood, and voice.	

Point to the sentence, "Dad is fixing the car in the driveway."

> *What is the helping verb in this sentence?* is
> *What is the main action verb?* fixing

Point to the sentence, "We are studying math in school."

> *What is the helping verb in this sentence?* are
> *What is the main action verb?* studying

> *Each of these sentences has two verbs. The main verb is the one that shows action. The "to be" verb is helping the main verb. It is called a helping verb.*

Identifying the Parts of Speech in Sentences

✎ *33.4 Identifying Parts of Speech –* **Let's look at the sentences in the second column more closely. The sentences are written in your workbook. Label the parts of speech as I write them on the board.**

> She is brushing her teeth.
>
> > *Who is brushing?* she, subject pronoun
> > *What is being said about she?* she is brushing, verb
> > *Notice that the verb is comprised of two words. Which word shows the action?* brushing
> > *"Is" is called a helping verb. It is a form of the "to be" verb that is helping to show that we are talking about something that is happening right now. We will label it HV.*
> > *What is she brushing?* teeth, direct object
> > *Whose teeth?* her, possessive pronoun adjective
> > *Is there a direct object receiving the action of the verb?* yes, transitive verb
> > *Divide the complete subject from the complete predicate.*
>
> SP   HV   TV   PPA   DO
> She / is brushing her teeth.

Dad is fixing the car in our driveway.

Who is fixing? Dad, subject noun
What is being said about Dad? Dad is fixing, verb
Notice that the verb is comprised of two words. Which word shows the action? fixing
What part of speech is the word "is?" helping verb
What is he fixing? car, direct object
Which car? the, article adjective
What is the word "in?" preposition
In what? driveway, object of the preposition
Which driveway? our, possessive pronoun adjective
Is there a direct object receiving the action of the verb? yes, transitive verb
Put parentheses around the prepositional phrase.
Divide the complete subject from the complete predicate.

SN   HV   TV   A   DO   P   PPA   OP
Dad / is fixing the car (in our driveway.)

We are studying math in school.

Who is studying? we, subject pronoun
What is being said about we? we are studying, verb
Notice that the verb is comprised of two words. Which word shows the action? studying
What is the helping verb? are
What are we studying? math, direct object
What is the word "in?" preposition
In what? school, object of the preposition
Is there a direct object receiving the action of the verb? yes, transitive verb
Put parentheses around the prepositional phrase.
Divide the complete subject from the complete predicate.

SP   HV   TV   DO   P   OP
We / are studying math (in school.)

Optional Grammar Practice

1. ✏ *33.5 Extra Practice: Helping Verbs* – Fill in the blank with the correct helping verb to complete the meaning of the sentence. Ⓚ Ⓥ Ⓐ

2. Miming - Have one student mime actions while another describes what is happening using present continuous tense. Ⓚ Ⓥ Ⓒ Ⓐ

3. What's Going on Around Here? Direct students to list as many things that are occurring in their surroundings as possible. This may be played out loud or in writing. If writing, set a timer for three to five minutes. Direct students to write present continuos tense sentences to describe their surroundings. Ⓥ Ⓒ Ⓐ

4. Create prepositional phrases using the Spelling Cards. Build prepositional phrases using a black preposition card + an article + a noun. Ⓚ Ⓥ Ⓒ Ⓐ

Composition

✏ *33.6 Present Continuous Story* – **Read the story in your workbook. It is told in present continuous tense.**

I am reading a book and waiting. The shop is fixing my car. The workers are taking a long time. Their team is going to lunch. I am still waiting.

What do you notice about the story? It sounds like it is happening now. The verbs all have an -ing.

Today you will write a story about yourself in present continuous tense. A story in present continuous tense sounds like you are telling us each event as it happens. Begin with:

I am ...

Let's make one up out loud.

For example: I am walking down the street. My friend is mowing her lawn. I am stopping to say, "Hello."

Let's make up a story using as many words as possible from the spelling list. How many can you use in one story that is happening right now?

✏ *33.7 Composition* – **Write a short story in your workbook. It must have at least five sentences. You must tell the story as if it is happening right now. Be sure to indent the first line.**

Vocabulary Development

Derivatives of Forget

forget

> **Today we will form new words with the word "forget."**

forget + able =

> **What new word is formed when we add -able to forget?** forgettable
> **Which rule do we need to consider first?** Double the last consonant when adding a vowel suffix to words ending in one vowel followed by one consonant, only if the syllable before the suffix is accented.
> **Does forget end in one vowel followed by one consonant?** yes
> **Are we adding a vowel suffix?** yes
> **Where is the accent in "forgettable?"** The accent is on the second syllable -get.
> **Is this the syllable before the suffix?** yes
> **Then what do we do?** double the T

forget + able = forgettable

> **Use forgettable in a sentence.** Answers will vary. Ex. That movie was easily forgettable.
>
> **What happens if we add the prefix un-?** unforgettable

un- + forgettable = unforgettable

> **Use unforgettable in a sentence.** Answers will vary. Ex. What an unforgettable party!

forget + ful =

> **What new word is formed when we add forget and -ful?** forgetful
> **Do we double the last T?** no
> **Why?** We are not adding a vowel suffix.

forget + ful = forgetful

forgetful + ly =

> **What new word is formed by adding -ly to forgetful?** forgetfully
> **Which rule do I need to consider?** Double the last consonant when adding a vowel suffix to words ending in one vowel followed by one consonant, only if the syllable before the suffix is accented.
>
> **Does "forgetful" end in one vowel and then one consonant?** yes
> **Are we adding a vowel suffix?** no
> **So what do we do?** Just add the suffix.

forgetful + ly = forgetfully

> **Use "forgetfully" in a sentence.** Answers will vary. Ex. She forgetfully left the store without her purse.

forgetful + ness =

> **What new word is formed when we add forgetful and -ness?** forgetfulness
> **Which rule do I need to consider?** Double the last consonant when adding a vowel suffix to words ending in one vowel followed by one consonant, only if the syllable before the suffix is accented.
>
> **Does "forgetful" end in one vowel and then one consonant?** yes
> **Are we adding a vowel suffix?** no
> **So what do we do?** Just add the suffix.

forgetful + ness = forgetfulness

> **Use forgetfulness in a sentence.** Answers will vary. Ex. Grandmother's forgetfulness is starting to concern me.

> ✎ *33.8 Vocabulary Development* – **Add the suffixes to the words in your workbook.**

Answer key: 1. beginner 2. beginning 3. preferable 4. fixed 5. forgetting 6. forgettable 7. presents 8. vacationing 9. received 10. teaming

Challenge - Roots

vacation

What does it mean to go on vacation? to leave home, school, or work and go someplace else for rest or fun

What is the root of vacation? vacate

vacate

vacant

What does vacate mean? to leave someplace empty, or to get out
What does vacant mean? empty
Vacate means to leave a house or a property empty.
How does this relate to vacation? When a family goes on vacation, the home is left empty.
When school is out for summer vacation, what happens to the building? It is vacant or empty.
Have you ever seen a sign at a hotel that says:

vacancies

no vacancy

What do these mean? Vacancies mean they have empty rooms that are available to rent. No vacancy means they do not have any empty rooms.

Dictation

✎ *33.9 Dictation – **Today's dictation will be a story. Rather than writing it as numbered sentences, I want you to write it as a paragraph. Make sure to indent the first line. I will read each sentence aloud two times. Repeat it back to me before you write it. When you are finished, I will read the next sentence.***

I received an unforgettable present from my grandmother. She gave me a vacation to the mountains. On the way, we visited my aunt, uncle, and cousins at their house. We took a boat down a river and saw many wild animals. I took several great photos. It was a big surprise!

Lesson 34

Phonograms:	
Exploring Sounds:	Words with a Silent L
Spelling Rules:	
Grammar:	Helping Verbs, Irregular Present Tense Verbs, Future Tense

PART ONE

Materials Needed: Phonogram Flash Cards from previous lessons and ⬚ si ⬚; Phonogram Game Cards.

Phonograms

Review

1. Drill the phonograms with flash cards.

2. ✎ *34.1 Phonogram Practice* – Dictate the following phonograms. For extra practice, have the students read them back. Write the correct answers on the board as the students check their answers.

1. gu	8. ir	15. ew
2. ie	9. ui	16. gn
3. ou	10. dge	17. kn
4. aw	11. ei	18. igh
5. igh	12. ey	19. ar
6. ur	13. eigh	20. oy
7. bu	14. augh	

3. Play Phonogram Snatch using the Phonogram Game Cards (*The Phonogram and Spelling Game Book*, 8).

Exploring Sounds

Words with a Silent L

Read the words as I write them on the board.

chalk

talk

walk

What letter is silent in these words? L

Today we will learn a few more common words with a silent L.

half   halve

What do these words mean? A half is two equal pieces. To halve is to cut something into two equal pieces.

What word does halve sound like? have
Where does the L come from? "Halve" is related to the root "half." They both have a silent L.

calf   calve

What do these words mean? A calf is a baby cow. When a cow gives birth to a calf, she calves.

could

would

should

What is similar between each of these word? They all include the phonogram ou saying /ü/. They all have a silent L followed by a D.

salmon

Lincoln

What do these say?

What is a salmon? a type of fish
Who is Lincoln? a former President of the United States

✎ *34.2 Words with a Silent L* – **Read the words in your workbook with silent L's.**

✎ *34.3 Words with a Silent L* – **Write the words that are the most important for you to remember on the lines in your workbook. Underline the L in a different color.**

Spelling Rule

Review the Voiced Phonogram SI

Show | si | .

> *What does this phonogram say?* /sh-ZH/
> *How are these sounds related?* /ZH/ is voiced and /sh/ is unvoiced.
>
> *I will write some words on the board that follow a pattern. See if you can discover the pattern.*

divide + ion = division

explode + ion = explosion

conclude + ion = conclusion

> *What do you notice about each of these words?* The roots all end in a D followed by a silent final E. We are adding the ending -ion. The D changed to the phonogram SI. The SI says /ZH/.
>
> *Is /d/ a voiced or an unvoiced sound?* voiced
> *The voiced /d/ turned into a voiced /ZH/ for spelling.*
>
> *What is the only way to spell /ZH/?* SI

Adding a Suffix to Any Word

> *We now have learned all the rules for adding suffixes to English words. What must we know before we add a suffix to a word in English?* whether the word ends in a silent final E, a single-vowel Y, or one vowel followed by one consonant
>
> ✎ *34.4 Adding a Suffix to Any Word –* **The flow chart in your workbook can aid you in adding a suffix to any word.**
>
> *What does the chart ask first?* Does it end with a silent final E?
> *If the answer is yes, you follow the arrow to the Silent Final E box.*
> *If the answer is no, you go on with the next question.*
>
> *Let's practicing adding suffixes to a few words using the flow chart.*

hobby + es =

> *What will we ask first?* Does it end in a silent final E? no
> *Then?* Does it end in one vowel followed by one consonant? no
> *Then?* Does it end in Y? yes
>
> *Then move to the box that says Single Vowel Y.*
> *What will we ask?* Does it end in a single vowel y? yes

Does the suffix begin with any letter except I? yes

Then change to Y to I and add the suffix.

hobby + es = hobbies

control + ing =

What will we ask first? Does it end in a silent final E? no
Then? Does it end in one vowel followed by one consonant? yes
Then move to the box that says One Vowel plus One Consonant.
Are we adding a vowel suffix? yes
Is the syllable before the suffix accented? yes
Then double the last consonant and add the suffix.

control + ing = con trol′ ling

divide + ing =

What will we ask first? Does it end in a silent final E? yes
Are we adding a vowel suffix? yes
Is dropping the E allowed by other spelling rules? yes

divide + ing = dividing

talk + ative

What will we ask first? Does it end in a silent final E? no
Does it end in one vowel followed by one consonant? no
Does it end in Y? no
Then just add the suffix.

talk + ative = talkative

change + able =

What will we ask first? Does it end in a silent final E? yes
Are we adding a vowel suffix? yes
Is dropping the E allowed by other spelling rules? No, G may say /j/ only before an E, I, or Y.
Then retain the E and just add the suffix.

change + able = changeable

✎ *34.5 Adding Suffixes – **Practice adding suffixes to the words in your workbook using the Adding a Suffix to Any Word Flow Chart.***

Optional Spelling Rule Practice

Review rules 1-30 using the Spelling Rule Flash Cards. Ⓥ Ⓐ

PART TWO

Using Spelling List 34 on pages 450-451, dictate each word following the steps included on pages Intro 42 - Intro 46.

Tips for Spelling List 34

Been

In some American dialects this word is commonly pronounced /bĕn/ or /bĭn/ despite the double E. Many English speakers with a British influence though clearly pronounce it /bēn/. This is a classic example of the usefulness of "Say to Spell." The spelling points to the pronunciation of "been" by some speakers and the origins of the spelling. Though Americans do not need to change their pronunciation, making these connections will heighten awareness of accents.

Could, Would, Should

Notice the relationship between each of these words. They each have a silent L and follow the same pattern for spelling.

Done

Exaggerate the vowel so that /dən/ sounds like /dŏn/ to help students create an auditory picture (*Uncovering the Logic of English,* 121-128).

Controlling

Encourage students to consider the root "control" before spelling "controlling." Ask them what suffix is being added and which rule governs adding a suffix to a word ending in one vowel followed by one consonant.

receive

	Word	Practice Sentence	Say to Spell	# of Syllables	Markings
1.	**been**	*I have been to that store.*	bēn	1	b<u>ee</u>n
2.	**could**	*What time could you leave?*	cüd	1	c<u>ou</u>ld
3.	**would**	*Would you like a piece of cake?*	wüd	1	w<u>ou</u>ld
4.	**should**	*Should we leave at noon?*	shüd	1	sh<u>ou</u>ld
5.	**have**	*May I have a glass of water?*	hăv	1	ha<u>ve</u>
6.	**do**	*Do you have time to work today?*	dö	1	dö
7.	**done**	*Have you done this dance before?*	dŏn	1	don<u>e</u>
8.	**does**	*She does not have a white shirt.*	dŏz	1	doe<u>s</u>
9.	**may**	*Thomas may join us for dinner.*	mā	1	ma<u>y</u>
10.	**might**	*We might go to the fair.*	mīt	1	mi<u>ght</u>
11.	**will**	*Evelyn will be at the party.*	wĭl	1	will
12.	**decide**	*We will need to decide soon.*	dē sīd	2	dē cīd<u>e</u>
13.	**decision**	*What is your decision?*	dē sĭ zhŏn	3	dē ci <u>sion</u>
14.	**controlling**	*What is controlling the temperature in this room.*	cŏn trōl lĭng	3	con trōl <u>ling</u>
15.	**tomorrow**	*Tomorrow we will go to the fair.*	tö mŏr rō	3	tö mor <u>row</u>

Spelling Hints	Part of Speech	Vocabulary Development
Say to spell /bēn/. Underline /ē/. For some people this is a say to spell word. Exaggerate the long /ē/ sound.	V	
Underline the /ŭ/ and put an x over it. /ow-ō-oo-ŭ/ said a sound that is an exception. Double underline the silent L.	V	
Underline the /ŭ/ and put an x over it. /ow-ō-oo-ŭ/ said a sound that is an exception. Double underline the silent L.	V	
Underline /sh/. Underline the /ŭ/ and put an x over it. /ow-ō-oo-ŭ/ said a sound that is an exception. Double underline the silent L.	V	
Underline the /v/ once and the silent final E twice. **12.2** English words do not end in V or U.	V	has, had, having
Put two dots over the /ö/. /ŏ-ō-ö/ said its third sound.	V	does, did, done, doing
Say to spell /dŏn/. Underline the silent final E twice. **12.9** Unseen reason.	V	
I do. He does. She does. It does. Add an ES to "do" to form does. Put a 2 over /s-z/. /s-z/ said its second sound /z/.	V	
Underline /ā/.	V	dismay, maybe
Underline /ī/. **28** Phonograms ending in GH are used only at the end of a base word or before the letter T. The GH is either silent or pronounced /f/.	V	
30 We often double F, L, and S after a single vowel at the end of a base word. Occasionally other letters also are doubled.	V	
Put a line over the /ē/. **4** A E O U usually say their names at the end of the syllable. Put a line over the /ī/ and double underline the silent final E. **12.1** The vowel says its name because of the E. **1** C softens to /s/ when followed by an E, I, or Y.	V	decided, decidedly, decider, undecided, deciding
Say to spell /dē sǐ zhŏn/. Put a line over the /ē/. **4** A E O U usually say their names at the end of the syllable. **1** C softens to /s/ when followed by an I. Underline /zh/. SI said /zh/ because of the voiced /d/ in decide. **17** SI is used only at the beginning of any syllable after the first one.	N	decisions, decisional, indecision
O said its long sound for no reason. Underline /ng/.	V	controlled, controller, controllable, controls, decontrol, decontrolling, noncontrollable, uncontrollable, overcontrol
Put two dots over the /ö/. /ŏ-ō-ö/ said its third sound. Underline /ō/ and put a 2 over it. /ow-ō/ said its second sound.	Adv	

PART THREE

Materials Needed: Red, green, and yellow colored pencils.

Grammar

Review

What is a noun? A noun is the name of a person, place, thing, or idea.

What are the six noun jobs? subject noun, direct object, indirect object, predicate noun, noun or direct address, object of the preposition

What is an adjective? Adjectives modify nouns and pronouns. Adjectives answer: What kind? How many? Which one? Whose?

What is an article? A, An, The. Tiny article adjectives that mark nouns and answer the question: Which?

Name the parts of a sentence. A sentence must have a capital letter, subject, verb, complete thought, and an end mark.

What is a verb? A verb shows action, links a description to the subject, or helps another verb.

What is an adverb? An adverb modifies a verb, adjective, or another adverb. An adverb answers: How? When? Where? To what extent?

What is a preposition? A preposition connects a noun or a pronoun to the rest of the sentence.

✎ *Spelling List 34 – **There is only one word in today's spelling list that is a noun. What is one way to test words to see if they are nouns?** * See if the word makes sense with "the _____."
What is the noun? decision
Label it with an N.
Write the plural form decisions.

✎ *Spelling List 34 – **There is one word in the list that is an adverb. It answers the question: When?*** * tomorrow
Label the adverb, Adv.
The rest of the words are verbs. Label them V for verb. You do not need to write the past tense form today.

Optional Spelling Cards

1. Dictate the words in List 34 for the students to write on index cards. Ⓚ Ⓥ Ⓐ

2. Ask the students to color a green border around the verbs, a red border around the nouns, and a yellow border around the adverbs. If a word can be used as more than one part of speech, color two borders. Ⓚ Ⓥ

Helping Verbs

Yesterday we learned that sometimes a main verb has a helping verb.

There are 23 helping verbs in English.

✎ *34.6 Helping Verb List –* **I will dictate the helping verbs. After you write the helping verbs in your workbook, I will write them on the board. In your workbook, begin by writing down the first column.**

am
is
are
was
were
be
being
been

Now write the next three words down the second column.

am	have
is	has
are	had
was	
were	
be	
being	
been	

Now write the next three words down the third column.

am	have	do
is	has	does
are	had	did
was		
were		
be		
being		
been		

Go down to the second table. In the first column write:

may
might
must

In the second column write:

may	*should*
might	*could*
must	*would*

In the third column write:

may	*should*	*can*
might	*could*	*will*
must	*would*	*shall*

How are all the helping verbs in the first column related? They are all forms of the "to be" verb.
How are the words in the second column related? They are all forms of the verb "to have."
How are all the words in the third column related? They are all forms of the verb "to do."
How about the fourth column? They all begin with M.
How about the fifth column? They all are spelled OULD, and they rhyme.
The sixth column? They are not related.

Let's recite the helping verbs together.

Use each of these words in a sentence out loud.

✎ *34.7 Helping Verbs – Helping verbs help other verbs. Using the chart in your workbook, form sentences aloud using a helping verb and another verb.*

Irregular Present Tense Verbs

I will write a chart on the board to review how to form the present tense verbs. Help me fill it in.

	First Person I	Second Person you	Third Person he, she, it	Plural we, they
decide				
control				

Do we need to add anything to "decide" in the first person? No. I decide.
How about the second person? No. You decide.
How about third person? Yes, we add an -s. He decides. She decides. It decides.
Do we add anything to form the plural? no

Continue with the word *control.*

	First Person I	Second Person you	Third Person he, she, it	Plural we, they
decide	I decide	you decide	he decides	we decide
control	I control	you control	he controls	we control

What rule are we following? To make a verb third person singular, add the ending -S, unless the word hisses or changes, then add -ES. Only four verbs are irregular.

An irregular verb does not follow the rule to add an -S to form the third person singular. Today we will learn the four irregular verbs in the present tense in English. They are: be, have, do and go.

	First Person I	Second Person you	Third Person he, she, it	Plural we, they
be				
have				
do				
go				

Help me to fill in the chart on the board.

	First Person I	Second Person you	Third Person he, she, it	Plural we, they
be	am	are	is	are
have	have	have	has	have
do	do	do	does	do
go	go	go	goes	go

What do you notice about each of the Third Person verbs? They all end in -S.

✎ *34.8 Irregular Verbs – Complete the sentences in the workbook with the correct form of the irregular verb.*

Future Tense

Today we will learn how to form the future tense.

We decide the answer.

How do we change this sentence to talk about the future? We will decide the answer.

We will decide the answer.

What did we do to change the sentence from present to future? add the word will

They walked.

Change this sentence to the future.

They will walk.

Future tense is simple to form in English.

✎ *34.9 Future Tense –* **Change each of the sentences in your workbook to future tense.**

Identifying the Parts of Speech in Sentences

✎ *34.10 Identifying Parts of Speech –* **Label the parts of speech as I write them on the board.**

The judge will decide the case on Monday.

Who will decide? judge, subject noun
Which judge? the, article adjective
What is being said about the judge? judge will decide, verb
Notice that the verb is comprised of two words. Which word shows the action? decide
What is "will?" helping verb
Decide what? case, direct object
Which case? the, article adjective
What is "on"? preposition
On what? Monday, object of the preposition
Is there a direct object receiving the action of the verb? yes, transitive verb
Put parentheses around the prepositional phrase.
Divide the complete subject from the complete predicate.

```
 A   SN      HV  TV  A  DO  P   OP
The judge / will decide the case (on Monday.)
```

We will go on vacation soon.

Who will go? we, subject pronoun

What is being said about we? we will go, verb

Notice that the verb is comprised of two words. Which word shows the action? go

What part of speech is the word "will?" helping verb

What is "on"? preposition

On what? vacation, object of the preposition

When ~~we~~ will we go? soon, adverb

Put parentheses around the prepositional phrase.

What question does "on vacation" answer? "Go where?"

The prepositional phrase "on vacation" is modifying the verb, "go." It is acting like an adverb.

Divide the complete subject from the complete predicate.

```
 SP    HV   V    P     OP        Adv
We  /  will go (on vacation) soon.
```

The noises across the hall will stop tomorrow.

What will stop? noises, subject noun

Which noises? the, article adjective

What is being said about noises? noises will stop, verb

What is the helping verb? will

What is the word "across"? preposition

Across what? hall, object of the preposition

Which hall? the, article adjective

Stop when? tomorrow, adverb

Put parentheses around the prepositional phrase.

Divide the complete subject from the complete predicate.

```
 A    SN      P    A   OP      HV  V   Adv
The noises (across the hall) / will stop tomorrow.
```

What changes when we write the sentence like this:

The noises will stop across the hall tomorrow.

It means the noises will be stationed across the hall, not that the noises across the hall will cease.

Optional Grammar Practice

1. Write the helping verbs on the board. Practice reciting them. Erase one. See if students can still recite the list. Continue erasing one each time until students can recite the list of helping verbs from memory. Ⓚ Ⓥ Ⓐ

2. Write a date in the future on the board. (For example, Saturday, December 31st, tomorrow...) Ask students, "What will you do ____?" Students may answer the question aloud using the future tense or write answers on paper. Ⓚ Ⓥ Ⓐ Ⓒ

3. Play Rummy Sentence using the Spelling Cards. Shuffle the Spelling Cards together. Deal seven cards to each player. Put the remaining cards in a draw pile face down. Students look at their cards. If they can make a complete sentence they lay down the cards in front of them. Two word sentences are worth 2 points, three words sentences 4 points, four word sentences 6 points, five word sentences 8 points, and six and more word sentences 10 points. Ⓚ Ⓥ Ⓐ Ⓒ

4. Write sentences using the irregular present tense verbs. Illustrate each sentence. Ⓚ Ⓥ Ⓒ

Vocabulary Development

Contractions

Today we will learn how to form contractions with the words: have, would, and will.

I + will =

What contraction is formed with the words I and will? I'll
Which sounds are left out? /w/ and /ĭ/.
The sounds which are omitted are replaced by an apostrophe.

I + will = I'll

she + will =

What contraction is formed with she and will? she'll

she + will = she'll

The contractions formed with "will" follow a pattern. What is the pattern? The W and I are replaced by an apostrophe.

✎ *34.11 Contractions – **Write the contractions formed with "will" in your workbook.***

I'll	he'll	it'll	they'll
you'll	she'll	we'll	

I + would =

How do we contract or shorten I would? I'd
Which letters are not heard? W O U L

I + would = I'd

they + would =

How do we form the contraction for "they would?" Write "they apostrophe D." Drop the W O U L.

they + would = they'd

What is the pattern for contractions using "would?" The W O U L is replaced with an apostrophe.

✎ *34.12 Contractions –* **Write the contractions formed with "would" in your workbook.**

I'd	he'd	it'd	they'd
you'd	she'd	we'd	

I + have =

How do we write the contracted form of "I have?" I've – Drop the H A and add an apostrophe.

I + have = I've

you + have =

What is the contraction for you have? you've – Drop the H A and add an apostrophe.

you + have = you've

We do not say "she have" or "he have." How does the word "have" change with the words he/she/it? He has. She has. It has.

What is the pattern for forming a contraction using "have?" Drop the H A and add an apostrophe.

✎ *34.13 Contractions –* **Write the contractions formed with "have" in your workbook.**

I've	they've
you've	
she's	
he's	
it's	
we've	

Optional Vocabulary Practice

✎ *34.14 Extra Practice: Contractions* – Play a matching game with the contractions in the book. Ⓥ Ⓚ Ⓐ Ⓒ

- Game 1 - Direct the students to cut out the cards and find the matching pairs.

- Game 2 - Flip all the cards upside down and play memory.

- Game 3 - Give one or two cards to each student. Direct them to find people who have the matching pair.

- Game 4 - Do not cut out the cards. Draw lines between the contractions and the phrases they represent.

Dictation

✎ *34.15 Dictation* – **Today's dictation will be a story. Rather than writing it as numbered sentences, I want you to write it as a paragraph. Make sure to indent the first line. I will read each sentence aloud two times. Repeat it back to me before you write it. When you are finished, I will read the next sentence.**

We heard a loud noise. Bang! Suddenly a tree fell to the ground. A runner was trapped. We helped him out from under the branches. We brought him to the hospital.

Composition

✎ *34.16 Composition* – Complete the sentences in your own words, using the sentence starters.

Lesson 35 — Assessment & Review

Materials Needed: red colored pencil.

1.   ✎   *35.1 Assessment* – Dictate the sentences to the students while they write them in their workbook.

    1. Do not forget the surprise party begins at twelve o'clock.

    2. "You'll receive the medicine from the hospital tomorrow," said Dr. Tom.

    3. The window near the ceiling is open and should be closed.

    4. Please turn off the lights beside the table.

    5. Our team races at the field across the street from the store.

    6. He's looking for the presents under the tree.

    7. The family will drive through the mountains tomorrow on their vacation.

    8. The winners could make the decision.

    9. The loud noises across the street suddenly stopped.

    10. He took the uncontrollable dog out of the house, around the corner, and toward the park.

2.   Direct the students to read the phrases aloud while you write them on the board. Sound out each word and model the thought process. The students should mark corrections in red. Encourage the students to discuss what they missed.

3.   Recheck the students' work. Note the words and concepts which need further practice.

4.   Did the students:

    _____ **use CEI correctly?**
    _____ **spell words ending in one vowel and one consonant correctly?**
    _____ **write contractions correctly?**

5.   ✎   *35.2 Reading* – Ask the students to read the following sentences. Note the words they did not read fluently.

    1. His mother said, "The decision was his alone."

    2. The water poured over the tub, down the stairs, around the corner, and out the door.

    3. He prefers fixing his own car.

    4. His apartment is above the store.

    5. I do not have any toothpaste left.

    6. She has been to that school.

    7. The land in Holland is below sea level.

    8. We live between two white houses.

    9. There are many sharp pieces of glass by the swing.

    10. She does not understand the answer.

    11. The students have done wonderful work this year.

    12. You might enjoy the books on the shelves.

    13. He said the program would start at eight o'clock.

6. ✎ *35.3 Words to Practice* – Ask the students to read the words in the list and mark which ones they would like to practice further.

7. Using the assessment and your knowledge as a teacher, identify words to dictate onto Spelling Word Cards.

1. ___ above	21. ___ for	41. ___ receive
2. ___ across	22. ___ forgetful	42. ___ sea
3. ___ any	23. ___ from	43. ___ several
4. ___ around	24. ___ have	44. ___ should
5. ___ been	25. ___ hospital	45. ___ stopped
6. ___ beginner	26. ___ look	46. ___ store
7. ___ below	27. ___ many	47. ___ suddenly
8. ___ beside	28. ___ may	48. ___ surprise
9. ___ between	29. ___ medicine	49. ___ team
10. ___ by	30. ___ might	50. ___ through
11. ___ ceiling	31. ___ mountain	51. ___ to
12. ___ controlling	32. ___ near	52. ___ tomorrow
13. ___ could	33. ___ noise	53. ___ took
14. ___ decide	34. ___ of	54. ___ toward
15. ___ decision	35. ___ off	55. ___ under
16. ___ do	36. ___ out	56. ___ vacation
17. ___ does	37. ___ over	57. ___ will
18. ___ done	38. ___ prefer	58. ___ window
19. ___ down	39. ___ present	59. ___ winner
20. ___ fix	40. ___ race	60. ___ would

SPELLING WORD REVIEW

1. Dictate the missed words onto Spelling Word Cards or index cards. Have the students highlight the part of the word that was difficult.

2. Choose from the review activities below or use another activity found in the *The Phonogram and Spelling Game Book.*

Optional: Spelling Word Practice

1. ✎ *35.4 Extra Practice: Word Search* – Create a Spelling Word Search. Dictate ten spelling words. The students write them in the grid and then fill in letters to hide the words. When finished, have the students exchange papers to find the words. (*The Phonogram and Spelling Game Book,* 52)

2. Write a sentence which uses the spelling words. Challenge students to find how many they can incorporate into one sentence.

3. Play You're My Editor (*The Phonogram and Spelling Game Book,* 56).

OPTIONAL SPELLING RULE REVIEW

Materials Needed: Spelling Rule Cards 14, 17, and 18; paper, pencil; whiteboard, marker, eraser; magnetic letters; Phonogram Game Cards.

Use the following mini-lessons to review as needed.

Spelling Rule 14

Spelling Rule	14
Double the last consonant when adding a vowel suffix to words ending in one vowel followed by one consonant, only if the syllable before the suffix is accented.	

1. Review the rule by reciting it and discussing the examples on the back of the card.

2. Write one syllable words on the board and practice adding suffixes as follows:

win + er = winner

run + ing = running

stop + ed = stopped

cap + s = caps (Do not double the last consonant because it is not a vowel suffix.)

pup + y = puppy

fun + y = funny

ship + ment = shipment (Do not double the last consonant because it is not a vowel suffix.)

fix + ed = fixed (Do not double the last consonant because X sounds like two consonants, K and S)

get + ing = getting

3. ✎ *35.5 Extra Practice: Adding Suffixes* – Complete the activity in the workbook.

4. Review finding the accent in multi-syllable words.

> **How do we find the accented syllable?** Listen for the strongest beat, or place your hand under your chin and feel which syllable the mouth drops open farther.
>
> ✎ *35.6 Extra Practice: Accent –* **Read the words in your workbook aloud. Mark the accented syllable.**

o' pen

for get'

buck' et

con trol'

ca' ter

com mit'

be gin'

cous' in

bul' le tin

pref' er ence

to mor' row

sud' den ly

> When adding a suffix to a multi-syllable word ending in one vowel and then one consonant, you must know where the accent is in the derivative. If we are adding a vowel suffix and the accent is on the syllable before the suffix, the consonant is doubled.

control + ing = con trol' ling

commit + ment = com mit' ment

(Do not double the last consonant because it is not a vowel suffix.)

commit + ing = com mit' ting

begin + er = be gin' ner

open + ed = o' pened

(Do not double the last consonant because the accent is not on the syllable before the suffix.)

> ✎ *35.7 Extra Practice: Adding Suffixes –* **Practice adding suffixes to multi-syllable words ending in one vowel followed by one consonant with the activity in the workbook.**

Answer key: 1. opener 2. committing 3. committee 4. controlled 5. controls 6. beginner 7. beginning 8. forgetting 9. forgetful 10. equipped 11. equipment 12. preferred 13. preference 14. preferable 15. medalist

5. Play the Adding Suffixes Game. Provide the students with white boards, markers, and erasers. Write a word on the board. Set a timer for one minute. Challenge the students to write as many derivatives as they can think of. Give one point for each word spelled correctly. Play to 30 points, or play a set number of words and see who has the most points.

drum	drip	hop	step
listen	zip	stop	net
begin	open	forget	control
fun	commit	limit	
run	offer	equip	

Adding a Suffix to Any Word

1.   ✎ *35.8 Extra Practice: Adding Suffixes Flow Chart* – Read through the chart. Discuss the various questions together.

I will write a word and a suffix on the board. Using the questions on the Flow Chart, tell me how to write the derivative. Then I will write it on the board.

l. ready + ness = readiness

"Ready" ends in single vowel Y. The suffix begins with a letter other than I. Therefore, we change the Y to I and add the suffix.

2. race + ing = racing

"Race" ends in a silent final E. The suffix begins with a vowel. Dropping the E is allowed by other spelling rules. Therefore, drop the E and add the suffix.

3. forget + ing = forgetting

"Forget" ends in one vowel followed by one consonant. The suffix begins with a vowel. The accent is on the syllable before the suffix. Therefore, double the last consonant before adding the suffix.

4. receive + er = receiever

"Receive" ends in a silent final E. The suffix begins with a vowel. Dropping the E is allowed by other spelling rules. Therefore, drop the E then add the suffix.

5. baby + es = babies

"Baby" ends in single vowel Y. The suffix begins with a vowel. Therefore, we change the Y to I and add the suffix.

6. service + able = serviceable

"Service" ends in a silent final E. The suffix begins with a vowel. Dropping the E is not allowed by other spelling rules. C softens to /s/ only before an E, I or Y. Therefore, retain the E and add the suffix.

✎ *35.9 Extra Practice: Adding A Suffix to Any Word* – *I will say a word that has a suffix added. Write the word in your workbook.*

1. **begins**
2. **ceilings**
3. **flying**
4. **controllable**
5. **deciding**
6. **heaviness**
7. **downer**
8. **fixing**
9. **unforgettable**
10. **stories**
11. **looked**
12. **mighty**

13. *mightiness*

14. *noisy*

15. *preferred*

16. *racing*

Spelling Rules 17 and 18

Spelling Rule	17
TI, CI, and SI are used only at the beginning of any syllable after the first one.	

Spelling Rule	18
SH spells /sh/ at the beginning of a base word and at the end of a syllable. SH never spells /sh/ at the beginning of any syllable after the first one, except for the ending -ship.	

1. Review the rules by reciting them and discussing the samples on the backs of the cards.

2. Remind the students to look to the roots to discover which Latin spelling of /sh/ is used. Say a word. Ask the students to name the root. Direct them to call out the base word and which Latin spelling of /sh/ is used in the derivative. *physician, partial, facial, confession, recession, commercial, Egyptian, clinician, exception, recession, election, confidential, infectious, racial, official, discussion, progression, tension*

3. Demonstrate how words that end in a voiced /d/ sound will be spelled with the voiced /ZH/ spelled SI. *divide - division, explode - explosion, conclude - conclusion*

4. Play the /sh/ Game. Say a word that uses SH, TI, SI, or CI to spell /sh/. Direct the students to write on a white board which spelling of /sh/ is used. Award one point per correct answer. Award one point for reciting the reason. Play to 10, 15 or 20 points.

   - **TI** – *action, intimidation, mitigation, motivation, adoption, deletion, creation, dilution, Egyptian, ignition, addiction, education, vibration, violation, direction, invention*

   - **SI** – *depression, discussion, impression, profession, compression, confession, expression, obsession, regression, transgression, confusion, tension*

   - **CI** – *racial, physician, clinician, mathematician, politician, technician, musician, facial, spacial*

   - **SH at the end of the word** – *fish, fresh, ash, blush, brash, bush, brush, clash, cherish, dash, crush, dish, foolish, gash, wash, push, rush, finish, slush, slash, leash, wish, marsh*

   - **SH at the beginning of the word** – *shadow, shade, shack, shaft, shady, shake, shall, shallow, shamble, shame, shampoo, shape, share, shark, sheriff, sharp, shawl, sheep, sheet, shell, shift, ship, shirt, shoe, shop, shore, shower, show, shrimp, shrink, shrub, shut, shuffle, shy, shuttle*

   - **Words that use the ending -ship** – *battleship, citizenship, authorship, relationship, horsemanship, readership, worship, warship, workmanship*

OPTIONAL GRAMMAR REVIEW

Contractions

> **Grammar Card 14.1**   **Apostrophe**
>
> **Use an apostrophe to denote the sound(s) omitted from a contraction.**

1. Review how to form contractions, demonstrating that the apostrophe replaces the sound that is omitted.

   I + will = I'll

   they + have = they've

   we + would = we'd

   he + would = he'd

   ✎ *35.10 Extra Practice: Contractions –* **Write the contraction.**

OPTIONAL PHONOGRAM ASSESSMENT & REVIEW

Phonograms

✎ *35.11 Phonogram Quiz –* Dictate the phonograms.

1. a	16. ur	31. oo
2. tch	17. f	32. ui
3. ough	18. au	33. l
4. b	19. g	34. ch
5. kn	20. ear	35. m
6. ow	21. wh	36. wor
7. c	22. h	37. ar
8. gn	23. igh	38. n
9. gu	24. ed	39. oy
10. ou	25. i	40. wr
11. d	26. oe	41. o
12. ir	27. j	42. oi
13. augh	28. ew	43. p
14. e	29. oa	44. ph
15. aw	30. k	45. ay

46. qu	56. eigh	66. ng
47. ai	57. u	67. ie
48. ei	58. cei	68. x
49. r	59. er	69. ee
50. sh	60. v	70. y
51. s	61. si	71. ti
52. ey	62. bu	72. ck
53. ea	63. dge	73. z
54. t	64. th	74. ci
55. or	65. w	

Optional Phonogram Practice

Practice the phonograms as needed using the following game suggestions or choose other games from *The Logic of English Phonogram and Spelling Game Book.*

1. ✎ *35.12 Phonogram Tic-Tac-Toe* (*The Phonogram and Spelling Game Book, 26*).

2. Practice the phonograms with Blind Writing (*The Phonogram and Spelling Game Book,* 23).

3. Play Team Up! using the Phonogram Game Cards (*The Phonogram and Spelling Game Book,* 14).

Lesson 36

Phonograms:	I says /ē/
Exploring Sounds:	Syllable Types
Spelling Rules:	7
Grammar:	Questions

PART ONE

Materials Needed: Phonogram Flash Cards from previous lessons, `i` and `y` ; Spelling Rule Card 7; Phonogram Game Cards.

Phonograms

Review

1. Drill the phonograms with flash cards.

2. ✎ *36.1 Phonogram Practice* – Dictate the following phonograms. For extra practice, have the students read them back. Write the correct answers on the board as the students check their answers.

1. ph	8. igh	15. wr
2. wor	9. oa	16. ti
3. ui	10. oe	17. si
4. ew	11. ei	18. ci
5. ow	12. ey	19. dge
6. ou	13. eigh	20. ie
7. ough	14. cei	

3. Play Dragon using the Phonogram Game Cards (*The Phonogram and Spelling Game Book,* 10).

Exploring Sounds

I says the Long /ē/ Sound

Show ☐ i *.*

What are the sounds of I? /ĭ-ī-ē-y/

Show ☐ y *.*

What are the sounds of y? /y-ĭ-ī-ē/

When does Y say the long /ē/ sound? at the end of a multi-syllable word
What happens to Y when we are adding a suffix? It changes to I.
What does the I say in these words? long /ē/

✎ *36.2 I says Long /ē/ – Read the words in your workbook aloud. Underline the suffix.*

fuzziest   *curlier*   *juicier*   *pickier*

Each of these words has had a suffix added to it. What letter did each of the base words end with? Y
What did the Y change to? I
What sound is I saying in each of these words? long /ē/

In Latin and in most Latin-based languages I says /ē/. When you see an I written in Latin, Italian, or Spanish it says /ē/.
In the 1400s English had a Great Vowel Shift which changed how we pronounce the vowels compared to other languages which use the same alphabet.

Say /ĭ/ and /ē/. What do you notice about the position of your mouth? It is the same, except the lips are pulled back more and more tense with /ē/ and the mouth is more relaxed with /ĭ/.

Since /ĭ/ and /ē/ are related sounds, you can see how the pronunciation may have shifted over time.

In words that have been imported into English, I sometimes retains the pronunciation /ē/. There are two primary places in words where I says the long /ē/ sound.

✎ *36.3 Foreign Words Ending in I – Read the words in your workbook. Where is I saying /ē/?*

ravioli   *broccoli*   *safari*   *salami*
chili   *ski*   *taxi*   *spaghetti*

I says /ē/ at the end of the word.
What is wrong with these words? English words do not end in I.
These words are all imports from other languages. Sometimes the original spelling is retained. There are very few words that fall into this category and they are all foreign. When you see a word that ends in I, you instantly know it is not an English word. Most of the time the I will say /ē/ at the end of the word.

✎ *36.4 I says Long /ē/ – Read the words in your workbook aloud with me. Slashes have been put between each syllable. Try to discover when I says the long /ē/ sound.*

me/di /um

he /li /um

ra/di/o

pat/i/o

stud/i/o

sta/di/um

am/phib/i/an

bac/ter/i/a

ab/bre/vi/a/tion

mem/or/i/al

mil/len/ni/um

his/tor/i/an

im/me/di/ate/ly

I says the long /ē/ sound at the end of the syllable before another vowel. It is always before the vowels A, O, U.

Spelling Rule   7

Y says long /ē/ only at the end of a multi-syllable word. I says long /ē/ only at the end of a syllable that is followed by a vowel.

Reading & Spelling Multi-Syllable Words

Today we will learn strategies to read multi-syllable words.

Before we begin, I want us to think about the parts of words.
What are the parts of a word? sounds/phonograms blended together, consonants, vowels, roots, suffixes, prefixes, syllables
What are the rhythmic beats of words called? syllables
Why do we need to know about syllables? Syllables tell us how to pronounce vowels. Single vowels are short in the middle of the syllable and long at the end of the syllable. Syllables limit the use of some phonograms.

Today we will learn tips for dividing a word into syllables and demonstrate how this helps to read long words.
What type of sound forms a syllable, a consonant or a vowel? vowel

Let's look together at some words and discover the types of vowels that are found and how the vowels affect the syllable.

I will write a word. Tell me the vowels and what you know about them by looking at the word.

sudden

The vowels are U and E. The vowels both say their short sounds.
Since there are two vowels, how many syllables are there? two
Where would you divide the syllable? between the D's
Why do they say their short sounds? U and E say their short sounds because they are in the middle of the syllable. A E O U usually say their names at the end of the syllable.

sud/den

> *Sudden demonstrates our first syllable type: a closed syllable. A closed syllable is one that ends in a consonant, thereby closing the vowel off from being at the end. When the syllable is closed, a single vowel in the syllable says its short sound.*
>
> ***What was the clue that the first vowel would be short?*** The syllable divides between the double consonants.

Vowel	Syllable Type	Hint
Single, short	*Closed*	*Double consonant*

> *A single vowel says its short sound in a closed syllable. One clue that a syllable is closed is a double consonant.*

pattern

> ***What are the vowels?*** The vowels are A and E. The U is short and the E is next to an R, so it says /er/.
> ***How many syllables?*** two
> ***Where would you divide the syllables?*** Between the T's.

pat/tern

> ***What type of syllable is the first syllable "pat?"*** It is a closed syllable, so the A says its short sound.
> ***Why does the E say /er/?*** It is next to an R.
> *Vowels next to an R are called R-controlled vowels. Though we often cannot hear the vowel clearly, R-controlled vowels still form another syllable.*

Vowel	Syllable	Hint
Single, short	*Closed*	*Double consonant*
R controlled	*R controlled*	*Vowel next to an R*

> *An R-controlled vowel is next to an R. It will say /er/.*

explain

> ***What are the vowels?*** The vowels are E and AI. The E is short and the AI says /ā/.
> ***How many syllables?*** two
> ***Where would you divide the syllables?*** Between the X and P
> ***What type of syllable is the first syllable "ex?"*** It is a closed syllable, so the E says its short sound.

ex/plain

> *AI is a multi-letter phonogram working together to make a single vowel sound. We will call this a multi-letter vowel syllable.*

Vowel	Syllable	Hint
Single, short	Closed	Double consonant
R controlled	R controlled	Vowel near an R
Multi-letter	Multi-letter Vowel	Multi-letter vowel phonogram

When you see a phonogram that looks like a multi-letter vowel phonogram, it may be a syllable with a multi-letter vowel.

little

What are the vowels? I and E. The I is short and the E is silent.
How many syllables? two
Where do you divide the syllables? between the T's

lit/tle

What type of syllable is the first syllable "lit?" It is a closed syllable, so the I says its short sound.
What is occurring in the last syllable? The L sound is somewhat like a vowel, so the E is added for the syllable.
Let's review the nine reasons for a silent final E. It makes make the vowel say its name, prevents a V or a U from being at the end, softens a C to /s/ or a G to /j/, ensures every syllable has a vowel, keeps a singular word from looking plural, makes the TH say its voiced sound /TH/, makes a word look bigger, distinguishes homophones, or may be present for an unseen reason.

When reading words, we need to be aware of final syllables with a silent final E. We will call these syllables Silent E syllables.

Vowel	Syllable	Hint
Single, short	Closed	Double consonant
R controlled	R controlled	Vowel near an R
Multi-letter	Multi-letter vowel	Multi-letter vowel phonogram
Silent E	Silent Final E	Word ending in E

table

What are the vowels? The vowels are A and E. The A is long and the E is silent.
How many syllables? two
Where do we divide the syllables? between the A and the B.

ta/ble

What type of syllable is the first syllable "ta?" The vowel is long because it is at the end of the syllable.
Which rule does this follow? A E O U usually say their names at the end of the syllable.

We will call this an open syllable. An open syllable ends in a vowel.

Vowel	Syllable	Hint
Single, short	Closed	Double consonant
R controlled	R controlled	Vowel near an R
Multi-letter	Multi-letter vowel	Multi-letter vowel phonogram
Silent E	Silent Final E	Word ending in E
Single, long	Open	

Now we will use this information to read two multi-syllable words.

illustrate

What are the vowels? I, U, A, and silent final E.
Beginning in the direction of reading and writing, where do you think the first syllable will break? between the L's

il/lustrate

What does the first syllable say? /ĭl/

Do you think the next syllable will break right after the U? no
Why not? There are three consonants following it, so it probably breaks between them.
So will the U be short or long? short
What will the next syllable say? /lŭs/ or /lŭst/

> Teacher Tip: *Do not be picky here. The goal is for the students to learn a strategy to decode. By reading the vowel sound correctly the exact place of the syllable break will not hinder their ability to read the word.*

il/lus/trate

Does the E make a new syllable? no
Why? It is a silent final E and it is not before an L so it must be there for one of the other reasons.
Why would you guess it is there? It is there to make the A say its name.
What does the last syllable say? /trāte/
Blend the whole word together. /ĭl lŭs trāte/ — illustrate

environment

How many vowels are there? four, E, I, O, E
How many syllables? four
Beginning in the direction of reading and writing, where do you think the first syllable will break? between the N and the V.
What does the first syllable say? /ĕn/
Why is the vowel short? It is a closed syllable.

en/vironment

> *After the second vowel there is only one consonant. Usually, if there is one consonant it goes with the next syllable, though this is not always true. What does the second syllable say?* /vī/ or /vĭ/. I may say /ĭ/ or /ī/ at the end of the syllable.

en/vi/ronment

> *Where will the next syllable divide?* between the N and M
> *What does the third syllable say?* /rŏn/
> *Why does O say its short sound?* The syllable is closed.

en/vi/ron/ment

> *What does the fourth syllable say?* /mĕnt/
> *Why does E say its short sound?* The syllable is closed.
>
> *What is the word?* /ĕn vī rŏn mĕnt/ — environment
>
> *This is a step-by-step approach to analyzing an unknown multi-syllable word.*

Spelling Rules

Optional Spelling Rule Practice

Review rules 1-30 using the Spelling Rule Flash Cards. Ⓥ Ⓐ

PART TWO

Using Spelling List 36 on pages 478-479, dictate each word following the steps included on pages Intro 42 - Intro 46.

Tips for Spelling List 36

What

Exaggerate the vowel so that /whət/ sounds like /whät/. The A is pronounced with a schwa sound /ə/ because the word "what" is a grammatical word which is not accented within the sentence (*Uncovering the Logic of English,* 126).

About

One of the difficulties with English spelling is that vowels in unaccented syllables often are pronounced as the schwa sound /ə/. In order to help students create an auditory picture of the word, it is helpful to exaggerate the unaccented vowel. Therefore exaggerate the vowel so that /ə bout/ sounds like /ā bout/.

To learn more about vowels in unaccented syllables and aiding students in creating an auditory picture of words, see *Uncovering the Logic of English,* 121-128.

PART THREE

Materials Needed: Grammar Cards 9.6, 9.9; Red, green, blue, yellow, and black colored pencils.

Grammar

Review

What is a noun? A noun is the name of a person, place, thing, or idea.

What are the six noun jobs? subject noun, direct object, indirect object, predicate noun, noun of direct address, object of the preposition

What is an adjective? Adjectives modify nouns and pronouns. Adjectives answer: What kind? How many? Which one? Whose?

What is an article? A, An, The. Tiny article adjectives that mark nouns and answer the question: Which?

Name the parts of a sentence. A sentence must have a capital letter, subject, verb, complete thought, and an end mark.

What is a verb? A verb shows action, links a description to the subject, or helps another verb.

What is an adverb? An adverb modifies a verb, adjective, or another adverb. An adverb answers: How? When? Where? To what extent?

What is a preposition? A preposition connects a noun or a pronoun to the rest of the sentence.

Question Words

Which words in today's spelling list are helpful for asking questions?

why	*where*	*who*	*which*
when	*what*	*how*	*whose*

What do you notice about these words? WH is used in almost all the question words.

WH is not a common phonogram. However, it is used in all the question words.

Use each of the question words in a sentence aloud.

✎ 36.5 *Question Words* – **Write the question words in your workbook.**

Questions

What are the three types of sentences we have learned so far? statements, commands, and exclamations

The fourth sentence type is the question. Sentences that ask a question are sometimes called interrogative sentences.

What does it mean to interrogate someone? Interrogate means to ask lots of questions.

	Word	Practice Sentence	Say to Spell	# of Syllables	Markings
1.	**why**	*Why do we need to add the sugar first?*	whī	1	w<u>hy</u>
2.	**when**	*When will they be here?*	whĕn	1	<u>wh</u>en
3.	**where**	*Where is my coat?*	whĕr	1	<u>wh</u>er<u>e</u>
4.	**what**	*What time is it?*	whät	1	whät
5.	**who**	*Who is coming over?*	whö	1	<u>wh</u>ö
6.	**how**	*How long do I need to practice?*	how	1	h<u>ow</u>
7.	**which**	*Which color do you think looks best?*	whĭch	1	<u>wh</u>i<u>ch</u>
8.	**whose**	*Whose house is it at?*	whöz	1	<u>wh</u>ös<u>e</u>²
9.	**medium**	*My daughter wears a medium.*	mē dē ŭm	3	mē di um
10.	**believe**	*Do you believe in Santa Claus?*	bē lēv	2	bē l<u>ie</u>v<u>e</u>
11.	**impossible**	*I think it is impossible.*	ĭm pŏs sĭ bl	4	im pos si b<u>le</u>
12.	**radio**	*Please turn up the volume on the radio.*	rā dē ō	3	rā di ō
13.	**about**	*We learned about reptiles in science class today.*	ā̄ bout	2	ā̄ b<u>ou</u>t
14.	**before**	*We need to eat lunch before we go.*	bē for	2	bē f<u>or</u>e
15.	**after**	*I need to go to work after breakfast.*	ăf ter	2	af t<u>er</u>

Spelling Hints	Part of Speech	Vocabulary Development
Underline /wh/. **6** When a one-syllable word ends in single vowel Y, it says /ī/.	Adv	
Underline /wh/.	Adv	whenever, whensoever
Underline /wh/. Underline the silent final E twice. **12.9** Unseen reason.	Adv	anywhere, elsewhere, everywhere, nowhere, somewhere, whereabouts, whereas, wheresoever, whereto, wherefore, wherewithal
Say to spell: /whăt/. Underline /wh/. Put two dots over the /ä/. /ă-ā-ä/ said its third sound.	Adv	somewhat, whatever, whatnot, whatsoever
Underline /wh/. Put two dots over the /ö/. /ŏ-ō-ö/ said its third sound.	Adv	whosoever, whose
Underline the /ow/.	Adv	however
Underline /wh/. Underline /ch/.	Adv	whichever
Underline /wh/. Put two dots over the /ö/. /ŏ-ō-ö/ said its third sound. Put a 2 over the /z/. /s-z/ said its second sound. Underline the silent final E twice. **12.9** Unseen reason.	Adv	
Draw a line over the /ē/. **4** A E O U usually say their names at the end of the syllable. **7** Y says long /ē/ only at the end of a multi-syllable word. I says long /ē/ only at the end of a syllable that is followed by a vowel.	Adj, N	
Draw a line over the /ē/. Draw a line under the second /ē/. Underline the /v/ once and the silent final E twice. **12.2** English words do not end in V or U.	V	believes, believing, believable, believably, believer, disbelieve, nonbeliever, unbelievable, unbelievingly
Underline the L. Double underline the silent final E. **12.4** Every syllable must have a vowel.	Adj	possible, impossibility, impossibly
Draw a line over the /ā/. **4** A E O U usually say their names at the end of the syllable. **7** Y says long /ē/ only at the end of a multi-syllable word. I says long /ē/ only at the end of a syllable that is followed by a vowel. Draw a line over the /ō/. **4** A E O U usually say their names at the end of the syllable.	N	radios
Say to spell /ā bout/. Put a line over the /ā/. A said the sound /ā/. **4** A E O U usually say their names at the end of the syllable. Underline /ou/.	P	hereabout, roundabout, runabout, thereabout, turnabout, whereabouts
Put a line over the /ē/. E said the sound /ē/. **4** A E O U usually say their names at the end of the syllable. Underline /or/. Double underline the silent final E. **12.9** Unseen reason.	P	beforehand
Underline /er/.	P	aftercare, afterglow, afterlife, afternoon, aftershave, aftershock, afterthought, afterward, hereafter, thereafter

---

Grammar Card 9.6

There are four types of sentences: statements, commands, exclamations, and questions.

Grammar Card 9.9   *Question*

A question ends with a question mark.

I will write a statement on the board. I want you to interrogate me about the statement. I will write your questions on the board.

Someone believes it is possible.

Who believes it is possible?

How is it possible?

Why do you believe it is possible?

When will it be possible?

What is possible?

Where is it possible?

Which one do they believe is possible?

Is it possible?

What punctuation mark is used at the end of a question? a question mark

Parts of Speech

✎ *Spelling List 36 –* **All of the question words are adverbs. Write a yellow Adv next to each one.**

✎ *Spelling List 36 –* **Label the part of speech for the remaining words in List 36.**

✎ *Spelling List 36 –* **Write the past tense of each verb and the plural form of each noun.**

Optional Spelling Cards

1. Dictate the words in List 36 for the students to write on index cards. Ⓚ Ⓥ Ⓐ

2. Ask the students to color a green border around verbs, a red border around nouns, a yellow border around adverbs, a blue border around adjectives, and a black border around prepositions. If a word can be used as more than one part of speech, color two borders. Ⓚ Ⓥ

Identifying Parts of Speech

✎ *36.6 Identifying Parts of Speech –* **Label the parts of speech in your workbook as I write them on the board.**

People will believe you.

Who believe? people, subject noun
What is being said about the people? people will believe, verb
Notice that the verb is comprised of two words. Which word shows the action? believe
What is "will?" helping verb
Believe whom? you, direct object
Is there a direct object receiving the action of the verb? yes, transitive verb
Divide the subject from the predicate.

SN   HV   TV   DO
People / will believe you.

We went on a lovely vacation with their family to the beach.

What is the subject of the sentence? we, subject pronoun
What is being said about we? we went, verb
What is the word "on?" preposition
On what? vacation, object of the preposition
Which vacation? a, article adjective
What kind of vacation? lovely, adjective
What is the word "with?" preposition
With whom? family, object of the preposition
Whose family? their, possessive pronoun adjective
What is the word "to?" preposition
To where? beach, object of the preposition
Which beach? the, article adjective
Put parentheses around the prepositional phrases.
Divide the subject from the predicate.

SP   V   P A Adj   OP   P PPA OP   P A OP
We / went (on a lovely vacation) (with their family) (to the beach.)

Eva will receive an award for her performance.

> **What is the subject of the sentence?** Eva, subject noun
> **What is being said about Eva?** Eva will receive, verb
> **Notice that the verb is comprised of two words. Which word shows the action?** receive
> **What is "will?"** helping verb
> **What will she receive?** award, direct object
> **Which award?** an, article adjective
> **What is "for"?** preposition
> **For what?** performance, object of the preposition
> **Whose performance?** her, possessive pronoun adjective
> **Is there a direct object receiving the action of the verb?** yes, transitive verb
> **Put parentheses around the prepositional phrase.**
> **Divide the subject from the predicate.**

```
 SN        HV  TV    A    DO    P   PNA       OP
Eva / will receive an award (for her performance.)
```

Challenge - Usage of Who and Whom

It is important to understand the correct usage of "who" and "whom." Though in many settings people misuse who in the place of whom, it is best to use them correctly at school and when applying for a job.

who   whom

> **To understand the usage of who and whom, let's mark the parts of speech in this sentence:**

Emma told David.

> **Who told?** Emma, subject noun
> **What is being said about Emma?** Emma told, verb
> **Whom did she tell?** David, direct object.

```
 SN   V    DO
Emma told David.
```

> **"Who" is used to ask about the subject of a sentence.**

Who told David?

Emma told him.

> **"Whom" is used to ask about the object, whether it is a direct object, indirect object, or object of the preposition.**

Whom did Emma tell?

Challenge - Usage of Who and Whom Continued

A trick to remember when to use "whom" is to use it if the answer "him" makes sense in the sentence.

Emma told him.

Notice that "him" and "whom" both end in the letter M.

We will now look at another example.
Tell me if I should use "who" or "whom."

_____ gave John the radio?

The answer is: "Who gave." They are asking about the subject of the sentence
We can see this by flipping the question around into a statement.

___He___ gave John the radio.

Could we say, "him gave?" no
What part of speech is "he" in this sentence? subject
Therefore we will use "who?" "Who" is used to ask about the subject of the sentence.

___Who___ gave John the radio?

About _____ did the official ask?

The answer is: "About whom did the official ask?" They are asking about the object of the preposition.
We can see this by flipping the question around into a statement.

The official asked about _____.

Could we say, "about him?" yes
What part of speech is "him" in this sentence? object of the preposition
Therefore we will use "whom?" "Whom" is used to ask about an object in the sentence.

The official asked about ___him___.

About ___whom___ did the official ask?

✎ *36.7 Who or Whom?* – **Complete the activity in the workbook.**

Answer key: 1. Who asked the question? 2. Whom did you invite to the party? 3. Before whom did you speak? 4. About whom was the book? 5. Who stole the radio? 6. Who believes this is the correct answer? 7. To whom it may concern

Composition

Writing Activity

Good writing answers questions and tells the reader a story or provides the reader information about something.

What do adjectives answer? What kind? How many? Which one? Whose?
What do adverbs answer? How? When? Where? To what extent?

I will write a simple sentence on the board. Then I will ask a question and I want you to add the answer to the sentence.

For example:

The family vacationed.

Where did the family vacation?

The family vacationed in Hawaii.

When did the family vacation?

Last year the family vacationed in Hawaii.

How did the family vacation?

Last year the family vacationed happily in Hawaii.

What kind of family vacationed?

Last year the close-knit family vacationed happily in Hawaii.

Expand each sentence by asking and answering questions.

1. Mother decided.

2. The workers transported.

3. Our son learned.

4. The officer acted.

✎ *36.8 Composition* – Write questions about the sentences in your workbook.

Vocabulary Development

Contractions Formed with Is

Tell me what contraction is formed and how to write it.

what + is =

What's. Drop the I and replace it with an apostrophe.

what + is = what's

Continue with the following words.

who + is = who's

there + is = there's

that + is = that's

Contractions Formed with Not

✎ *36.9 Contractions with Not – **Read the list of contractions in your workbook. What do you notice?** Each of them is formed with the word "not" and the O is replaced by an apostrophe.

weren't	*isn't*	*doesn't*	*won't*
hasn't	*couldn't*	*don't*	*didn't*
haven't	*can't*	*shouldn't*	
wasn't	*wouldn't*	*aren't*	

Look closely. Can you find one contraction that is an exception and does not follow the rule? won't

will + not = won't

This contraction is an exception. It is spelled exactly how we pronounce it.

✎ *36.10 Contractions – **Write the contractions in your workbook.***

Usage: Who's and Whose

who's

What does "who's" mean? Who is.

whose

What does whose mean? Who does it belong to.
Which one should I use in the following sentences?
Hint: See if "who is" makes sense. If it does, use "who's" with an apostrophe.

_____ *whispering?*

_____ *books are these?*

Who's whispering? This sentence makes sense with "who is." Therefore, we use the contraction.

Whose books are these? This sentence shows the books belong to someone, so we use the form that shows possession.

Who's whispering?

Whose books are these?

Challenge - Derivatives of "Where"

The word "where" is found in twenty-one compound words. Challenge the students to think of a derivative and use it in a sentence. Write it on the board. Discuss the meaning.

anywhere	whereat	wheresoever
elsewhere	whereby	whereto
everywhere	wherefore	whereunto
nowhere	wherefores	whereupon
somewhere	wherein	wherever
whereabouts	whereof	wherewith
whereas	whereon	wherewithal

Dictation

✎ *36.11 Dictation* – Read each sentence twice. Ask the students to repeat it aloud, then write it in their student workbooks.

1. I believe that is impossible.

2. Where are the directions?

3. What is your name?

4. Will we go before dinner?

5. Who's practicing after them?

6. He is listening to the radio.

Lesson 37

Phonograms:	our
Exploring Sounds:	Distorted U Sound
Spelling Rules:	
Grammar:	Coordinating Conjunctions Compound Sentences

PART ONE

Materials Needed: Advanced Phonogram Card our ; Phonogram Game Cards, cloth bag.

Phonograms

Advanced Phonogram - *our*

The seventy-four basic phonograms describe 98% of English words. The advanced phonograms are used in fewer words, less common words, or in more advanced words. The students who understand the concept of a phonogram will begin to recognize additional phonograms in their reading and spelling words.

Show the phonogram our .   /er/

> **What do you notice about this phonogram?** It is related to the other spellings of /er/. It is an R controlled phonogram. It is written with the multi-letter phonogram OU /ow-ō-oo-ŭ/.

> **All of the words that use the phonogram** our **are derived from French.**

✎ *37.1 The Advanced Phonogram OUR –* **Read the words in your workbook. Underline the French spelling of /er/.**

adjourn	flourish	nourish
courtesy	journal	sojourner
courage	journey	tournament

Do you know why there are so many French words in English?
The reason is because in 1066 the French Normans conquered England. When the French Normans ruled England, they brought their language and culture with them. Many words were added to English. They were spelled using the French phonograms to reflect their origin.

Many of these French-based words have a different spelling in the United States than in Britain.

✎ *37.2 American and British Spelling – Read the American and British spellings of each word in your workbook. Underline the phonogram used to spell /er/.*

American Spelling	British Spelling
color	colour
behavior	behaviour
labor	labour
neighbor	neighbour
honor	honour
valor	valour
enamor	enamour
favor	favour
flavor	flavour
glamor	glamour

Do you know why these words are spelled differently in the United States than in England? Around 1783 a man named Noah Webster wrote a book to teach spelling to children in the United States.

What had happened just a few years before 1783? In 1776 the United States won the Revolutionary War and became independent from Great Britain.

Since the United States was a new country, Noah Webster wanted to make the spelling of English more American and less British, therefore he changed some of the spellings. One of them was the French spelling of /er/.

Unfortunately, he was not consistent. He only changed the spelling for words ending in our *. He left the French spelling in the middle of a few words.*

✎ *37.3 Writing the Phonogram – Write the French Spelling of /er/ five times in your workbook.*

Review

Drill the phonograms with flash cards.

1. ✎ *37.4 Phonogram Practice* – Dictate the following phonograms. For extra practice, have the students read them back. Write the correct answers on the board as the students check their answers.

1. our	8. ir	15. ew
2. ie	9. ui	16. gn
3. ou	10. dge	17. kn
4. aw	11. ei	18. igh
5. igh	12. ey	19. ar
6. ur	13. eigh	20. oy
7. bu	14. augh	

2. Play Rotten Egg (*The Phonogram and Spelling Game Book, 13*).

Exploring Sounds

Distorted URE Sounds

Say /t/.
Now say /ūr/.
Now put them together /tūr/.
Now say them together, faster and faster.
What does it turn into? /cher/

Say the sound /s/.
Now say /ūr/.
Now put them together /sūr/.
Now say /sūr/ faster and faster.
What sound does it turn into? /sher/

Say the sound /z/.
Now say /ūr/.
Now put them together /zūr/.
Now say /zūr/ faster and faster.
What sound does it turn into? /ZHer/

The long /ū/ sometimes distorts the /s/, /z/, and /t/ sounds. These words will need extra attention for spelling purposes.

✎ *37.5 Distorted U – Read the examples in your workbook. Pronounce each word as if each sound is clearly articulated. Then blend them together quickly.*

closure	sugar	moisture	feature
measure	sure	adventure	creature
treasure	picture	mixture	texture
pleasure	nature	culture	

Read the words again. Highlight the distorted sound.

Reading & Spelling Multi-Syllable Words

What are the five syllable types to consider when reading a multi-syllable word?

1) closed

2) open

3) silent final E's

4) multi-letter vowel

5) R-controlled

Let's analyze two words together:

consideration

Let's analyze the word in the direction of reading and writing.
What is the first vowel? O
What comes after it? N, S
Where do you think the first syllable will break? between the N and S
What does the first syllable say? /cŏn/

con /sideration

What is the next vowel? I
What comes after I? D, E, R
Where will we likely divide the syllable? after the I
Why? When there is only one consonant, it usually goes with the beginning of the next syllable.
What does I say at the end of the syllable? I may say /ĭ/ or /ī /at the end of the syllable.
What does the second syllable say? /sĭ/ or /sī/

con /si /deration

Where does the R belong? With the E. It is the phonogram /er/.
What does this syllable say? /der/

con /si /der /ation

What is the next vowel? A
What follows the A? T, I
Is TI a phonogram? yes
Where should we divide the syllable? after the A
What does A usually say at the end of the syllable? /ā/

con /si /der /a /tion

What are the next two letters? TI
What does it say? /sh/
What does the final syllable say? /shŏn/

con / si / der / a / tion

>**Blend the whole word together.** /cŏn sĭ der ā shŏn/ — consideration

>**What is the root of this word?** consider
>**What does it mean to consider?** to think about carefully
>**What do you think consideration means?** It is the act of considering or think about something carefully.
>**Use it in a sentence.** Answers will vary. He gave careful consideration to the decision.

improvement

>**Let's analyze the word in the direction of reading and writing.**
>**What is the first vowel?** I
>**What comes after it?** M, P
>**Where will we probably divide the syllable?** between the M and P
>**What does the first syllable say?** /ĭm/

im / provement

>**What is the next vowel?** O
>**What comes after O?** V, E
>**We need to consider if this is a silent final E with a suffix, or if this is a vowel for the next syllable.**
>**Since there is V, what is one reason this word may have a silent final E?** for the V
>**If it is for the V, where will we likely divide the syllable?** after the E
>**Why?** It is probably a silent final E because English words do not end in V.
>**How might this syllable be pronounced?** The O could say its name because of the E, or it could say /ŏ/ or /ö/.
>**Knowing your options is the key.**
>**Try each one.** / ĭm prōv/, / ĭm prŏv/, / ĭm pröv/.
>**Which one makes the most sense?** / ĭm pröv/

im / prove / ment

>**What is the next vowel?** E
>**What does the final syllable say?** /mĕnt/

>**Blend the whole word together.** /ĭm pröv mĕnt/ — improvement

>**What is the root of this word?** improve
>**What does it mean to improve?** to make something better
>**Use "improvement" in a sentence.** The improvements to the house increased its value.

Optional Spelling Rule Practice

Review rules 1-30 using the Spelling Rule Flash Cards. Ⓥ Ⓐ

PART TWO

Using Spelling List 37 on pages 494-495, dictate each word following the steps included on pages Intro 42 - Intro 46.

Many of the words in Part Two of Lesson 37 require more analysis. Lead the students step by step through the thought process for spelling multi-syllable words such as *memorization, equipment*, and *encouraging*.

Tips for Spelling List 37

Sugar, Sure, Unusual, Measure, Picture

Each of these words has a long /ū/ that distorts the consonant that comes before it. Aid students in memorizing the spellings by exaggerating each sound for Say to Spell (*Uncovering the Logic of English*, 127).

/shə ger/ becomes /sū gär/

/sher/ becomes /sūr/

/ŭn ū ZHəl/ becomes /ŭn ū zū ăl/

/mĕ zher/ becomes /mĕ zūr/

/pĭc cher/ becomes /pĭc tūr/

Again

The word "again" demonstrates both an unaccented vowel which says the schwa sound /ə/, as well as a word where the vowel is distorted in some American accents. In order to help students create an auditory picture of the word, it is helpful to exaggerate vowels so that /ə gĕn/ sounds like /ā gān/. Note that some people already clearly pronounce the second vowel as long /ā/.

To learn more about vowels in unaccented syllables and aiding students in creating an auditory picture of words, see *Uncovering the Logic of English*, 121-128.

PART THREE

Materials Needed: Grammar Cards 7, 7.1, 9.13; Red, green, and yellow colored pencils.

Grammar

Review

What is a noun? A noun is the name of a person, place, thing, or idea.

What are the six noun jobs? subject noun, direct object, indirect object, predicate noun, noun of direct address, object of the preposition

What is an adjective? Adjectives modify nouns and pronouns. Adjectives answer: What kind? How many? Which one? Whose?

What is an article? A, An, The. Tiny article adjectives that mark nouns and answer the question: Which?

Name the parts of a sentence. A sentence must have a capital letter, subject, verb, complete thought, and an end mark.

What is a verb? A verb shows action, links a description to the subject, or helps another verb.

What is an adverb? An adverb modifies a verb, adjective, or another adverb. An adverb answers: How? When? Where? To what extent?

What is a preposition? A preposition connects a noun or a pronoun to the rest of the sentence.

✎ *Spelling List 37 –* **Label the nouns in red, the adjectives in blue, the verbs in green, and the adverbs in yellow.**

✎ *Spelling List 37 –* **Write the past tense of each verb and the plural form of each noun.**

Optional Spelling Cards

1. Dictate the words in List 37 for the students to write on index cards. Ⓚ Ⓥ Ⓐ

2. Ask the students to color a green border around verbs, a red border around nouns, a yellow border around adverbs, and a blue border around adjectives. If a word can be used as more than one part of speech, color two borders. Ⓚ Ⓥ

Word	Practice Sentence	Say to Spell	# of Syllables	Markings
1. **also**	*You also need to pack a warm coat.*	äl sō	2	äl sō
2. **too**	*This is too salty.*	too	1	t<u>oo</u>
3. **memorize**	*It is important to memorize the phonograms and spelling rules.*	mĕm ōr īz	3	mem <u>or</u> īz<u>e</u>
4. **memorization**	*Memorization of the phonograms is important for learning to spell.*	mĕm ōr ī zā shŏn	5	mem <u>or</u> īz ā <u>tion</u>
5. **equipment**	*Hockey equipment is expensive.*	ē quĭp mĕnt	3	ē <u>quip</u> ment
6. **encouragement**	*She needed encouragement to finish the race.*	ĕn ker āj mĕnt	4	en <u>cour</u> āge ment
7. **easy**	*That was an easy test.*	ēz ē	2	<u>ea</u>²sy
8. **sugar**	*The recipe calls for one cup of sugar.*	**sū** gär	2	sū <u>g</u>ar
9. **sure**	*Are you sure you want to go?*	**sūr**	1	sūr<u>e</u>
10. **unusual**	*That is an unusual color.*	ŭn ū **zū** al	4	un ū ²<u>s</u>u al
11. **measure**	*The nurse will measure your height.*	mĕ **zūr**	2	m<u>ea</u>² ²<u>s</u>ūr<u>e</u>
12. **picture**	*That is a beautiful picture.*	pĭc **tūr**	2	pic tūr<u>e</u>
13. **again**	*I need to call him again.*	**ā** gān	2	ā g<u>ai</u>n
14. **happen**	*The accident happened at one o'clock.*	hăp pĕn	2	hap pen
15. **sweet**	*This cake is too sweet.*	swēt	1	sw<u>ee</u>t

Spelling Hints	Part of Speech	Vocabulary Development
Put two dots over the /ä/. /ă-ā-ä/ said its third sound before an L. Put a line over the /ō/. 4 A E O U usually say their names at the end of the syllable.	Adv	
Underline /oo/.	Adv	
Underline /or/. Draw a line over the /ī/. Double underline the silent final E. 12.1 The vowel says its name because of the E.	V	memorized, memorizes, memorizable
Underline /or/. Draw a line over the /ī/. Draw a line over the /ā/. 4 A E O U usually say their names at the end of the syllable. Underline the /sh/. 17 TI, CI, and SI are used only at the beginning of any syllable after the first one.	N	
Draw a line over the /ē/. 4 A E O U usually say their names at the end of the syllable. Underline /qu/.	N	
Encourage + ment. Underline the /er/. Draw a line over the /ā/. 2 G may soften to /j/ when followed by an E, I or Y. 13 Drop the silent final E when adding a vowel suffix only if it is allowed by other spelling rules..	V, Adj	encourage, encouraging, encouraged, encourager, encourages
Underline /ē/. Put a two above the /z/. /s-z/ said its second sound /z/. 7 Y says long /ē/ only at the end of a multi-syllable word.	Adv	easily, easier, easiest, easygoing, easiness, uneasy
Say to spell /**sū** gär/. Draw a line over the /ū/. 4 A E O U usually say their names at the end of the syllable. Underline the /är/.	N	sugary, sugarcane, sugarcoated, sugarcoat, sugared, sugarless, sugarplum, sugarloaf
Say to spell /**sū**r/. Draw a line over the /ū/. Double underline the silent final E. 12.1 The vowel says its name because of the E.	Adv	surely, surefire, surest, ensure, reassure, insure
Say to spell /ŭn ū **zū** al/. Draw a line over the /ū/. 4 A E O U usually say their names at the end of the syllable. Put a 2 over the /z/. Draw a line over the /ū/. 4 A E O U usually say their names at the end of the syllable.	Adj	usual, unusually
Say to spell /mĕ **zū**r/. Underline the /ĕ/. Put a two over it. /ē-ĕ-ā/ said its second sound /ĕ/. Put a 2 over the /z/. Draw a line over the /ū/. Double underline the silent final E. 12.1 The vowel says its name because of the E.	V	measurement, measuring, measured, measures
Say to spell /pic **tū**r/. Put a line over the /ū/. Double underline the silent final E. 12.1 The vowel says its name because of the E.	N, V	pictured, picturing, pictures, picturesque
Say to spell /ā g**ā**n/. Underline the /ā/.	Adv	
All first sounds.	V	happening, happens, happenstance
Underline /ē/.	N	sweets, sweetly, sweetness, bittersweet, sweeten, sweetener, unsweetened, presweetened, sweetbread

Introducing Coordinating Conjunctions

✏ *37.6 Coordinating Conjunctions – **I will dictate seven words for you to write in your workbook. None of them are difficult to spell.***

for	*nor*	*or*	*so*
and	*but*	*yet*	

These word are the seven coordinating conjunctions.

coordinating conjunction

This may sound like a big name for these very small words, but let's analyze these words for a few minutes. When you learn a new vocabulary word, it is a good idea to think about the roots and meaning of the word and then to analyze the spelling. This will help you to remember the words more efficiently. The few minutes you spend up front learning a new word will save you a lot of time in the future needing to look it up, misunderstanding its meaning, and misspelling it.

What does it mean to coordinate your clothes or your schedule? To make them match, to go together, to work together.

Coordinate means to act together in an orderly way

What word do you see within the word conjunction? junction
What is a junction? Where two things meet together, an intersection.

✏ *37.7 Junctions – **Look at the images in your workbook. One is a train junction, the other is a freeway junction.***
What does a junction do? It joins two or more roads or tracks together.

A conjunction is a word. What does a conjunction do? Joins other words together.

What is a conjunction?

Grammar Card 7   C

Conjunctions connect words, phrases or sentences together. There are two types of conjunctions: coordinating and subordinating.

A coordinating conjunction joins words, phrases, or sentences that match or coordinate together.

Grammar Card 7.1   C

Coordinating conjunctions connect related words, phrases, or sentences together. Use a comma before a coordinating conjunction: and, but, or, for, nor, yet, so.

---

coordinating

> Now let's look at the logic of the spelling of the word "coordinating."
> How many syllables in /co or di na ting/? five
>
> What letter is used to spell the /k/ sound? C before an O
> What is saying the long /ō/ sound? O at the end of the syllable
> What is the rule? A E O U usually say their names at the end of the syllable.
>
> Where will the second syllable likely break? between the R and the D
> What is the second syllable? /or/
>
> Where will the third syllable likely break? After the I. There is only one consonant and it will probably go with the next syllable.
> What does I say at the end of the syllable? /ĭ/ or /ī/
> What is the third syllable? /dĭ/ or /dī/
> Where will the fourth syllable likely divide? before the T
> What will the A say and why? A will say /ā/ at the end of the syllable.
>
> What is the final syllable? /tĭng/
>
> For spelling purposes, what do you need to memorize to spell this word? That it begins with a C. The first two syllables are /cō or/.
>
> Though we have not covered this, CO is a common prefix added to Latin root words. It means together. For example co-authors write together, co-workers work together, etc.

conjunction

> What is first vowel in "conjunction?" O
> Where you do think the first syllable breaks? between the N and the J
> What is the first syllable? /cŏn/
>
> What is the second vowel? U
> What comes after the U? N, C, T, I
> Do you see a possible phonogram? TI
> Where do you think the syllable will break? between the C and T
> What is the second syllable? /jŭnc/
>
> What will the final syllable say/? /shŏn/
>
> Why do we need to use a J and not a G? Because G may soften to /j/ only before an E, I or Y, and the /j/ sound is followed by a U.
>
> Is there anything difficult about spelling the word conjunction? no

Using Coordinating Conjunctions

Now that we have explored the term "coordinating conjunction," let's learn how they are used.

We have already learned about joining groups of words together in a list with a conjunction. For example:

I ate an apple, a banana, and an orange for lunch.

Would you like an apple, a banana, or an orange for lunch?

Which words in these sentences are in a list? apple, banana, orange
How are they joined together? with commas and the words "and" and "or'

Today we will learn how to join sentences with coordinating conjunctions.

Morgan rode her bike to school, and Paige walked to work.

What two sentences do you see in this sentence? Morgan rode her bike to school. Paige walked to work.
How are they joined together? They are joined with a comma and the word "and."

When we join two related sentences together with a conjunction, we must put a comma first.

I need to go to sleep now, for I have to get up early tomorrow.

What two sentences are joined by the coordinating conjunction? I need to go to sleep now. I have to get up early.

What is the coordinating conjunction? for

Since these sentences are related, they may be joined by the conjunction "for."
What comes before the conjunction? a comma

✎ *37.8 Coordinating Conjunctions –* **Read the sentences in your workbook. Circle the comma and underline the coordinating conjunction.**

Tom was not in class today, nor will he be here tomorrow.

Evan received three letters from the school, but I did not receive any.

She must finish her homework before six o'clock, or she will have to miss the movie.

My younger sister loves to travel, yet she did not want to go on this trip.

Eli was late, so we started without him.

Sentences combined with a coordinating conjunction and a comma are called compound sentences.

> **Grammar Card 9.13**
>
> **A compound sentence contains two complete sentences joined together with a comma followed by a coordinating conjunction.**

✏️ *37.9 Joining Sentences – **Join the sentences in your workbook using one of the coordinating conjunctions.***

✏️ *37.10 Grammar Rule – **Write "coordinating conjunction" on the line in your workbook. Write a short definition in your own words. Write a rule that states where to put the comma.***

Usage To, Too, Two

What words have we learned before that sounds like "too?" to, two

two

What does this form of two mean? the number two
How can you remember that? Twelve, twin, twice are related words and you can hear the W sound.

What does "to" with one O mean? It is a preposition and connects another noun to the rest of the sentence.

T-O-O has two meanings. First it means "also." For example: "My sister loves to skate. I do too." I could have said, "My sister loves to skate. I do also."

The second meaning is "too many." I have too many papers on my desk.
I like to remember that when I have too many of something I need to use too many O's.

Sam has a red bicycle. Luke has a red bicycle _____.

Which form of "too" do I need? t-o-o
Why? "Luke has a red bicycle also" makes sense.

Sam has a red bicycle. Luke has a red bicycle too.

We own _____ many hats.

Which form do we need here? T-O-O because it also means "too many"

We own too many hats.

I went _____ the funeral.

Which form do we need here? T-O because it is a preposition connecting funeral to the rest of the sentence

I went to the funeral.

I read _____ books this week.

Which form do we need here? T-W-O because it is a number.

I read two books this week.

✎ *37.11 To, Two, and Too – **Complete the activity in your workbook.***

Optional Grammar Practice

1. Challenge students to see if they can recall the seven coordinating conjunctions. Write them on the board as they name them. Challenge the students to write them all from memory. ⓀⓥⒶ

2. The Compound Sentence Challenge - ⓀⓋⒶ©
    - Write the following sentences on ten index cards. *1. The cat ran across the street. 2. Six men yelled for help. 3. Hand me a measuring cup. 4. That is an unusual picture. 5. She gave me an encouraging note. 6. We memorized one hundred facts. 7. The cookies have too much sugar. 8. People in the south drink sweet tea. 9. The company bought all new equipment. 10. Our math problems were too easy.*
    - Place the index cards face down in a pile in front of the students. Set a timer for three minutes.
    - Direct the students to choose one card and in three minutes write as many compound sentences using their chosen sentence and one or more coordinating conjunctions. At the end of three minutes:
    - Award one point for each sentence that correctly uses: *and, but.*
    - Award two points for each sentence that correctly uses: *or, for.*
    - Award three points for each sentence that correctly uses: *nor, yet, so.*

3. Team Compound Sentence Challenge – Use the same rules as above; however, divide students into two groups. Provide students three to five minutes to write a list of original simple sentences on index cards. The teacher checks to make sure each sentence is written correctly. When the time is up, each team chooses a sentence and passes it to the other team. The timer is set for two to three minutes. The team must write as many compound sentences as possible that incorporate the original sentence. Award points as directed above.

Dictation

✎ *37.12 Dictation* – Read each sentence twice. Ask the students to repeat it aloud, then write it in their student workbooks.

1. We need to memorize all the answers, or we will not do well on the test.

2. Measure the sugar carefully, so it is not too sweet.

3. The letter from my teacher was encouraging, and it helped me believe I could do it.

4. I need all the equipment, or I cannot take the pictures.

5. Why did that happen again?

6. Which question was unusually easy?

Composition

Today we will write some sentences with coordinating conjunctions. To coordinate means that the sentences must belong together.

Write the students' answers on the board.

We need a subject. Who do we want our sentence to be about? For example:

A good student

What is being said about the good student?

A good student studies everyday

Now we need to choose a coordinating conjunction.

A good student studies everyday so

What goes before the coordinating conjunction? comma

A good student studies everyday, so

Now we need another subject that coordinates with "a good student." Often this will be a pronoun that refers to the subject.

A good student studies everyday, so she

She what?

A good student studies everyday, so she does not forget her lessons.

✎ *37.13 Composition* – **Write three sentences that use a coordinating conjunction. I will ask you questions and provide directions. You write the answers to build your sentence. Who or what?**

What is being said about your subject?
Choose a coordinating conjunction.
What do you write before the conjunction?
Choose a pronoun that refers back to your subject.
What is being said about ___?

Now try to write a sentence with a coordinating conjunction without my guidance.

Vocabulary Development

What is the root of encourage? courage

What is the prefix that has been added to courage to make encourage? en-

EN- is a prefix that means "make, or put into."

How does this relate to the meaning of encourage? Encourage literally means to put in courage.

Can you think of any other words that begin with en-? As you name a word, tell me how it relates to the meaning of the prefix en-.

List them on the board as the students name them.

enclose to put in a closed space

enact to put in an act

encase to put in a case

encamp to make, or put into a camp

endear to make dear

engage to make a pledge *(The root "gage" means a pledge. Consider how this relates to engagement.)*

enliven to make alive

endanger to put in danger

envelope to make it folded up *("Velope" means to fold, thus to "develop" means to unfold.)*

How does the meaning of a word change if I add the prefix dis-?

dis + courage =

Discourage is the opposite of encourage. It means to take away someone's courage.

What do you think the prefix dis- means? to take away

What words can you think of that begin with the prefix dis-? Tell me how it relates to the meaning of the prefix dis-.

disadvantage away from advantage

disagree away from agreeing

disallow away from allowing

dislike away from liking

discontinue away from continuing

discover away from covering *("Cover" means to hide. To "discover" means to take the cover away.)*

disgrace away from grace

dishonest away from honesty

dismount away from being mounted

disrespect away from respect

disappoint away from appointing *("Appoint" means to resolve, to agree.)*

disconnect away from a connection

discredit to take away someone's credibility

✎ *37.14 Vocabulary –* **Add the prefixes to the words in your workbook. Discuss the meaning of each word as it relates to the prefix.**

Lesson 38

Phonograms:	aigh
Exploring Sounds:	I says /y/
Spelling Rules:	
Grammar:	Subordinating Conjunctions Dependent Clauses

PART ONE

Materials Needed: Phonogram Flash Cards from previous lessons and Advanced Phonogram Card aigh , Basic Phonogram cards i , and y ; Whiteboard, marker, eraser.

Phonograms

Advanced Phonogram - *aigh*

Show the phonogram aigh . /ā/

> ***What do you notice about this phonogram?*** It is related to two letter /ā/ that you may not use at the end of English words — AI. It is also related to OUGH, IGH, AUGH. It follows the rule, Phonograms ending in GH are used only at the end of the base word or before the letter T.

> ***This is an advanced phonogram because it is found in only one word.***

> *straight*

> ✎ *38.1 AIGH – **Write straight in your workbook. Underline the /ā/ of straight.***

Review

1. Drill the phonograms with flash cards.

2. ✎ *38.2 Writing* – Write straight five times while saying the sounds aloud.

3. ✎ *38.3 Phonogram Practice* – Dictate the following phonograms. For extra practice, have the students read them back. Write the correct answers on the board as the students check their answers.

1. ir	8. ay	15. ey
2. ur	9. gu	16. ew
3. ear	10. cei	17. ui
4. er	11. ci	18. eigh
5. our	12. dge	19. kn
6. ai	13. ei	20. wh
7. aigh	14. ti	

4. Play Eraser Race (*The Phonogram and Spelling Game Book*, 28).

Exploring Sounds

When I Says /y/

Show   i .

What are the sounds of this phonogram? /ĭ-ī-ē-y/

Today we will discover when I says its consonant sound /y/.

✎ *38.4 I says /y/ –* **Read the words in your workbook.**

onion	billion	genius
union	stallion	valiant
opinion	savior	
million	senior	

How many syllables are in onion? two
Do vowels or consonants form syllables? vowels
Syllables are formed when we open our mouths to say the vowels.
Based upon the number of vowels, how many syllables might you guess are in the word
"onion?" three

Now say /ĭ/ and /y/. What do you notice about the position of your mouth? It is the same though the tongue drops down to say /y/ and it stops the sound.

The /ĭ/ and /y/ sounds are related.

When do you notice that the I says /y/? I says /y/ at the beginning of a syllable in the middle of a word. Most commonly, I says /y/ before an O.

Reading & Spelling Multi-Syllable Words

What are the five syllable types to consider when reading a multi-syllable word?

1) *closed*
2) *open*
3) *silent final E*
4) *multi-letter vowel*
5) *R-controlled*

electricity

Let's analyze the word in the direction of reading and writing.
What is the first vowel? E
What comes after it? L, E, C
Where will we probably divide the syllable? after the E
What does the first syllable say? /ē/

e/lectricity

What is the next vowel? E
What comes after E? C, T
Where will we probably divide the syllable? after the C
What does the second syllable say? /lĕc/

e/lec/tricity

What is the next vowel? I
What comes after i? C, I
Where will we probably divide the syllable? after the I
What does the third syllable say? /trĭ/ or /trī/.
Try to sound out the word to this point. Which one would you guess?

The next two letters are CI. This could be the phonogram /sh/. However /sh/ is always followed by a vowel. Is CI followed by a vowel? no

Then it is a C followed by an I. What does it say? /sĭ/

What does the final syllable say? /tē/

Why does the Y say /ē/? Y says long /ē/ only at the end of a multi-syllable word.

Sound out each syllable, then blend them together. /ē-lĕc-trĭ-cĭ-tē/ — electricity

What is the root of electricity? electric

historian

Let's analyze the word in the direction of reading and writing.
What is the first vowel? I
What comes after the I? S, T
Where will the syllable likely be divided? between the S and the T
What does the first syllable say? /hĭs/

his/torian

What is the second vowel? O
What comes after O? R
Could OR be a phonogram? yes
What does the second syllable say? /tōr/

his/tor/ian

What is the next vowel? I
What comes after the I? A
Is this a phonogram? no
What is likely happening? It is an I saying the long /ē/ sound. I says long /ē/ at the end of the syllable before another vowel.

his/tor/i/an

What does the final syllable say? /ăn/

Sound out each syllable, then blend them together. /hĭs tōr ē ăn/ — historian

---

Optional Spelling Rule Practice

Review rules 1-30 using the Spelling Rule Flash Cards. Ⓥ Ⓐ

PART TWO

Using Spelling List 38 on pages 510-511, dictate each word following the steps included on pages Intro 42 - Intro 46.

Tips for Spelling List 38

Eye

The word *eye* in English is very unusual. Draw the student's attention to the fact that the Y is spelling the long /ī/ sound and that both E's are silent.

Against

The word "against" demonstrates both an unaccented vowel which says the schwa sound /ə/, as well as a word where the vowel is distorted in some American accents. In order to help students create an auditory picture of the word, it is helpful to exaggerate vowels so that /ə gĕnst/ sounds like /ā gānst/. Note that some people already clearly pronounce the second vowel as long /ā/.

To learn more about vowels in unaccented syllables and aiding students in creating an auditory picture of words, see *Uncovering the Logic of English*, 121-128.

Question

Hints: *Question* can be a very difficult word to spell because the last syllable is pronounced /chĭn/ or /chŭn/. When teaching this word, it is important to consider the logic behind its spelling. Use the following dialog.

> **What is the root of question?** quest
> **How do we add the suffix -ion?**

> *quest + ion =*

> **Just add the ending**

> *quest + ion = ques tion*

> **Say "question" how it is literally spelled.** /quĕs shŭn/
> **Now say /quĕs shŭn/ more and more quickly. Did it morph into /quĕs chĭn/?** yes
> **Sounds change when they are near one another. Why is question spelled with a TI?** The root is quest.

> **How are quest and question related in meaning?** A quest is a search for something. By asking a question you are searching for the answer.

	Word	Practice Sentence	Say to Spell	# of Syllables	Markings
1.	**because**	*He needs a new shirt because his ripped.*	bē cäz	2	bē cau²se
2.	**although**	*Although I think it is a good idea, I would like more time to think about it.*	äl thō	2	äl thou²gh²
3.	**since**	*Since he has started working, he has solved six problems.*	sĭns	1	since
4.	**while**	*While we wait, let's play a game.*	whīl	1	while
5.	**whenever**	*Whenever you want, we can leave.*	whĕn ĕv er	3	when ev er
6.	**until**	*Until mom gets home, you need to play quietly.*	ŭn tĭl	2	un til
7.	**unless**	*Unless you clean your room, you will not be able to go to the party tomorrow.*	ŭn lĕs	2	un less
8.	**eye**	*The doctor examined my left eye.*	ī	1	eye
9.	**combination**	*Iced tea and lemonade are a great combination for a cold beverage.*	kŏm bĭn ā shŏn	4	com bin ā tion
10.	**question**	*Please answer the questions at the end of the chapter.*	quĕs shŏn	2	ques tion
11.	**against**	*Why is she so against the project?*	ā gānst	2	ā gainst
12.	**straight**	*Draw a straight line.*	strāt	1	straight
13.	**immediately**	*I need to know the answer immediately.*	ĭm mē dē āt lē	5	im mē di āte ly
14.	**million**	*The business made five million dollars last year.*	mĭl lyŏn	2	mil lion
15.	**country**	*Which country is north of Italy?*	cŭn trē	2	coun⁴ try

Spelling Hints	Part of Speech	Vocabulary Development
Draw a line over the /ē/. **4** A E O U usually say their names at the end of the syllable. Underline the /ä/. Put a 2 over the /z/. /s-z/ said its second sound. Underline the E twice.	C	
Put two dots over the /ä/. Underline /TH/. Put a 2 over it. /th-TH/ said its second sound. Underline /ō/ and put a 2 over it. /ŏ-ō-oo-ow-ŭf-ŏf/ said its second sound.	C	
Underline the /s/. Double underline the silent final E. **12.3** The C says /s/ and the G says /j/ because of the E.	C	
Underline /wh/. Draw a line over the /ī/. Double underline the silent final E. **12.1** The vowel says its name because of the E.	C	awhile, meanwhile, worthwhile, whiles
Underline /wh/. Underline /er/.	C	
All first sounds.	C	
30 We often double F, L, and S after a single vowel at the end of a base word. Occasionally other letters also are doubled.	C	
This is a very unusual word. Which phonogram says /ī/? Y The E's are both silent.	N, V	eyes, eyed, eyeing, cockeye, eyeball, eyebrow, eyelet, eyelash, eyestrain, eyewitness, eyeglasses, eyeful
Say to spell /kŏm bĭn ā shŏn/. Combine + ation. Draw a line over the /ā/. **4** A E O U usually say their names at the end of the syllable. Underline the /sh/. **17** TI, CI, and SI are used only at the beginning of any syllable after the first one.	N	combine, combined, combining, combinable, combiner, recombine, uncombined
The root is quest. The /s/ followed by /sh/ morphs into a /ch/. Underline /qu/. Underline /sh/. **17** TI, CI, and SI are used only at the beginning of any syllable after the first one.	N, V	questioned, questions, questionable, questioning, questioner, questionnaire, unquestionable, unquestioning
Say to spell /ā gānst/. Underline the /ā/.	Adv	
Underline the /ā/.	Adj	straightforward, straightaway, straightedge, straighten, straightlaced, straightjacket, straightest, straighter
Say to spell /ĭm mē dē āt lē/. Draw a line over the /ē/. **4** A E O U usually say their names at the end of the syllable. I said /ē/ at the end of the syllable. Draw a line over the /ā/. Double underline the silent final E. **12.1** The vowel says its name because of the E.	Adj	immediate, immediateness
In the second syllable, I is saying its consonant sound /y/.	Adj, N	millions, millionaire
Underline the /ŭ/ and put a 4 over it. /ŭ-ū-oo-ü/ said its fourth sound.	N	countries, countrywide, countrywoman

PART THREE

Materials Needed: Grammar Cards 7.2, 7.3, 7.4, 9.14, 10.2; red, green, yellow, blue, and gray colored pencils;

Grammar

Review

What is a noun? A noun is the name of a person, place, thing, or idea.

What are the six noun jobs? subject noun, direct object, indirect object, predicate noun, noun of direct address, object of the preposition

What is an adjective? Adjectives modify nouns and pronouns. Adjectives answer: What kind? How many? Which one? Whose?

What is an article? A, An, The. Tiny article adjectives that mark nouns and answer the question: Which?

Name the parts of a sentence. A sentence must have a capital letter, subject, verb, complete thought, and an end mark.

What is a verb? A verb shows action, links a description to the subject, or helps another verb.

What is an adverb? An adverb modifies a verb, adjective, or another adverb. An adverb answers: How? When? Where? To what extent?

What is a preposition? A preposition connects a noun or a pronoun to the rest of the sentence.

Introducing Subordinating Conjunctions

✎ *38.5 Sentences and Fragments –* ***We will read together the sentences and phrases in your workbook. Tell me if it is a sentence or a fragment. If it is a complete sentence, put an S after it. If it is a fragment, put an F after it.***

I memorized my math facts.

When I memorized my math facts.

He rode in an airplane.

Although he rode in an airplane.

I want to surprise my friend.

Unless I want to surprise my friend.

Evan and Sam hiked up the mountain together.

Because Evan and Sam hiked up the mountain together.

Finish your science.

If you finish your science.

I walk the dog.

Whenever I walk the dog.

Molly went to the store.

Since Molly went to the store.

Which words are stealing away the completeness of the sentence?

when	*unless*	*if*	*since*
although	*because*	*whenever*	

✎ *38.5 Sentences and Fragments* – **Underline these words in the sentences in your workbook.**

Words that steal away the complete sense of a sentence are called subordinating conjunctions.

subordinating conjunction

Notice the prefix sub-. What other words can you think of begin with sub-?

subtract	*subzero*	*submarine*	*subway*

Based upon these words, what would you guess that sub- means? below or take away

What is a conjunction? a word that joins two words, phrases, or sentences together

Subordinating conjunctions take away the completeness of one sentence so that it can be joined to another sentence.

Grammar Card 7.2	SC
Subordinating conjunctions join two sentences together by turning one sentence into a dependent clause (or sentence fragment).	

By taking away the completeness of the sentence, they make one part of the sentence dependent upon the rest of the sentence. This is called a dependent clause. It is dependent upon the other sentence to complete its meaning.

Grammar Card 10.2	Clause
A dependent clause includes a subordinating conjunction, subject, and verb. A dependent clause does not express a complete thought.	

If Clara finishes her homework, she will go to the baseball game.

Clara will go to the baseball game if she finishes her homework.

Look carefully at these two sentences. What is the same? They use the same phrases.

What is different? The clause with the subordinating conjunction "if" has moved to the end of the sentence.

How are they punctuated differently? When the sentence begins with "if" and the dependent clause, you need a comma. When "if" and the dependent clause are placed second, you do not need a comma.

Grammar Card 7.3

When a sentence begins with a dependent clause, separate it from the rest of the sentence with a comma.

Grammar Card 7.4

When a sentence ends with a dependent clause, no comma is needed.

Sentences that include a dependent clause are called complex sentences.

Grammar Card 9.14   *Complex Sentence*

A complex sentence contains an independent clause joined with one or more dependent clauses.

✎ *38.6 List of Subordinating Conjunctions – **Read the list of subordinating conjunctions in your workbook. Choose one. Make up a sentence using it aloud. Practice making five to ten sentences which include subordinating conjunctions.***

✎ *38.7 Sentences – **Combine the sentences using a subordinating conjunction. Remember, when a sentence begins with a subordinating conjunction, use a comma. When the dependent clause is at the end, there is no comma.***

Answer Key

1. Although that is a good combination, I do not want to try it.

2. While I waited for the eye doctor, I read a book.

3. You may miss the announcement unless you listen to the radio this afternoon.

4. When Spain plays Brazil, I will cheer for Spain.

5. That sweater is too small for him because it is a size medium.

✎ *38.8 Grammar Rule –* **Write "subordinating conjunction" in your workbook. Write a short definition. Write seven examples of subordinating conjunctions.**

✎ *Spelling List 38 –* **Words 1-7 are conjunctions. Label them with Conj. in gray.**

✎ *Spelling List 38 –* **Label the remaining parts of speech.**

✎ *Spelling List 38 –* **Write the past tense of each verb and the plural form of each noun.**

Identifying Parts of Speech

✎ *38.9 Identifying Parts of Speech –* **Together we will identify the parts of speech. Write the parts of speech in your workbook as I write them on the board.**

> *While Father went to the store for more milk, I made dinner.*
>
> **How many clauses are there?** two
> **How many subjects and verbs would we expect?** two subjects and two verbs
> **What is the subject of the first clause?** Father, subject noun
> **What is being said about Father?** Father went, verb
>
> **What is the word "to?"** preposition
> **To what?** store, object of the preposition
> **Which store?** the, article adjective
>
> **What is the word "for?"** preposition
> **For what?** milk, object of the preposition
> **How much milk?** more, adjective
>
> **What is the subject of the second clause?** I, subject pronoun
> **What is being said about I?** I made, verb
> **Made what?** made dinner, direct object
> **Since there is a direct object in this clause, what type of verb is it?** transitive verb
>
> **What is while?** subordinating conjunction
>
> **Put parentheses around the prepositional phrases.**
>
> ```
>    SC    SN    V    P  A  OP    P  Adj  OP   SP  TV  DO
> While Father went (to the store) (for more milk), I made dinner.
> ```

We must leave immediately because class starts in three minutes.

How many clauses are there? two
How many subjects and verbs would we expect? two subjects and two verbs

What is the subject of the first clause? we, subject pronoun
What is being said about we? we must leave, helping verb and verb
Leave when? immediately, adverb

What is the word "because?" subordinating conjunction

What is the subject of the second clause? class, subject noun
What is being said about class? class starts, verb
What is the word "in?" preposition
In what? minutes, object of the preposition
How many minutes? three, adjective

Put parentheses around the prepositional phrases.

SP   HV   V   Adv   SC   SN   V   P Adj   OP
We must leave immediately because class starts (in three minutes.)

I listen to the radio until I leave for school.

How many clauses are there? two
How many subjects and verbs would we expect? two subjects and two verbs

What is the subject of the first clause? I, subject pronoun
What is being said about I? I listen, verb

What is" to?" preposition
To what? radio, object of the preposition
Which radio? the, article adjective

What is the word "until?" subordinating conjunction

What is the subject of the second clause? I, subject pronoun
What is being said about I? I leave, verb
What is the word "for?" preposition
For what? school, object of the preposition

Put parentheses around the prepositional phrases.

SP V   P A   OP   SC SP V   P OP
I listen (to the radio) until I leave (for school.)

Optional Grammar Practice

1. The Compound/Complex Sentence Challenge – ⓀⓥⒶⒸ

- Write the following sentences on ten index cards. *1. Good students ask questions. 2. She has straight, black hair. 3. The twins have brown eyes. 4. The company made ten million dollars last year. 5. His family is traveling out of the country. 6. That is a good combination. 7. We will leave immediately after lunch. 8. Monkeys live in Africa. 9. Turn on the radio. 10. We had a surprise party.*

- Place the index cards face down in a pile in front of the students. Set a timer for three minutes.

- Direct the students to choose one card and in three minutes write as many compound or complex sentences using their chosen sentence and one or more coordinating or subordinating conjunctions. At the end of three minutes:

- Award one point for each sentence that correctly uses: *and, but.*

- Award two points for each sentence that correctly uses: *or, for, nor, so.*

- Award three points for each sentence that correctly uses: *a subordinating conjunction.*

2. Team Compound/Complex Sentence Challenge – Use the same rules as above, however, divide students into two groups. Give students three to five minutes to write a list of original simple sentences on index cards. The teacher checks to make sure each sentence is written correctly. When the time is up, each team chooses a sentence and passes it to the other team. The timer is set for two to three minutes. The team must write as many compound or complex sentences as possible that incorporate the original sentence. Award points as directed above.

Dictation

✎ *38.10 Dictation* – Read each sentence twice. Ask the students to repeat it aloud, then write it in their student workbooks.

1. Although you may have the radio on, please turn it down.

2. Since the horse lives in the country, we do not see it often.

3. My brother was against going until he heard about the surprise.

4. The boy carefully drew a straight line while the girl talked.

5. Which combination of toys do you want to bring?

6. I have a question about the letter I received from school.

Composition

To practice writing sentences with subordinating conjunctions, we will begin by choosing which subordinating conjunction we want to use.

Let's begin with "although."

Although

Now we need a subject for our sentence. (Allow the students to pick.) For example:

Although the store

What is being said about _____?

Although the store is next door to our house

Although means that we are about to say something that is surprising or contrary to what you might expect based upon the first sentence.

Although the store is next to our house, we never shop there.

We can also flip the order of the two sentences.

We never shop there although the store is next to our house.

Notice the difference in punctuation.

✎ *Composition 38.11 – In your workbook, choose one of the subordinating conjunctions and write a sentence using it. Then rewrite the sentence by reversing the order. Do the same with a second complex sentence.*

Vocabulary

Today we will practice writing compound words that include the words "eye" and "straight."

✎ *38.12 Compound Words – Using the list in your workbook write the new word that is formed. Then use it in a sentence aloud.*

Answer Key: *eyeball, eyelash, eyebrow, eyeglasses, eyewitness, eyesight, straightforward, straightedge, straightlaced, straightaway, straightjacket*

Lesson 39

Phonograms:	SC
Exploring Sounds:	Multi-Syllable Words
Spelling Rules:	Review
Grammar:	Subordinating Conjunctions

PART ONE

Materials Needed: Phonogram Flash Cards from previous lessons and Advanced Phonogram Card ⬚ SC . Three sets of Phonogram Game Cards.

Phonograms

Advanced Phonogram - *sc*

Show the phonogram ⬚ SC . /s/

What do you notice about this phonogram? S and C both say /s/. However, C only says /s/ before an E, I, or Y.

When do you think it would be used? It will be used only before an E, I, or Y. Otherwise, the C would say /k/.

✎ *39.1 The Advanced Phonogram SC –* ***Read the words in your workbook which use the two-letter Latin spelling for /s/. Underline the SC.***

scene	*scepter*	*scissors*	*discern*
science	*discipline*	*ascent*	
scent	*fascinate*	*descend*	

Review

1. Drill the phonograms with flash cards.

2. ✎ *39.2 Writing the Phonogram* – Write the new phonogram five times while saying the sound aloud.

// 519

3. ✎ *39.3 Phonogram Practice* – Dictate the following phonograms. For extra practice, have the students read them back. Write the correct answers on the board as the students check their answers.

1. ai	8. augh	15. oa
2. cei	9. aigh	16. oo
3. ck	10. oe	17. ow
4. dge	11. ea	18. tch
5. sc	12. ear	19. wor
6. au	13. gn	20. wr
7. our	14. gu	

4. Play Speed (*The Phonogram and Spelling Game Book,* 11).

Reading & Spelling Multi-Syllable Words

What are the five syllable types to consider when reading a multi-syllable word?

1) closed
2) open
3) silent final E
4) multi-letter vowel
5) R-controlled

opportunity

Let's begin to analyze the word in the direction of reading and writing.
What is the first vowel? O
What comes after it? P, P
Where will we probably divide the syllable? between the P's
What does the first syllable say? /ŏp/

op/portunity

What is the second vowel? O
What comes after it? R, T
Is it possible that OR is a phonogram? yes
Where will we probably divide the syllable? between the R and the T
What does the second syllable say? /pōr/

op/por/tunity

What is the third vowel? U
What comes after it? N, I
Where will we probably divide the syllable? after the U — When there is only one consonant it usually goes with the syllable after it.
What does the third syllable say? /too/ or /tū/
Why does U say its long sound? A E O U usually say their names at the end of the syllable.

op/por/tu/nity

> ***What is the fourth vowel?*** I
> ***What comes after it?*** T, Y
> ***Where will we probably divide the syllable?*** after the I — When there is only one consonant it usually goes with the syllable after it.
> ***What does the fourth syllable say?*** /nĭ/ or /nī/
> ***Why?*** I may say /ĭ/ or /ī/ at the end of the syllable.

op/por/tu/ni/ty

> ***What will the final syllable say?*** /tē/
> ***Why?*** Y says the long /ē/ sound at the end of a multi-syllable word.
>
> ***Blend the word together.*** /ŏp ōr too nĭ tē/ — opportunity

responsible

> ***Let's begin to analyze the word in the direction of reading and writing.***
> ***What is the first vowel?*** E
> ***What comes after it?*** S, P
> ***Where will we probably divide the syllable?*** between the S and the P
> ***What does the first syllable say?*** /rĕs/

res/ponsible

> ***What is the second vowel?*** O
> ***What comes after it?*** N, S
> ***Where will we probably divide the syllable?*** between the N and the S
> ***What does the second syllable say?*** /pŏn/

res/pon/sible

> ***What is the third vowel?*** I
> ***What comes after it?*** B, L, E
> ***Where will we probably divide the syllable?*** after the I — BLE is a final syllable with a silent final E needed for the syllable.
> ***What does the third syllable say?*** /sĭ/ or /sī/

res/pon/si/ble

> ***What will the final syllable say?*** /bl/
> ***Why is there a silent final E?*** Every syllable must have a written vowel. The /l/ sound is similar to a vowel sound and so an E is added.
>
> ***Blend the word together.*** /rĕs pŏn sĭ bl/ — responsible

Spelling Rules

Optional Spelling Rule Practice

Review rules 1-30 using the Spelling Rule Flash Cards. ⓋⒶ

PART TWO

Using Spelling List 21 on pages 524-525, dictate each word following the steps included on pages Intro 42 - Intro 46.

Calendar, Dollar, Motor

Exaggerate the /ar/ and /or/ so that /kăl ĕn der/ sounds like /kăl ĕn där/; /dŏl ler/ sounds like /dŏl lär/; and /mō ter/ sounds like /mō tōr/.

Century

Draw attention to the root of "century" which is "cent" and means one hundred. The long /ū/ distorts the T. Exaggerate the sounds for spelling purposes so that /sĕn **cher** ē/ sounds like /sĕn **tū** rē/ (*Uncovering the Logic of English,* 127).

Another

The word "another" demonstrates both an unaccented vowel which says the schwa sound /ə/, as well as a word where the vowel is distorted in some American accents. In order to help students create an auditory picture of the word, it is helpful to exaggerate vowels so that /ən əth er/ sounds like /ăn ŏth er/.

To learn more about vowels in unaccented syllables and aiding students in creating an auditory picture of words, see *Uncovering the Logic of English,* 121-128.

PART THREE

Materials Needed: Red, green, yellow, and black colored pencils; A penny for the vocabulary demonstration.

Grammar

Review

What is a noun? A noun is the name of a person, place, thing, or idea.

What are the six noun jobs? subject noun, direct object, indirect object, predicate noun, noun of direct address, object of the preposition

What is an adjective? Adjectives modify nouns and pronouns. Adjectives answer: What kind? How many? Which one? Whose?

What is an article? A, An, The. Tiny article adjectives that mark nouns and answer the question: Which?

Name the parts of a sentence. A sentence must have a capital letter, subject, verb, complete thought, and an end mark.

What is a verb? A verb shows action, links a description to the subject, or helps another verb.

What is an adverb? An adverb modifies a verb, adjective, or another adverb. An adverb answers: How? When? Where? To what extent?

What is a preposition? A preposition connects a noun or a pronoun to the rest of the sentence.

What is a conjunction? A conjunction connects words, phrases, or sentences together.

Subordinating Conjunctions Continued

✎ *39.4 Subordinating Conjunctions – I will read a subordinating conjunction. I want you to write it in your workbook, then use it in a sentence out loud.*

as long as	*in order that*	*by the time*
as though	*now that*	*as soon as*
even if	*rather than*	*just in case*
even though	*so that*	*the first time*
if only	*in the event that*	

✎ *39.5 Sentences – Read the sentences in your workbook. Underline the two clauses, then highlight the words that are acting as subordinating conjunctions.*

Hint: which half of the sentence does not make complete sense? Which words need to be removed to turn the clause into a complete sentence? That word is the subordinating conjunction.

As long as <u>the stadium is empty</u>, <u>we can sit together</u>.

Even if <u>you stop the motor</u>, <u>it will not make a difference</u>.

	Word	Practice Sentence	Say to Spell	# of Syllables	Markings
1.	**earth**	*The earth is about 240,000 miles from the moon.*	erth	1	<u>earth</u>
2.	**stadium**	*We watched the soccer game at the stadium.*	stā dē ŭm	3	stā di um
3.	**construction**	*There is a lot of road construction in town this summer.*	cŏn strŭc ˙shŏn	3	con struc <u>tion</u>
4.	**science**	*Science class begins at ten o'clock.*	sī ĕns	1	<u>scī</u> en<u>ce</u>
5.	**motor**	*Electric motors are available.*	mō tōr	2	mō <u>tor</u>
6.	**motion**	*I get motion sickness when I ride in the backseat of the car.*	mō shŏn	2	mō <u>tion</u>
7.	**motive**	*What was his motive for committing the crime?*	mō tĭv	2	mō ti<u>ve</u>
8.	**problem**	*Problem number one was easy.*	prŏb lĕm	2	prob lem
9.	**enough**	*That is enough salt.*	ē nŭf	2	ē n<u>ough</u>⁵
10.	**calendar**	*I will need to check my calendar.*	kăl ĕn där	3	cal en d<u>ar</u>
11.	**century**	*A century is one hundred years.*	sĕn **tū** rē	3	cen tū ry
12.	**dollar**	*I found a one dollar bill.*	dŏl lär	2	dol l<u>ar</u>
13.	**difference**	*Find the difference between them.*	dĭf fer ĕns	3	dif <u>fer</u> en<u>ce</u>
14.	**together**	*The family went to the fair together.*	tö gĕTH er	3	tö ge<u>th</u>²er
15.	**another**	*She needs another piece of paper.*	ăn ŏther	2	an o<u>th</u>² er

Spelling Hints	Part of Speech	Vocabulary Development
Underline /er/. Underline /th/.	N	earths, earthly, earthen, earthed, earthy, earthier, earthiest, earthling, earthquake, earthrise, earthward, earthworm, unearth
Draw a line over the /ā/. **4** A E O U usually say their names at the end of the syllable. **7** Y says long /ē/ only at the end of a multi-syllable word. I says long /ē/ only at the end of a syllable that is followed by a vowel.	N	stadiums
Underline the /sh/. **17** TI, CI, and SI are used only at the beginning of any syllable after the first one.	N	construct, constructed, constructible, constructionally, constructionist, constructor, deconstruct, reconstruct
Underline /s/. Draw a line over the /ī/. **5** I and Y may say /ĭ/ or /ī/ at the end of the syllable. Underline the /s/. Double underline the silent final E. **12.3** The C says /s/ and the G says /j/ because of the E.	N	sciences, scientific, scientist, pseudoscience, prescience, unscientific
Draw a line over the /ō/. **4** A E O U usually say their names at the end of the syllable. Underline the /ōr/.	N, V	motors, motorbike, motorboat, motorcade, motorize, motorist, motorway, motion
Draw a line over the /ō/. **4** A E O U usually say their names at the end of the syllable. Underline the /sh/. **17** TI, CI, and SI are used only at the beginning of any syllable after the first one.	N	motions, commotion, emotion, emotional, locomotion, motionless, promotion, emotionalize, emotionless
Draw a line over the /ō/. **4** A E O U usually say their names at the end of the syllable. Underline the /v/ once and the silent final E twice. **12.2** English words do not end in V or U.	N	motives, motivate, motivational, emotive, locomotive, motivated, unmotivated
Say to spell / prŏb lĕm/. All first sounds.	N	problems, problematic, problematically, subproblem
Draw a line over the /ē/. **4** A E O U usually say their names at the end of the syllable. Underline the /ŭf/. Put a 5 over it. /ŏ-ō-oo-ow-ŭf-ŏf/ said its fifth sound.	Adj, Adv	
Say to spell / kăl ĕn där /. **1** C softens to /s/ when followed by an E, I or Y. Otherwise C says /k/. Underline the /är/.	N	calendars
Say to spell /sĕn tū rē/. **1** C softens to /s/ when followed by an E, I or Y. Otherwise C says /k/.	N	centuries
Say to spell / dŏl lär/. Underline /är/.	N	dollars
Underline the /er/. Underline the C. Double underline the silent final E. **12.3** The C says /s/ and the G says /j/ because of the E.	N	differ, different
Put a 3 over the /ö/. /ŏ-ō-ö/ said its third sound. Underline the /TH/ and put a 2 over it. /th-TH/ said its second sound. Underline /er/.	Adv	altogether
Say to spell /ăn ŏther/. Underline /TH/ and put a 2 over it. / th-TH/ said its second sound. Underline /er/.	Adj, P	

I will not spend another dollar even though _you say it is a good deal._

She marched into the store as though _she owned it._

In the event that _Dad arrives home in the next hour, we will leave on vacation today._

Bring an umbrella with you in case _it begins to rain._

By the time _the earth has orbited around the sun one time, the moon has orbited around the earth more than thirteen times._

What do you notice about the coordinating conjunctions? They consist of more than one word.

Identifying Parts of Speech

✎ *39.6 Identifying Parts of Speech –* **Together we will identify the parts of speech. Write the parts of speech in your workbook as I write them on the board.**

Even though I studied hard for the science test, I received a poor grade.

How many sentences are there? two
How many subjects and verbs would we expect? two subjects and two verbs

What is the subject of the first clause? I, subject pronoun
What is being said about I? I studied, verb
Studied how? hard, adverb

What is "for?" preposition
For what? test, object of the preposition
What kind of test? science, adjective
Which test? the, article adjective

What is the subject of the second clause? I, subject pronoun
What is being said about I? I received, verb
Received what? grade, direct object
What type of verb is it? transitive verb
What kind of grade? poor, adjective
Which grade? a, article adjective

What is "even though?" subordinating conjunction
Put parentheses around the prepositional phrases.

  SC   SP   V   Adv   P A Adj OP SP TV A Adj DO
Even though I studied hard (for the science test,) I received a poor grade.

As long as they are constructing the new stadium, we cannot drive down this street.

How many sentences are there? two
How many subjects and verbs would we expect? two subjects and two verbs

What is the subject of the first clause? they, subject pronoun
What is being said about they? they are constructing, helping verb, verb
Constructing what? stadium, direct object
What type of verb is it? transitive verb
What kind of stadium? new, adjective
Which stadium? the, article adjective

What is the subject of the second clause? we, subject pronoun
What is being said about we? we cannot drive, helping verb, verb
What is "down?" preposition
Down what? street, object of the preposition
Which street? this, adjective
What is "as long as?" subordinating conjunction
Put parentheses around the prepositional phrases.

```
  SC      SP  HV    TV    A  Adj  DO   SP   HV   V
As long as they are constructing the new stadium, we cannot drive
   P   Adj  OP
(down this street.)
```

Even though he has saved fifty-five dollars, it is not enough.

How many sentences are there? two
How many subjects and verbs would we expect? two subjects and two verbs

What is the subject of the first clause? he, subject pronoun
What is being said about he? he has saved, helping verb, verb
Saved what? dollars, direct object
What type of verb? transitive verb
How many dollars? fifty-five, adjective

What is the subject of the second clause? it, subject pronoun
What is being said about it? it is, verb
Is what? enough, predicate adjective
Notice that "it" is being described as "enough"
This means "is" is a linking verb.
What kind of enough? not, adjective
What is "even though?" subordinating conjunction

```
   SC       SP  HV  TV      Adj      DO   SP LV Adj  PA
Even though he has saved fifty-five dollars, it is not enough.
```

Composition

Today we will write sentences using subordinating conjunctions.

Choose one of the subordinating conjunctions found in 39.4 Subordinating Conjunctions *in your workbook. I will write it on the board.*

For example:

By the time

Now choose a subject.

By the time my sister

Ask yourself what is being said about "my sister?"

By the time my sister gets home

Write a comma.

By the time my sister gets home,

Choose a related subject.

By the time my sister gets home, I

Ask what is being said about "I?"

By the time my sister gets home, I will already be asleep.

We can also invert the order of the clauses.

I will already be asleep by the time my sister gets home,

Does this sentence need a comma? No, the comma is only needed when the subordinating clause is first.

✎ *39.7 Composition –* **Now follow this process two more times and write your own sentences in your workbook.**

Vocabulary

Hold up a penny.

The word cent is the Latin word for hundred. Why do you suppose this is called a cent? Because there are one hundred cents in a dollar.

I will write some words on the board. Look for the word cent in each. If you know the definition, tell me.

cent

century — one hundred years

percent — parts of one hundred

centipede — a bug with a hundred legs (or a lot of legs)

centurion — a Roman solider who was in charge of one hundred men

centennial — a one hundred year celebration

centimeter — one hundredth of a meter

centiliter — one hundredth of a liter

centigram — one hundredth of a gram

When you encounter new words that you do not know the meaning of, it is helpful to look for familiar roots.

✎ *39.8 Latin Roots* – **Read the words in your workbook.**

motor	*locomotive*	*immovable*
motion	*emotion*	*mobile*
motionless	*motel*	*mobility*
motive	*movie*	*automobile*
motivate	*move*	*bookmobile*
motivation	*movable*	*immobile*
motorist	*movement*	*immobilize*
promote	*remove*	*snowmobile*
demote	*removal*	
remote	*unmovable*	

What do you notice about each of these words? They all have "mot," "mov," or "mob."

Each of these words is based upon a Latin root. Latin words change based upon their job within a sentence. These grammatical parts came into English with the words.

Tell me the definitions of the words you recognize.

Do you see a theme in the meanings of these words? They are all related to movement.

Discuss the meaning of each word and how it relates to the root.

motor — something that produces motion

motion — movement

motionless — without movement

motive — what moves someone to an action

motivate — to encourage someone to move

motivation — something that motivates

motorist — someone who drives a moving vehicle

promote — to move up

demote — to move down

remote — far away from other people or cities

locomotive — a self propelled vehicle or engine

emotion — feelings (consider the phrase, "I feel moved.")

motel — motor + hotel; a roadside hotel

movie — pictures that move

move

movable — able to be moved

movement — motion

remove — to move away

removal — the act of removing

unmovable — not able to be moved

immovable — not able to be moved

mobile — able to be moved

mobility — quality of being mobile

automobile — a car, it moves automatically

bookmobile — a moving library

immobile — not able to be moved

immobilize — to put something/someone in a state where they cannot move

snowmobile — a moving machine that drives on snow

✎ *39.9 Synonyms* – **Which words in the list are synonyms or share the same meaning? Write the words in your workbook.**

mobile   moveable

unmovable   immovable   immobile   motionless

motion   movement

Today's words demonstrate the importance of looking for patterns and roots in words.

Dictation

✎ *39.10 Dictation* – Read each sentence twice. Ask the students to repeat it aloud, then write it in their student workbooks.

1. Now that we live here, the road construction is a problem for us.

2. Though I found twenty-five dollars, it is not enough.

3. She is unusually motivated.

4. We will study motors in science class today.

5. The construction workers did not have enough time because it rained too much.

6. Did our families go to the stadium together?

SPELLING ASSESSMENT

Materials Needed: red colored pencil.

1. ✎ *40.1 Assessment* – Dictate the sentences to the students while they write them in their workbook.

   1. I don't have any questions about the problems, but my brother has two questions.

   2. Who memorized all the combinations?

   3. Since I only have twenty dollars and thirty-five cents, it is impossible for me to buy new equipment.

   4. What is the difference between these radios?

   5. Even if you saw what happened, do not judge their motives.

   6. Although science is my favorite class, I also enjoy math.

   7. If you add too much sugar, it'll be too sweet.

   8. Do not look straight at the sun, or you will hurt your eyes.

   9. Are you sure there is room in the stadium for one million people?

   10. Whenever my teacher encourages me, I believe I can do it.

2. Direct the students to read the phrases aloud while you write them on the board. Sound out each word and model the thought process. The students should mark corrections in red. Encourage the students to discuss what they missed.

3. Recheck the students' work. Note the words and concepts which need further practice.

4. Did the students:

   ____ *use a comma before a coordinating conjunction?*
   ____ *use a comma after a subordinate clause when it comes at the beginning of a sentence?*
   ____ *put no comma before a subordinate clause when it comes at the end of the sentence?*
   ____ *write contractions correctly?*

5. ✎ *40.2 Reading* – Ask the students to read the following sentences, phrases and words. Note the words they did not read fluently.

   1. Nine million people live in the country of Sweden.

   2. A century is one hundred years.

   3. When you see them together, will you take a picture for me?

   4. The earth is beautiful.

   5. After the construction is finished, we will have more room.

   6. Which section do I need to practice again?

   7. Our team will play against Century High School.

   8. She will not be happy until she has another pet.

   9. Before you leave, I'd like to ask you something.

   10. This shirt is a medium.

11. Why won't this motor work?

12. I learned the new motions easily because they are so easy.

13. She is good at memorization.

14. While it was an unusual situation, they still should have responded immediately.

15. Where was the accident?

16. The calendar is in the kitchen.

6. ✎ *40.3 Words to Practice* – Ask the students to read the words in the list and mark which ones they would like to practice further.

7. Using the assessment and your knowledge as a teacher, identify words to dictate onto index cards.

1. ____ about		29. ____ medium
2. ____ after		30. ____ memorization
3. ____ again		31. ____ memorize
4. ____ against		32. ____ million
5. ____ also		33. ____ motion
6. ____ although		34. ____ motive
7. ____ another		35. ____ motor
8. ____ because		36. ____ picture
9. ____ before		37. ____ problem
10. ____ believe		38. ____ question
11. ____ calendar		39. ____ radio
12. ____ century		40. ____ science
13. ____ combination		41. ____ since
14. ____ construction		42. ____ stadium
15. ____ country		43. ____ straight
16. ____ difference		44. ____ sugar
17. ____ dollar		45. ____ sure
18. ____ earth		46. ____ sweet
19. ____ easy		47. ____ together
20. ____ encouragement		48. ____ too
21. ____ enough		49. ____ unless
22. ____ equipment		50. ____ until
23. ____ eye		51. ____ unusual
24. ____ happen		52. ____ what
25. ____ how		53. ____ when
26. ____ immediately		54. ____ whenever
27. ____ impossible		55. ____ where
28. ____ measure		56. ____ which

57. _____ while

58. _____ who

59. _____ whose

60. _____ why

SPELLING WORD REVIEW

Materials Needed: Index cards, highlighter, timer, whiteboard, markers, eraser.

1. Dictate the missed words onto index cards. Have the students highlight the part of the word that was difficult.

2. Choose from the review activities below or use an activity found in the *The Phonogram and Spelling Game Book*.

> 1. Play Spelling Snap (*The Phonogram and Spelling Game Book*, 36).
>
> 2. Write the words using Rainbow Writing (*The Phonogram and Spelling Game Book*, 48).
>
> 3. Practice the words by typing them on a computer.

OPTIONAL SPELLING RULE REVIEW

Use the following mini-lessons to review the concepts as needed.

Spelling Rule 14

Spelling Rule	14
Double the last consonant when adding a vowel suffix to words ending in one vowel followed by one consonant, only if the syllable before the suffix is accented.	

1. Review the rule by reciting it and discussing the samples on the back of the card.

2. Write one syllable words on the board and practice adding suffixes as follows:

bat + er = batter

fan + ed = fanned

fog + y = foggy

mom + y = mommy

pit + ed = pitted

run + ing = running

wet + er = wetter

fix + ing = fixing (X has two sounds /k/ and /s/.)

fax + ed = faxed

mix + er = mixer

quit + ing = quitting (QU is a phonogram. U is not a vowel here.)

quiz + ed = quizzed

sing+ ing = singing

pick + ed = picked

mad + ly = madly

ship + ment = shipment

3. ✎ *40.4 Extra Practice: Adding Suffixes to One-Syllable Words* – Practice adding suffixes to one syllable words ending in one vowel followed by one consonant with the activity in the workbook.

4. Review finding the accent in multi-syllable words.

> **How do we find the accented syllable?** Listen for the strongest beat, or place your hand under your chin and feel on which syllable the mouth drops open the farthest.
> **Let's practice finding the accented syllable in the following words.**
> **I will write a word on the board. Say the word aloud and tell me which syllable is accented.**

e quip'	*re turn'*
can' cel	*re sell'*
of' fer	*a bout'*
ac' cent	*les' son*

> **When adding a suffix to a multi-syllable word ending in one vowel and then one consonant, you must know where the accent is in the derivative. If we are adding a vowel suffix and the accent is on the syllable before the suffix, the consonant is doubled.**

medal + ion = me dal' lion

medal + ist = med' al ist (Do not double the consonant. The accent is on the wrong syllable.)

omit + ing = o mit' ting

prefer + ing = pre fer' ring

prefer + ence = pref' er ence (Do not double the consonant. The accent is on the wrong syllable.)

rebel + ion = re bel' lion

occur + ed = oc curred'

offer + ed = of fered (Do not double the consonant, the accent is on the wrong syllable.)

allow + ance = al low'ance (Do not double the consonant, it ends in a multi-letter phonogram.)

saw + ing = saw'ing (Do not double the consonant, it ends in a multi-letter phonogram.)

5. ✎ *40.5 Extra Practice: Adding Suffixes to Multi-Syllable Words* – Practice adding suffixes to multi-syllable words ending in one vowel followed by one consonant with the activity in the workbook.

OPTIONAL GRAMMAR REVIEW

Use the following mini-lessons to review the concepts as needed.

Coordinating Conjunctions and Compound Sentences

> **Grammar Card 7**   C
>
> **Conjunctions connect words, phrases or sentences together. There are two types of conjunctions: coordinating and subordinating.**

> **Grammar Card 7.1**   C
>
> **Coordinating conjunctions connect related words, phrases, or sentences together. Use a comma before a coordinating conjunction: and, but, or, for, nor, yet, so.**

> **Grammar Card 9.13**   *Compound Sentence*
>
> **A compound sentence contains two complete sentences joined together with a comma followed by a coordinating conjunction.**

1. Review the rules by reciting them and discussing the samples on the backs of the cards.

2. Review these sample sentences on the board. Emphasize the comma before the conjunction.

Mom went to the store, and dad stayed home.

I memorized the first two immediately, but the last one took more time.

Is this a good combination, or would that be better?

She is not encouraging, nor do I want to spend time with her.

3. ✎ *40.6 Extra Practice: Coordinating Conjunctions* – Join the sentences in your workbook using a

comma and a conjunction.

Subordinating Conjunctions and Complex Sentences

Grammar Card 7.2	C
Subordinating conjunctions join two sentences together by turning one sentence into a dependent clause (or sentence fragment).	

Grammar Card 10.2
A dependent clause includes a subordinating conjunction, subject, and verb. A dependent clause does not express a complete thought.

Grammar Card 9.14
A complex sentence contains an independent clause joined with one or more dependent clauses.

1. Review the rules by reciting them and discussing the samples on the backs of the cards.

2. ✎ *40.7 Extra Practice: Sentences and Fragments* – Direct students to write an S next to the complete sentences and an F next to the fragments. If it is a fragment, underline the subordinator that steals the completeness of the sentence.

3. Discuss the following sentences. Notice that when the subordinate clause is first, a comma is used. Discuss how when the subordinate clause is second, a comma is not needed.

   While Grandfather listens to the radio, we clean the kitchen.

   We clean the kitchen while Grandfather listen to the radio.

   Although I believe it is impossible, I will try my hardest.

   I will try my hardest although I believe it is impossible.

   As soon as grandpa took the picture, I wanted to see it.

   I wanted to see the picture as soon as grandpa took it.

4. ✎ *40.8 Extra Practice: Subordinating Conjunctions* – In you workbook, practice reversing the order of the two clauses in the sentences.

OPTIONAL PHONOGRAM ASSESSMENT & REVIEW

Phonograms

40.9 Extra Practice: Phonogram Practice – Dictate the phonograms.

1. a	20. or	39. ci	58. ei
2. igh	21. o	40. th	59. i
3. m	22. ou	41. r	60. wr
4. ir	23. ay	42. ck	61. v
5. ai	24. ough	43. s	62. eigh
6. kn	25. d	44. ti	63. er
7. ar	26. ow	45. dge	64. j
8. z	27. bu	46. g	65. w
9. ng	28. p	47. ea	66. ew
10. oa	29. oy	48. ui	67. k
11. b	30. ch	49. ur	68. ey
12. au	31. ph	50. ear	69. x
13. n	32. e	51. t	70. l
14. oe	33. sh	52. wh	71. gn
15. oi	34. cei	53. ed	72. y
16. c	35. qu	54. h	73. gu
17. augh	36. si	55. ee	74. ie
18. oo	37. f	56. wor	
19. aw	38. tch	57. u	

Optional Phonogram Practice

Practice the phonograms as needed using the following game suggestions or choose other games from *The Phonogram and Spelling Game Book.*

1. Play Last One! (*The Phonogram and Spelling Game Book,* 12).

2. Play Teacher Trouble (*The Phonogram and Spelling Game Book,* 29).